EMOTIONAL

LANDSCAPES

STUDIES OF WORLD MIGRATIONS

Marcelo J. Borges and Madeline Hsu, editors

*A list of books in the series appears
at the end of the book.*

EMOTIONAL LANDSCAPES

LOVE, GENDER, AND MIGRATION

Edited by
Marcelo J. Borges, Sonia Cancian, and Linda Reeder

UNIVERSITY OF ILLINOIS PRESS
Urbana, Chicago, and Springfield

© 2021 by the Board of Trustees
of the University of Illinois
All rights reserved
1 2 3 4 5 C P 5 4 3 2 1
♾ This book is printed on acid-free paper.

Library of Congress Control Number: 2020948386
ISBN 978-0-252-04349-9 (hardcover)
ISBN 978-0-252-08539-0 (paperback)
ISBN 978-0-252-05237-8 (e-book)

CONTENTS

ACKNOWLEDGMENTS vii

INTRODUCTION
    Marcelo J. Borges, Sonia Cancian, and Linda Reeder 1

CHAPTER 1. What's Love Got to Do with It?
Language of Transnational Affect in the Letters
of Portuguese Migrants
    Marcelo J. Borges 19

CHAPTER 2. "The Letter Said That My Wife
Had Died": Bigamy in Argentina in the Era
of Mass Migration
    María Bjerg... 39

CHAPTER 3. "People Cannot Live on Love Alone":
Negotiating Love, Gender Roles, and Family
Care between Slovenia and Egypt
    Mirjam Milharčič Hladnik............................... 57

CHAPTER 4. Love, Mobility, and Fate
in Turn-of-the-Century Berlin
    Tyler Carrington 75

CHAPTER 5. Brotherly Love: The Forging of an Italian-
Argentine Brotherhood in Argentina, 1880–1920
    Elizabeth Zanoni 91

CHAPTER 6. "Let Them Deport Me, I Will Come
Back to Him Again": Romance, Affective Relations,
and the US Deportation Regime, 1919–1935
Emily Pope-Obeda 112

CHAPTER 7. The Emotions of War: Italian
Emigrant Soldiers and Love of Country
Linda Reeder 131

CHAPTER 8. Maintaining Relationships and
Creating Epistolary Personae: (Not) Articulating
Emotions in the Letters of a Viennese Family
of the Mid-Twentieth Century
Suzanne M. Sinke 147

CHAPTER 9. Love at the Threshold of War
and Migration: A War Orphan's Story
Sonia Cancian 163

CHAPTER 10. Love, Sex, Feelings: Marriage
and Transatlantic Migration in Postwar Germany
Alexander Freund 184

CHAPTER 11. "When I Came to Canada,
All I Did Was Cry": Emotions and Migration
of Greek Women in Postwar Montreal
Margarita Dounia 201

CHAPTER 12. Stories of Love and Marriage in
the Modern British Diaspora: Themes of Change
and Continuity
A. James Hammerton 220

CHAPTER 13. "I Can Express My Feelings with
Just a Tweet": Language, Emotion, and the Digital
Divide among Immigrant Families in Italy
Roberta Ricucci 238

EPILOGUE
Donna R. Gabaccia 259

CONTRIBUTORS 269

INDEX 275

ACKNOWLEDGMENTS

This project has been a long time in the making, and benefited from the advice, critiques, and insights of scholars and friends on multiple continents. To all who have worked on this project, we say thank you. To all the contributors, we thank you for your patience and hard work. We dedicate this book to Donna Gabaccia, whose ideas inspire all we do. A special thanks to James Engelhardt, former acquisitions editor at the University of Illinois Press, for his support, unfailing good humor, and equanimity throughout the process. Finally, thank you to our coeditors who made this process a pleasure.

EMOTIONAL LANDSCAPES

Introduction

MARCELO J. BORGES,
SONIA CANCIAN,
AND LINDA REEDER

On September 2, 2015, a photograph of three-year-old Syrian refugee Aylan Kurdi's lifeless body washed up on the shores of the Mediterranean went viral, spreading through social networks and into the media, accompanied by calls for a more robust humanitarian response to the growing refugee crisis and by ferocious condemnation of the European Union's (non)actions. After a summer of photographs circulating of the drowned and the desperate, the image of Aylan was the one that sparked a deep emotional response and became a powerful political symbol. Two months later, in the wake of horrific bombings in Paris and calls to close national borders, social media once again invoked Aylan in their cries to stop conflating refugees and migrants with terrorists. The photograph showing Aylan's body abandoned on the sand took on an iconic power in debates over migration and refugees because of its *emotional* power: attached to his red shirt and blue shorts was a mother's love and a father's grief. Gently carried in the arms of the Turkish police officer, Aylan's body invoked the western Christian traditions of innocence, sacrifice, and love contained in a pietà. The emotional power of the photograph shifted European public opinion from "being inimical to 'migrants' to empathetic to 'refugees.'"[1] An internet search for "refugee" results in images of men and women holding tight to their children as if their capacity to love as fathers and mothers attests to their humanity and our compassion. If you type "migrant" into an internet search bar, however, the results are significantly different:

piled into boats, crowded into camps, migrants appear as an undifferentiated, threatening crowd. A few family photos are scattered amid the images of unattached young men, sparking our deep dread of the violent, unassimilable foreigner, exacerbated by ever-present fears of terrorism. The fear swirling around our understandings of migration is anchored in the same gendered emotional space as the love that underpins the images of refugees. Unattached from wives or children, the mobile man is suspicious. In the western imagination, the absence of tangible proof of a man's paternal or heterosexual conjugal affection makes it impossible to judge his capacity to love a country. In a world that generally sees the transnational movement of people as inherently disloyal, love attests to an individual's capacity to be loyal.[2]

These dueling contemporary narratives of love and fear that shape our responses to mobility are not new. Love has long stood at the heart of the stories of migrants, refugees, and exiles. The weight of love lost, found, embittered, and celebrated is woven into the stories told by those who cross borders and oceans and those who greet them on the far shores. Although often buried under legal, economic, and historical analyses, journalists, politicians, and critics have long been quick to seize on the affective languages surrounding migration as a means of humanizing or dehumanizing migrants within broader political debates. In the nineteenth century, the fearsome images of unattached men or women immigrants stood in contrast to the sympathetic images of destitute families—one designed to evoke fear, the other compassion. Despite the centrality of emotions in our collective understanding of migration, there has been little historical analysis of how these emotional landscapes of migration are enmeshed in the gender norms shaping personal and political understandings of migration. This is the driving force behind the writers in this book—to explore the relationships among gender, mobility, and love in historical perspective. This exploration took the form of a series of conference sessions that provided space for contributors to exchange ideas, compare historical experiences in different cultural contexts, and shape their individual studies. Indeed, the genesis of this project stretches back further in time, to 2003, when Donna Gabaccia called for new research initiatives focusing explicitly on how the intimate world shapes the political, on the ways in which affective ties "mediate within and among structures of family, community, and nation."[3] In a subsequent collection of essays published in 2011, Donna Gabaccia and Loretta Baldassar traced how mobility complicated the intimate emotional bonds linking individuals to each other, and to the wider imagined community of nations.[4] Combined, these essays offered new ways to understand how ideas of motherhood, sexuality, and desire altered the contours of social categories (class, gender, race, and ethnicity) and notions of national belonging in the mobile world of Italians. The power of this work is in the way it anchors the exploration of transnational domestic spaces in the bodies (mothers, fathers, children, lovers) of those who migrate and those who remain. *Emotional Landscapes* seeks to complement this work by shifting attention to the emotions that link these bodies, to better understand the role of emotions in general, and love in particular, in the reconfiguration of intimate and collective relations in a mobile world.

By placing love at the center of the phenomenon of mobility, the chapters in this anthology study how changing affective languages define gender norms that shape migration processes that have connected Europe, the Mediterranean, the Americas, Australia, and Africa since 1880. The anthology focuses on the centrality of love, with its attendant constellation of emotions (loss, grief, guilt, nostalgia, hate, euphoria, and joy, among others), and its power to define and transform individual experiences of mobility in relation to self, family, and nation. It further explores how intimate emotional languages merge with public discourses surrounding modernity, urbanization, and patriotism. This book seeks to understand how multiple languages of love shaped the emotional landscapes fashioned by the experiences of migrant men and women, and how it created meaning for them, their families, and their societies in a mobile world. Our interest in exploring the sentimental, sexual, and political meanings of love underscores the multifaceted ways in which discourses of love served to validate intimate, familial, communal, and political experiences of separation and loss, ultimately privileging certain categories of migrants (refugees, labor migrants, lovers, wives, and children) over others.

Theoretical Framework

The historian of emotion faces an array of definitional and intellectual difficulties. What is an emotion? How is emotion generated? Are emotions instinctual, irrational responses to some sort of stimulus, either external (for example, a physical threat) or internal (such as a traumatic memory), or are they products of societal norms and expectations?[5] Cognitive psychologists generally hold that emotions are the products of conscious and unconscious judgments, based on perceptions of whether an external stimulus brings pleasure or pain. Emotions follow from the conclusions of psychological appraisals of physical affects. Different people respond to physical stimuli in different ways, shaped by rational analysis, personal experiences, and prevalent communal notions of acceptable emotional responses. Social constructionists reject the notion that emotions are physiological responses to external stimuli, existing outside of language, cultural norms, or social practices. The "feelings" associated with a perceived threat are purely products of social norms. The divisions between social constructionists and cognitive psychologists, while important for psychology, proved less significant for scholars working in other fields. For scholars in the humanities and social sciences, these psychological theories provided a way of positioning emotions as linking individual experiences to those of a larger collective.[6]

Informed by works in cultural studies, feminist philosophy, gender history, and the history of sexuality showing how changing meanings of desire, love, and attachment transformed fundamental social relations, culture, and political institutions, scholars from multiple disciplines have come to recognize that the contingent meanings of love, lust, anger, and fear give meaning to social and political change. The physical origins of some "feelings" could be deemed instinctual and universal, but how they are expressed, labeled, and validated shifts over time and place. Feelings and emotions are experienced in a dynamic biocultural interaction. As Rob Boddice reminds us in a recent survey of the history of emotions, "our relation to the objects of perception, much as with our relation to the objects of emotion (our associations), is filled by the brain."[7]

In the 1990s, affect became the central conceptual frame for a wide range of scholarship across disciplines that examined how affective expressions informed notions of individual and collective attachment, institutional development, and politics. Running through affect studies was the strong sense that affect was separate from emotion. Many in affect studies argued that unlike emotions, which were intimate, interior, individual articulations of feeling, affect was a social, collective, exterior expression. In the past decade or so, scholars, particularly, from the humanities, have questioned the usefulness of this inside/outside division, which seemed to replicate an older mind/body dualism.[8] Instead, historians and philosophers hinted at ways in which emotion and affect were mutually constitutive, where the articulations of individual feelings merged into broader affective languages. This anthology continues in this vein, exploring the complex links between emotion and affect in a mobile world.[9]

Although still conflicted on the definition of emotions, historians have increasingly recognized that emotional/affective expressions, like political or economic languages, are critical to understanding social, cultural, and political change.[10] Following on Peter and Carol Stearns's pioneering discussion of "emotionology" (focusing on the standards that promoted or hindered different emotional expressions in the past, and its social and institutional consequences), historians slowly began to consider the analytical possibilities of the emotional lens.[11] By considering emotion as an analytic category, scholars have identified new historical narratives, highlighting moments of change that make visible alternate chronologies and historical actors, largely invisible in conventional political or social histories.[12] Historians of the premodern period have most enthusiastically embraced the possibilities of emotion as a viable category of analysis, and a driver of cultural, social, political, and economic change. Barbara Rosenwein's work on medieval Europe, for example, offers a convincing critique of Norbert Elias's argument that the transition to modernity was marked by a tempering of raw emotion, offering a number of examples of self-control and restraint in premodern Europe.[13] Ute Frevert's work exploring the emergence and disappearance of emotions over time adds to the literature by forcing us to reconsider the meaning of emotions, and to focus attention on why certain emotions, or "emotional economies," disappear or are "lost" among some groups or societies (for example, honor), replaced by others.[14] Frevert suggests that, in Europe, the nineteenth century was marked by the rise of empathy/sympathy "as civil society's primary emotional resource."[15] It is no coincidence that this "sympathetic" economy accompanied the rise of the nation-state and the emotional character of the new imagined national body. Underlying Frevert's work are fundamental questions that shape our own project: Why do "emotional economies" shift? Who shifts them? How do people learn the new rules? What happens to those who fail to learn?

Although Frevert utilizes the term "emotional economies," for our purposes, Rosenwein's idea of emotional communities combined with William Reddy's notion of "emotional regime" provide a more flexible frame to explore the multiple ways love informs mobility.[16] Rosenwein urged scholars to consider the ways that certain historical eras are marked by multiple emotional communities, "groups in which people adhere to the same norms of emotional expression and value—or devalue—the same or related emotions."[17] These coexisting communities (monastic, courtly, military, and peasant) provide a range of emotional options, at times contradictory and, at other moments, complementary. Much of the work inspired by Rosenwein's insights illuminated the contours of distinct communities, making visible new historical agents, and identifying new moments of social or cultural transformation. The hierarchical relations between the communities are less distinct. Power dynamics that shape these communities fade to the background.

Reddy's theoretical construct of "emotional regimes" centers on power.[18] He argues that at any given moment, a dominant emotional regime circumscribes the range of possible expressions, pushing certain feelings and emotional displays to the margins, or even erasing them completely. The various expressions of emotion, what Reddy calls "emotives" (evoking the performative quality of emotions and their capacity to enact change), are formed in response to the constraints of social/political expectations and intimate, individual experience. By tracing how groups navigate through this world of feeling, Reddy argues that identifying moments when new emotives become visible provides new ways to understand political, cultural, and social change. Reddy's work focused on a dialectical relationship between the dominant emotional regime and those formed in reaction to the regime. The dominant regime can obscure the gendered, sexed, raced, and age diversity of emotional communities that form the emotives of the "regime" and run through intimate, personal relations. However, Reddy's model offers useful insights into the ways emotions link individual bodies to the national collective. For historians of migration interested in emotions as a subject, or as a category of analysis, Reddy's work offers a theoretical frame focusing on the space where the dominant emotional regime converges with multiple emotional communities including intimate/private familial spaces, transnational communities, and sending communities. By following one emotion through these diverse communities, our project seeks to explore how these various "emotives" of love inform political understandings and intimate experiences of migration.

In an effort to keep focused on the relations among the multiplicity of actors (including migrants, those who remain behind, politicians, critics, and receiving societies at large), we propose to use the term "emotional landscapes" as a way to bring into the frame the multiplicity of communities and pay attention to shifting power dynamics between emotional regimes and the new emotives formed through mobility. Framing the discussion on a wider landscape hopefully enables scholars to focus on the emotional intersections among the multiple emotional communities of family/village, nation, emigrant/immigrant societies.

The idea of "landscapes" brings into light a central dimension of the migration experience that makes it particularly well suited for an approach that privileges the lens of emotion: its multi-connectivity in spatial, cultural, and temporal terms. Indeed, the nature of migration makes it a good lens through which to analyze the effects of emotions. Migrants change places and cultural contexts, forging new relations in the societies of settlement while remaining connected with societies of origin, and positioning themselves temporally in multiple ways (in relationship with the present that makes them migrants, the past of the home left behind, and the future represented by the potential attainment of the objective that prompted them to migrate). This is a dynamic, open-ended process that lives on after the act of migration when the move is revisited over a migrant's life course (questioned, reconsidered, reinforced) and every time it is repeated (or such a possibility is considered) through return, reunification, and multiple moves. As Paolo Boccagni and Loretta Baldassar state, "the significance of the [migrants'] emotional experience... lies in [its] potential to dis-embed, translocate, and re-embed emotions, on the one hand; in the interaction between different ways of cultivating and managing emotions, as affected by different societal backgrounds (i.e. sending and receiving), on the other."[19] This multiplicity of connections to spatial, cultural, and temporal spaces is experienced at the level of the self and in its historical context (social, cultural, political) in a dynamic, dialectical relationship that shapes and is shaped by emotions. Using this perspective, we consider "the self," to use Maruška Svašek's words, as "a multiple, relational being-in-the-world that is captured by his or her surroundings, engaging with past, present, and future situations."[20]

The experiences of the self in the world, and the attitudes and norms that shape them, are also gendered. Even though purported differences between the sexes were commonly deployed in early discussions of emotions and their relationship to nature and culture, or to the body and the mind, the relationship between gender and emotions is an area of historical inquiry that has been largely marginal.[21] Historians of emotion often seem to take for granted the gendered dimension of emotions, and focus on the ways in which emotions shape gender, and in turn how gender shapes emotions. We must pay close attention to the intersectionality of these categories of analysis. By focusing on the role of emotion in constructing gender as a category of analysis (as opposed to work, society, or culture) and on gendered readings of migrants' emotional attitudes and practices, this volume moves beyond the historical scholarship on love and migration. Taken together, not only do the contributions in this anthology deepen our understanding of the gendered nature of migration in a long historical perspective since the late nineteenth century, they also show how love, gender, and migration are interwoven in complex ways in the day-to-day and life courses of men and women and their families.[22] As Nicola Mai and Russell King argue, it is not only necessary to recognize migrants as emotional and sexual beings, but equally important, to consider "the intersectionality of love, sex, and emotion in framing mobility behavior" as "distinct, yet overlapping domains"; and as experiences that are "culturally, socially, and economically sited and interdependent, both 'at home' and 'away.'"[23] The gendered nature of migration is, therefore, better understood within the larger idea of emotional landscapes as a way to capture the multiplicity of spatial and temporal connections that characterize migrants' lives.

Love, Mobility, and Gender

The essays collected in this anthology highlight the multifaceted and complicated ties between emotion and gender in a mobile world. Arranged in roughly chronological order, they reveal the impact of technology, capital, wars, and state-building on the construction of transnational emotional landscapes experienced by migrants in the nineteenth and twentieth centuries. They make visible the bonds linking intimate displays and deployments of love to the normative languages enacted in the public world. The transformations discussed in these chapters are specific to migration to and from Europe and the Americas, Australia, and Africa, and within Europe. These diverse geographies connected by mobility and transnational lives had a profound effect on the emotional dispositions and practices of migrants and their families. In dynamic interaction, the experience of migration, and the values and mores of societies of origin and settlement, contributed to shaping diverse emotional landscapes. Equally important were tensions created by changing conceptions of self and society, family and nation, and gender norms and relations, in a fluid political and cultural context marked by mobility.

Bureaucratic and capitalist languages drew on the intimate affective languages circulating among mobile communities to generate loyalty, notions of belonging, and diasporic identities. The weight of the written word in mobile languages of love reconfigured familial dynamics and constituted new forms of femininity and masculinity. Distance fueled fears of social decay, loosening of obligations, and betrayal. At the same time, distance generated new spaces for affective performances. The violence of the wars of the twentieth century strengthened the ways in which states and family drew on affective languages to construct notions of belonging across distances, infusing prewar expressions of love with a deep sense of loss, abandonment, and nostalgia for an imagined homeland. In the aftermath of wars and throughout the last decades of the twentieth century, a sharp shift in the relationship between love and migration emerged that complicated ideas of obligation and love in connection with individual, family, and societal projects in contexts of mobility. No longer did languages of love describe migration as an expression of love and sacrifice, but instead, love seemed to drive migration in new ways. The circulation of public and intimate languages of love and mobility in the prewar world became a constitutive element of the ways in which European people in Europe and abroad understood migration in the postwar world. More than mutually exclusive, however, different conceptions of the role of love as affected by or affecting migration should be considered within a broader spectrum with variations, adaptations, and overlaps along changing geo-cultural, gender, class, and generational lines.

New methods of communication that accompanied the rise of transoceanic migrations in the late nineteenth and early twentieth centuries altered intimate affective ties between husbands and wives, siblings, and parents and children. European migrations led to an expansion of letter-writing, which, in turn, altered established forms of emotional expression. The shift to letters proved deeply disrupting to communities where love was expressed through the physical interactions of men and women in their quotidian tasks of daily life—work, chores, and meals. The gendered implications of these languages of love are particularly apparent in the chapters of Marcelo J. Borges and Mirjam Milharčič Hladnik. In Portugal and Slovenia, normative expressions of love for men included provisioning and protecting in ways proclaimed worthy by the community at large. For women, love was tied to caring for houses and bodies, maintenance of familial and kin ties, and the regulation of sexuality. This love enacted every day, at home and in the streets, had little verbal or literary form. Migration required couples and communities to translate these physical acts into written form. As Borges observes, words connected to money became the tangible expressions of the physical performances of love. These same struggles to articulate gendered ideals of love among couples appear among the *aleksandrinke*, the women from Slovenia who left to work in Egypt in the 1920s analyzed by Milharčič Hladnik. Verbal affective expressions reshaped communal notions of love, and arguably, the content itself, introducing new written and performative vocabularies of affection.

The lines between intimate expressions of love blurred with bureaucratic languages of belonging. In the letters written by Portuguese men to bring their wives to join them, Borges explores the ways that new articulations of love made their way into the official records, reinforcing gender norms identifying men with productivity and protection now expressed in terms of sacrifice, struggle, and absence. This combination of languages is visible in the records of bigamy trials in late-nineteenth-century Buenos Aires. María Bjerg notes how accepted understandings regarding the power of love and appropriate expressions made it possible for Italian and Spanish women to emigrate on their own, defying community gender norms. Their love stories proved acceptable to custom agents suspicious of women traveling alone, and enabled them to cross borders. Bjerg explores how immigrant women, once abroad, evoked sentiments of male sacrifice, obligation, and familial duty alongside images of abandonment and helplessness to claim rights in Argentinian courts. It is apparent that the accused men also played with shifting, mobile affective languages. In the courtroom, migrant men evoked alternative forms of masculinity that challenged the centrality of obligation, duty, provisioning, and protection. They claimed that the dislocation of migration and their isolation generated a deep emotional need for love and affection, and for physical, sexual love. Accused of failing in their manliness, at least in terms of their conjugal duties, these men drew on emotional expressions to construct a narrative of personal and public redemption.

Throughout these essays, it is clear that both those who migrated and those who remained behind deployed a multiplicity of languages and expressions of love to further individual and collective interests. In Portugal, Italy, and Argentina, wives worried about their husbands overseas appealed to the mayors or priests to remind their husbands of their obligations and duties. They brandished proof of their continued "love" in the care of their children, property, and careful management of the family's resources. At times, women who remained behind also wielded the implicit threat and fears articulated in the popular tropes of sexual betrayal and abandonment to justify their own emigration or the transfer of their affections elsewhere. The experience of aleksandrinke women in Slovenia altered the traditional division of labor mobility by leaving men behind, creating a need to negotiate new gender roles within a moral framework of family responsibility. The combination of languages of love reinforced sympathy for the mobile woman as a wife and mother, and suspicion of unattached women migrants.

Public languages of love reshaped physical spaces in a mobile world. Urban spaces emerged as sites of new emotives articulated through newspapers, fiction, and material goods. This is evident in the immigrant worlds of late-nineteenth-century Buenos Aires, as well as in the rapidly changing social world of early-twentieth-century Berlin described by Tyler Carrington. Migration to urban centers carved out new social spaces in boardinghouses, tenements, bars, and parks. For the new arrivals, both men and women, these spaces proved emancipatory. Freed from the surveillance of family, kin, and community, migrants in cities were enabled to enact new emotional practices and subjectivities, resting in larger part on personal desire and sexual pleasure, and increasingly divorced from economic interests. Desire, companionship, emotional intimacy, took on a greater weight in the migrant's calculus of love. Among the fastest-growing cities in Europe, Berlin in 1905 provides a particularly vivid example of the possible new expressions and performances of love. Young men and women poured in from the countryside seeking work in the city's expanding economy. Pressed together on the streets and sidewalks, residents complained about the constant movement of people, the collisions between strangers, and, at the same time, the new distances. Far from small-town social regulatory mechanisms, these strangers remained strangers. Through magazines, newspaper columns, and fiction a new kind of urban, modern love emerged: the fortuitous, chance encounter between strangers that could morph into romantic, sexual, passionate love. The new visions of love countered dominant ideas about male and female respectability, and reconceptualized notions of home and community, where emotional well-being covered over the economic realities of marriage and family. Love blossomed in trams, in dance halls, and at the cinema, seemingly outside the boundaries of traditional social networks. These visions of urban mobility and unloosed sexuality proved both threatening and emancipatory, providing models for new forms of femininity (the new woman) and masculinity (unhitched from domesticity), but also reinforced a public rhetoric casting suspicion on the morality of migrants and cities in equal measure.

If Berliners looked to newspapers to find new kinds of romantic relations, Elizabeth Zanoni suggests that Italian migrants found new kinds of fraternal and familial affective ties in advertisements for Italian products in foreign lands. Transnational markets drew on languages of love and emotional belonging to sell their goods along with distinct racialized and gendered ideas of immigrant men and women. In the transoceanic migrant community, commercial interests fused with notions of political belonging. In Buenos Aires, sentimental notions of racial fraternity justified preferences for Italian immigrants and improved their standing in the community in relation to other groups in the larger immigrant population because they belonged to an international community of purportedly Latin character. As the analysis of Italian migrants in Buenos Aires shows, migrants had to navigate and adapt creatively to contending notions of emotional attachment that were not only rooted in individual and family logics but also in sometimes contending claims for ethnic and national allegiance. The expansion of a consumer society added another dimension to this tension created by multiple belongings and identities. As a result, migrants and their families had to adapt to living in multiple emotional landscapes with their own emotional logics, claims, and vocabularies.

The growth of international migration, and the emergence of mobile populations and transnational communities during the second half of the nineteenth century and at the turn of the twentieth century, coincided with a consolidation of the power of nation-states that sought to regulate labor flows and its demographic consequences. States had to adapt to the challenges posed by geographically mobile populations who moved across multiple borders (national, cultural, political) as receiving nations rushed to claim migrants' allegiances. They did so in the context of competing notions of duty, belonging, and identity for which emotional vocabularies were also deployed. By the early twentieth century, affective ties and expressions of love became a means of legitimizing expulsions, woven into deportation laws. As Emily Pope-Obeda argues, in the case of the United States, love stories stood at the center of stories of forced expulsions, used to challenge or rationalize a deportation order. Stories of love run amok or families torn apart course through the deportation records themselves and the journalistic accounts of the most sensational cases. As in Zanoni's world, love became a means of regulating racial, gender, and sexual relations. In Pope-Obeda's work, however, attention is focused on individuals rather than the collective body.

The disruptions attendant with war tightened the links between love and mobility. In Linda Reeder's chapter on Italian male migrants called to arms, and in Suzanne M. Sinke's close reading of the Hine family letters, we learn how the exigencies of war pushed state bureaucracies and family members to draw on articulations of love and sacrifice to navigate the complexities of global conflict. The wars of the twentieth century generated massive migrations. Paradoxically, these wars also hardened borders. How love and its rhetorical powers shaped emigrants' desire to return and fight for their homeland in relation to gendered notions of citizenship is at the heart of Reeder's analysis. Relatedly, Sinke's gendered reading of a Viennese family's transnational communication and the shaping of an emotional community during World War II demonstrates the extent in which (not) writing emotions was critical among exiled family members. The long-term consequences of the complicated ways in which war altered mobility and underlying intimate relations is also highlighted in Sonia Cancian's telling of her mother's life as a war orphan (a term used in Italy to include those who lost a father in the war), first left by her mother in a charity school, and then left again when her mother and stepfather migrated to Canada. Maria's experiences of multiple migrations, separations, and reunions affected the intimate emotional bonds between mother and daughter. Here we see how memories of past migration experiences created a more capacious meaning of love, encompassing sadness, hurt, and experiences of loss and resilience. The idea of "distant love" that runs through Cancian's work makes visible the artifice underlying notions of "forced" and "voluntary" family separations, suggesting that viewed through emotions, whether caused by war or work, familial separations are painful.

In the aftermath of the war, the relationship between mobility and love shifted. If the earlier works explored the ways mobility created new intimate spaces and altered the meaning of love, in the postwar period, new technologies, Cold War politics, and immigration regulations made love into a driver of migration. People migrated to find romantic love, to reunite with a lover or spouse, or rejoin their parents or children. Sexual and familial love appears to justify decisions to travel across oceans or move to faraway cities. By emphasizing the centrality of family bonds and obligations, even making it the basis for sponsorship and reunification, the regulatory power of emigration and immigration states contributed to the consolidation of this connection. Alexander Freund's chapter explores the ways in which the state, church, and private charities drew on imagery of a heteronormative love that shaped postwar German migration. Although the creation of a transatlantic "marriage marketplace" reflected the political and social desires to redefine and discipline gender within the context of postwar Germany, migration schemes also offered new kinds of opportunities for women. The ways in which love-driven migration altered the gendered nature of transnational mobilities by sexualizing women migrants and shifting the emotional tonalities of love are also visible in the histories of Greek women in postwar Canada. The ways in which coercion, familial love, and choice are all enmeshed in a woman's decision to marry an emigrant is visible in the oral histories collected by Margarita Dounia. Through these stories emerges a love weighted by nostalgia, anger, and homesickness, but also tinged with the hope of a new independence and autonomy.

Although informed by an array of diverse desires (individual, familial, erotic, and pragmatic), personal circumstances, financial constraints, and migratory regulations favoring family unification or short tourist stays, the experiences of the German and Greek women told by Freund and Dounia echo through James Hammerton's essay on the modern British diaspora. Toward the end of the last century, we see how the elevation of love to primary motivator of migration reconfigured gender norms and family relations, and transformed the emotional landscape of transnational mobility. Hammerton's study focusing on the "mobility-hungry generation" of the 1980s asks us to reconsider the significant role new kinds of communication and transportation play in shaping the emotional underpinnings of mobility. Increased disposable income combined with more vacation time could transform a holiday into a permanent move. What Hammerton terms a "mobility of modernity," marked by the material changes in the last decades of the twentieth century, ushered in a new sort of transnational movement, privileging self-fulfillment, exploration, and personal well-being over employment. These stories of falling in love on holiday ask us to think differently about the emotional life of migrants.

The significance of technology stands at the center of Roberta Ricucci's contribution. Shifting our focus from the migrants to the means of communication, Ricucci asks us to consider the impact of information and communication technologies on challenging and creating the emotional contours of contemporary migration. Ricucci's study introduces intergenerational differences linked to migrant experience, focusing on the ways in which multiple languages (digital, verbal, and physical) create a varied emotional lexicon within migrant communities. New communication technologies and mobile communication are shifting the emotional landscape of migrants and transnational living, creating new possibilities for affective expressions and intimacy across borders. As in the expansion of letter-writing and the shift to epistolary language in the second half of the nineteenth century, migrants and their families are adapting to the possibilities and testing the limits of these new forms of communication and, in the process, redefining their emotional practices and lexicon. As in the past, these experiences vary across cultures, societies, and social groups, and along generational and gender lines.

Emotional Landscapes tells us much about the forms of verbal, physical, and spatial emotional geographies underpinning the gendered nature of mobility. Space is at least as important as distance in considering the ways emotions gender migration. It is in the spaces of the initial separation, the detachment, that love appears as a means of making sense of the feelings of loss, dislocation, and fear. In some cases, it is visible in the renegotiation of intimate affective ties between husbands and wives, siblings, and parents and children. Love seems to suggest alternate chronological frameworks marking transnational migration. In general, scholars of modern migration tie shifting patterns of migration to the imposition of restrictive legislation limiting the mobility of workers. To what extent did the older languages linking migrant masculinity to "money," "letters," and "memories" combined with new romantic languages play a part in shaping arguments for and against these regulations? Emotions also show the arbitrary nature of divisions between rural/urban, transoceanic, and transnational. One other conclusion is that though the forms of love change, creating new definitions of the "good" and "bad" migrant, the ways in which affective bonds continue to define the good and bad have remained remarkably constant across time and types of migration. The chapters in this anthology cover a wide range of historical experiences connected through mobility in Europe, North America, Latin America, the Mediterranean world, Africa, and Australia. By identifying ways in which the emotional experiences of migrant men and women have shaped and were shaped by migration in this interconnected world, these essays contribute to an analytical framework for comparative work in other sociocultural and political contexts marked by migration.

NOTES

1. Farida Vis and Olga Goriunov, "The Iconic Image on Social Media: A Rapid Response to the Death of Aylan Kurdi," Visual Social Media Lab, November 1, 2015, http://visualsocialmedialab.org/blog/the-iconic-image-on-social-media-a-rapid-response-to-the-death-of-aylan-kurdi.

2. Linda Reeder, "The Making of the Italian Husband in Nineteenth-Century Italy," in *Italian Sexualities Uncovered, 1789–1914*, ed. Valeria P. Babini, Chiara Beccalossi, and Lucy Riall (London: Palgrave Macmillan, 2015), 272–90; Suzanne Desan, *The Family on Trial in Revolutionary France* (Berkeley: University of California Press, 2004); Doris Sommer, *Foundational Fictions: The National Romances of Latin America* (Berkeley: University of California Press, 2007); Jyoti Puri, *Encountering Nationalism* (Oxford: Blackwell, 2003); Aleardo Zanghellini, *The Sexual Constitution of Political Authority: The "Trials" of Same-Sex Desire* (New York: Routledge, 2015); Sin Yee Koh, *Race, Education, and Citizenship: Mobile Malaysians, British Colonial Legacies, and a Culture of Migration* (Basingstoke, UK: Palgrave Macmillan, 2016) ; Choo Chin Low, "The Politics of Emigration and Expatriation: Ethnicisation of Citizenship in Imperial Germany and China," *Journal of Historical Sociology* 29, no. 3 (2016): 385–412; Mikos Papastergiadis, *The Turbulence of Migration: Globalization, Deterritorialization, and Hybridity* (Cambridge: Polity Press, 2000).

3. Donna R. Gabaccia, "Honor and Shame in a Mobile World," unpublished paper, 2003.

4. Donna R. Gabaccia and Loretta Baldassar, eds., *Intimacy and Italian Migration: Gender and Domestic Lives in a Mobile World* (New York: Fordham University Press, 2011).

5. For recent introductions to and appraisals of the field of the history of emotions, see Susan J. Matt and Peter N. Stearns, eds., *Doing Emotions History* (Urbana: University of Illinois Press, 2014); Jan Plamper, *The History of Emotions: An Introduction* (New York: Oxford University Press, 2015); Barbara H. Rosenwein and Riccardo Cristiani, *What Is the History of Emotions?* (Cambridge: Polity, 2018); Rob Boddice, *The History of Emotions* (Manchester: Manchester University Press, 2018); and Piroska Nagy, "History of Emotions," followed by a comment by Ute

Frevert and a response by Piroska Nagy, in *Debating New Approaches to History*, ed. Marek Tamm and Peter Burke (London: Bloomsbury Academic, 2019), 189–215. See also the interviews with three of the key scholars that have shaped the field of emotion history, in Jan Plamper, "The History of Emotions: An Interview with William Reddy, Barbara Rosenwein, and Peter Stearns," *History and Theory* 49, no. 2 (2010): 237–65.

6. Barbara H. Rosenwein, "Worrying about Emotions in History," *American Historical Review* 107, no. 3 (2002): 836–37.

7. Boddice, *History of Emotions*, 134.

8. For example, the work of Monique Scheer on emotional practices (within the framework of practice theory) has provided an influential line of inquiry proposing an alternative to the mind/body, conscious/unconscious dualities. See Monique Scheer, "Are Emotions a Kind of Practice (and Is That What Makes Them Have a History?)," *History and Theory* 51, no. 2 (2012): 193–220.

9. For more information on the debates around affect and emotion see Birgitt Röttger-Rössler and Jan Slaby, *Affect in Relation: Families, Places, Technologies* (New York: Routledge, 2018), 1–28; "Affect/Emotion: Orientation Matters. A Conversation between Sigrid Schmitz and Sara Ahmed," *Freiburger Zeitschrift für Geschlechter Studien* 22, no. 2 (2014): 97–108; Sara Ahmed, *The Cultural Politics of Emotion* (New York: Routledge, 2015); and Sara Ahmed, *The Promise of Happiness* (Durham, NC: Duke University Press, 2010).

10. For examples, see the general discussions of the evolution of the history of emotions cited in note 5.

11. Peter N. Stearns and Carole Z. Stearns, "Emotionology: Clarifying the History of Emotions and Emotional Standards," *American Historical Review* 90, no. 4 (1985): 813–36.

12. Susan J. Matt and Peter N. Stearns, "Introduction," in *Doing Emotions History*, ed. Matt and Stearns, 9.

13. Rosenwein, "Worrying about Emotions"; Barbara H. Rosenwein, *Emotional Communities in the Early Middle Ages* (Ithaca, NY: Cornell University Press, 2006); Barbara H. Rosenwein, *Generations of Feelings: A History of Emotions, 600–1700* (New York: Cambridge University Press, 2016); Maureen C. Miller and Edward Wheatley, eds., *Emotions, Communities, and Difference in Medieval Europe: Essays in Honor of Barbara H. Rosenwein* (New York: Routledge, 2017).

14. Ute Frevert, *Emotions in History—Lost and Found* (Budapest: Central European University Press, 2011).

15. Frevert, *Emotions in History*, 12.

16. William M. Reddy, *The Navigation of Feeling: A Framework for the History of Emotions* (New York: Cambridge University Press, 2011).

17. Rosenwein, *Emotional Communities*, 2.

18. Reddy, *Navigation of Feeling*, 45.

19. Paolo Boccagni and Loretta Baldassar, "Emotions on the Move: Mapping the Emergent Field of Emotion and Migration," *Emotion, Space, and Society* 16 (2015): 75.

20. Maruška Svašek, "On the Move: Emotions and Human Mobility," *Journal of Ethnic and Migration Studies* 36, no. 6 (2010): 868.

21. Boddice, *History of Emotions*, 92–99; Joanna Bourke, *What It Means to Be Human: Reflections from 1791 to the Present* (Berkeley, CA: Counterpoint, 2011), 94–97, 136–43.

22. Social scientists working on contemporary migrations have begun to pay more attention to the interplay between gender and emotion. This is, in part, a result of the growing feminization of migration that began in the second half of the twentieth century. Most works have focused on migration experiences in which women are important protagonists, such as transnational marriages and care work. For an overview, see Ann Brooks and Ruth Simpson, *Emotions in Transmigration: Transformation, Movement, and Identity* (New York: Palgrave Macmillan, 2013). Examples of these studies include: Jennifer S. Hirsh, *A Courtship after Marriage: Sexuality and Love in Mexican Transnational Families* (Berkeley: University of California Press, 2003); Nicole Constable, *Romance on a Global Stage: Pen Pals, Virtual Ethnography, and "Mail-Order" Marriages* (Berkeley: University of California Press, 2003); Rhacel Salazar Parreñas, *Servants of Globalization: Migration and Domestic Work*, 2nd ed. (Stanford, CA: Stanford University Press, 2015); Loretta Baldassar and Laura Merla, eds., *Transnational Families, Migration, and the Circulation of Care: Understanding Mobility and Absence in Family Life* (New York: Routledge, 2014). In regard to the work on correspondence, emotions, and migration in this volume, see also Sonia Cancian, *Families, Lovers, and Their Letters: Italian Postwar Migration to Canada* (Winnipeg: University of Manitoba Press, 2010) and the contributions in the Special Issue on Migrant Letters, ed. Marcelo J. Borges and Sonia Cancian, *History of the Family* 21, no. 3 (2016), for a historical and interdisciplinary approach.

23. Nicola Mai and Russell King, "Love, Sexuality, and Migration: Mapping the Issue(s)," *Mobilities* 4, no. 3 (2009): 297, 300.

CHAPTER 1

What's Love Got to Do with It?

Language of Transnational Affect in the Letters of Portuguese Migrants

MARCELO J. BORGES

The unprecedented increase in transoceanic migrations in the second half of the nineteenth century was a major catalyst for an explosion in letter-writing and for the expansion of letter-writing to the working classes.[1] Through letters, migrants and their families made sense of their separation and kept connected with each other and with the broader purpose of migration as a family project, contributing to the creation of what David Gerber characterizes as a "singular transnational space."[2] This chapter explores this epistolary language, focusing on expressions of responsibility and sacrifice as gendered manifestations of transnational affect among Portuguese families separated by migration, in particular married couples living apart and parents who left their children behind. Epistolary language was the vehicle through which they managed the emotion work of migration; communicated vital information to cope with their temporary separation; weighed options and possibilities for the future; and discussed expectations and behaviors within a narrative framework of family and marital love that combined emotional and material well-being.

Migration was a widespread phenomenon in late-nineteenth- and early-twentieth-century Portugal. Portuguese workers participated in a variety of migratory circuits in the Americas, Portuguese Africa and other colonial territories, and Europe. Brazil attracted the vast majority of transatlantic migrants (ranging from 90 percent in the 1890s to 70 percent in the 1920s), followed by the United States and Argentina.³ This was a gendered labor strategy characterized by a predominance of migrant men, who constituted close to 80 percent of departures from continental Portugal between 1886 and 1930.⁴ For married migrants, this strategy relied on the active role of wives who stayed home to take care of the household, work the land if they lived in rural villages, and invest money sent from abroad.⁵ The gendered nature of Portuguese migrations contributed to a prevalent pattern of family separation rooted in a longstanding culture of migration with expectation of return.⁶ A parallel movement of family reunification also emerged, but transatlantic migration continued to be overwhelmingly male.⁷

The significance of correspondence in keeping family ties alive, in particular among husbands and wives separated by migration, is illustrated by the literary depictions of scenes of women waiting for the arrival of the mail from abroad in rural towns throughout Portugal. In the novel *A morgadinha dos Canaviais* (The Canaviais heiress, 1868), Júlio Dinis described the arrival of the mail carrier in a village in northern Portugal as an "ant-like movement of people."⁸ "Today is the arrival of the mail from Brazil, nobody can calm the populace down," explains the local postal manager to the protagonist, who is visiting from the city and therefore unfamiliar with the commotion created by the arrival of the mail among the local population.⁹ This scene resembles others portrayed by writers in different times and places of emigration. In the novel *Viúvas de vivos* (Widows of the living, 1947), set in central Portugal, Joaquim Lagoeiro described the contrasting emotions experienced by the wives of migrant men as they waited the arrival of the post. "There were those who, despite their lost men not having written for many years, were still there, without blinking; waiting, always waiting," he observed.¹⁰ Once names began to be called, the fortunate who received news "would later exhibit the letter, full of vanity."¹¹

The discussion that follows examines letters submitted in passport applications of women or minors to prove marital or parental consent of husbands or fathers abroad. For women, this requirement was in place from 1863 to 1969.¹² Personal letters were commonly used as proof of authorization until the 1920s, when they were replaced by a standardized form. They became known as call letters (*cartas de chamada* in Portuguese). The corpus under analysis consists of over 2,200 such letters from the 1870s to the 1920s from regions with significant migration throughout Portugal.¹³ These letters were part of larger epistolary exchanges kept by families separated by migration and thus representative of personal correspondence in contexts of migration.¹⁴ They constitute, to borrow Mark Seymour's characterization of love letters found in Italian judicial records, "normal exceptions"—exceptional because of their bureaucratic use, "but very probably quite representative in other respects."[15] The main limitation of call letters is that they include only the voice of the person who calls, which in this case is overwhelmingly male (from husbands to their wives). If indirect, however, women's perspectives are not absent. These letters were part of broader epistolary conversations and it is possible to identify significant traces of the voices of correspondents in writers' answers, challenges, and reactions. In addition, the prospect of an imminent family reunification often resulted in explicit discussions of migration as a family project, the responsibilities of husbands and wives, and the emotional and material underpinnings of their transnational lives.

Transnational Affect

For Portuguese families separated by migration, the epistolary language became the building block of transnational affect. As sociologists Amanda Wise and Selvaraj Velayutham argue for current international migrations, a full understanding of the migration experience requires us to include a consideration of the "non-material conditions" that keep networks and relations alive.[16] Wise and Velayutham propose to look beyond the "traffic"—that is, the material aspects of migration—and focus on affects and emotions to help bring to light "what compels groups to remain with and continue to reproduce transnational social fields."[17] This approach is equally revealing for nineteenth- and twentieth-century labor migrations. Like contemporary circuits of global migrations, these moves were characterized by varied types of mobility that connected home villages and local economies with the wider world, including cycles of male migration with return and temporary family moves, some of which became long-term or permanent relocations. The experience of migration and transnational living required families to engage in considerable emotional work. Keeping family bonds alive also meant connecting migrants back to the homeland, especially through remittances, which, in Portugal, were equally vital for the household and the national economy. As a result, migrants' transnational affect was also reinforced by national emotional regimes that equated love of family with love of country.[18] Even though cases of lost husbands and abandoned families existed, as attested by popular culture and historical accounts, such behavior was considered by the societies of origin as a transgression of the values of transnational affect that expected bonds to be nurtured as the foundation of family migratory projects.[19]

Interest and emotion are both integral parts of migration projects. As a reaction to earlier portrayals of migrants as mere pawns of larger political and economic forces, and with the intent of highlighting migrants' agency and volition, scholars turned their analyses to migrants' economic strategies. But, as Paolo Boccagni and Loretta Baldassar argue, an exclusive focus on the rationality of migrants' motivations risks obscuring other factors involved in migration that could be considered irrational. As the authors explain, "[e]ven when emotions are considered . . . there is a tendency to see them as largely inconsequential 'soft stuffing' to the 'hard' issues that really matter."[20] For Boccagni and Baldassar, looking at the emotional underpinnings of migrants' experiences provides "an important corrective to the notion of migrant as *homo economicus*."[21] Further, taking into account the material and emotional dimensions of the migrant experience is also necessary because such an approach aligns more closely with migrants' own conception of the migratory project. As their letters make clear, migrants rarely treated emotion and interest as mutually exclusive categories nor kept them as distinctly separate narrative themes. Sentiments influenced economic decisions, and these decisions were in turn made in the context of larger emotional logics. Migrants made use of a combined language of interest and emotion to discuss motivations, decisions, strategies, and behavior as well as to reflect on their consequences. In this blended narrative, family love often took the form of securing material well-being, and economic decisions were explained in emotional terms.

An initial characterization of the language of transnational affect in migrant letters requires an identification of words and their usage. Words are central to an understanding of past emotions, but we need to be aware of changing meanings and contexts.[22] This chapter approaches the language of transnational affect among Portuguese migrant families at different levels—from word frequencies and key terms in context to thematic clusters and narrative strategies—and it situates language in the larger cultural and historical context.

The following words emerge as the top ten nouns in the complete corpus (which comprises over 900,000 words): letter, money, health, company, family, God, day, mother, children, and house/home. Some of these words are common in the openings and closings of personal letters, thus contributing to their frequency; but they also represent central concerns of families separated by migration: desire for fluid communication, and discussions about material well-being, health, family members, and home. The word "money" appears as a very close second to "letter," with a frequency of more than 4,000 times each; these two words represent 0.48 percent and 0.46 percent of the corpus. But if we also consider common equivalents for money (such as diminutives, slang terms, and specific currencies), explicit references to money grow from about 4,100 to about 7,100. In contrast, the word *amor* (love in Portuguese) is used 196 times (0.02 percent); and if we add the word *amizade* (friendship), which was often used to talk about love or affection, the proportion increases slightly to 0.03 percent of the corpus (143 times). Word frequencies constitute but a first step toward uncovering the characteristics of the emotional lexicon of migrant letters. They provide an indication that economic interest was a central concern for the writers of these letters and that this concern was fully integrated into the language of affect.

Narrative of Responsibility

Expressions of family and marital love appear in these letters in a variety of forms. A close reading of the letters brings to light key terms as well as narrative patterns and strategies used by writers to maintain and re-create emotional bonds, and to restate the significance of migration as a family endeavor. The use of recognizable themes and recurrent language in thousands of individual letters indicates the existence of a shared understanding of what constituted affection and commitment for families living apart because of migration. These ideas were usually communicated in the form of expressing expectations and obligations. Among them, dependability and responsibility were key concerns for migrant husbands and fathers. These expectations translated into specific obligations: not to forget their families, to keep up regular communication, to provide for their families through remittances, to save money, and to build a future together through reunification in the place of immigration or by returning home. Since the letters in this corpus were used as call letters, temporary or long-term family reunification abroad was the preferred plan.

The worry about migrants forgetting and abandoning their wives and children is present in many letters. It was a fear that letter-writing itself was meant to assuage. It was far more common for writers to talk about not forgetting their families than it was for them to talk about remembering them. This is illustrated by the higher frequency of the verb *esquecer* (to forget) compared to the verb *lembrar* (to remember) in all its forms: they appear 769 times (0.08 percent) and 392 times (0.04 percent), respectively. Not to forget meant writing regularly and providing for their families. Writers made regular use of a common term for gift by referring to the money they sent home as a *lembrança*, that is, as a "souvenir," further underscoring the connection between writing/sending money and remembering their families.[23] Therefore, the rhythm of writing was habitually punctuated by the possibility of remittances. This sentiment is clearly expressed in the following example drawn from a letter from Brazil sent by António to his wife, Graça: "I know you are amazed because I have not written to you; I received your letters and saw everything you tell me in them; the fact that I have not written is not because I have forgotten but because I know [*me lembra*] that letters are only paper, and since so far I have written two letters without anything of value in them, I have not written sooner for that reason."[24] António sent ten thousand réis with this letter, apologizing for its not being as large a sum as he would have liked because of unfavorable economic conditions, adding "not everything goes the way we imagine it."

Letters and remittances were the most tangible expressions of migrants' continued commitment to their family and to their shared migration project. The arrival of money from abroad was a validation of the decision to migrate and a justification for the emotional and practical costs of living apart. The value of remittances went beyond the strictly monetary; its significance was also moral and emotional.[25] Writers commonly refer to sending money home in terms of duty and obligation (*dever, obrigação*). This sentiment is clear in the language of the following passages that appear in letters by migrants from the districts of Porto and Braga working in Brazil: "I have fulfilled my duty [*dever*] because I have sent you everything that I have earned"; and "when I came here, I knew what my obligation [*obrigação*] was, I may be left without money, but there will be no lack of money for you, God willing."[26]

In contexts of family migration, sending money was a fulfillment of masculine roles. Migrant men were keenly aware of their expected role as defined by family members and by the community at large. An effective channel for social mores, gossip acted as a powerful check. "If a man comes here and he is lucky and sends lots of money, then there is no man like him," reflected Luíz in a letter to his wife, Maria de Jesus, "because he is hardworking and thrifty ... but if a man is unlucky and sends little money, then he is a failure [*estragado*] and lazy or he spends money on women; that is the way people talk."[27] As Luíz's characterization suggests, this was an expectation that defined the migrant not only as a husband and father, but also as a man. It is in this context that we need to read the reaction of his countryman António to what he perceived as his wife's criticism of the fulfillment of his role as a husband and a man when he wrote from São Paulo: "I know well that what you expected is for me to send you more money, but you need to understand that here I don't just collect it by the handful. Look, I have worked a lot to get what I have, and I think that I have fulfilled my obligation well. In the middle of a crisis like this one, I have been a man ... in order to earn money for us to eat."[28] For migrants, remembering and providing were clear manifestations of marital affection characterized as a manly duty.

Some writers also made explicit references to love as part of their discussions of obligation and talked about remittances as manifestation of marital love (*amor, amizade*). For example, this was the sentiment expressed in a letter from Albino when he informed his wife that he had made arrangements for her to receive five pounds and added: "Forgive me for it being so little, as it is only a small a token [*lembrança*] so that you know that I have not stopped loving you [*ainda não lhe perdi o amor*]."[29] This connection could also act as a double-edged sword, as when wives used the association between remittances and love to question their husbands' behavior. A migrant from Olhão (Faro) reacted strongly to such an equation by his wife, which included suspicions of infidelity: "You say that, if I send you money, it is because I love you and, if I don't send you [money], it is because I don't love you."[30] He went on to express that, despite what his wife may imagine, life abroad was difficult and it was not easy for a man by himself to save money, thus encouraging her to join him. As these examples illustrate, remittances were central to migrant families in economic and emotional terms.

The impact of the money sent home by migrants went beyond individual households and local economies.[31] Contemporary observers remarked how the Portuguese economy benefited greatly from migrants' fulfillment of their roles as husbands, fathers, and sons that materialized in remittances. This association was vividly described by Portuguese journalist Mariano Pina. In an 1896 book recounting his experiences in Brazil, Pina wrote a passionate defense of the benefits of emigration for Portugal that associated love of family to love of country.[32] Pina presents a moving account of the long lines of Portuguese migrants at the banks of Rio de Janeiro to exchange money the day before the mail steamers were to depart for Portugal. "That people ... was composed exclusively of Portuguese men," he wrote, "of tireless, honorable, and kind workers from our land ... good sons, good husbands, good brothers, who were bringing the fruit of their savings, a good portion of the excessive labor they do every day, every hour; they were bringing the gold they earned with so much effort in these faraway lands to send it to their old parents, to their families, so they could make the lives of their loved ones easier, more comfortable, sweeter."[33] For Pina, these "blessed people" were deeply committed to their loved ones in their villages in rural Portugal—"the place where the eyes of their exiled souls always direct their gaze" and where they hoped to return one day.[34] The cultural and social importance of the idea of return, the gender imbalance of migration, the moral expectations of family and community, and the economic and emotional significance remittances had among migrant families kept migrant savings flowing back to Portugal for many decades.

Narrative of Sacrifice

The language of responsibility that constituted the foundation of the expression of marital affect in migrant letters had another important pillar in the language of sacrifice. Its use underscored the writer's capacity to overcome difficult personal and material conditions, and to forgo individual needs to achieve the goals of migration. It was also often used for its "mirror effect," calling the reader to emulate the writer and do likewise according to expected behaviors and accepted gender norms. This narrative strand is a central component in these letters, which reinforced the overall idea of the migrant as a provider. It often appears in connection to references to the effort required for securing resources to meet family needs and to send money home. The goal was to remind the recipient of the letter of the toil behind the monetary assistance they received from abroad. This message was also an important one to convey when remittances were lower than expected or not as regular as desired. These references are meant to explain circumstances, actions, and decisions, but they were also imbued with emotional connotations.

A systematic reading of the letters indicates the existence of some recurring expressions that shaped this narrative. Starting with the term "sacrifice" itself, concordance analysis reveals that most of the times it appears (either as a noun or a verb: *sacrifício, sacrificar*), writers use it in this context and with this particular meaning.[35] "Make do as well as you can with that money," wrote a migrant from Rio de Janeiro to his wife in Lamego (Viseu), "God knows the sacrifices I made to send it to you."[36] Related terms used in the letters to convey similar ideas include: suffering and to suffer (*sofrimento, sofrir*), effort (*esforço*), struggle or fight (*luta*), and toil (*trabalhos*). The following passages illustrate some uses of these expressions in the letters to talk about the migration experience: "Here I am, fighting, fighting against this dark life, thinking of you and my son"; "Poor he who is in need, who does not have any remedy but to suffer"; "I suffer everything to see if I can earn some money"; "You can see the struggles of a father in this world."[37] Another recurring term is "cost" (*custar*), used as a way to express how something was obtained with effort. In this case, hard work and sacrifice are presented as the "cost" migrants had to pay to be able to send money, a cost whose value cannot be fully captured by the monetary worth of remittances or by references to wages or exchange rates (information that was also frequently included in the letters). A migrant from Cantanhede (Coimbra), residing in São Paulo, conveyed these ideas of cost and sacrifice by using a dramatic comparison: "Money is like blood," he wrote, "earning it requires much effort [*custa a ganhar*]."[38] This common turn of phrase appears in other letters as a way to highlight migrants' dedication and hard work, albeit usually in less dramatic ways. "Money is nice but earning it takes a lot of effort [*custa muito a ganhar*]," wrote another migrant from Brazil; for his part, a migrant working in Ludlow, Massachusetts, cautioned his wife to take good care of the money he was sending, adding "and don't think this is a joke, because it takes a lot of effort to earn it [*custa muito a ganhar*]."[39]

In addition to these recurrent expressions, the letters exhibit some recognizable thematic clusters that communicated the message of sacrifice by focusing on migrants' dedication to work, on the physical consequences of their working and living conditions, and on migrants' frugal and self-denying lifestyle.[40] This message was reinforced by the use of expressions and images that underscored the demanding nature of migrants' labor; among them, the use of a quantifier ("I work a lot") or of comparisons with the toil of forced laborers, such as beasts of burden ("like a donkey") or non-Europeans ("like a black man" or "like a Moor").[41] Other ways to convey this sentiment was to draw on images of religious or political sacrifice such as Calvary, purgatory, or exile.[42] Particularly salient in these thematic clusters is the notion of physical sacrifices associated with migration. Migrants lamented their lack of time to attend to personal needs, to write, or to rest. References to poor health and to the strained physical state of writers served to embody the consequences of separation and hard labor, and were meant to elicit emotional responses from the reader. A familiar pattern appears with regularity in the letters in which references to health and physical affliction serve to explain the impossibility of sending money or to highlight how the writer was able to overcome this impediment and secure money to provide for his family (working despite physical limitations or humiliating himself by having to ask others for money). Thus, both keeping up regular correspondence and sending money become measures of a migrant's effort to nurture family bonds and to provide for his family. This rhetorical strategy served to highlight that migrants sacrificed for something larger than their individual objectives; they did so for the well-being of their families. In this way, sacrifice turns into self-sacrifice, a dimension that becomes particularly clear in the many epistolary references to thriftiness and frugality as important characteristics of a responsible migrant's behavior.

The excerpts below illustrate some of the many ways in which writers combined elements from these thematic clusters to express the narrative of sacrifice:

> I received your letter... and did not write to you on the same day because ... I wanted to send you three pounds.... You need to wait for a letter which will arrive soon with the order to receive them.... You cannot imagine the sacrifices I am making for you and the children.... As you know, I did not grow up working in retail... but I was able to overcome all difficulties and today I am licensed as a merchant.... [W]hen there is a need, one does whatever it takes.... I can't leave the store at all, except on Sundays to go to church, and for that I need to close the doors.... I work without rest [*agarrado ao trabalho*] from sunrise to ten at night, sacrificing everything because of you... and I will die working to see if one day you can live with greater satisfaction. (Manuel to his wife, Maria dos Prazeres)[43]

> Regarding my illness, I am doing better. It is not tuberculosis, like all of you thought. I was sick and I did not take good care of myself just to save money, and I got bronchitis. If I treat it, maybe it will go away. You can see how much I have worked and saved to see if one day I can become a man.... And tell your parents that their son-in-law is not like they think; like those men who go after women. Tell them that he goes one or even two months just wearing boots without socks. And for what? So he can see if he can achieve something. (António to his wife, Deolinda)[44]

> I am sending you two bills of exchange for a total value of 150,000 réis. ... If you decide not to come, take care of the money. Remember that I am earning it honorably, with the effort of my work and with sacrifice for my health.... Forgive me if this letter is written in haste, slumber is overtaking me. (Francisco to his wife, Emília)[45]

The prevalence of these expressions suggests that migrants felt their families back home did not fully appreciate the challenges migrants encountered and their efforts to overcome them. Images of the riches awaiting migrants abroad were common in Portugal's popular culture. They were part of an imaginary that developed over decades of emigration and, in the case of Brazil, one that went back to centuries of colonial experience. Migrants' own desires to show how well they have done abroad also contributed to these deep-rooted images. This is illustrated by the prevailing stereotype of the successful migrant who struck it rich—popularly known as the *brasileiro* or the *americano*—and who displayed his good fortune in the form of new construction and through celebrated donations to local schools and hospitals.[46] In more modest ways, thousands of families throughout Portugal could always point to new plots of land, home improvements, or new animals acquired with money earned abroad.[47] Images of migration as an easy path to economic success had an adverse effect on the evaluation of migrants' actions and perceived character when it did not materialize according to expectations. In this view, if Brazil or "America" were lands of boundless riches and opportunities, and if the migrant was not sending money home often enough or at the expected level, then he only had himself to blame.

The narrative of sacrifice was necessary to counter this view and give credit to migrants' work. At the same time, it served to protect migrants' character as responsible family members in moments of hardship when hopes and expectations were not met. "Brazil is for everyone, but not everyone is for Brazil," wrote Joaquim to his wife, Piedade.[48] This phrase aptly captures the sentiment of many letter writers who felt their experiences were being measured against unrealistic tales of easy riches achieved with little effort. We do not have Piedade's side of the epistolary conversation, but we learn from Joaquim's letter that she had asked her husband to arrange everything for them to be reunited in Rio de Janeiro. Joaquim decided to oblige, but he warned his wife not to believe all "the empty talk" (*palavreado*) she has heard in the village about Brazil, adding that only after seeing it for herself will she learn "what Brazil is really like" and realize that "money is not made here while sleeping." In this way, Joaquim expresses a sentiment that appears in many letters: migrants are able to provide for their families because of hard work and sacrifice, and not because the bounties of the land are available to them just for the taking. Comparisons with other migrants were often used by wives and family members to express dissatisfaction and question migrants' commitment, work ethic, or capacity. But comparisons worked both ways, as some writers reacted by questioning the performance of other potential or real migrants if they were in their place. This was the response of Manuel, a migrant from Sernancelhe (Viseu) working in Rio de Janeiro, in a 1918 letter in which he reacted to accusations from his father, father-in-law, and wife that he was not doing enough to save and send money. "You tell me . . . that José, Amelia's husband, has sent a lot of money. He sends it home but owes it here. I could also do like that, but it is only with the power of my sweat. . . . Let's hope that those who are there are working as hard as I am."[49]

Family pressure intensified emotional responses, as illustrated by a letter from António, a migrant from the rural parish of Conceição (Faro). António reacted angrily to his in-laws' questioning of his character, work ethic, and competence as a family provider. He discredited his accusers by questioning their knowledge about what life as a migrant was really like and their own aptitude to succeed in the challenging circumstances of working away from home:

> I don't know what they expect me to have done in the short time that I have been here. Only if your family imagines that here money is lying around in the streets. Add up all the money that I have sent you and ask those who talk about me how much more they could have done in the time that I have been in this land. I would like to see some of those stupid people who talk like that in this place; they would probably be crying, not knowing where to earn a dime to eat. . . . And you write me that if you don't ask me for money I would not have sent you any [*não teria essa lembrança*]. You have no reason to talk like that because it is true that I have not been able to send more but at the same time I have not been here for a long time.[50]

The basic idea common to these and other epistolary uses of the narrative of sacrifice is that people back home talked too lightly about migration and its rewards without any understanding of its true cost. These strong reactions reinforced the main idea of the migrant as a responsible provider, and served to underline that achieving results in the form of savings required dedication, hard work, and putting family interests above individual ones.

Because of the gendered nature of overseas labor migration, and the historically gendered understanding of family responsibilities, the message of sacrifice transmitted in these letters may appear highly masculine. But the few examples of female writers that are part of this corpus indicate that a comparable rhetorical strategy, associated to similar images and emotions, was used by migrant women who were family providers, such as widows or single mothers.[51] This is illustrated in the language used by Maria dos Remédios, a female migrant from Lamego (Viseu), when she wrote from Rio de Janeiro to the person in charge of the children she left home: "I am worn out [*acabada*] and my eyesight is already failing me due to the excess of work . . . because of those two unfortunate children."[52] For her part Carlota, a female migrant from the neighboring village of São João de Fontoura (Resende, Viseu), presents a different migration experience but a comparable use of the common language of sacrifice to describe it. Carlota had migrated to São Paulo to join her sons, leaving her daughters to the care of her mother in Portugal. She explained her situation as follows: "I suffer more and more every day. . . . Some days I only have a tea. . . . I leave home every night three hours after midnight and I have to go alone as far as from there to Vila Verde." And then she added a telling reflection about the false images of migration as a path to easy riches that were common in the places of origin. "When somebody returns home with a few coins in their pockets they brag about it, but it is when one arrives here [in Brazil] that sees how it really is." Carlota was calling her daughters to join them in Brazil; but warned them: "In this land one works night and day."[53] A comparable assessment, but on a darker note, appears in a letter from a female migrant in Rio de Janeiro to her mother, who is caring for her son in Portugal: "Today, I don't have family, friends, anything. Everything is so far away. Here I go from home to work. I come back from work at seven in the evening and leave again at six in the morning. . . . I don't care because this is my lot in life [*minha sorte*]. And I keep going and going until one day I am consumed and I put an end to my existence. I have not done that already because I need to look after my son."[54]

The discussion in this chapter has focused on the expressions of transnational affect by labor migrants and, in particular, on the understandings of marital and family affect by husbands and fathers who wrote the majority of the call letters. However, these letters also illuminate the emotional expectations and decisions of the wives of migrants who stayed behind. Several thematic clusters emerge in the corpus revealing the ideal behavior of wives. Above all, wives were expected to show an unambiguous attachment to the strategy of male labor migration. Characterized by June Hee Kwon as forms of "unwaged affective labor," waiting and taking care of household and family constituted the most visible forms of this attachment.[55] Important thematic clusters of wives' expected behavior included: writing regularly, obeying their husbands' decisions, acting and looking respectable, protecting their marriage, being responsible with the money earned abroad, and, in more general terms, helping their husbands achieve the goals of migration. Since the letters under analysis here functioned as call letters, many of these aspects of wives' marital duty were evaluated and discussed in the context of possible reunification. Married women were not legally obligated to follow their husbands beyond the borders of Portugal; therefore, husbands deployed material and emotional reasons to present a persuasive case to their wives. Their arguments ranged from practical and economic reasons, to expressions of marital love and reciprocity, to the threat of infidelity and even abandonment.[56]

Emotions on the Move

Looking at the language of affect in the migration experience provides a fertile perspective to consider the interactions between emotions and space in contexts of mobility. As scholars of the history of emotions have shown, emotions are connected not only with time but also with place. The variability of emotions according to space and context has been analyzed through concepts like emotional communities, regimes, and styles.[57] The narrative strategies used in Portuguese migrant letters open a window into the emotional work that migrant families engaged in as they built, maintained, negotiated, and sometimes mended the bonds of transnational affect. A gendered language of marital and family affect that blended such concepts as love, interest, sacrifice, and reciprocity provided the script for this emotional work. Emotions and interest were an integral part of this language, as illustrated in this chapter by the analysis of the material and emotional costs of remittances and by function of the epistolary narratives of responsibility and sacrifice.

Through migration, families adapted to shifting emotional landscapes. What constituted a responsible husband and a dutiful wife, ideas of marital affect and of parental and filial obligations, and their emotional underpinnings were rooted in the emotional regimes of the migrants' societies of origin. The experience of migration and its emotional tensions heightened these feelings and challenged these notions. For couples separated by migration, the family was the emotional community that anchored the emotional expressions and practices of migrant letter writers and their recipients back home—a family that was physically separated and whose bonds were tested by the tensions of transnational living. The script of transnational affect built over epistolary conversations—and silences—was guided by a shared understanding of migration as a family project. Even when new emotional attachments occurred (as in the case of discussions of "lost" husbands and infidelity), they were considered within the framework of the moral foundations and expected gender roles of the transnational family. This script re-created dominant sociocultural values of and ideas of gendered responsibilities and emotions of turn-of-the-century Portugal. By and large, the gendered expectations of family obligations and marital responsibilities that formed the foundations of this script of transnational affect among migrant families conformed to dominant bourgeois ideals.[58] Migration was seen by these families as a way to fulfill expected roles and conform to socially accepted norms. But by separating families and giving new spaces for women as household managers, producers, and de facto heads of households while men were away, migration itself challenged this normative foundation. It is possible that family relocation to a different country in time diminished some of the moral and emotional power of the local societies of origin, but this experience is not visible through these letters, which capture the experiences and sentiments of families while they were separated. The emotional system that is mobilized in the letters to make sense of the transnational living among Portuguese families was rooted in the values and cultural norms of the places of origin, but it was not static. It was challenged and reshaped by the experience of migration itself, by the changing identities and roles of husbands and wives living temporarily apart, and by influences from the societies of immigration.

NOTES

Research and analysis for this chapter have been generously supported by the following institutions and programs: Dickinson College's Research and Development Committee and the Kalaris Family Fellowship; Central Pennsylvania Consortium–Andrew W. Mellon Foundation Grant; the EURIAS Fellowship Program, cofunded by the EU Marie Curie Actions, under the 7th Framework Programme.

1. War mobilization constituted another major force behind the expansion of popular writing. See Antonio Gibelli, "Emigrantes y soldados: La escritura popular como práctica de masas en los siglos XIX y XX," in *La conquista del alfabeto: Escritura y clases populares*, ed. Antonio Castillo Gómez (Gijón, Spain: Ediciones Trea, 2002), 189–223; Martyn Lyons, *The Writing Culture of Ordinary People in Europe, c. 1860–1920* (New York: Cambridge University Press, 2013).

2. David A. Gerber, *Authors of Their Lives: The Personal Correspondence of British Immigrants to North America in the Nineteenth Century* (New York: New York University Press, 2006), 92.

3. For an overview, see Marcelo J. Borges, "Portugal, Modern Era Migration," in *The Encyclopedia of Global Human Migration*, ed. Immanuel Ness with Peter Bellwood (New York and Oxford: Wiley-Blackwell, 2013).

4. Maria Ioannis Baganha, "Migração transatlântica: Uma síntese histórica," in *Desenvolvimento económico e mudança social: Portugal nos últimos dois séculos, homenagem a Miriam Halpern Pereira*, ed. José Vicente Serrão et al. (Lisbon: Imprensa de Ciências Sociais, 2009), 410–12.

5. On average, from 1885 to 1930, 48.1 percent of emigrant men were married and 1.2 percent widowers (or in a few cases, divorced). The proportion of married men grew considerably in the second half of the 1920s, when they represented an average of 55 percent of migrant men (plus 1.8 percent who were widowers or divorced). These figures consider all migrant men, regardless of age. *Anuario estatístico 1884–1886, 1900, 1921, 1923–1924, 1925–1930* (Lisbon: Imprensa Nacional, 1886–1931); *Emigração portuguesa 1901–1912* (Lisbon: Imprensa Nacional, 1904–1913); *Movimento da população 1887, 1889–1896, 1909–1921* (Lisbon: Imprensa Nacional, 1889–1924).

6. Caroline B. Brettell, "Emigrar para voltar: A Portuguese Ideology of Return Migration," *Papers in Anthropology* 20, no. 1 (1979): 1–20.

7. João Evangelista, *Um século de população portuguesa* (Lisbon: Publicações do Centro de Estudos Demográficos, 1971), 125–26.

8. Júlio Dinis, *A morgadinha dos Canaviais* (1868; rpt. Porto: Porto Editora, 2004), 49. All translations from Portuguese to English are mine.

9. Dinis, *A morgadinha dos Canaviais*, 49.

10. Joaquim Lagoeiro, *Viúvas de vivos*, 3rd ed. (1947; rpt. Lisbon: Editorial Minerva, 1973), 105.

11. Lagoeiro, *Viúvas de vivos*, 105.

12. Carlos Vieira Ramos, *Legislação portuguesa sobre emigração e passaportes* (Lisbon: Typographia Adolpho de Mendonça, 1913), 21; Elina Guimarães, "A mulher portuguesa na legislação civil," *Análise Social*, 3rd ser., 22, nos. 92–93 (1986): 557–77; Maria Manuel Stocker de Sousa and Maria Cristina Perez Dominguez, *Women in Portugal*, Women in Europe Supplement No. 11 (Brussels: European Union Commission, 1982).

13. The letters in this corpus are the result of an examination of an estimated 100,000 passport application dossiers in the following regional archives: Braga, Castelo Branco, Coimbra, Faro, Leiria, Lisbon, Madeira, Porto, Viseu, and Castelo Branco. All letters were transcribed and annotated for content analysis using the qualitative data analysis software MaxQDA.

14. Some scholars have warned about the limitations of this type of private document put to bureaucratic use, but the blurry lines between private and public are inherent to personal and family letters in general. For a critique, see Werner Stangel, "Consideraciones metodológicas acerca de las cartas privadas de emigrantes españoles desde América, 1492–1824: El caso de las 'cartas de llamada,'" *Jahrbuch für Geschichte Lateinamerikas* 47 (2010): 11–35. For the connection between public and private, see Janet Gurkin Altman, *Epistolarity: Approaches to a Form* (Columbus: Ohio University Press, 1982); David Barton and Nigel Hall, eds., *Letter Writing as a Social Practice* (Amsterdam: John Benjamins Publishing Company, 2000); Gerber, *Authors of Their Lives*; Sonia Cancian, *Families, Lovers, and Their Letters: Italian Postwar Migration to Canada* (Winnipeg: University of Manitoba Press, 2010).

15. Mark Seymour, "Epistolary Emotions: Exploring Amorous Hinterlands in 1870s Southern Italy," *Social History* 35, no. 2 (2010): 150.

16. Amanda Wise and Selvaraj Valayuntham, "Towards a Typology of Transnational Affect," Working Paper No. 4 (Sydney: Centre for Research on Social Inclusion, Macquarie University, 2006), 2.

17. Wise and Valayuntham, "Towards a Typology of Transnational Affect," 2.

18. Miriam Halpern Pereira, *A política portuguesa de emigração, 1850–1930* (Lisbon: A Regra do Jogo, 1981); Brettell, "Emigrar para voltar"; Caroline B. Brettell, "The Emigrant, the Nation, and the State in Nineteenth- and Twentieth-Century Portugal: An Anthropological Approach," *Portuguese Studies Review* 2, no. 2 (1993): 51–65. The chapters by Linda Reeder and Elizabeth Zanoni in this volume further explore connections between familial love, patriotism, and gendered ideas of citizenship in contexts of migration in the Italian case.

19. See the study of María Bjerg in this anthology for a discussion of this perspective focused on cases of transatlantic bigamy in contexts of migration. For examples among Portuguese migrants in Brazil, see Cristina Donza Cancela and Daniel Souza Barroso, "Casamentos portugueses em uma capital da Amazônia: Perfil demográfico, normas e redes sociais (Belém, 1891–1920)," *História Unisinos* 15, no. 1 (2011): 66–69. For a discussion of "forgetful" husbands in the context of Portuguese migration, see Marcelo J. Borges, *Chains of Gold: Portuguese Emigration to Argentina in Transatlantic Perspective* (Leiden, the Netherlands: Brill, 2009), 193–96, 226.

20. Paolo Boccagni and Loretta Baldassar, "Emotions on the Move: Mapping the Emergent Field of Emotion and Migration," *Emotion, Space, and Society* 16 (2015): 77.

21. Boccagni and Baldassar, "Emotions on the Move," 77.

22. Susan J. Matt, "Recovering the Invisible: Methods for the Historical Study of the Emotions," in *Doing Emotions History*, ed. Susan J. Matt and Peter N. Stearns (Urbana: University of Illinois Press, 2014), 42–44; Barbara H. Rosenwein, "Problems and Methods in the History of Emotions," *Passions in Context: International Journal for the History and Theory of Emotions* 1 (2010): 12–24, http://www.passionsincontext.de; Barbara H. Rosenwein, *Generations of Feelings: A History of Emotions, 600–1700* (New York: Cambridge University Press, 2016), 3–10.

23. As a *lembrança* commonly refers to a small gift, this term sometimes was used to express that the amount of money sent home was not as large as it could be expected or as the sender would have desired.

24. Letter 1677, António to his wife Graça, Rio de Janeiro, Brazil, 9/11/1897, Arquivo Distrital de Braga [hereafter ADB], Governo Civil [Civil Government], Processos de Passaporte [Passport Applications], file 1885, 10/9/1897. Since all letters come from passport applications handled by the Civil Government authorities, I have omitted this information in subsequent notes.

25. For an analysis of economic matters and emotional language in migrant correspondence from other European countries, see Sonia Cancian and Simone Wegge, "'If It Is Not Too Expensive, Then You Can Send Me Sugar': Money Matters among Migrants and Their Families," *History of the Family* 21, no. 3 (2016): 350–67.

26. Letter 832, Manuel to his wife Maria Clara, Rio de Janeiro, Brazil, 5/12/11, Arquivo Distrital do Porto [hereafter ADP], dossier 1748, file 43, 6/1/1912; Letter 1930, Eduardo to his wife Rosa, Bagé, Rio Grande do Sul, Brazil, 30/7/1911, ADB, file 17808, 1/9/1911.

27. Letter 1103, Luíz to his wife Maria de Jesus, Rio de Janeiro, Brazil, 9/15/1910, ADP, dossier 1720, file 944, 10/17/1910.

28. Letter 815, António to his wife Joaquina, São Paulo, Brazil, 7/10/1918, Arquivo Distrital de Coimbra [hereafter ADC], IID/GC/ILFS/10/1/696, file 502, 11/2/1918.

29. Letter 21, Albino to his wife Maria Joaquina, Pará, Brazil, 25/5/1903, Arquivo Distrital de Viseu [hereafter ADV], box 2044, file 81, 20/7/1903.

30. Letter 1313, José to his wife Maria, place unknown, Brazil, 4/6/1907, Arquivo Distrital de Faro [hereafter ADF], uncatalogued, file 3, 4/1/1908. Other examples in Letter 356, Manuel to his wife Bernarda, Pará, Brazil, 1/12/1900, ADC, IID/GC/ILFS/8/1/412, file 214, 3/12/1900; Letter 1736, António to his wife Susana, ADB, place unknown, Brazil, date unknown, file 13589, 1/19/1914.

31. Pereira, *A política portuguesa de emigração*, 36–57; Rick Chaney, *Regional Emigration and Remittances in Developing Countries: The Portuguese Experience* (New York: Praeger, 1986); Baganha, "Migração transâtlantica," 410–12.

32. Mariano Pina, *Portugal e Brazil* (Lisbon: Antiga Casa Bertrand–José Bastos, 1896).

33. Pina, *Portugal e Brazil*, 137.

34. Pina, *Portugal e Brazil*, 138–39.

35. Concordance is a concept from corpus linguistics that refers to a list of a particular term in a corpus in the context in which it appears. I created concordance lists for several key words analyzed in this chapter as a first step in identifying which other words particular terms were associated with. For an introduction to concepts from corpus linguistics, see Paul Baker, *Using Corpora in Discourse Analysis* (London: Bloomsbury, 2006).

36. Letter 226, Miguel to his wife Henriqueta, Rio de Janeiro, Brazil, 7/5/1918, ADV, box 2430, file 35, 10/30/1918.

37. Letter 634, Manuel to his wife Maria, Niterói, Rio de Janeiro, Brazil, 10/30/1905, ADC, IID/GC/ILFS/8/3/483, file 1985, 12/7/1905; Letter 603, Joaquim to his wife Maria, Santos, São Paulo, 9/24/1890, ADC, IID/GC/ILFS/7/2/293, file 1097, 10/14/1890; Letter 1593, José to his wife Basília, Provincetown, MA, USA, 7/5/1916, ADF, box 169, dossier 1, 8/4/1916 II; Letter 2003, José to his wife Olívia, Pará, Brazil, 4/8/1904, Arquivo Distrital de Viana do Castelo, box 1904, file 311, 5/5/1904.

38. Letter 649, António to his wife Maria da Assunção, São Paulo, Brazil, 9/13/1916, ADC, IID/GC/ILFS/10/1/689, file 384, 5/30/1917.

39. Letter 2182, Manuel to his wife Genoveva, Cravinhos, São Paulo, Brazil, 1/?/1896, Arquivo Distrital de Lisboa, box 62, N.T. 2487, file 2647 A, 3/20/1896; and Letter 458, António to his wife Maria do Carmo, Ludlow, MA, USA, 8/30/1915, ADC, IID/GC/ILFS/9/5/676, file 569, 10/18/1915.

40. Mentions to work, working, or to work as a synonym for effort or difficulty appear in close to a third of the letters (29 percent).

41. The latter were common expressions in popular speech connected to Portugal's Christian-Muslim confrontation and colonial expansion. See E. de Moura Correia and Persília Teixeira, *Dicionário prático de locuções e expressões correntes* (Porto: Papiro Editora, 2007) and Sérgio Luís de Carvalho, *Nas bocas do mundo*, 2nd ed. (Lisbon: Planeta, 2014), 97.

42. Examples of these images in Letter 79, Manuel to his wife Maria Josefina, Lorena, São Paulo, Brazil, 3/71888, ADV, box 1871, file 147, 1/21/1889; Letter 823, José Maria to his wife Emília, Buenos Aires, Argentina, 9/16/1909, ADP, dossier 1710, file 35, 2/3/1910; Letter 841, Manuel to his wife Maria, Rio de Janeiro, Brazil, 9/19/1911, ADP, dossier 1751, file 981, 3/5/1912; Letter 603, Joaquim to his wife Maria José, Santos, São Paulo, Brazil, 9/24/1890, ADC, IID/GC/ILFS/7/2/293, file 1097, 10/14/1890; Letter 1448, António to his wife Maria da Conceição, Buenos Aires, Argentina, 4/19/1918, ADF, box 848, 8/23/1918; and Letter 1897, Abílio to his wife Teresa, Rio de Janeiro, Brazil, 9/12, unknown year, ADB, file 29292, 5/2/1914.

43. Letter 1883, Barbacena, Minas Gerais, Brazil, 10/3/1892, ADB, file 26638, 8/9/1892.

44. Letter 772, Niterói, Rio de Janeiro, Brazil, 7/3/1919, ADC, IID/GC/ILFS/10/2/713, file 1917, 11/17/1919.

45. Letter 849, Rio de Janeiro, Brazil, 7/2/1912, ADP, dossier 1762, file 734, 8/24/1912.

46. Jorge Fernandes Alves, *Os brasileiros: Emigração e retorno no Porto oitocentista* (Porto: Gráficos Reunidos, 1994); Comissão Nacional para as Comemorações dos Descobrimentos Portugueses, *Os brasileiros de torna-viagem no noroeste de Portugal* (Lisbon: CNDP, 2000); Maria Beatriz Rocha-Trindade and Domingos Caeiro, *Portugal-Brasil, migrações e migrantes, 1850–1930* (Lisbon: Edições Inapa, 2000).

47. Helen Graham has estimated that, during the first two decades of the twentieth century, remittances could have represented "about two-thirds of a single industrial worker's average annual wage ... and a much larger proportion for an agricultural worker." Helen Graham, "Money and Migration in Modern Portugal: An Economist's View," in *Portuguese Migration in Global Perspective*, ed. David Higgs (Toronto: Multicultural History Society of Ontario, 1990), 83.

48. Letter 315, Joaquim to his wife Maria da Piedade, Rio de Janeiro, Brazil, 3/7/1912, ADV, box 1983, file 140, 5/11/1912.

49. Letter 70, Manuel to his wife Gracinda, Rio de Janeiro, Brazil, 9/11/1918, ADV, box 2375, file 17, 2/21/1919.

50. Letter 1357, António to his wife Rita de Jesus, Buenos Aires, Argentina, 7/8/1895, ADF, box 146, dossier 1, file 62, 9/16/1895.

51. Mirjam Milharčič Hladnik's chapter in this volume further explores the importance of love and duty to family in the case of a female labor migrant from Slovenia to Egypt.

52. Letter 888, Maria dos Remédios to her sister Palmira, Rio de Janeiro, Brazil, 6/14/1918, ADP, dossier 1869, file 876, 9/22/1919.

53. Letter 1067, Carlota to her mother, São Paulo, Brazil, 2/9/1910, ADP, dossier 1712, file 957, 4/21/1910.

54. Letter 1315, Isabel to her mother, Rio de Janeiro, Brazil, 5/19/1915, ADF, uncataloged, file 196, 8/11/1915.

55. June Hee Kwon, "The Work of Waiting: Love and Money in Korean Chinese Transnational Migration," *Cultural Anthropology* 30, no. 3 (2015): 495.

56. For a more developed analysis, see Marcelo J. Borges, "For the Good of the Family: Migratory Strategies and Affective Language in Portuguese Migrant Letters, 1870–1920s," *History of the Family* 21, no. 3 (2016): 368–97.

57. Benno Gammerl, "Emotional Styles—Concepts and Challenges," *Rethinking History* 16, no. 2 (2012): 161–75; Rosenwein, "Problems and Methods"; Rosenwein, *Generations of Feelings*; William M. Reddy, *The Navigation of Feeling: A Framework for the History of Emotions* (Cambridge: Cambridge University Press, 2001); Jan Plamper, *The History of Emotions: An Introduction* (New York: Oxford University Press, 2015).

58. M. de Lourdes Lima dos Santos, *Para uma sociologia da cultura burguesa em Portugal no século XIX* (Lisbon: Editorial Presença–Instituto de Ciências Sociais, 1983); Irene I. Vaquinhas, "A família, essa 'pátria em miniatura,'" in *História da vida privada em Portugal: A época contemporânea*, ed. Vaquinhas (Lisbon: Círculo de Leitores–Temas e Debates), 118–51.

CHAPTER 2

"The Letter Said That My Wife Had Died"

Bigamy in Argentina in the Era of Mass Migration

MARÍA BJERG

Andresa Barrachina and Rafaela Fioretto were just two of the hundreds of thousands of immigrants arriving in Buenos Aires between the 1880s and the 1920s. Unlike many of their fellow travelers seeking work or adventure, Andresa and Rafaela left their homes looking for their husbands, discovered they had been betrayed by their husbands' bigamy, and sought justice in Argentine courts. Their stories illustrate how emotions pervaded transnational relations, and how multiple meanings of love and its mutations into myriad other, less positive, feelings shaped migration. In the context of migration and family—a site of intimacy and affection, but also one of disagreement, contest, deceit, and heartbreak—bigamists and betrayed spouses reveal the complexities of leaving one's family and of being left behind.[1]

The cases of Andresa and Rafaela are not exceptional, but representative of a corpus of eighty trials for bigamy involving European immigrants in the period 1871–1920.[2] The analysis of this corpus brings to light stories of love, disillusionment, separation, reunion, abandonment, and search for redress. Although these criminal records often reveal the texture of migrants' marital relationships and the emotions they entailed, we ought to be aware of the records' particular features as historical sources. In addition to the fact that the voices of litigants, witnesses, suspects, and accused were mediated by what court officials recorded, historians agree that judicial sources are fragmented narratives that capture extraordinary moments in which victims and defendants must explain how an incident that tears their lives apart has occurred.[3] Scholars have also underscored that judicial discourses are, by their very nature, incomplete, not only as a result of the influence exerted on them by the fear, lies, and embarrassment of defendants, plaintiffs, and witnesses, but also because the questions put by judges often differ from those put by historians.[4] However, despite their opacity and fragmentary condition, I argue that the criminal records used in this chapter shed light on the encounter of immigrants with the emotional standards of the new society in a situation of power disparity.[5] In a territory where the border between the intimate from the public was blurred, bigamy cases allow us to explore how individuals shaped their emotional narratives by expressing—or restraining—their feelings, sometimes following, sometimes going against social norms.

This chapter is divided in four parts. The first two focus on the stories of Andresa and Rafaela. For this narrative I have mostly relied on the information obtained from court records. In addition, I have searched for data in vital records, migration records, and population censuses to re-create the life trajectories of these migrants. The next section departs from the stories to explore the ways individuals responded to the emotional standards of a foreign society. Finally, the fourth section explores how the distance and novelty of migration transformed personal and collective sentiment.

The Spanish Seamstress, a Woman of Discreet Feelings

In the summer of 1881, Father José Novota, a Spanish priest from Zaragoza, received his compatriot Andresa Barrachina and her eleven-year-old daughter, Facunda Aldaz, in his parish in the city of Buenos Aires. Andresa brought a letter of introduction from a relative of Novota living in Pamplona (where the woman and the girl were from), a copy of the document certifying her marriage to Luis Aldaz, and the birth certificate of Facunda. Andresa had traveled from Spain to find out the whereabouts of her husband, with whom she had lost contact for almost a decade.[6]

Luis Aldaz had emigrated in 1871. During his first two years in Argentina he had corresponded briefly but lovingly with his wife, and then stopped writing. His family never heard from him again nor did they have any news of his fate, except for the rumor that had recently reached Pamplona about his forthcoming wedding with another woman, despite his being still legally married to Andresa.

The first letter Andresa received from Luis was written in September 1871. By then, eight months had passed since his departure. In this letter, he explained the reason for his delay in communicating, saying that he had wanted to write to her only when he could confirm to her that he had found a good job. The letter indicated that he was living in the interior of the province of Buenos Aires, where he had started working as a laborer in a railway gang a few weeks before. Luis apologized for not sending "a single ounce since this is my first month here I couldn't save," and promised to send some money in the next letter so that Andresa could buy a dress for Facunda, "[whom] I miss very much . . . her memory makes me cry like a child at night."[7] In the last paragraphs, perhaps to ward off suspicions or ease any jealousy harbored by his wife, Luis added that he didn't like Argentine women at all, and that he considered them "not so pretty, and very lazy." He ended the letter by saying to Andresa: "You are the woman of my heart, and I never forget you."

Two months later, a second letter from Luis arrived in Pamplona. It contained a portrait of Luis and some money "to buy Facunda a floral dress, and for helping both of you, along with what you earn from your sewing, to get through the winter . . . you must manage this sum I am sending you carefully, it's the product of my hard work."[8] After this letter, there was a final missive written in February 1873. It consisted of a brief note in which Luis excused himself for not being able to arrange for Andresa and their daughter to join him in Argentina. He explained: "I never forget you and my dear daughter, and I don't lack the will of bringing you here, but I don't have a way to do it, for lack of money."[9]

Together with these letters from Luis, Andresa also arrived in Buenos Aires with the address of Luis Goñi, a man from Pamplona who had settled in the city, and who had been living in Spain when she and Luis had celebrated their wedding. As Andresa later explained, it was Goñi who told her that Luis had remarried. After learning of her husband's actions, Andresa decided to sue Luis for bigamy.

Before the judge, Goñi declared that six years before, Luis Aldaz had expressed a willingness to send for his family, but then "he began to hide the fact that he was married, because he was courting another woman with whom I heard rumors he married nine months ago."[10] The witness also provided information on the whereabouts of Luis. By mid-August 1881, the justice of the peace of Juárez, a rural town about 400 kilometers south of Buenos Aires

City, informed the court that in March 1881, Luis Aldaz, aged thirty-four and at that time a rural police officer, had married Justina Amarante, an Argentine woman aged twenty-one.[11] Three months later, the bigamist was arrested and taken to Buenos Aires.

After such a long separation, the reunion between Andresa and Luis took place in the gloomy setting of a prison. That encounter is an eloquent representation of the rough path through which Andresa entered Argentine society as an immigrant. At the time, thousands of European women traveled to reunite with their husbands. Many of those reunions were the last phase of an experience in which estrangement, anxiety, and misunderstandings were very likely present. Certainly, migration affected all couples, forcing many to renegotiate their bonds and feelings. Individuals were transformed by a variety of conflicting emotions: fear and euphoria, love and disaffection, pleasure and anger. Once couples had reunited, they needed to re-create their affective bonds, and resume a common language of intimacy.[12] However, for women who were sent for by their husbands, their entry into the new society was a less emotionally arduous passage than the one experienced by Andresa and other European women who had migrated on their own, fearing that nobody was waiting for them. Driven by the abandonment and the treachery of their husbands, these wives were compelled to start their lives in the new country while coping with cumbersome legal procedures that forced them to speak of things that would have remained unsaid had a destabilizing event not occurred.

Unfortunately, the judicial record does not give details of the day when Andresa visited her husband for the first time in prison. What feelings must have assaulted her when she was about to face a man who not only had betrayed her but who was by then almost a stranger? What emotions did Luis feel on the eve of this encounter? Was he seized by the fear that his wife's spitefulness would be so implacable as to block any chance for him to recover his freedom?

After six months in prison, the bigamist appeared before the judge. Surely his statement did not differ much from the one he had improvised for Andresa in the penitentiary. Although Luis admitted committing bigamy, he argued that when he remarried he thought his first wife had died.[13] Eager to convince the authorities of his innocence, and fully aware that his freedom depended not only on his word but also on evidence, Luis presented three letters showing that he had written to Andresa in Spain on several occasions in an attempt to find out her whereabouts since he had no news of her. The letters had been sent from Pamplona by three of his friends. Containing different degrees of detail, the letters provided the same answer to his concern: Andresa had moved from Pamplona to Zaragoza in mid-1878 and "here, rumor has it that she was ill with consumption and that she had died in the house of some aunt and uncle of hers, where Facunda might be."[14]

It is quite clear that Luis did not write to Pamplona because he was driven by the desire to reestablish contact with his wife, but because of the possibility that his decision to remarry straddled the thin line dividing legal actions from criminal actions. To marry again, he needed some certainty that his first wife had forgotten him, and that the distance and the long silence between them had put an end to their marriage.

Suspecting the letters were apocryphal and that Luis had made up a hoax, the prosecutor demanded a three-year sentence on the charge that he had committed two crimes, adultery and bigamy.[15] But a month later, Andresa submitted a declaration to the judge stating that, after several conversations with her husband, she was convinced of his innocence because "when I left Pamplona in 1878," she wrote, "the word spread that I had died, and the people who told him this, acted driven by the rumor ... [and] being convinced that it was this mistake what led my husband to marry again, and trusting his sincerity and good faith, I drop all charges."[16] A few weeks later, the defendant was released. Seemingly, he and Justina resumed their married life together. Indeed, the 1895 national census of population recorded that they had had two children, both born after 1883, the year that he had regained his freedom.[17]

What led Luis Aldaz to commit bigamy? Perhaps he had no choice but to marry Justina. She had been born into a prominent local family. The Amarante were integrated into the social core of what was then known as *gente decente* (decent people), a people who watched over the female sexual conduct, demanded chastity of their women, and valued marriage.[18] In the 1860s and early 1870s, Justina's father, Paulino Amarante, had been a major of the National Guards, and he had close ties of friendship and godfathership with some of the most conspicuous landowners and military officers of the province of Buenos Aires.[19] In fact, the godfather of Justina was Lieutenant Colonel Benito Machado, a figure of national fame because of his military performance in the fight against the indigenous population and the expansion of the frontier.[20]

How did Justina face the news that her husband was already married in Spain? What was the reaction of her family to such a dishonor? The judicial record leaves these questions unanswered. Justina was not summoned to testify, and therefore, we cannot assess her reaction. However, a detail from the court record illuminates the role Justina's family probably played. At the outset of the trial, Luis presented a pauper's appeal requesting a public counsel. But in the middle of the case, when the prosecutor asked for a three-year prison sentence, Luis fired the public defender. Instead, Aristóbulo del Valle, a prestigious lawyer and politician, was hired.[21] Although there are no traces of Justina or her family in the court record, the change in lawyer suggests the Amarante family intervened. Their class privilege and network afforded Luis the possibility of hiring a more reputable attorney.[22]

The behind-the-scene presence of Justina's family most likely restricted Andresa's liberty to express her feelings.[23] Intimately, she might have felt a turbulence of conflicting emotions (love, disillusionment, anger), emotions she might have felt compelled to restrain in public in response to the intervention of Justina's family. Self-control and pardon seem to have been the options available to her. An ambiguous figure, strong and conceding at the same time, Andresa ended up living in a country that she had entered by the heavy door of the judicial system.[24]

As for Justina, the dishonor she experienced as a result of the court case had affected her family. The presence of a renowned lawyer suggests that the Amarantes were not indifferent to the lawsuit details, nor to the course taken by Justina's life afterward. They intended to keep up social appearances, pretending that what had occurred was just a misunderstanding, although the argument presented by Luis—that he had married again believing he was a widower—might have seemed foolish to them. For Justina, to carry on with the marriage assuming inadvertent bigamy had been a one-time mistake in the life of a man who had, in the words of his first wife, "acted in good faith," was perhaps the least dramatic way to save the family honor.[25]

An Irascible Italian Woman in the Cosmopolitan City

In December 1879, Domingo DeBartolo, a twenty-two-year-old day laborer, and Rafaela Fioretto, an eighteen-year-old peasant, married in the village of Marano Marchesato, in the province of Cosenza, Italy. By 1882, the couple had one child, and Rafaela was pregnant a second time. That year, Domingo left his family in the care of his parents-in-law and emigrated to South America with the promise to his wife that he would return.[26]

Rafaela and her husband maintained a regular correspondence during the first years, but in 1885, the exchange of letters came to an end. A few years later, rumors that Domingo had remarried began to circulate in and around Marano Marchesato. In 1899, Rafaela traveled to Argentina.

For nearly seven months, she searched for Domingo in Buenos Aires. At first, the vague directions, and perhaps the complicity of Domingo's fellow countrymen prevented Rafaela from tracking him down, that is, until one afternoon in June 1900, when he turned up at the tenement house where Rafaela lived. Confronted with the rumor, Domingo confirmed there was another woman, but denied the rumor of a second marriage: "DeBartolo told her he didn't want to live there because it was a miserable place, and looked for another room to rent... there her husband said his name was José Cecilio, and when asked by his wife about that false identity he explained that it was because he had a mistress and was afraid she could bother him."[27] Despite this confession of infidelity, the couple resumed their married life. Perhaps, Rafaela thought it was natural that after so many years of separation her husband had another relationship, and perhaps felt relieved to learn that it was just a lover and not a wife. However, one month later, Julia Macaya, a twenty-one-year-old Argentine dressmaker, showed up in the tenement house claiming to be Domingo's legitimate wife with a marriage certificate to prove it. Rafaela's initial stupefaction soon gave way to a furious attack. The impact of the news and the lack of documents that proved that she was married to the same man resulted into a scandalous incident of insults and physical violence. Rafaela's rage was so great that it prompted the neighbors to call the police. She was thus arrested.[28]

Domingo used Rafaela's fury to his advantage to convince Julia, as the record states, that the woman "was not his wife but a mistress deranged by spitefulness... she [Julia] believed him because at that time Fioretto did not have any document to prove she was also married to DeBartolo."[29] A few days later, Julia accepted Domingo's return to the house they shared.

Soon after her arrest, Rafaela began what probably seemed endless visits to the consulate and the courthouse until she finally received her marriage certificate from Italy. When DeBartolo's clumsy hoax was revealed and the judicial process began, he argued that when he married Julia he thought Rafaela had died. The defendant declared that he had corresponded with his wife and sent money to her until 1885. He claimed that he had asked Rafaela to join him in Buenos Aires in 1885, but she had insisted that he return to Italy as he had promised her. Because she "refused to obey," he stopped writing her. In 1889—he further declared—he received a letter from a friend of his informing him that Rafaela had passed away. Following this news, Domingo claimed, he wrote several times to his parents-in-law, but never received an answer.

The discrepancy between the declarations of the two parties resulted in a face-to-face confrontation in which Rafaela confessed that the friend's letter was a stratagem to make Domingo return to Italy. But the admission of that trick was not enough to mitigate the verdict. In June 1901, the court sentenced Domingo to four-and-a-half years in prison. The judge took into consideration the point raised by the prosecutor, that is, the adulterous conduct of the bigamist was an aggravating circumstance, because Domingo had resumed conjugal life with his first wife when she arrived in Buenos Aires while being married to Julia.

The sentence was appealed and, concerning the aggravating circumstance, the defense attorney declared: "Having resumed a conjugal life with his first wife . . . I do not consider it unlawful . . . it cannot aggravate the situation of the accused at the time of the sentence, because in the face of the unexpected appearance of the wife whom he believed to be dead, he intended to avoid the emotions of the moment, delaying the catastrophe."[30] The Court of Appeals dismissed the charge of adultery and considered the time elapsed between the commission of the crime and the trial as a mitigating factor. As a result, Domingo's sentence was reduced to three-and-a-half years of imprisonment. Unlike Luis Aldaz, DeBartolo received no leniency from either of his wives, and at the end of the trial Julia filed a lawsuit for the marriage to be annulled.

The stories of these two bigamists reveal how distance and time challenged the maintenance of kin ties, damaged marital bonds, undermined the will, and consumed the emotional resources necessary for a family migration project to stay the course. If that had been the initial agreement between Andresa and Luis, and between Rafaela and Domingo, the perspective of a family reunion vanished for different reasons. In the context of migration and separation, love gave way to disaffection, trickery, and disloyalty, and other emotions like anguish, rancor, and rage emerged in this new anatomy of relationships.

Longing to Be Together?

In the last decades, scholars who have focused on the convergence of migration and emotions have emphasized the positive relationships, the affection, the role of kinwork and of an imaginary co-presence.[31] From this perspective, the estrangement and the longing for loved ones might have emotionally influenced both those who migrated and those who remained behind. All of them employed resources to prevent distance from dissolving family ties. Marriages remained standing through epistolary exchanges in which affective semantics converged with manifestations of love and practical advice on the management of money, the care of animals and crops, and the education of children. Fiancées and future wives mitigated passion by exchanging letters—some of them poetically inspired, others more rudimentary but no less effusive—in which correspondents, knowing that distance conspired against ardor, nurtured their passion by evoking common memories and imagining their reunion in the future.[32] Many parents of migrants discovered the hidden emotional potential of letters, and children received gratifying expressions of gratitude while at the same time were tacitly or explicitly urged to fulfill the social mandate of looking after their parents.[33]

Letters certainly had the capacity to shorten distance and time, and to transport thoughts, objects (a dried flower, a photograph, a postcard), and emotions. For engaged couples, spouses, parents, and children, to read again and again the same letter, to look at every detail in a portrait, or to send and receive remittances were ways of forging emotional closeness and reassuring the maintenance of relationships rendered vulnerable by separation.[34] However, if the bonds of migrants with the affective life of their place of origin depended to a great extent on epistolary exchanges, it should also be taken into account that often the route of the letters had to follow the extraordinary spatial mobility of the male workforce. The phenomenon of migration within migration, that is, relocations in countries of destination, affected millions of men who did not have a fixed residence. That unstable context might have restricted the continuity of the epistolary exchange because letters got lost on the way, or waited for a long time at the consular offices before reaching the hands of their addressees, if at all. Before long, the conversation became interrupted, and the affection slowly faded into a void of silence.

Rather than revealing emotions different from those found in the letters exchanged by migrant families, judicial records allow us to see these same emotions from a different angle.[35] As intimate narratives, letters may be placed on the opposite pole from judicial records, a typical public source. However, if we consider that during the transoceanic migrations of the nineteenth and early twentieth centuries, most migrants were semi-illiterate or illiterate, we need to take into account that these migrants often wrote letters with the assistance of another person.[36] Furthermore, in rural and small-town Europe, correspondence was intensely communal and it was not uncommon to read letters in public.[37] Viewed from this angle, the intimate nature of the epistolary narrative appears compromised.

Regardless of the degree of intimacy, however, scholars agree that letters do not reflect only individual choices, subjectivity, efforts of self-fashioning, and feelings, but also broad cultural categories and prevailing rules about emotions. This intertwining between feelings and norms is also found in judicial records. Nevertheless, the manner they interact differs because these sources make evident a more heterogeneous array of social actors whose relations are mediated by state power. Whereas in personal narratives, individuals may have sometimes written to conform to norms and rules, other times, they wrote in defiance. In the court, however, they were prompted to comply with the conventions regulating emotions. Hence, judicial records allow us to explore the intersectionality of emotional standards and the ways in which individuals expressed and navigated their feelings in a public context characterized by asymmetrical power relationships.

Love—albeit sometimes transfigured into negative emotions—seems to have been the common denominator of the stories narrated above. However, a closer look at the emotional language used in the trials reveals that the protagonists' conception of love had little to do with a romantic idea of marriage. For example, in Luis's letters, he rarely deploys intimate and romantic language. Instead, the narrative pulsates with notions of responsibility encouraging husbands to work hard and send remittances and urging wives to administer the household finances properly.[38] The testimonies of Rafaela and Domingo reflect these notions. Rafaela expected Domingo to be fully committed to the pact they had sealed at his departure. But, when he changed his mind and, instead of returning, called for her to join him, and she refused, he then interpreted Rafaela's attitude as an act of defiance and a breach of marital obligations.

After a long period without news from their husbands, the rumors of their betrayals reached Andresa and Rafaela, compelling them to cross the Atlantic to claim their rights as wives. The two women had endured abandonment and broken promises; however, neither of them seemed to be willing to abide the loss of status that would accompany the publicly acknowledged failure of a marriage. If matrimony was a legally and socially recognized union, what would happen to their status of married women if their husbands remarried?

When they left Europe, neither Andresa nor Rafaela could have imagined they would be forced to claim their status and their rights as wronged wives in the courthouse. In fact, at first, both sought to come to terms with their husbands within the familiar space of their intimate domain, where they could express their emotions based on a shared language of intimacy. However, when the circumstances prompted them to sue their husbands as bigamists, they were urged to take into consideration the emotional conventions of the judicial institution, and of society at large in the new country. That is clear in the story of Rafaela who, after having resumed marital life, learned about her husband's bigamy through Domingo's second wife. Her spontaneous reaction was an outburst of rage, and the first to condemn it were the neighbors of the tenement house. That was Rafaela's first step on the long path of learning how to behave according to the norms of the new society. She soon understood—with the aid of the lawyer, who surely instructed her—that sudden, impulsive anger could not be exposed publicly, as it did not comply either with expectations of womanly behavior, or with the emotional standards of the host society. Tellingly, when she testified before the judge, she started her statement evoking that episode and apologizing for her "improper behavior."

Disillusionment and anger may have been the driving forces underlying Andresa's decision to sue the man who had disregarded her; however, her intention to forgive him seemed to hide behind her negative feelings. The several visits paid to Luis in prison at the beginning of the process suggest that she might have been intending reconciliation. However, when a prestigious lawyer took over Luis's defense, Andresa's ability to manage her emotions and to navigate among conflicting feelings came to an end. Although there is no evidence that she was threatened to withdraw the lawsuit, she probably experienced helplessness and fear toward her husband's new in-laws. Class, gender, solitude—added to her condition as a foreigner—left Andresa unarmed to proceed with a battle whose end may have originally been to regain love.

The fuzzy figures of the bigamists' second wives make it difficult to grasp their emotions. For example, among his male in-laws, Luis's deviant conduct triggered strategies that seemed to disregard Justina's feelings. She might have felt betrayed and spited, but in her case a game of appearances was demanded to safeguard her well-respected family from public opprobrium. Thus, silence and mastery of emotions were essential for Justina. She had to stay away from the trial and accept her husband again. The emotional standards prevailing among the "decent classes" seemed to have been more rigid for her than for the bigamist. Perhaps, privately, Luis had to pay a heavy price to his in-laws for his failure but, in exchange, he regained his freedom, his marriage, and his job.[39]

As a woman from the popular classes, Julia seems to have had a wider degree of liberty to manage her emotions. Unlike Justina, Julia was involved in the process and, in court, she could publicly express her anger for having been doubly cheated, when she married Domingo assuming he was unmarried, and when she pardoned him believing Rafaela was just a mistress. Probably her lawyer also suggested she show dispassion and determination in her request to the court for the most severe punishment possible to the man who, as she is quoted stating, had "ruined my life."[40] In addition to a long reclusion, Julia requested the annulment of the civil marriage. Although the latter was legally cumbersome, if not impossible, by bringing it up she expressed the depth of her rancor and spite.

While women were compelled to restrain their emotional repertoire, men were able to justify their actions in terms of passion, love, and fear. A more unrestricted expression of emotions shaped the language shared by defendants and lawyers. For example, in his testimony, Domingo underscored his fear of Rafaela's scandalous behavior; and, in the plea, the lawyer's argument to exculpate his client revolved around love, passion, and misunderstanding: "[DeBartolo] got married in the belief he was a widower . . . after a long period of uprooting and solitude when he was deprived from family and homeland . . . affection and passion aroused driving him, like any decent man, to marry and form a family, an undeniable right for every man . . . a family that helped develop roots in this country."[41]

Changing Feelings

The analysis of these bigamy trials allows us to delve into the emotional landscapes of migration and to explore the relationship between gender, mobility, and love, one of the main aims of this book. On the one hand, the experience of unfaithful husbands and their wives sheds light on the variety of emotional styles that seem to have coexisted in turn-of-the-century Argentina. Although negative emotions such as rage were more likely to be condemned when the impassioned subject was a female, society—as far as the cases let us hypothesize—seemed to have been fairly open, setting few limits to emotional navigation, even in presumably rigid realms enforced by the state such as the justice system.

On the other hand, a closer look at bigamy trials reveals the limits of the affective transnational domain created by millions of people engaged in epistolary conversations. Probably the most obvious of those limits was imposed by the everyday dynamics of big cities. To men like Luis and Domingo, managing in parallel their adaptation to Buenos Aires and their marital life, suspended and awaiting an uncertain reunion, was not a simple task. The force of novelty conspired against the bonds that tied them to their families, and the past became blurred in front of the power of the fluid landscape of the urban world. The lure of freedom, the casual sexual relations, and the dangerous appeal of prostitutes: all of it awakened new passions.[42]

A labile universe where more than a half of the population was composed of young foreign men, turn-of-the-century Buenos Aires promised anonymity and secrecy. The city was the setting of a new sociability based on spontaneous, occasional, and fleeting relationships.[43] Bars and streets were more attractive than the miserable room in a tenement house, while a dirty tent by the side of a railroad track or a shed used as a dormitory for a gang of harvesters could hardly emulate a home. These experiences must have left a mark on the subjectivity of those men, whose identities and emotions must have changed along with their migration project. In that process, the relation between the migrants' universe of origin, their present, and their expectations changed.

Disembarked in an unknown city that deprived them of the physical presence of their families, these men's emotional landscape was dominated by an unstable and changing morality to which they were certainly not accustomed in their places of origin.[44] But if we look at Buenos Aires not in a panoramic perspective but from the tenement houses or from the ethnic neighborhoods where immigrants coming from a same European locality converged, the promise of anonymity of the street relationships vanishes. In the narrow setting of everyday life, where everyone knew each other, it was difficult to avoid prying eyes and gossip.[45] The social control by countrymen could be as stifling in an Argentine cosmopolitan town as in a rural village in southern Europe. In these circumstances, women left behind could learn quite easily about the moral lapses of their husbands.

Migration also imposed changes on the lives of women. When their husbands emigrated, they assumed productive roles and coped with the requirements of managing a home. Household and extra-household responsibilities, illness of themselves or their children, death, and alterations in the structure of the extended family imposed challenges and brought change. For instance, Andresa coped with consumption by moving with her daughter from Pamplona to Zaragoza. It was a long time since her husband had stopped writing her, and she had probably lost all hope that he would call for her. But when the rumor that Luis would marry again reached her, she decided to cross the Atlantic herself. We don't know what happened that pushed her to undertake such an unpredictable venture like that of regaining her husband on another continent. Was she still in Zaragoza? Had she lost the support of their uncle and aunt? Were their parents still alive? The underlying reasons for Rafaela's decision are not clear, either. We know, however, that a significant change had occurred in her life: her parents died a few years before her journey to Argentina. This loss narrowed her affective circle and, at the same time, emancipated her from patriarchal control. It is also possible that her part of the inheritance, in the form of monetary compensation, provided her with the resources to pay for the tickets to Buenos Aires.

A delicate interweaving of situations caused changes in women's lives. In absence of their husbands, many spouses remained subject to the patriarchal regime under the control of their fathers and brothers, a vigilance through which migrants moderated their worries about the sexual conduct and the fidelity of their wives.[46] But paradoxically, migration expanded their spaces of autonomy, either because men entrusted wives with many extra-household tasks, or because, when abandoned, women had to face bigger workloads outside the home to ensure their subsistence. In the tension between vigilance and autonomy, female roles and the representations of family life were changing, influenced by the rhythm of the successive aftershocks of the "small earthquake" caused by migration.[47]

Nevertheless, when women lost track of their spouses, or when they learned about their betrayals, it was not easy to cross the Atlantic to find out their whereabouts, and, even more challenging, to take them to court. We should bear in mind that many women were illiterate peasants. Expressions like *esquecidos* (referring to the men disappeared in the large mass of immigrants), "widows of the living," or "widows in white" were common in some European regions like Galicia, southern Portugal, and the south of Italy, places of substantial migration to Argentina.[48] Although the last two expressions allude to the liminal state between the husband's migration and the family reunion more than to abandoned women, it is reasonable to ask how many of them were the legitimate wives of bigamists, who didn't have the emotional and material resources to follow the route of Andresa and Rafaela, who could not get a passport without marital authorization,[49] or who simply didn't wish to incur the costs of uprooting and chose to forget their forgetful husbands.

NOTES

1. For a discussion of families as sites of disagreement and contestation in context of migration, see Loretta Baldassar and Donna R. Gabaccia, "Home, Family, and the Italian Nation in a Mobile World: The Domestic and the National among Italy's Migrants," in *Intimacy and Italian Migration: Gender and Domestic Lives in a Mobile World*, ed. Loretta Baldassar and Donna R. Gabaccia (New York: Fordham University Press, 2011), 3. For a general discussion of migration to Argentina see María Bjerg, *Historias de la inmigración en la Argentina* (Buenos Aires: Edhasa, 2009).

2. In this corpus, 94 percent of the bigamists are foreigners, mostly Spanish and Italian male immigrants.

3. Arlette Farge, *Le goût de l'archive* (Paris: Le Seuil, 1989), 10.

4. For a discussion on the convergences and divergences between historians and judges concerning the treatment of evidence, see Carlo Ginzburg, *The Judge and*

the Historian: Marginal Notes on a Late-Nineteenth-Century Miscarriage of Justice, trans. Anthony Shugaar (London: Verso, 1999).

5. For a discussion about how historians have explored emotional codes and standards of past societies see Susan J. Matt and Peter N. Stearns, "Introduction," in *Doing Emotions History*, ed. Susan J. Matt and Peter N. Stearns (Urbana: University of Illinois Press, 2014), Kindle edition; William M. Reddy, *The Navigation of Feeling: A Framework for the History of Emotions* (New York: Cambridge University Press, 2001); Ute Frevert, *Emotions in History: Lost and Found* (Budapest: Central European University Press, 2011).

6. *Barrachina v. Aldaz por bigamia*, 351–2–81, Juzgado del Crimen de la Capital, 1881, Archivo Histórico de la Provincia de Buenos Aires.

7. *Barrachina v. Aldaz*, 23.

8. *Barrachina v. Aldaz*, 24.

9. *Barrachina v. Aldaz*, 25.

10. *Barrachina v. Aldaz*, 36.

11. The Justice of Peace of Juárez to the Investigating Judge, Letter and authenticated copy of marriage certificate attached, August 18, 1881, in *Barrachina v. Aldaz*, 47.

12. A good example of the resignification of bonds and affection among immigrant couples is found in María Brunswig de Bamberg, *Allá en la Patagonia* (Buenos Aires: Javier Vergara, 1999). The book is a compilation of the letters written by German migrant Ella Hoffmann, who arrived in Argentina in 1923. After three and a half years of separation, she traveled in the company of her children to reunite with her husband, who was the manager of a sheep ranch in Patagonia. Ella's letters were addressed to her mother. The correspondence from her first year in Patagonia offers insight on the emotional implications of the couple's reunion and the conscious and unconscious effort she and her husband made to reestablish the relationship and a common language.

13. *Barrachina v. Aldaz*, 50.

14. Baldomero Navacíes to Luis Aldaza, Letter, December 4, 1879, in *Barrachina v. Aldaz*, 51.

15. *Barrachina v. Aldaz*, 6.

16. *Barrachina v. Aldaz*, 82.

17. Censo Nacional de Población de la República Argentina de 1895, Ciudad de Buenos Aires, population schedule, sección 21, subdivisión 33, p. 418, orden N° 15, Justina Amarante de Aldaz; digital image, FamilySearch, accessed October 15, 2016, https://familysearch.org.

18. A feature of Latin American family practice and sexuality dating back to colonial times, concubinage was still a widespread practice in nineteenth-century Argentina. The historiography of the family has identified the existence of a double pattern of family organization in which factual unions and illegitimate children (mostly among popular sectors and in the rural areas) coexisted with legally married

couples (a more common option among the so-called decent classes). Marriage-like relationships and assembled families in which children of previous unions converged were common practices, although part of society rejected them. These two kinds of family arrangements have been, very roughly, associated with social stratification and status, settlement patterns, territorial mobility, and church and state control. Among urban upper and middle classes, marriage was valorized; while among lower and subaltern classes, sexual unions and children born out of wedlock were much more common. On family and sex in colonial Latin America see Asunción Lavrín, *Sexuality and Marriage in Colonial Latin America* (Lincoln: University of Nebraska Press, 1989). For Argentina, see José Luis Moreno, *Historia de la familia en el Río de la Plata* (Buenos Aires: Sudamericana, 2008).

19. Major Paulino Amarante to the Justice of Peace of Tandil, Letter, July 31, 1864, Archivo Histórico Municipal de Tandil.

20. Parroquia Nuestra Señora de los Dolores, Libro de Bautismo, 1859, Amarante Justina, digital image, FamilySearch, accessed September 29, 2016, https://familysearch.org. Melina Yangilevich, "Construir poder en la frontera: José Benito Machado," in *Vivir entre dos mundos: Las fronteras del sur de la Argentina, siglos XVIII y XIX*, ed. Raúl Madrini (Buenos Aires: Taurus, 2006), 195–226.

21. *Barrachina v. Aldaz*, 54.

22. Del Valle was born in Dolores, the same town where the Amarante family was from.

23. Reddy, *Navigation of Feeling*, 122–30.

24. In 1895, the national census of population recorded Andresa and her daughter settled in La Plata, the brand-new capital of the province of Buenos Aires. Facunda had recently married a German musician.

25. On honor as a gendered emotional disposition deeply ingrained in nineteenth-century society, see Frevert, *Emotions in History*, 70–89.

26. Rafaela's testimony before the police, in *Fioretto Rafaela v. DeBartolo Domingo por bigamia*, Juzgado del Crimen, Expediente B89, 1901, Archivo General de la Nación Argentina, 8.

27. Rafaela's testimony before the judge, in *Fioretto v. DeBartolo*, 16.

28. *Fioretto v. DeBartolo*, 8.

29. Julia's testimony, in *Fioretto v. DeBartolo*, 25.

30. *Fioretto v. DeBartolo*, 51.

31. Micaela di Leonardo, "The Female World of Cards and Holidays: Women, Families, and Work of Kinship," *Signs* 12, no. 3 (1987): 440–53; Loretta Baldassar, "Missing Kin and Longing to Be Together: Emotions and the Construction of Co-presence in Transnational Relationships," *Journal of Intercultural Studies* 29, no. 3 (2008): 247–66.

32. Sonia Cancian, "My dearest love . . . Love, Longing, and Desire in International Migration," in *Migrations: Interdisciplinary Perspectives*, ed. Michi Messer, Renee Schroeder, and Ruth Wodak (Vienna: Springer Verlag, 2012), 175–86.

33. María Da Orden, *Una familia y un océano de por medio: La emigración gallega a la Argentina: Una historia a través de la memoria epistolar* (Barcelona: Anthropos, 2010), 72–80.

34. David A. Gerber, *Authors of Their Lives: The Personal Correspondence of British Immigrants to North America in the Nineteenth Century* (New York: New York University Press, 2006), 2.

35. For further discussion on the emotional language of migrant letters, see the chapters by Marcelo J. Borges, Mirjam Milharčič Hladnik, and Suzanne M. Sinke in this anthology.

36. Antonio Gibelli and Fabio Caffarena, "Le lettere degli emigrante," in *Storia dell'emigrazione italiana*, Vol. 1, *Partenze*, ed. Piero Bevilacqua, Andreina De Clementi, and Emilio Franzina (Rome: Donzelli, 2001), 569; Marcelo J. Borges and Sonia Cancian, "Reconsidering the Migrant Letter: From the Experience of Migrants to the Language of Migrants," *History of the Family* 21, no. 3 (2016): 283.

37. Marcelo J. Borges, "For the Good of the Family: Migratory Strategies and Affective Language in Portuguese Migrant Letters, 1870s–1920s," *History of the Family* 21, no. 3 (2016): 370.

38. Borges, "For the Good of the Family," 370. In this article, Borges analyzes in depth the role of responsibility and money in the epistolary language of immigrants. Further discussion of this topic in the context of narratives of marital obligation and sacrifice can be found in Borges's chapter in this anthology.

39. In 1895, the national census of population still recorded him as police officer, the same position he held before the trial.

40. *Fioretto v. DeBartolo*, 25.

41. *Fioretto v. DeBartolo*, 52.

42. Donna Guy, *Sex and Danger in Buenos Aires: Prostitution, Family, and Nation in Argentina* (Lincoln: University of Nebraska Press, 1991).

43. Sandra Gayol, *Sociabilidad en Buenos Aires: Hombres, honor y cafés, 1862–1910* (Buenos Aires: Del Siglo, 2000), 94–100.

44. Pablo Ben, "La ciudad del pecado: Moral sexual de las clases populares en la Buenos Aires del 900," in *Moralidades y comportamientos sexuales: Argentina 1880–2011*, ed. Dora Barrancos, Donna Guy, and Adriana Valobra (Buenos Aires: Biblos, 2014), 95–113. On urban modernity and migration see also Tyler Carrington's chapter in this anthology.

45. On social control and gossip, see among others Robert F. Harney, "Men without Women: Italian Migrants in Canada, 1885–1930," in *The Italian Immigrant Woman in North America*, ed. Betty Boyd Caroli, Robert F. Harney, and Lydio F. Tomasi (Toronto: Multicultural History Society of Ontario, 1977), 79–102; Borges, "For the Good of the Family."

46. For a discussion of changes in women's lives when their husbands emigrate, see Caroline B. Brettell, *Men Who Migrate, Women Who Wait: Population and History in a Portuguese Parish* (Princeton, NJ: Princeton University Press, 1986); Sally

Cooper Cole, *Women of the Praia: Work and Lives in a Portuguese Coastal Community* (Princeton, NJ: Princeton University Press, 1991); Linda Reeder, "When the Men Left Sutera: Sicilian Women and Mass Migration, 1880–1920," in *Women, Gender, and Transnational Lives: Italian Workers of the World*, ed. Donna R. Gabaccia and Franca Iacovetta (Toronto: University of Toronto Press, 2002), 45–75.

47. Here I paraphrase De Clementi's reference to the effects of return migrants. See Adreina De Clementi, "Gender Relations and Migration Strategies in the Rural Italian South: Land, Inheritance, and Marriage Market," in *Women, Gender, and Transnational Lives*, ed. Gabaccia and Iacovetta, 76–105.

48. Marcelo J. Borges, *Chains of Gold: Portuguese Migration to Argentina in Transatlantic Perspective* (Leiden, the Netherlands: Brill, 2009), 194; Caroline B. Brettell, *Anthropology and Migration: Essays on Transnationalism, Ethnicity, and Identity* (Lanham, MD: AltaMira, 2003), 153; Linda Reeder, *Women in White: Migration and the Transformation of Rural Italian Women, Sicily 1880–1920* (Toronto: University of Toronto Press, 2003).

49. Women may have tried to work around the law or manipulate officials, but most were unsuccessful when requesting passports without the authorization of their husbands. See Victoria Calabrese, "Land of Women: Basilicata, Emigration, and the Women Who Remained Behind, 1880–1914" (PhD diss., City University of New York, 2017).

CHAPTER 3

"People Cannot Live on Love Alone"

Negotiating Love, Gender Roles, and Family Care between Slovenia and Egypt

MIRJAM MILHARČIČ HLADNIK

Felicita Koglot migrated to Alexandria, Egypt, in 1921 when she was twenty-two years old. She was a Slovenian from Goriška, a contested region inhabited by peoples with complex identities and loyalties. She left from the nearby port of Trieste, which had, together with the westernmost part of the Slovenian national territory that included her village, just been annexed to Italy after the end of the disastrous Great War.[1] Felicita's decision to emigrate was not motivated by the hardship of war or political instability, but by love. She was engaged to Franc Peric, the oldest son of a big family from the same village, Bilje.[2] Like many other young women, Felicita wanted to marry with enough money saved to provide essentials for the couple's life together. Egypt offered lucrative opportunities, therefore Felicita joined numerous women from the region, called the *aleksandrinke* (Alexandrian women), and embarked for the port city of Alexandria. Felicita entered the tight network of translocal and transcultural life of the aleksandrinke, who worked as domestic helpers, cooks, nannies, governesses, and wet nurses for affluent bourgeois families. She joined this region-specific women's migration circuit motivated by general political and economic reasons prevalent in the Goriška region in the interwar period, but above all she aspired to meet family obligations and followed intimate plans. Through an analysis of the correspondence between Felicita and Franc during their separation, this chapter highlights the importance of letters in maintaining intimate and collective ties in contexts of migration. In this correspondence, love emerges as a crucial feeling and a tool in preserving the relationship amid the challenges created by separation and changes in personal, familial, and gender roles. The analysis that follows explores how love defined subjective experiences of migration in relation to self, loved ones, family, and community. In addition to the relationship of the letter writers, this epistolary love story illuminates the broader family and community systems of migration at play in the sociopolitical contexts of two very different, yet closely connected worlds—the villages of Goriška, Slovenia, and the urban centers of Egypt in the 1920s.

Felicita and Franc: An Epistolary Love Story

Felicita migrated to Egypt twice. She first left in 1921, and through her migration network quickly found a job as a nanny for a family in Alexandria. She saved money, returned home after three years, married Franc, moved into his family's household—as was the custom for new brides—and gave birth to a girl named Danila.[3] In 1928, when Danila was three years old, Felicita and Franc decided she should migrate again. For the next three years, she worked as a nanny with a family in Cairo, occasionally visiting Bilje while traveling to Europe with her employers, and returned home for good in 1931. This kind of migration cycle was nothing unusual in a region in which most families had someone abroad: be it in Egypt, Argentina, the United States, or Switzerland—the latter close enough for Bilje's construction workers, Franc among them, to go there for seasonal work.[4]

Felicita and Franc discussed a wide range of topics in their correspondence—among them, the intensifying political repression at home and political tensions in Egypt; relationships with employers; her difficulties getting paid in a timely fashion; the care she received from her employers when she was ill; the exchanges of gifts and the dispatches of goods like grapes, wine, and ham for the Egyptian family; the activities of local ethnic organizations established by the Slovenian Catholic church in Egypt, whose events Felicita attended regularly; and changes in everyday life in Bilje, Alexandria, and Cairo. However, I will focus on the intimate world that this correspondence illuminates. My selection of letters reveals the epistolary love story spanning six years in two periods of migration, and highlights four topics that are relevant to understand the emotional dynamics experienced by the couple: love and longing, doubts and concerns, gossip and rumors, and family relationships. I have chosen these topics of epistolary conversation to present the main goal of the correspondence: to preserve and strengthen social and family solidarity, and above all, the young couple's intimate relationship.

I view the preservation and strengthening of this relationship through the perspective of the (temporary) rearrangements of the normative gender roles and attitudes created by migration. Apart from the challenges to emotional ties caused by the years of separation, Felicita and Franc's experience was characterized by two different familial dynamics and gender roles' constellations. In the first three years, Felicita was engaged, but single, with no children and also no work experience outside the home. During her second stay in Egypt, she was a more confident and experienced worker, a wife, and the mother of a small child. She established an intense relationship with the family and with the children for whom she cared, Marika and especially Fredi. In the first period, Franc was young, single, and engaged to a migrant woman. In the second period, however, he was a married man and a father; yet having an absent wife and mother of your child was not a traditional and prescribed family ideal. Though it was common in these villages for wives and mothers to migrate, and in many cases be the main breadwinners, rearranging gender roles and negotiating embedded sensibilities of femininity and masculinity were not simple tasks.[5] The correspondence exchanged by Felicita and Franc offers us a glimpse into how they negotiated their new roles and navigated the challenges created by the tension between socially prescribed gender expectations and their transformation in the migration process.

Correspondence in the Research of Emotions and Gendered Mobility

We must understand the preservation of the emotional ties and the negotiation of the normative gender roles visible in the epistolary dialog between Felicita and Franc in the context of the controversy that female labor migration caused at the individual, family, and community level.[6] From the second half of the nineteenth century until 1940, when it came to an end because of World War II, *aleksandrinstvo*, as the phenomenon of female migration to Egypt is called, represented an important financial resource for the Goriška region.[7] Migration to Egypt was spurred by the economic prosperity created by the opening of the Suez Canal in 1869 and by the profitable Egyptian cotton industry. Prosperous Egyptian cities witnessed an influx of cotton merchants and other wealthy families as well as many migrant workers from Europe, including aleksandrinke.[8]

A complex phenomenon, aleksandrinke encompassed diverse patterns of women's migration, reemigration, circular and chain migration, and, above all, different personal experiences. The emotional underpinning of experiences varied considerably according to the type of work and the migrants' personal circumstances. There were clear differences between women who worked as nannies and wet nurses and women who did other types of work; between a few women who had their children with them and the majority who left them at home in Goriška; between single women and those who were wives and mothers. Regarding children, there are a few testimonies of abandoned children whom nobody cared for, but many more testimonies of less traumatic childhoods.[9] The different responses of men, spouses, and fathers to the mass migration of women varied from a caring role they embraced without hesitation or performed with the help of kin, to a retreat to the most reckless behavior of drinking and spending the money sent to them by their daughters, fiancées, or wives.

Even if the decisions to go to work in Egypt were the result of family deliberations, the fact that women became breadwinners threatened prescribed gender roles and caused what Rhacel Salazar Parreñas calls "the gender paradox": the more changes of traditional family and gender roles are necessary because of the absent women, the more persistent everyone involved is in preserving them.[10] The fact that migrant women were far from the tight social control of family and village prompted public opinion and policy makers to attack them regularly. The Catholic Church and local priests condemned the practice as a threat to morality and used gossip about the supposedly immoral behavior of aleksandrinke to preach against the migration of women. They linked women's migration to the danger and fear of moral corruption, ignoring the economic and political causes of migration.[11] The institutions and discourses that supported the denigration of women migrants were far from limited to the Church. Dirk Hoerder argues that the discourse of disdain and moral condemnation of female work and migration was deeply rooted in nineteenth- and twentieth-century nationalism, and has not yet been overcome. The reduction of women to the role of "mothers of the nation" was intense in all political and ideological varieties, and it was institutionalized on the legislative, cultural, and ideological levels. For this very reason, the concrete experiences, achievements, contributions, and importance of female migrants had to be silenced, overlooked, forgotten, or wrapped into traumatic intimate memories.[12]

For women who migrated to Egypt, where they were mostly well respected and well paid, migration had a profound impact on their public image as unconventional female characters whose reputation fluctuated between "silent thankful adoration and loud moral condemnation."[13] As such, it brought with it rearrangements of the traditional roles within families, of the value of women's work within the rural economy, and of the emotional system of the community. The concept of emotional community as suggested by Barbara H. Rosenwein applies, in this case, to a social community of families from the cluster of villages in the Goriška region where all were affected by this specific female migration. As Rosenwein argues, this concept allows a researcher "to uncover systems of feeling, to establish what these communities (and the individuals within them) define and assess as valuable or harmful to them (for it is about such things that people express emotions); the emotions that they value, devalue, or ignore; the nature of the affective bonds between people that they recognize; and the modes of emotional expression that they expect, encourage, tolerate, and deplore."[14] Autobiographical sources that convey experiences and emotions of ordinary people and their everyday lives help us gain this perspective.

Since the 1980s, the importance of emotions has been recognized not only in histories of emotions, but also in migration studies.[15] The use of diaries, auto/biographical texts, letters, photographs, and life narratives has been extensive in migration studies in the past few decades.[16] Samuel Baily and Franco Ramella assert the research importance of letters when they state: "We must use letters for what they can uniquely document—personal insights and feelings. Letters provide the subjective perspective on the immigrant experience."[17] Personal correspondence reveals the complexity of individual and family decisions, everyday choices, cultural negotiations and social experiences, and above all personal interpretations, intimate feelings, and the infinite series of emotions triggered by decisions about separation among those who left and those who stayed behind.

There are several methodological limitations regarding letters as a source. Susan J. Matt mentions the unclear relationship between words and feelings, and the question of audience: "Writings, even private scribbles and diaries, are composed for an audience. That fact shapes what is included and what is left out, what is accented, and what is unstressed."[18] The chronology of the letters is also never an easy issue: there might be letters that should have arrived earlier but did not due to various circumstances; some are without dates, some with the date but not the year; and there might be missed letters or unanswered ones.[19] David Gerber calls our attention to another methodological challenge, which he terms the "epistolary masquerade," describing it as a problem of silence and untruths. He stresses that "immigrant letters are not principally about documenting the world, but instead about reconfiguring a personal relationship rendered vulnerable by long-distance, long-term separation. It is in the service of that goal that the letter develops its content, so that goal, profoundly illusive in its own way because it springs from the most profound recess of human needs and emotions, needs to be understood as the source of the aspirations of the parties involved."[20]

Nevertheless, correspondence reveals "the voice of the past" and the emotions of their migrating protagonists.[21] As Sonia Cancian argues, "letters take us inside the minds and hearts of ordinary people whose personal and family identities and circumstances were most affected by the realities of international migration."[22] This is exactly what we find in the correspondence of Felicita Koglot and Franc Peric: it is rich in content and extensive in the number of letters, postcards, photographs, and numerous references to packages that made up the exchanges of emotions, concerns, longings, doubts, and hopes in the decade between 1921 and 1931 from both sides.[23] I had the privilege to read and analyze a part of this vast correspondence: 110 letters written by Felicita to Franc and 122 letters sent by Franc to Felicita. During my research on the aleksandrinstvo phenomenon, I met many relatives and descendants of aleksandrinke, and one of them was Neda R. Bric, the granddaughter of Felicita and Franc Peric, who let me use her well-kept family correspondence for research purposes and provided additional background in several conversations.[24]

Uniting through Letters: Dreaming and Longing

The motif of an engaged couple's romantic love filled the correspondence immediately after Felicita left in February 1921. In a letter sent to Franc "just before Easter," Felicita wrote:

> Oh, how happy I was tonight, dreaming that Zorka [her roommate and friend] and I returned home and that you all came toward us on the road, but when we were only a few steps apart and I'd already thought how we would greet and kiss, Madam called me to go to the baby. Such a pity! Let's hope that this, like all in the world, passes; these three years pass and if God preserves our health we also live to see that happy reunion. How often do I picture that happy moment when the steamship approaches the dock. Ah, I mustn't ponder, because this goal is far, far away. You know, now I understand the saying that abroad more tears

are shed than water is drunk. Just know that at times my heart wants to break with homesickness!²⁵

Franc wrote his answer on Easter Sunday, pouring his sadness into words: "To ease the bitterness of today I decided to write you this letter. First, please accept thousands of heartfelt greetings and kisses. It is a holiday, everything is beautiful, the procession at the resurrection mass was beautiful. Everyone is happy, everyone is brave, only my heart is terribly sad because it has lost its greatest treasure that it loves."²⁶ These lamentations went on in the correspondence throughout the whole year. In August 1921, Felicita wrote: "Please know that when I was reading your letter I cried bitter tears. Why is God punishing us so much; I am truly afraid for you all, that you will suffer hunger. My God, every time I sit down to eat, I think of you, that here I have [food], and you over there, God knows."²⁷ A month later her beloved replied even more inconsolably: "I don't know what would happen if I sent you any of those letters I write when I think of you too much, when I'm sad, when I can find no solace. If you felt like me in your heart you'd cry like I do, or you'd say, this man is stupid."²⁸ However, besides the hurting, longing, and sadness they also exchanged joy, expectations, and details about their dreams, especially Felicita. In the same letter from August 1921, alongside tears and fears, there were also encouraging words:

> How we used to watch the moon and the stars thinking of the days to come. Know that even now I look at the moon and the stars and I think that perhaps you are watching them at the same time and think we see them the same way. Unfortunately, we're far apart from each other, but know that in our thoughts we're always together, aren't we? I often see you in my dreams, and I find some consolation in this.²⁹

Far from unique, the topic of looking to the same stars and the recounting of the dreams seem to be common motifs in the correspondences between lovers and couples separated by migration. Cancian has found references to the same topics in her study of Italian migration to Canada after 1945. She argues, "it seems that the act of dreaming functioned both to trigger the imagination of correspondents and to bridge the distance between lovers through a recounting of the experience."³⁰ It also seems that the recounting of dreams served the purpose of expressing erotic longing and fueled further desire for the absent lover.³¹

Separation also created uncertainty. Only nine months after the departure and a month after words of sad passion and longing were exchanged, a very different topic appeared in the couple's correspondence. A letter expressing doubts, suspicions, and jealousy arrived from Franc, and Felicita obviously felt compelled to answer it decisively:

> As for me, have no worries, because I have neither the freedom nor the parties, nor anything at all to get myself in any danger. And the thought of home and my beloved encourages me . . . and I cannot wait for that moment that we see each other again. What, have you already tried it, as you write that you feel when you hold a girl or even hug her, it feels like hugging a tree? I'm curious. I've not sullied myself, not with the slightest thing, and God make it stay this way.[32]

The personal, intimate doubts Franc expressed in his letters were penned in the context of a general suspicion about aleksandrinke that resulted from a combination of intense moral condemnation voiced by priests and widespread gossip within the tight-knit communities of the villages. Franc wrote about gossip extensively as well as about other events and social changes at the level of local communities and individuals. He wanted to produce epistolary closeness and simultaneity with his beloved fiancée.[33] The letters from November 1921 provide good examples of this double objective: Franc reported to Felicita about nasty gossip, but also sent endless confessions of love. He wrote that on a rainy Sunday he had done nothing else but read her letters over and over: "My beloved Felička, one of my favorite letters of yours is the one you gave to me that last Sunday in our field when we went to Gorica, do you still remember? I will never forget you, nor the places where we were together."[34] Felicita also wrote back sweet words: "I was pleased to get your lovely letter this week again. Thank you from my heart. I'm glad that you respond to me regularly. I hope that now that long winter evenings have arrived you will have more time to unite with me through letters."[35] Nevertheless, the romantic "uniting" through correspondence turned again to the bitterness of moral suspicions and gossip. Felicita wrote at the end of 1921:

> I was pleased to receive your letter, but as I was reading it such sadness came over me that I couldn't be happy at all. Because your writing reveals that you're very upset [with me] and are even doubting [me]!! I think that nobody can say a bad word about me for leaving. Do not curse Egypt, because people cannot live on love alone, and where there's poverty it's often a cause for arguments in married life, and praise God that He gave me a chance to earn some money. . . . As I understand from your writing, it might appear that because we're in a so-called bad city, we're all the

same. You're wrong, when we're free, we go to the nuns, and there we play, sing, and that's all the joy we have.³⁶ My heart aches, because I think if we saw each other, you'd look at me with suspicion and not like before.³⁷

In defending herself against suspicions and insinuations, Felicita writes in this letter about the tight connection between emotions and interest.³⁸ She understands money as a prerequisite for marital happiness and well-being because love is not enough to guarantee happiness, and poverty can destroy it. Despite realistic and mature epistolary conversations about this problem, letters from 1922 brought more gossip. Another difficult topic appeared in these letters, namely the complicated relationship between the members of the two families, especially between Felicita's mother and Franc. Over the years, even when already married, the tension between Franc and his mother-in-law would grow as we will see in the letters from the second period of separation. In August 1922, Franc wrote a harsh letter regarding this matter:

> As for your picture, I swear I didn't get it. If you care to, resend it!? Further, you're *insulting* [his underline] me if you say things like that regarding your family, that I probably don't go there very often, or even not at all. Now that you haven't written to me in a while, I was there every week, I asked if they had anything from you. Finally on Saturday they received your letter which your mother let me read. And when I reached the lines that were about me, I felt more than one knife in my heart. I'll leave these things be for today, perhaps more about them next week. I will just tell you this, you listen to people too much, and I think there is no uglier sin in the world than these old chin-waggers from Bilje.³⁹

Despite the tension created by distance, time of separation, gossip, the public accusations about aleksandrinke, and family difficulties, the following letters show that the love between Felicita and Franc prevailed. Deploying a familiar strategy, in September 1923, Felicita yet again expressed her love and doubts simultaneously: "Please know that although I love you with all the love that one can love with, if I knew that you'd be happier not marrying, of course I'd be miserable, there are no words to describe it, but I'd please you."⁴⁰ But shortly after, in a letter from October 3, she shared her happy dreams with him: "The night before last I dreamed that I came home and I saw you from afar plowing with the horses, I thought to myself 'He'll come,' and you did, but just to say hello ... And then I told you, see, three years passed in a moment, and I'm here again. It was such a pity to wake up from dreams like that."⁴¹

Optimism and happiness predominated in the correspondence as Felicita's departure from Egypt and return home came closer. Felicita summarized the three-year separation in positive, hopeful terms, in a letter from February 1924:

> So today as I write this, three years have passed since I stepped on Egyptian soil. Three years and yet they've gone by quickly, no? A lot of water under the bridge, a lot of tears, but our love is still firm, like a rock. Ours is that ditty: everything in this world passes, everything comes to an end, only love goes without changing, faithful love, forever there. So three years, now I'm calculating another three months, and if God grants us health, we'll pick the first cherries together.[42]

They did pick cherries together that spring, got married, and had a baby girl, Danila, the next year. As we can understand from the correspondence in the second migration period and from the oral testimonies of their granddaughter, they were happy. However, the Italian state's forced "Italianization" of the Slovenian population gradually worsened the political and economic situation in the Goriška region. This was undoubtedly one of the main reasons that Felicita and Franc decided she would leave again.[43]

Enduring through Letters: Weeping and Consoling

The correspondence started again on a sad day in February 1928, when Franc returned home after watching Felicita set sail from Trieste for the second time. He described his suffering vividly in his first letter, written at the moment that the second period of separation began:

> You have no idea how sad I came home. I couldn't even speak when I stepped into the house or when I saw Danilka. I thought I'd not make it until the hour when it's time for bed. But with a lot of attention and suffering I managed until 7 o'clock and me and Danilka went into our once so dear, but now lonely room. Oh, if only she could tell you, once you return, how many tears were shed that night, that we could both wash in them in the morning, Danila and I. The day was better, the second evening was still a little bad, but now I'm good. Danilka is fine, don't worry, you have no idea how many kisses she sends you every day.[44]

At the intimate, emotional level of couples and children, the migration of women complicated life as much as it made it easier. Women's everyday physical and emotional care was absent but with the money they sent from Egypt there was enough food on the table, taxes and loans that put farms in danger were paid, houses were repaired or enlarged, and a new field or a vineyard purchased. Working abroad was a "blessing" but it all came at a high emotional price on the individual and family levels. Felicita described this complexity in her letter, addressing her daughter and husband, in December 1928.

> Honestly, I don't know if we'll ever be happy again. Like you write, perhaps if we cover our ears and fuse our eyes so we don't feel what's going on around us. In this way, we could still savor our previous happiness. Still, I wish indescribably to hold you both in my arms in the embrace of marital happiness. My heart hurts when you write about Nila that she asks for her mother when she comes home. Oh, child, if you only knew how your mama wants to see you and hug you and love you fiercely, but it's all in vain. God knows how much time will pass before this happens. Because the times are getting worse and blessed are the families who have members around the world.[45]

Felicita and Franc were loving parents who adapted to the challenges created by migration and family separation. In their correspondence, we see how Franc as a father and husband did not have a problem with the rearrangements of traditional and prescribed gender roles or with the expression of emotions.[46] He took care of their daughter lovingly, and understood Felicita's dire situation as a mother, being so far away from her child. In March 1929, he wrote to her the following compassionate lines:

> Truth be told, mommy, it hurts me that you cannot hear and see how our beloved daughter is growing. . . . it's impossible to tell you how I yearn for you, my beloved wife, and how Danila is also all pensive and upset when I tell her about you, her precious mommy, and how mommy loves her, and how she cares and sacrifices herself. . . . My love for you, I hope I don't have to convey it anymore, because surely you don't doubt that I love you with all my might and that I yearn for you as the thirsty yearn for water.[47]

It is obvious that being parents did not mean that they stopped expressing their love and passion as a couple. Yet, it all became more difficult as the gossip continued and family problems intensified. In 1929, Franc joined the seasonal migration to Switzerland where construction workers from Bilje and neighboring villages worked every year. Thus, Danila stayed with his family and relatives. His 1929 work season ended in December, and he reported to Felicita very bad news from home:

Please note that they all talk about your mother, how she is the way she is, and everybody's surprised how she can be like that. I've never spoken ill to her, I've put up with it patiently, I've cried, you and I, we've both cried to console ourselves, but now I'm so fed up with everything that I don't know if I'll be able to keep quiet about everything when I go over there. Come what may! She's gone too far, I don't know what would happen if someone else was in my place. And I'm advising you, too, not to write to her, not to send her anything, because, mother or not, she's not worth it.

I know that this insults you, Felička, but I've heard from reliable people that she wants to alienate you from me, and that she wants to disgust my entire family toward you without any of us doing anything bad to her. These days, I've not had a happy hour. All days and nights I am wrought with worries. And instead of looking forward to your return, it scares me, our much-awaited reunion! And this is the truth, mommy, I know very well, that there will be no peace.[48]

Apart from the growing problems with his wife's mother, Franc had difficulties being back in the village and having to readapt to its traditional ways. Perhaps he felt what so many women felt when they returned home from Egypt—unexpected alienation and isolation. Instead of happiness, aleksandrinke often felt that they no longer belonged there. The difficulties upon returning home were caused by changed identities brought about by the new experience of independence and dignity, by the acquired knowledge of foreign languages and an urban, higher class lifestyle, and by traveling the world and Egypt. Upon arriving home, women had to again accept the prescribed gender norms, the required social control, and the rural, farming way of life. For aleksandrinke there was another problem: the adjustment to the interpretation of their experience as morally questionable, which remained as a collective trauma deeply embedded in the community until recently.[49] Feelings of inadequacy were also common among returned seasonal workers like Franc. These feelings were compounded by the absence of wives, in the case of married men whose wives were working abroad. Franc confided to Felicita his feelings of isolation: "I feel very bored, no company, I like it best to keep at home. My old mates, they don't fit right." And he mentioned the sorry fact that hard-earned money from Egypt was trickling down the throats of ungrateful, indifferent, or even frustrated and suspicious husbands in the local bars. He indignantly described his peers as "only drunkards and scroungers."[50]

Franc's detailed descriptions of Zurich in the next year's correspondence, when he was again a seasonal builder, are particularly noteworthy. In the midst of describing to her the beauty of Zurich's surroundings, he dreams about seeing her soon:

> Since I got your picture yesterday I've missed you so much; if it were possible I'd fly to you, but it's in vain to even think about it when we're so far apart. You know what I've been thinking, for example, if it happened like you mentioned in your last letter that they'd both go to Paris [the couple she worked for], ask them to take you with them as far as Zurich, and give you the money they'd spend for the hotel over there, and for the entire time they're in Paris you could be here and we'd have a good time.[51]

They did not meet and stay together in Zurich. Their reunion had to wait until another cherry-picking season in Bilje in 1931, when Felicita finally came home and never left again.[52]

Conclusion: "Our Love Is Still Firm, Like a Rock"

Correspondence is considered one of the central documents to study "history from the inside out," and to understand the solidarity, bonds, experiences, and emotions of individuals involved, whether they stay or migrate.[53] The analysis of correspondence offered in this text provides an insight into the complexity of feelings of love as driving forces behind the decisions and everyday negotiations in translocal and transcultural settings. The correspondence Felicita and Franc kept during the years of separation helped them maintain and strengthen their relationship. The selected epistolary topics convey expressions of love, loyalty, and devotion that were exchanged to preserve the relationship even in times of disagreements, resentment, and misunderstandings. These hard times were further complicated by the couple's family problems as well as by external issues such as public gossip and attitudes instilled by the Church and the community, and by the social, economic, and political realities in Europe and Egypt at this turbulent time. Testimonies of their "epistolary emotions" reveal how gender and migration were interconnected in the correspondence of a young couple involved in the phenomenon of aleksandrinstvo.[54] The selected letters offer a glimpse of the subtle and complex emotional landscape resulting from the rearrangement of gender roles and of the embedded sensibilities of femininity and masculinity caused by migration.

Apart from the relationship of the writers of the letters, my main goal was to show how their love story was part of the larger family and community system of migration in the social and political context of two different, yet connected worlds—Goriška villages and Egyptian cities. They were connected by women and men, who loved, cared, hoped, and feared on both sides of the Mediterranean. They were aware that no matter how strong their love was, migration and separation were a necessary challenge of their pursuit of happiness. As Felicita put it in her letter to her beloved Franc, "people cannot live on love alone."

NOTES

This research was funded by the Slovenian Research Agency (research core funding P5-0070).

1. The Slovenian ethnic territory was a part of the Habsburg Empire for centuries. It was divided after World War I: The biggest part became a constitutional entity of the new Kingdom of Yugoslavia and the western part (including the Goriška region), became part of the Kingdom of Italy with the signing of the Rapallo Treaty. The population suffered greatly under the forced "Italianization" and repression of the Fascist regime from 1921 to 1943. This involved economic, social, and cultural measures: devastating tax policy, the prohibition of the use of Slovenian language, name changes, the banning of all Slovenian organizations, prosecutions of intellectuals, forced migration, imprisonments, and killings. After World War II, the western territory (including the Goriška region, but without the city of Gorizia/Gorica, which remained a part of Italy) became an integral part of Slovenia, the northernmost republic of the Socialist Federal Republic of Yugoslavia, and in 1991 it became an independent state.

2. Bilje is a relatively large village with orchards and vineyards, and centuries-old brickyards. Many buildings were damaged or destroyed during the Isonzo Front of World War I. For political and economic reasons, migration was widespread. There was hardly any household that did not have one or more of its female members working in Egypt.

3. In the letters, her name appears in different loving variations: Neli, Dani, Danilka, Nila, Nini, etc.

4. Franc migrated for seasonal work in 1929, in the context of a worsening political situation and a generalized economic crisis.

5. On the concept of sensibility, see Daniel Wickberg, "What Is the History of Sensibilities? On Cultural Histories, Old and New," *American Historical Review* 112, no. 3 (2007): 669. See also the study of Margarita Dounia in this anthology who describes the drastic changes in gender roles when women migrate and the emotional complications these migrations cause. She also presents the specific emotional trajectory of the separation from children, which was the case for many women migrants from Goriška and for Felicita as well.

6. The rearrangement of socially prescribed gender roles is one of the basic characteristics of migration that has been extensively researched in recent de-

cades by several scholars, for example, Donna R. Gabaccia, *From the Other Side: Women, Gender, and Immigrant Life in the U.S., 1820–1990* (Bloomington: Indiana University Press, 1994); Floya Anthias and Gabriella Lazaridis, eds., *Gender and Migration in Southern Europe: Women on the Move* (Oxford: Berg, 2000); Luisa Passerini, Dawn Lyon, Enrica Capussotti, and Ionna Laliotou, eds., *Women Migrants from East to West: Gender, Mobility, and Belonging in Contemporary Europe* (New York: Berghahn Books, 2010). Suzanne M. Sinke conceptualized and defined this process of rearrangements of gender roles with the term "social reproduction." In her own words, she uses this term "[t]o describe how people put those roles back together, sometimes replicating, sometimes revising, sometimes totally reformulating their ideas of what women and men should do." Suzanne M. Sinke, *Dutch Immigrant Women in the United States, 1880–1920* (Urbana: University of Illinois Press, 2002), 1.

7. See Ana Barbič and Inga Miklavčič Brezigar, "Domestic Work Abroad: A Necessity and An Opportunity for Rural Women from the Goriska Borderland Region of Slovenia," in *Gender, Migration, and Domestic Service*, ed. Janet H. Momsen (London: Routledge, 1999), 164–77.

8. See Francesca Biancani, "Globalisation, Migration, and Female Labour in Cosmopolitan Egypt," in *From Slovenia to Egypt: Aleksandrinke's Trans-Mediterranean Domestic Workers' Migration and National Imagination*, ed. Mirjam Milharčič Hladnik (Göttingen, Ger.: V and R Unipress, 2015), 207–28.

9. On children in the context of aleksandrinstvo, see Daša Koprivec, "Aleksandrinke in Egypt: Between Condemnation and Adoration," in *Going Places: Slovenian Women's Stories on Migration*, ed. Mirjam Milharčič Hladnik and Jernej Mlekuž (Akron, OH: University of Akron Press, 2014), 105–35. We also need to consider the emotional experiences of the children the aleksandrinke cared for, and their testimonies of how Slovenian nannies marked their lives and identities. See Ellis Douek, *A Middle Eastern Affair* (London: Peter Halban, 2004).

10. Rhacel Salazar Parreñas, *Servants of Globalization: Women, Migration, and Domestic Work* (Stanford, CA: Stanford University Press, 2001) and Rhacel Salazar Parreñas, *Children of Global Migration: Transnational Families and Gendered Woes* (Stanford, CA: Stanford University Press, 2005).

11. See the chapter of Alexander Freund in this anthology for a discussion on social discourses of gender and the moralistic rhetoric that state and church mobilize to control women. Moralistic accusations and condemnations of women migrants from Goriška to Egypt caused a collective trauma of families in the region that lasted until recently. For more on the recent attempts to reevaluate this specific women's migration by the local population of Goriška and the descendants of women migrants, see Mirjam Milharčič Hladnik, "Trans-Mediterranean Women Domestic Workers: Historical and Contemporary Perspective," in *From Slovenia to Egypt*, ed. Milharčič Hladnik, 11–38.

12. Dirk Hoerder, "Re-remembering Women Who Chose Caregiving Careers

in a Global Perspective: Mothers of the Nation or Agents in Their Own Lives?" in *From Slovenia to Egypt*, ed. Milharčič Hladnik, 117–30.

13. Milharčič Hladnik, "Trans-Mediterranean Women Domestic Workers," 12.

14. Barbara H. Rosenwein, "Problems and Methods in the History of Emotions," *Passions in Context: Journal of the History and Philosophy of the Emotions* 1, no. 1 (2010): 11.

15. William M. Reddy, "Historical Research on the Self and Emotions," *Emotion Review* 1, no. 4 (2009): 302–15.

16. Samuel L. Baily and Franco Ramella, eds., *One Family, Two Worlds: An Italian Family's Correspondence across the Atlantic, 1901–1922* (New Brunswick, NJ: Rutgers University Press, 1988); Solveig Zempel, *In Their Own Words: Letters from Norwegian Immigrants* (Minneapolis: University of Minnesota Press, 1991); Sonia Cancian, *Families, Lovers, and Their Letters: Italian Postwar Migration to Canada* (Winnipeg: University of Manitoba Press, 2010); Bruce S. Elliot, David A. Gerber, and Suzanne M. Sinke, eds., *Letters across Borders: The Epistolary Practices of International Migrants* (New York: Palgrave Macmillan, 2006); Alistair Thomson, *Moving Stories: An Intimate History of Four Women across Two Countries* (Manchester: Manchester University Press, 2011); Mirjam Milharčič Hladnik, "A Slovenian Bride in Cleveland: Emotions in Letters," in *Going Places*, ed. Milharčič Hladnik and Mlekuž, 21–67.

17. Baily and Ramella, *One Family, Two Worlds*, 4.

18. Susan J. Matt, "Current Emotion Research in History: Or, Doing History from the Inside Out," *Emotion Review* 3, no. 1 (2011): 117–24.

19. On "fragmentation" of correspondence, see Zempel, *In Their Own Words*, xiii–xiv.

20. David A. Gerber, "Epistolary Masquerades: Acts of Deceiving and Withholding in Immigrant Letters," in *Letters across Borders*, ed. Elliot, Gerber, and Sinke, 143.

21. The expression comes from Paul Thomson, *The Voice of the Past: Oral History* (Oxford: Oxford University Press, 1988).

22. Cancian, *Families, Lovers, and Their Letters*, 5.

23. This is rarely the case as usually only one side of correspondence is preserved. See Elliot, Gerber, and Sinke, eds., *Letters across Borders*, 3.

24. I would like to express my gratitude to Neda R. Bric for access to this correspondence, our long conversations, her help in understanding family relations, and her trust. All the letters in this chapter are from her family archive. For my previous work about this migratory experience, see Milharčič Hladnik, *From Slovenia to Egypt*.

25. Felicita to Franc, before Easter 1921, no date.

26. Franc to Felicita, Easter day 1921.

27. Felicita to Franc, August 18, 1921.

28. Franc to Felicita, September 29, 1921.

29. Felicita to Franc, August 18, 1921.

30. Cancian, *Families, Lovers, and Their Letters*, 136.

31. However, in his extensive research of epistolary practices of Irish immigrants in Australia and their loved ones in Ireland, David Fitzpatrick found the reporting of a dream also between friends and relatives. In the dreams, they were happily united again or "the dream signified not a happy conjunction but a supernatural warning of disaster or death, travelling faster than the promptest telegram." David Fitzpatrick, *Oceans of Consolation: Personal Accounts of Irish Migration to Australia* (Ithaca, NY: Cornell University Press, 1994), 494.

32. Felicita to Franc, November 1, 1921.

33. Many studies have helped us to understand that this "simultaneity" is an essential part of the subjective experience of the migration process—of those who leave and those who stay. See Peggy Levitt and Nina Glick Schiller, "Conceptualizing Simultaneity: A Transnational Social Field Perspective on Society," *International Migration Review* 38, no. 3 (2004): 1002–39.

34. Franc to Felicita, November 7, 1921. Gorica is the main town of the region (Gorizia in Italian); the region is named after it in Slovenian: Goriška.

35. Felicita to Franc, November 30, 1921.

36. On their free days, Slovenian women got together at the "nun's place" in Cairo and Alexandria, where they participated in different cultural events and maintained a tight network of support. The Slovenia Women's Christian Union, the sisters of the Order of Saint Francis and of Christ the King (called school sisters), who managed the Franz-Joseph Asylum (later called Saint Francis Asylum), and the Catholic Association of Saint Cyril and Metod had been active in Egypt since 1908.

37. Felicita to Franc, December 26, 1921.

38. See the study of Marcelo J. Borges in this anthology for many examples of how emotions and interest, love and money, are connected and intertwined in migration decisions and processes.

39. Franc to Felicita, August 5, 1922.

40. Felicita to Franc, September 18, 1923.

41. Felicita to Franc, October 3, 1923.

42. Felicita to Franc, February 1924 (no day).

43. Her case was far from unique. Village and family life adapted to the migration of women. Family, relatives, friends, and neighbors took care of children when mothers (and fathers) left and even in the case of those who went as wet nurses the community had a system of support that worked well.

44. Franc to Felicita, February 14, 1928.

45. Felicita to Franc, December 5, 1928.

46. The fact that women and men are equally articulate and passionate in conveying emotions on paper is also found in Cancian's analysis. Cancian, *Families, Lovers, and Their Letters*, 142. I have argued the same in the analysis of the Udovič-Valenčič-Hrvatin family correspondence. In this correspondence, the brother and the sister who migrated to Cleveland in the United States expressed equally mov-

ing emotions in the letters to their mother and family in the Slovenian village of Jelšane. Milharčič Hladnik, "A Slovenian Bride in Cleveland," 21–67.

47. Franc to Felicita, March 18, 1929.

48. Franc to Felicita, December 4, 1929.

49. This trauma has been collectively dealt with through the Society for the Preservation of the Cultural Heritage of the Alexandrian Women. In 2005, the descendants of aleksandrinke in Slovenia organized themselves into this society, started to collect testimonies and material heritage, and, a year later, opened a participatory museum in the village of Prvačina, in the Goriška region, in order to establish the perception of aleksandrinke as courageous, successful, and determined saviors of their families. See the website of the museum and the society: http://www.aleksandrinke.si/eng/. See also, Milharčič Hladnik, *From Slovenia to Egypt*, especially pt. 3.

50. Franc to Felicita, December 4, 1929.

51. Franc to Felicita, August 30, 1930.

52. In many cases, the love for the children in the care of an aleksandrinka and the love of those children for her did not cease with her departure. The existing love and affection created translocal emotional ties that, in many cases, lasted until the death of the aleksandrinka and even through generations, with her descendants. Upon her arrival home, Felicita put Fredi's photograph on a shelf in the dining room and it stayed there. Bric remembers that for them, Felicita's grandchildren, Fredi was their "cousin." Neda R. Bric, e-mail message to author, October 15, 2016.

53. The expression belongs to Susan Matt. See Matt, "Current Emotion Research."

54. For a discussion of epistolary emotions, see Mark Seymour, "Epistolary Emotions: Exploring Amorous Hinterlands in 1870s Southern Italy," *Social History* 35, no. 2 (2010): 148.

CHAPTER 4

Love, Mobility, and Fate in Turn-of-the-Century Berlin

TYLER CARRINGTON

Love was in motion in the turn-of-the-twentieth-century city. In Berlin, electric trams whizzed commuters to and from jobs where men and women now worked side-by-side and found in each other potential mates; bustling train stations shuttled Berliners out to suburban dance halls where love flourished; transportation hubs like the Friedrichstrasse station funneled in provincials drawn by the city's manifold romantic possibilities; and busy boulevards teemed with intimate strangers who might just be soulmates if Fortuna's smile happened to hit them at the right time.

The search for love was also shifting in the modern metropolis—love being a moving target, it seemed, for an unlucky many. Berliners were fond of recalling how finding a partner earlier had been much simpler.[1] Now, they said, one at best stumbled upon love over the telephone or via a fortuitous encounter or, failing that, penned a matrimonial ad in the classifieds. Judging the suitability of a mate now seemed to require either the services of a "professional" (new matchmakers with scientific "systems") or various other homespun methods.[2] There was, in short, a great deal of talk about how love from "back then" was out of date in the modern city where both the pace of modern life and the ever-new faces of strangers were, Berliners thought, "nowadays" rendering the standard romantic methods old and ineffective.

If love was ever-shifting and so often in motion, turn-of-the-century men and women can be excused for expressing frustration with the metropolis's countless obstacles to finding love, as they so often did: publicly, in newspaper reader's forums; artistically, in short stories and poems; and privately, in diaries, memoirs, and correspondence. Surely, though, the experience cannot have been so consistently vexing. Indeed, more often than not, they must have found what they were looking for—or at least a substitute (the "first-best," in the parlance of the day) who offered a modicum of companionship or at least some financial assistance in the "struggle for existence." Marriage rates in the metropolis were indeed slightly higher than in Germany as a whole, even if this was primarily because of the overall younger population of cities like Berlin.[3]

On the other hand, urban migrants had a lot working against them, and their frustrations were real. What, then, do we make of Berliners' endless complaining about love's elusiveness; the way they lamented their city's stodgy romantic normativities; or their dreamy "what-ifs" about connecting with a stranger on the street?

This chapter traces the origins of Berliners' dreams about strangers and of fated encounters and suggests that the city's painful mixture of opportunity and opposition led urban migrants to yearn for a more pragmatic, individualistic approach to love, one that might allow them to break with prevailing ideas about respectability and find an intimate partner amid the whirr of the new metropolis. However, because traditional respectability was so deeply rooted and highly prized in turn-of-the-century society—and because it was leveraged to quash these new romantic approaches—newcomers to Berlin in turn became fascinated by the idea of fate and the fortuitous encounter. Fate, chance, and "what if?" formed a new language of love that opened up an imaginative space of normative mobility, one in which they could imagine breaking free from traditional masculinity and femininity and seizing for themselves the manifold amorous possibilities created by the motion of the modern city.

Mobility and love were thus their own problem and solution, for while the constant movement of cities and the entrenchment of traditional beliefs about respectability seemed to frustrate the blossoming of urban romances, this very mixture of movement and stasis prompted Berliners to create a new language of love that offered a certain liberation. Love, in this way, was not simply the punching bag of the modern world, not something merely acted upon and shaped by the countervailing forces of the modern city, modern life, and modernity itself. Love was its own force and was, indeed, creative of something new.[4] As we will see here, love was at once constricted by and creative of mobility.

The Dizzying Motion of the Modern City

Berlin was not Europe's largest city, but its exponential growth at the turn of the century gave it a unique flair. Berlin exploded from under a half million in 1850 to two million in 1905, making it the fastest-growing major European capital in the nineteenth century.[5] Most of this growth came in the form of single young men and women who were drawn from surrounding provincial towns by the manifold opportunities and excitements of the modern industrial city.[6] Statistical yearbooks and histories of migration reveal that slightly more men than women came to Berlin and that roughly three-quarters of newcomers were between fifteen and thirty-five years old.[7] Of these, very few were married (for example, of newcomers aged twenty to twenty-four, only 2 percent of men and 9 percent of women were already married),[8] and most were either working-class laborers and domestic servants or petit-bourgeois typists and clerks.[9]

Berlin was constantly growing, constantly moving to accommodate these thousands of newcomers each month. It was a dynamic city, and alongside the steady influx of provincials into the giant Berlin Friedrichstrasse train station, Berlin was in perpetual motion with its residents moving around the city at a dizzying pace. A remarkable and frequently cited statistic suggests that one half of all Berliners moved apartments within Berlin every six months.[10] Statistical yearbooks bear this out,[11] and anecdotal evidence comes from both early sociological studies of the city's widespread housing squalor, as well as pastors complaining that a good half of their parishioners changed their addresses each year.[12]

Berlin was also a sort of revolving door for newcomers, and while the data of the Berlin Statistical Office of course shows an overall surplus of new arrivals to those leaving the city (and thus population growth), the margins were often surprisingly small (in 1904, for example, 13 percent of all Berliners were new arrivals that year, but 12 percent of Berlin's population left the city). And women were even more likely to be on the move than men.[13] Much of this city-countryside movement was dictated by the demands (or scarcities) of work, family, and other opportunities.[14] The average foray into the city was in fact just three months, probably because of the absence of meaningful family connections for most migrants.[15] Indeed, most metrics for extended family structures (cohabitation of elderly with their offspring, marriage rates and ages, size of extended families) suggest that newcomers to the city were mostly on their own.[16] This was both destabilizing and, in terms of expected behaviors, values, and practices, actually somewhat liberating.

All of this movement occasioned a great many encounters: one passed countless faces on the street while commuting to work, sat next to strangers on the streetcar, and lived sometimes shoulder-to-shoulder in packed apartment buildings. And while the nature of the encounters themselves was not new, Berliners' responses to them were. They complained constantly about little collisions on the street, getting scratched or poked by an excessively elaborate hat in the omnibus, and having to listen to fellow commuters' chatter while riding "the electric" to work each morning. Those calm enough to offer advice usually suggested that one should simply try to tune out her fellow urbanites and put on a face of indifference—what the famous sociologist Georg Simmel, himself a Berliner, alternatingly called "a mental attitude . . . of reserve" and a "blasé outlook."[17]

Coping mechanisms such as these may have been effective ways of getting to work or to the corner store with one's nerves intact, but they were apparently less suitable for the more meaningful aspects of life, especially love and intimacy, which were scarcely attainable by shutting oneself off from the world. Indeed, as the nineteenth century slid into the twentieth, Berliners were, more and more, considering alternative paths to love, ways to find intimacy and connection in a city that seemed to be full of strangers. This included intimate relationships formed in dance halls, romances discovered while playing sports or at the office, and even connections made via matchmakers and the newspaper classified ads.[18] Each of these alternative paths was more or less easy to access, legal, and, generally speaking, tolerated; but for middle-class tastes, which ruled the day for most Berliners (especially those on the margins of the middle class), there was something unsavory about meeting this way, something that smacked of depravation and desperation—or, worse, prostitution. Thus, actually making use of these new methods was quickly cordoned off by the arbiters of respectability, to wit, fathers, older brothers, judges, police officers, clergy, and even the state itself.

Berlin as Cupid

Among these new and risky approaches to finding love in the big city was a type of longing or desire for the otherwise so irksome strangers Berliners encountered on a regular basis, and turn-of-the-century urban literature shows Berliners imagining the exciting possibility of fleeting urban relationships—strangers passing strangers—turning into something more, something lasting and intimate, something romantic. This may all sound terribly improbable, hoping against hope, waiting to be struck by lightning, and, of course, it was.

But men and women alike nevertheless continued to talk about and place a remarkable degree of hope in these chance encounters, and it is compelling to ask why, to ask what they saw in these unlikely connections.

As it happens, fate (in German, *Zufall*, fortuity) was an aspect of city life that Berliners referenced again and again, and even more common than complaints about isolation or annoying urban collisions was the trope of the "missed connection." Indeed, there was, alongside a very prevalent narrative of loneliness and of random encounters in the modern metropolis, alongside the longing this engendered, a sense, even a hope that these brief chance meetings might lead to romance. Berlin was in fact full of stories about fortuitous encounters arranged or at least enabled by the big city with its masses in constant movement. This talk of fate was in some ways part of a larger shift (discussed at length in a great many histories of love) toward the importance of love at the beginning of relationships—this as opposed to love playing only a secondary role in courtship, indeed, as something that came later, if at all;[19] but fortuitous encounters were different than the ascendant love marriage. They were more immediate, more of the moment, and more quintessentially urban. There was a sense that at any time, at any point, one might run into his soulmate or even simply someone who might soften the pains of isolation in the metropolis. These were known as *Strassenbekanntschaften*, street acquaintances with whom one shared a brief—though often intense—connection. Walter Benjamin famously called this type of meeting "love at last sight,"[20] though Charles Baudelaire deserves the credit for poeticizing this type of relationship already in the 1860s in his poem "To a Passer-By" ("À une passante").[21]

Whatever their provenance or first coinage, these relationships were utterly and importantly different than love relationships and love marriages, for these were distinctly urban fantasies. Talk of fated love and fortuitous meetings may exist to a certain extent in folklore and mythology of much earlier times, but in those cases, it is the work of the gods or of a magic potion or, most spectacularly, of heroic feats like pulling swords from stones and slaying dragons. Here, by contrast, it was the simple reality of the city, the movements of multitudes. Significantly, however, it was also the frustrations and restrictions of turn-of-the-century life that fed this fascination with chance meetings.

The typical, turn-of-the-century newspaper version of the fortuitous encounter usually involved a young man meeting his future wife because they both walked the same route into work each morning or both rode the same streetcar.[22] But most stories were slightly more involved (and farfetched) than this. One story in the popular daily newspaper the *Berliner Morgenpost*, for example, featured a man who accidentally grabs the wrong briefcase while leaving the streetcar on his way to work. In the briefcase is a picture of a beautiful girl, and he ultimately tracks her down and marries her.[23] Chance encounters at the post office were another common plot of short stories, as were twists of fate whereby, for example, a working-class boy who was spurned by a middle-class girl finds success as a businessman and later reconnects with her because he happens to employ her son (he, of course, promptly marries the woman).[24]

But Berliners did not limit themselves to just writing fiction about fated encounters. They even took to casting real-life events in the language of fate and fortuitous encounters. In one case presented as genuine news, a man who had recently sat for a portrait and given the photographer permission to display the photo in his display window heard from his friends that there was a picture of a beautiful woman next to his. Upon seeing the portrait himself and being so impressed by the woman's beauty, he got her name from the photographer and ended up marrying her. The newspaper writer attributed this to the power of fate.[25] In another, it was a penny vending machine that was supposed to predict a person's future mate by spitting out, at random, a picture of a seemingly anonymous Berliner. Wilhelm Strebel, the inventor of the machine, had at some point acquired a pile of old personal photograph negatives at an auction and used them to build his device, which he rented to various bars and restaurants throughout the city. The machine, which was reportedly especially popular among young women, produced for a penny or two a real photograph reproduced from one of these randomly selected negatives. Trouble arose, however, when a woman received the picture (by fate, the newspaper writer remarked casually) of someone she actually knew and who, upon hearing that his photo was being used thusly, sued Strebel.[26]

Berliners' obsession with—indeed, their faith in—meetings like these eventually became so pervasive that even physicians began noticing it. In his 1907 book on the psychology of love, *Love and Psychosis*, Dr. Georg Lomer suggested that while young people were especially predisposed to believe in love at first sight, neither age nor life experience could protect people from being struck by lightning, as he put it. This kind of love, he continued, appeared to come out of thin air, when really it was the product of the fortuitous combination of various circumstances.[27] Fate, in this way, was employed as a medical and scientific explanation for love.

Newspapers fed the flame, knowing fate made for great copy. The columnists of the *Berliner Morgenpost* newspaper took up the topic of street acquaintances in an article in 1909, opening with the thesis that city people were failing to make meaningful connections. Berliners, it suggested, struggled to find mates with whom they shared a certain "poetry," but not because poetic love was a fantasy; rather, because they were looking in the wrong places. Each day, the article claimed, people meet each other in the street, in the theater, in the café, and they may well be made for each other. Take, for example, the young woman walking home from work one day. She appears to be deep in thought, "perhaps she is even dreaming of the person she noticed on one of her recent Sunday outings . . . , perhaps somewhere on the tram, in the suburbs. . . . But she had not been able to approach him because there was no opportunity and because it would not look right" for a girl to approach a man she did not know. Perhaps if they had been in "society," in polite company. . . . "But on the street, in a train . . . that would never fly!"[28]

Now let us imagine, the article continued, there is a young man out walking, as well. This man is walking in the hopes of finding someone. This has, in fact, become a routine of sorts for him, but not because he is a "Don Juan." He is, rather, "one of the many who wake up each day with full hearts and look for their soulmates but return each evening with empty hands." He has "already a hundred times looked around in his small milieu but could not find a single soul who could make his life poetic." "How happy he would be," it continued, "if he had found his soulmate! How often has he found instead the true curse of his suffering." But it is not his fault that he is alone. It is, rather, "the big city with its colorful cluster of . . . people who appear as if whirled together; the big city that keeps those who belong from finding each other." So this man has taken to the streets, as it were, to use the one advantage of the metropolis—its masses—in his favor. By now he recognizes the look on her face—namely that she will not stop on her own—and knows he has to get her to stop. So he catches up to her and stammers out an attempt at an approach: "May the lady forgive me that I bother her . . . the urgent desire to get to know you . . . sudden encounter and unexpected feelings of warmth . . . I ask politely for the honor of accompanying you." The young woman, it says, "doesn't have a heart of stone—yes, she too felt something in the man's eyes; she would even like to accept his accompaniment, but . . . 'My father does not allow street acquaintances [*Strassenbekanntschaften*].'" And so ends the brief contact between the man and the woman—"they who just found each other"—and since she is a respectable woman, she thanks him and heads on her own in the direction of home. "This is the poetry and tragedy of street acquaintances that do not come to fruition," the article concludes.[29]

Daily newspapers, which were so widely read, had immense power and influence when it came to setting and routinizing Berliners' emotional lexicon, their go-to terms to describe emotional encounters or ascribe to them a certain meaning or provenance (such as "fate"); so we might expect the newspapers to have either fallen hard for the idea of successful chance encounters or, as murky reflections of hegemonic respectability, stuck unwaveringly to the narrative of the city's overwhelming power to divide and disappoint. However, what we find instead is a striking ambivalence about chance meetings, indeed, a mix of descriptions of fortuitous encounters that clicked and those that failed—some, even, that somehow featured both success and failure.

One journalist referred in a discussion of the unspoken language of love to the power of a lingering glance on the street between a man and a woman but quickly concluded the fictional intimacy of his protagonists bitterly: a day after their visual flirtation, "he" sees "her" walking with another man, and she does not so much as look his way.[30] Another story featured the fortuitous encounter of former lovers in Berlin's central park, the Tiergarten. Long ago, the man had broken off their engagement because his financial situation required that he think of himself and put off any marriage that did not bring with it an immediate windfall (through a dowry, for example). Having since established himself, he is now ready to marry her, he says, and he has in fact been looking for her for years. "Fate ultimately helped me find you again," he tells her as he pleads for her to renew their engagement. But it is too late: she has already married and tells him coolly that, in any case, his love had not been true.[31]

Romantic Roadblocks of the City

This was, it seems, the painful reality to which one awoke after the dream of the fortuitous encounter. As exciting as these encounters were in the imagination, the truth for most Berliners was that they were plainly off-limits and needed to be relegated to the realm of the imagination. Indeed, problems with these types of relationships (or, more accurately, the very idea thereof) stemmed from longstanding, mostly middle-class beliefs about the proper paths to love—paths that stuck closely to the traditionally sanctioned methods of family connections, courtships begun at popular but mostly chaste balls and house parties, and sensible economic or strategic partnerships made by heavy-handed fathers and mothers. Indeed, where the sheer movement and momentum of the modern metropolis manifested itself so perfectly in the chance meetings of strangers on streetcars and on busy boulevards, turn-of-the-century codes of masculinity and femininity functioned as roadblocks, halting as they did the amorous possibilities of these movements and asserting a rather staid, inflexible regime of respectability vis-à-vis love, romance, and intimacy.

In this sense, Berliners hardly needed the good Dr. Lomer to tell them about their "psychosis," as it were; they had, in fact, already diagnosed themselves and were debating the prudence, propriety, and safety of letting oneself believe in the possibility of love at first sight (and, more importantly, acting upon this belief by approaching or allowing oneself to be approached by a stranger).

The aforementioned 1909 column about the failed encounter on the street occasioned the following week a passionate reader's letter from a woman saying she was truly glad someone was treating this subject in such a reasonable manner. "It is foolish," she wrote, "that we should still think about this in such a small-town, provincial way." Provincial, of course, stood for outdated, old-fashioned, clueless. "I used to think . . . it was improper for a woman to react to the attempted approach of unknown men," she continued, but over time "I realized that I perhaps ruined my chance at happiness because of this." The woman went on to describe her own "missed connection," a love that might have been. She had moved to Berlin from the provinces and, like so many others, had a hard time meeting anyone. One day while riding the streetcar she noticed that the man sitting across from her appeared to be interested in her and was, in fact, quite obviously trying to work up the nerve to start a conversation with her. The woman for her part ignored him and plunged deeper into her newspaper. She might well have chalked up this experience to the frequent (and aforementioned) annoyances of unwanted urban encounters, except that it happened again the next day. This time she got up and moved to the balcony of the streetcar, hoping he might take the hint. He did not. In fact, undeterred, the man ratcheted up his efforts, and try as she might to avoid getting in the same streetcar as he, the man seemed always to manage to make it into her streetcar, even if it meant almost comically ramming himself onto a nearly packed car.[32]

Three years passed thusly, and the man showed remarkable persistence. One evening the woman was at a concert of the philharmonic orchestra and saw by chance an old work colleague. She had always known the woman to be single, like herself, but now she had a man with her—her husband, it turned out. She recognized the man, actually: it was the man from the streetcar. As it happened, they had met the same way—only in this case the woman had been undeterred by social conventions about streetcar acquaintances—and had gotten married. The happy couple later invited her over to their apartment, and she saw first-hand how nice of a gentleman this man really was.[33] The woman concluded by arguing that many young women—in particular those who came, as she had, to Berlin from the provinces and had no family connections in the big city—simply lacked any other means of meeting men and that Berliners should not look down on women who entertained the possibility of a street acquaintance.

The reader forum of the *Berliner Morgenpost* (a mostly left-leaning paper) reflected a similar eagerness to debate the propriety of this sort of dating or courting. In 1904, it featured a host of letters from men and women who responded with a unanimous "yes" to the question of whether it was proper for a man to approach a woman on the street. In one response, a woman argued in verse her point that "To profit you must risk / Without fear and without hesitation / I'd ridicule the world!" But the editors of the *Berliner Morgenpost* were less convinced and, in a rare act of open intervention in the readers' forum, called on Berliners to consider the matter more carefully.[34] Not surprisingly, the paper was filled the following week with the responses of older, more conservative readers who still considered such a street acquaintance unthinkable. "We knew that people have not lost their moral compass," the editors concluded, satisfied that Berliners were, in fact, still happy to remain inside the familiar walls of middle-class respectability.[35] The advice column of the more conservative *Berliner Lokal-Anzeiger* provided similarly traditional counsel to a mother asking if it was a good idea for her daughter to show up at a café for a rendezvous with a man she had met on the commuter train. "Even if a rendezvous in a café is not a capital crime, it does display a certain amount of trust—trust that is questionable after such a fleeting acquaintance," the columnist wrote sternly.[36]

The debate about the propriety of street-level intimacy is indicative of the way Berliners felt about love and dating in the big city more generally. Their initial response to the question of whether it was appropriate for young, single people to meet others in such an unsupervised, random way was poetic and enthusiastic, quite like so many journalists and authors portrayed the resulting relationships of such encounters through rose-colored glasses. And, to be sure, some Berliners truly believed this (and acted accordingly). The sheer number of swindlers who seized upon gullible and starry-eyed single men and women on the street and in the streetcar—and there are indeed far too many cases to even begin to list them here—stand as evidence of this fact.[37] Yet more conservative voices ultimately prevailed and quickly centered the moral compass of the newspaper-reading public, just as Berliners generally continued to eschew the pursuit of romance that veered from the traditional path of the nineteenth century. The very idea of respectability, of middle-class propriety, then, functioned as fences lining this path, indeed, as emotional roadblocks to the romantic mobility the metropolis offered to young people, and women, especially. The preservation of middle-classness, of a differentiation between Berliners of a certain moral and economic posture and the workers whose proximity and potential power was so unsettling—the urgency of this preservation required the regulation of all aspects of life, and this included (and, indeed, often focused on) love.

* * *

Why did men and women find the idea of the fortuitous encounter so alluring even though it was so clearly an affront to hegemonic ideas about male and (especially) female respectability? Why did they so enjoy thematizing and hoping for love that would appear out of thin air or strike one as a lightning bolt while walking down the street when they were generally so careful to avoid making these fantasies a reality? To be sure, it was partly because such stories of chance and of unlikely romance were simply compelling and juicy, and Berliners fell in love with the idea of falling in love on the street and in the streetcar because, on one level, it fit with and even enhanced their pride in Berlin as a modern metropolis that was incredibly big and disorientatingly fluid. Just as newspapers reported on (and readers gobbled up reports about) the chaos of the city and constant and bewildering movement of its two million residents, so also did they seize on the theme of chance meetings and the (im)possibility of finding love on the street because it fed the larger narrative of the metropolis.

It was also in some ways a coping mechanism not unlike the blasé attitude that affected, as Simmel claimed, all urban dwellers. Berliners enjoyed reading and fantasizing about fortuitous encounters because the difficulty of finding a mate frankly drove them to believe it or at least consider it as good a possibility as any. After all, the woman who rued having perhaps missed her "life's happiness" because she had not entertained the timid advances of a fellow streetcar passenger did so as a woman who wanted to find a mate and wanted to get married but had failed. And she was but one of thousands who had failed to make connections in the city.

On a different level, Berliners' obsession with fate and the fortuitous encounter was an attempt at a sort of mobility in a time when the strictures of respectability prevented Berliners from moving freely—meeting on the street, in office corridors, and on streetcar balconies. "Fate" as a way of speaking about love—a "language of love," as it were—in a way reconfigured the space of the city, transforming streets, alleyways, and corridors into places where men and women could move about and try on a new moral, romantic, and sexual ethic. The chance meeting that could not be was more than simply a modern aesthetic, more than the compelling narrative of city life as fleeting and contingent, and more than a last resort at love. As is clear from the debates and discussions on the topic, Berliners who fantasized about actually making the fortuitous encounter a reality were transgressing a whole host of spatial, linguistic, moral, and class boundaries, and in this transgression (and the resulting hemming and hawing about whether to turn fantasy into reality) we start to see some of the tensions of middle-class life and sensibilities in the modern city.

There were a few people who used the stories—real and imaginary—of random, fated connections as blueprints for their own lives, and these were men and women who had lost faith in the religion of middle-classness and were willing to forgo the stability of the middle-class existence for a degree of love and intimacy.[38] "Fate," the buzzword peddled so ubiquitously by newspapers and invoked so frequently by Berliners, was in this sense merely a stand-in for "nontraditional" or "risky," serving to cast romantic entrepreneurialism as the work of something (chance) or someone (Cupid?) over which Berliners themselves had no control, actions for which Berliners could not be held responsible. In this way, fate as discourse and explanation offered a pass to the street: men could be something other than workers or consumers (indeed, they could be potential lovers and partners), and women out on the street could be something other than prostitutes (they could be potential lovers and partners, not to mention workers, commuters, and, more generally, independent women).

And yet the arbiters of respectability (fathers, politicians, judges, and other male voices in the public sphere) were careful to hold these Berliners accountable for this sort of entrepreneurialism, and talk of fated encounters retreated gradually to the pages of fiction as Berliners had their hands slapped for acting out these fantasies of fated meetings. Indeed, most found the cliff on the margins of this middle-class respectability to be too steep, too dangerous to risk it. To be sure, men had greater freedom than women to have it both ways, to take a chance on the fortuitous encounter without damage to their reputation. Fate's ticket to public urban movement had a much greater valence for men than women. And working-class Berliners no doubt faced less scrutiny with regard to street relationships than those in the middle class, even if many middle-class reform efforts were plainly morally patronizing. But people—and especially women—who were in between, who were either trying to adopt a lifestyle befitting a new arrival to the middle class or struggling to hang on to the pieces of a crumbling bourgeois identity certainly had less freedom to indulge in fortuitous encounters.

From first meeting to marriage, city people, and especially new migrants to the city, found that intimacy in the modern metropolis was difficult to find and just as hard to hold on to. As this chapter has suggested, Berliners expressed their frustration at being lonely, at not having enough money to marry or to be a desirable mate, and at a lack of opportunities to meet other single people. They also displayed a fascination—one born out of this frustration, and one enabled by the emotional lexicon of newspaper copy—with fate and the fortuitous encounter. This created an important imaginative space of adventure outside the bounds of traditional masculinity and femininity, even if it did not, except for in the example of a few men and women, ever become more than a fantasy. Tracing Berliners' interest in fate and the fantastical mixed with the everyday adds another layer to the story of urbanization and modernity at the turn of the century, and it gives city people a degree of imaginative and emotional agency not afforded them in studies of the city as dangerous or alienating.

It also suggests something about the experience of arriving in new urban environment, attempting to moor oneself to piers of employment, reliable housing, and, perhaps most importantly, love and intimate connection, and finding little or no purchase, nothing solid. Marshall Berman, borrowing a line from Marx, famously described the experience of modernity as one where "all that is solid melts into air," indeed, where we "struggle to make ourselves at home in a constantly changing world."[39] This was, in many ways, the experience of all urbanites, even those few who were born Berliners, those who had some measure of family support, existing networks of friends and acquaintances, and a familiarity with the city itself. Most Berliners were new, however, and while their experience of the big city was not always painful and lonely—indeed, most Berliners ended up marrying at some point—it is telling that Berliners were so interested in fate and fortuity, something beyond the realm of the city's seemingly antiromantic logic. Of course, even though fate was somehow separate from the city, the antithesis to the predictable, logical rhythm of the city, its mechanisms nevertheless relied on these same urban movements, for fate only brought people together whom the city had already set in motion. Love and mobility were thus intertwined: the mobility of the turn-of-the-century city—the movement of its residents and arrival of many others—was at once that which isolated or atomized them and, as the common urban trope went, that which might, by sheer fortuity, connect them.

NOTES

Material from this chapter was originally published in Tyler Carrington, *Love at Last Sight: Dating, Intimacy, and Risk in Turn-of-the-Century Berlin* (New York: Oxford University Press, 2019), and has been reproduced by permission of Oxford University Press. (http://global.oup.com/academic). For permission to reuse this material, please visit http://global.oup.com/academic/rights.

1. Wilhelm Brönner, "Der Kampf um die neue Liebe," *Geschlecht und Gesellschaft* 1, no. 1 (1906): 7–14.

2. Carry Brachvogel, "Elektrische Frauen," *Berliner Morgenpost*, October 21, 1906, no. 247.

3. Catherine L. Dollard, *The Surplus Woman: Unmarried in Imperial Germany, 1871–1918* (New York: Berghahn Books, 2009).

4. See Stephanie Coontz, *Marriage, a History: How Love Conquered Marriage* (New York: Penguin, 2006); or, more generally, Susan J. Matt and Peter N. Stearns, "Introduction," in *Doing Emotions History* (Urbana: University of Illinois Press, 2014), 5ff.; Susan J. Matt, "Current Emotion Research in History: Or, Doing History from the Inside Out," *Emotion Review* 3, no. 1 (2011): 117–24.

5. Thomas Hall, *Planning Europe's Capital Cities: Aspects of Nineteenth-Century Urban Development* (London: Spon, 2005), 300.

6. Paul Puschmann and Arne Solli, "Household and Family during Urbanization and Industrialization: Efforts to Shed New Light on an Old Debate," *History of the Family* 19, no. 1 (2004): 1–12.

7. *Statistisches Jahrbuch der Stadt Berlin* (Berlin: P. Stankiewicz' Buchdruckerei, 1905), 81.

8. *Statistisches Jahrbuch der Stadt Berlin 1905*, 21.

9. *Statistisches Jahrbuch der Stadt Berlin 1905*, 82.

10. Lutz Niethammer and Franz Brüggemeier, "Wie wohnten Arbeiter im Kaiserreich?" *Archiv für Sozialgeschichte* 16 (1976): 84.

11. *Statistisches Jahrbuch der Stadt Berlin* (Berlin: P. Stankiewicz' Buchdruckerei, 1907), 82.

12. Albert Südekum, *Großstädtisches Wohnungselend*, vol. 45 of *Großstadt-Dokumente*, ed. Hans Ostwald (Berlin, 1908), 17; Eugen Baumann, "Die zunehmende Beweglichkeit der Bevölkerung," 14, quoted in Hugh McLeod, *Piety and Poverty: Working-Class Religion in Berlin, London, and New York* (New York: Holmes and Meier, 1996).

13. *Statistisches Jahrbuch der Stadt Berlin 1905*, 80.

14. David I. Kertzer and Dennis P. Hogan, "On the Move: Migration in an Italian Community, 1865–1921," *Social Science History* 9, no. 1 (1985): 20. See also Clé Lesger, Leo Lucassen, and Marlou Schrover, "Is There Life Outside the Migrant Network? German Immigrants in XIXth Century Netherlands and the Need for a

More Balanced Migration Typology," *Annales de Démographie Historique* 2 (2002): 29–50.

15. James Harvey Jackson, *Migration and Urbanization in the Ruhr Valley, 1821–1914* (Boston: Humanities Press, 1997).

16. For example, Steven Ruggles, *Prolonged Connections: The Rise of the Extended Family in Nineteenth-Century England and America* (Madison: University of Wisconsin Press, 1987); Michael Anderson, *Family Structure in Nineteenth-Century Lancashire* (Cambridge: Cambridge University Press, 1971), 152–60; Rolf Gehrmann, "German Towns on the Eve of Industrialization: Household Formation and the Part of the Elderly," *History of the Family* 19, no. 1 (2004): 13–28; Katherine A. Lynch, "The European Marriage Pattern in the Cities: Variations on a Theme by Hajnal," *Journal of Family History* 16, no. 1 (1991): 79–95; Michel Oris, "The Age at Marriage of Migrants during the Industrial Revolution in the Region of Liège," *History of the Family* 5, no. 4 (2000): 391–413.

17. Georg Simmel, "The Metropolis and Mental Life," in *The Blackwell City Reader*, ed. Gary Bridge and Sophie Watson (Oxford: Wiley-Blackwell, 2002), 15.

18. More information about this topic, see Carrington, *Looking for Love*.

19. For example, Coontz, *Marriage, a History*; Matt and Stearns, "Introduction"; Christina Simmons, *Making Marriage Modern: Women's Sexuality from the Progressive Era to World War II* (New York: Oxford University Press, 2009), especially chap. 3; Simon May, *Love: A History* (New Haven, CT: Yale University Press, 2011); Marcus Collins, *Modern Love: An Intimate History of Men and Women in Twentieth-Century Britain* (London: Atlantic, 2003); Lisa Appignanesi, *All About Love: Anatomy of an Unruly Emotion* (New York: W. W. Norton, 2011); Andrew J. Cherlin, *The Marriage-Go-Round: The State of Marriage and the Family in America Today* (New York: Alfred A. Knopf, 2009), chap. 3; Lawrence Stone, *The Family, Sex, and Marriage in England, 1500–1800* (New York: Harper Torchbooks, 1979); Edward Shorter, *The Making of the Modern Family* (London: Collins, 1976).

20. Walter Benjamin, *Illuminations*, trans. Harry Zohn (New York: Schocken Books, 1968), 169.

21. Charles Baudelaire, "To a Passer-By," in *The Flowers of Evil*, trans. and ed. William Aggeler (Fresno, CA: Academy Library Guild, 1954), 311.

22. Heinrich Teweles, "Aller Liebe Anfang," *Berliner Morgenpost*, August 1, 1908, no. 179.

23. Hugo Klein, "Furcht vor der Liebe," *Berliner Morgenpost*, April 26, 1904, no. 97.

24. Aimée Gaber, "Sehnsucht," *Berliner Morgenpost*, October 23, 1910, no. 291; A. Burg, "Fritz Wendekamp's Jugendliebe," *Berliner Morgenpost*, September 3, 1907, no. 206.

25. "Der Photograph als Heiratsvermittler," *Berliner Lokal-Anzeiger*, August 22, 1906, no. 425.

26. "Das Bild des Zukünftigen," *Berliner Morgenpost*, February 5, 1907, no. 30.

27. Georg Lomer, *Liebe und Psychose* (Wiesbaden, Ger.: Bergmann, 1907), 12–13; Pascal, "Ein Buch über die Liebe," *Berliner Lokal-Anzeiger*, June 15, 1907, no. 299.

28. M. Warwar, "Straßenbekanntschaften," *Berliner Morgenpost*, October 3, 1909, no. 257.

29. Warwar, "Straßenbekanntschaften."

30. Aribert, "Die Liebessprache," *Berliner Morgenpost*, August 16, 1905, no. 191.

31. Reinhold Ortmann, "Wiedersehen," *Berliner Morgenpost*, September 6, 1904, no. 209.

32. "Das Publikum: Straßenbekanntschaften," *Berliner Morgenpost*, October 10, 1909, no. 264.

33. "Das Publikum: Straßenbekanntschaften."

34. "Das Publikum: Das Ansprechen auf der Strasse," *Berliner Morgenpost*, May 1, 1904, no. 102.

35. "Das Publikum: Das Ansprechen auf der Strasse," *Berliner Morgenpost*, May 12, 1904, no. 111.

36. "Briefkasten: Konditorei," *Berliner Lokal-Anzeiger*, May 8, 1904, no. 215.

37. In fact, I stopped counting after finding well over 100 cases of swindlers who had played on Berliners' eagerness to end their loneliness. Each story was more or less the same with just the names and places differing from case to case. Some were quite bizarre, though; for example, the case where a man posing as a doctor found various "patients" in the hospital who believed love had found them. "Eine Bekanntschaft von der Strasse," *Berliner Morgenpost*, January 6, 1903, no. 4.

38. Manfred Hettling and Stefan-Ludwig Hoffmann, "Zur Historisierung bürgerliche Werte," in *Der bürgerliche Werthimmel Innenansichten des 19. Jahrhunderts*, ed. Hettling and Hoffmann (Göttingen, Ger.: Vandenhoeck and Ruprecht, 2000), 9.

39. Marshall Berman, *All That Is Solid Melts into Air: The Experience of Modernity* (New York: Penguin Books, 1982), 6.

CHAPTER 5

Brotherly Love

The Forging of an Italian-Argentine Brotherhood in Argentina, 1880–1920

ELIZABETH ZANONI

In 1910, Argentine and Italian political elites gathered in Rome to celebrate Argentina's centennial. *La Patria degli Italiani*, Argentina's largest Italian-language newspaper, covered the commemorative events in detail for its readers back in Buenos Aires. At the celebration, Guido Fusinato, president of the Italian Colonial Institute, founded six years earlier to promote Italian expansion worldwide, spoke of the "unshakable foundation of brotherhood" between Argentines and Italians, a brotherhood based on sympathy, justice, and honesty that "affirms and reinforces unions of sentiments and harmony of interests" between the two countries. He closed his speech by sending Argentines, on behalf of Italians, "our loving brotherly greeting."[1] In framing the relationship between Argentines and Italians as one based on brotherly love, Fusinato expressed the common assumption among Italian elites in Italy and Argentina during the late nineteenth and early twentieth centuries that the two countries shared a uniquely intimate bond.

This chapter explores the ways in which Italians in Argentina used migrant publications to construct gendered and racialized conceptions of familial love between Italians and Argentines as "brotherly people."[2] A focus on brotherly love offers an alternative lens for studying the history of international relations between migrant-sending and -receiving countries. Such sentiments forged "from below" in migrant publications were just as important to the creation of international allegiances and national identities as were the supposedly rational and serious decisions made by statesmen "from above."[3] While removed from the high realms of diplomacy and trade, everyday articulations of brotherly love show how migrant periodicals forged alternative "emotional landscapes" to reflect and manage larger social, economic, and political aspects of international migration.[4] Italian-language newspapers depicted foreign relations between Italy and Argentina and between Italians and Argentines as family relations, as relations between "Latin brothers," to justify migration, to promote favorable attitudes about and support for Italy and its migrants, and to rebuke unbrotherly destinations like the United States.

Beyond providing readers with practical information, migrant newspapers functioned as transnational cultural spaces where immigrants created and reinforced community norms and ties that linked migrants to their home regions and nations.[5] Indeed, the transatlantic worlds within which Italian migrants operated is evidenced, for example, in the news articles and op-ed pieces from and on Argentina and Italy, in the published ship manifests of Italian imports arriving to Buenos Aires and other Argentine port cites, and in the use of both Spanish and Italian. Migrant newspapers were also exceedingly public and collaborative mediums where writers and readers together produced and sometimes challenged new meanings of nationhood, race, ethnicity, and gender.[6] The press's very public quality, however, did not mean it was devoid of sentiments like love and hate often associated with intimate settings, and—as many of the chapters in this collection explore—with more private sources like personal correspondence.[7] Italian-language newspapers talked about "private" topics such as marriage, divorce, and parenthood, and moreover used affective language in their discussions of seemingly public discourses on immigrant incorporation, diplomacy, and international commerce, subjects often treated by scholars as disconnected from mobile people's emotional worlds.

Expressions of brotherly love in *La Patria* competed with other expressions of sentimental solidarities among Italy's people worldwide. The widely circulated commercial daily mainly represented the interests of middle-class and elite *prominenti*, prominent members of the Italian community, those in the skilled trades and professional classes. However, the paper also promoted the interests of the Italian community more generally, including the working classes and their efforts toward labor reform. Prominenti's class status derived in part from Argentina's two-class system, in which native-born Argentines gravitated toward law, politics, and landownership, permitting migrants and their descendants to dominate the growing middle classes of industrialists, business owners, merchants, and other white-collar positions by the early twentieth century.[8] The mainstream *La Patria*, while supportive of republican ideals, was a generally nationalistic and moderately monarchist paper; the paper was especially invested in cultivating a sense of common national identity and pride among Italy's heterogeneous peoples in Argentina, and in this it echoed the desires of Italian political elites at home who believed their nation's global reputation and empire-building initiatives depended on uniting Italians at home and abroad.[9] And yet, Argentina was also home to an active, multiethnic and multinational community of socialists, communists, and anarchists with their own periodicals and visions of fraternity. These newspapers, such as the left-leaning *L'Italia del Popolo* and the anarchist *La Questione Sociale*, offered radical visions of brotherly solidarity for Italian speakers rooted in global networks of proletarian laborers who sometimes rejected nationalism and the nation-state as a base for building worker unity.[10] While this chapter focuses on *La Patria* as the largest, most popular commercial daily, it is critical to remember that conceptions of fraternity forged in its pages competed with myriad alternative, coexisting "emotional communities," and that the overarching ideological assumptions and economic and political interests reflected in *La Patria* mediated the paper's emotional terrains.[11]

Brotherly love helped explain and celebrate a history of steady male-predominant Italian migration to Argentina. Migration to Argentina during the late nineteenth and early twentieth centuries was overwhelmingly male. With few exceptions, between 1880 and 1930, male Italian migrants to Argentina fluctuated between 60 and 65 percent of the total.[12] The hundreds of thousands of Italian male *golondrine* or seasonal "birds of passage" worked as manual laborers and increasingly as middle-class professionals in cities such as Buenos Aires, Rosario, and Córdoba, and in agricultural and husbandry work as day laborers and sharecroppers on Argentina's fertile pampas.[13] The heavily male character of Italian migration to Argentina was a result of gendered divisions of labor in both Argentina and Italy, which increasingly characterized positions in heavy industry and commercial agriculture as exclusively male.[14] Although men arrived to Argentina without their wives and children, most remained deeply enmeshed in transnational family economics in which husbands, brothers, and sons migrated as part of a larger family strategy to augment their social standing back home.[15] Single men, therefore, arrived with gendered community and economic obligations to families in Italy, although as María Bjerg's chapter on bigamy cases in Argentina shows, such distance could also challenge or dissolve transnational marital norms and obligations.[16]

Therefore, such gendered conceptions of sibling love between Italians and Argentines as brotherly, rather than sisterly, in migrant publications matched the gendered nature of Italian transoceanic mobility during the age of mass migrations.

The language of brotherly love helped the migrant press justify the predominance of Italian migrants in Argentina and praise the contributions migrants made to their host country. In 1910 *La Patria* highlighted "the intimate relations of interests and sentiments that unite Italy to the great country [Argentina] where its children find, as is said, a second homeland and carry in exchange a continuous, precious contribution of the vigorous and refined Latin blood, of commercial and industrial genius and of honest work."[17] Basilio Cittadini, editor of *La Patria*, pointed to Argentine immigration law, which kept the doors open to Italians, as evidence that Argentina welcomed Italians with open arms and invited them "to assume its share of partnership in the common work of civilization, of intellectual and economic evaluation of the Nation as it marches toward its highest destiny."[18] Because relationships between Argentines and Italian migrants were so regularly conceptualized as affective brotherly bonds, the migrant press depicted disagreements between migrants and Argentines, or instances of discrimination against migrants, as family discord. In response to Argentine criticism of migrants who sent their earnings home to Italy instead of investing them in Argentina, *La Patria* portrayed such Argentine denunciations as a familial affront. The paper reminded its readers of the "many years of cohabitation and friendly collaboration" between Italian migrants and Argentines who have "come together as brothers in solidary of work and ideals" to form "pleasant sentimental bonds." As brotherly people, the paper concluded, "We are equal and we should treat each other equally."[19] In framing the relationship between Argentines and Italians as rooted in familial intimacies, the Italian-language press often represented criticism against migrants not merely as political and economic offenses, but as personal and disloyal insults against kin.

This familial language used to describe the relationship between Italian migrants and Argentines and Italy and Argentina bore some similarities to that used in more formal Italian and European colonial contexts. Historians have noted how the leaders of European imperial powers such as France, Britain, Germany, the Netherlands, and Italy used patriarchal family metaphors to include colonial subjects into the larger imperial community while simultaneously excluding them from the national family as racialized and juridical "others," especially as increasing numbers of nonwhite colonial and formal colonial subjects migrated to the metropole.[20] Despite Italy's low standing among Europe's great imperial powers and its limited geographical reach, Italian colonialism, as Ruth Ben-Ghiat and Mia Fuller acknowledge, "had no less an impact on the development of metropolitan conceptions of race, national identity, and geopolitical imaginaries."[21] Furthermore, unlike its European competitors, Italy's colonial pursuits proceeded alongside massive Italian emigration within Europe and to overseas destinations like Argentina. As Mark Choate and others have argued, Italian elites at the turn of the twentieth century viewed emigration and colonialism as inextricably linked.[22] The voluntary and informal demographic settlements in countries like Argentina, Italian political leaders believed, complemented Italy's more formal attempts at territorial conquest in East and North Africa, as both promoted Italian cultural and commercial expansion worldwide.[23]

La Patria and other commercial migrant publications sometimes echoed the language of Italian elites in Italy who asserted Italians' superiority over Argentines, and who depicted migration to Argentina as an extension of Italian expansionist aims in Africa.[24] And yet, the variegated understandings and workings of race and family in Europeans' African and Asian colonies differed from the Italian-Argentine context. In the pages of *La Patria*, gendered and familial conceptions of brotherly love collided with racialized ideas of *Latinità*, or Latinness, and Latin civilization to shape unique affective ties produced through mass Italian emigration. The paper insisted that Italians and Argentines were not simply brothers, but that they were "Latin" brothers, both "children of the Latin race," who shared similarities in language, religion, family arrangements, and cultural values.[25] This brotherhood was not metaphorical or exclusively cultural. This fraternal bond, *La Patria* insisted, was rooted in blood. Italian migrants depicted the "blood ties" linking Italian migrants and Argentines as intensifying emotional attachments between people of the two countries, thus making Argentina one of the most logical places for Italian emigration. Italian migrants' ideas about Latinità were formed against the backdrop of global conversations among pseudoscientists who categorized the peoples of the world within a system of hierarchical and unequal castes; skin color, character traits, and social ills from poverty to illiteracy were believed to be rooted in the inheritable defective germ-plasm of inferior races. To these racial scientists, Italians occupied a somewhat ambiguous place within these evolving racial classifications. Southern Italians in particular were seen as belonging to a degenerate race, separate from northern Italians; at the same time, however, Italians continued to be affiliated with the triumphs marking the birth of Western civilization, including the Roman Empire, the Renaissance, and the Age of Exploration.[26]

Even while scientific elites worldwide increasingly conceived of Italians, particularly southern Italians, as racially inferior, migrants themselves tapped into somewhat similar but distinct ideas about race in Argentina, where skin color, socioeconomic status, and ancestry mixed with assumptions about European cultural superiority to define racial hierarchies.[27] This racialized Latinità, based on the notion that similarities between Italians and Argentines were grounded in common biological ancestry, functioned to validate both Italian migrants' inclusion in and Italy's influence over Argentine society. Indeed, race and civilization collided in declarations of Italo-Argentine brotherhood, especially during public events like the Argentine Centennial when Italian migrants and elites in Italy depicted Argentines and Italians as both Latin and European. *La Patria* reported on a speech by Ernesto Nathan, mayor of Rome, who stated that Argentina, like Italy, "descended from the Latin trunk" and that Argentines and Italians shared "in commonality of aspirations, health, thought, and affection for its ancient mother." He concluded by offering the Argentine president Roque Sáenz Peña a "pledge of affectionate fraternity" between Italy and Argentina.[28] Similarly, *La Patria* reported on a speech made by Italian criminologist Enrico Ferri, who celebrated Argentina as an "offshoot of Latin civilization."[29] Historic connections between Italy, Spain, and the Viceroyalty of the Río de la Plata based on Spain's longstanding presence in and control over territories that would become Italy, and on sixteenth- and seventeenth-century-Spanish colonization (facilitated by merchants and explorers from Italy's northern city-states), further solidified the blood ties linking Italians and the descendants of Spanish colonial settlers and migrants in Argentina.[30] It was the voyages of Genoa native Christopher Columbus, *La Patria* regularly reminded its readers, which led to the first European settlements in the lands that would come to make up the countries of Central and South America; similarly, the paper frequently paid tribute to the Italian general and nationalist Giuseppe Garibaldi, leader of the Italian Legion that helped defeat Juan Manuel de Rosas, the dictatorial governor of the Province of Buenos Aires, before returning home to fight in the Italian unification movement.[31] Including eminent Italian male migrants like Columbus and Garibaldi in the foundational myths of Argentine and Latin American history bolstered the racial commonalities at the heart of the Italian-Argentine brotherhood.

As Europeans, *La Patria* suggested, Italian migrants allowed their Latin brothers in Argentina to simultaneously claim a certain Europeanness associated with western civilization and whiteness that Argentine political elites believed was central to Argentine nation-building. The paper, for example, reported on a speech made by Davide Spinetto, president of the Rotary Club in Buenos Aires, who identified Argentines and Italians as both "branches of European civilization" and that Italians represented the most robust "graft" of that civilization in Argentine society. Articles like these reminded readers that Italian migrants facilitated Argentina's entrance in the "civilized sphere" through their economic, industrial, and cultural contributions to their host country.[32] In the commercial realm, too, Italians depicted themselves bestowing upon their Argentine brothers, who represented a "civilization in formation," the trappings of Europeanness.[33] The success of the Domingo Tomba winery, founded by Venetian migrants Antonio and Domingo Tomba in Mendoza, and comparable to the great wineries of Italy and France, demonstrated that "Argentina in every way wants to emulate the ancient nations," an advertisement touted.[34]

References to this fraternal love between Latin brothers became an increasingly important rhetorical strategy against the backdrop of Argentine elites' changing attitudes toward Italian migrants. While many nineteenth-century Argentine liberals had championed European migration as key to the creation of Argentine modernity, others, starting in the early twentieth century, increasingly divorced Italians from desirable forms of Europeanness embodied in "Anglo-Saxon" and "Nordic" migrants from northern and western Europe.[35] As Argentines increasingly saw the masses of mainly poor, seasonal migrants as a threat, rather than an aid to building the Argentine nation, *La Patria* continued to characterize migrants as Italian, Latin, *and* European while suggesting that Argentina's acceptance into the coveted European family came through Italian migrants, their Latin "brothers." The press insisted that Italy and Italians had a deep love for Argentina, and that this explained not only Italian migration to Latin America but also Argentina's intimate relationship with Europe. "In no other country of Europe is Argentina as sincerely loved as it is loved in Italy, and this is because the heart of the nation beats in unison with the Argentine heart," wrote *La Patria* in 1910; it would be Italy, and Italy alone among European countries, that, through its heartfelt fondness and shared racial bonds, would keep Argentina linked to Europe.[36] And yet, as one of many "Latin" migrant groups to Argentina, Italians competed with Spanish, Portuguese, French, Greek, and other migrant groups, who also considered themselves Latin and European, for the affection and loyalty of their Argentine brothers.[37] Italians certainly had the demographic advantage as the largest foreign-born group in the country during this time, but the presence of other migrants, especially the large community of Spaniards, meant that Italians did not have a monopoly on the gendered and racialized solidarities underpinning brotherly love. As Jose Moya has shown, early-twentieth-century reactionary movements against liberalism and cosmopolitanism sparked among some Argentine nationalists a reevaluation of the relationship between Argentina and Spain, their former colonial oppressor. Argentines used Spanish immigrants, once maligned for their backwardness, to help manufacture a transatlantic Hispanism based in part on the shared cultural backgrounds and Hispanic *raza* (race) of Argentines and Spaniards. To Argentine traditionalists and notable Spanish immigrants, Hispanism justified the rejection of Italians as non-Iberian foreign interlopers and heralds of dangerous US-dominated Pan Americanism. Spanish and Italian migrants clearly competed for the prestige and respect of their host country, and they employed the language of race and family to fabricate solidarities and exclusion.[38]

Like the advertisement for the Tomba winery, commercial iconography for products made by Italians in Argentina, as well as those imported from Italy, especially foodstuffs like wine, liquors, olive oil, pasta, and cigarettes, served as another site for forging bonds of brotherhood between Italians and Argentines. Advertisements and trademarks for Italian goods sometimes paired illustrations of well-known Italian and Argentine men side-by-side in ways that suggested a kinlike relationship joined them together. A 1907 trademark for Emanuele Gianolio's "America" brand vinegar from Genoa presented Christopher Columbus bordered by images of Latin American revolutionary figures including Simón Bolívar, Domingo Faustino Sarmiento, José de San Martín, and José María Paz y Haedo (see figure 5.1). By pairing Columbus, Italy's most illustrious emigrant, with nineteenth-century Latin American leaders, the trademark collapsed time and space in gendered ways to show economic and political relationships based on trade and exploration as embedded in personal partnerships, however fictitious, between Latin brothers of both nations' pasts.

Other visual imagery produced for Italians and Argentines hinted at the way brotherly love, most often portrayed as platonic family affection, could morph into sexual intimacies between men. The cover of *Italia e Argentina* (*Italy and Argentina*) published by the Italian Colonial Institute on the occasion of Argentina's centennial celebration featured an illustration of two nubile male youths, one representing Italy, the other Argentina, bearing the flags of their respective countries (see figure 5.2). They stare playfully at each other, and while a *fasce*—the bundle of sticks often joined with an axe blade that served as an ancient Roman symbol of strength and unity—separate the men, Italy appears to reach out and caress Argentina's forearm; Argentina's other arm holds the country's red-tipped flag erect and it is secured between

FIGURE 5.1. Trademark for Emanuele Gianolio vinegar. Archivio Centrale dello Stato, Ministero dell'Industria, del Commercio e dell'Artigianato, Ufficio Italiano Brevetti e Marchi, fasc. 8593, 1907. Courtesy of the Archivio Centrale dello Stato.

FIGURE 5.2. Istituto Coloniale Italiano, *Italia e Argentina* (Bergamo: Officine dell'Istituto Italiano d'Arti Grafiche, 1910), cover. Courtesy of the Archivio Centrale dello Stato.

the young man's legs.[39] Images of nude men and homosocial male worlds were commonplace in ancient Greek and Roman art as masculine symbols of virility and sexuality, among other social and cultural symbols; images such as the cover of this commemorative volume that projected overtly homoerotic messages about the love uniting Italians and Argentines show the varied, rather than singular, manifestations or meanings of intimate bonds cultivated through international migration and diplomacy.[40]

Despite rising skepticism about Italian migrants among some Argentine elites, Argentines also utilized metaphors of brotherly love to understand and discuss the relationship between the two countries. For example, *La Patria* reported on a speech given by Angelo Bottero from the Argentine Consulate in Turin, Italy. After extolling the work being done in Turin to equalize trade relations between Italy and Argentina, which Bottero described as "works of brotherhood," Bottero admitted that "Argentina and Italy were indissolubly united in my heart, by the spirit of patriotism and of solidarity that I have found in Italian-Argentines living in Turin."[41] *La Patria* published excerpts from various Spanish-language newspapers in Argentina on the occasion of Argentina's centennial to showcase a brotherly love built through decades of migration, one that Argentines as well as Italians valued. An article titled "Genuine Fraternity" appearing in the Argentine daily *La Nación* noted that celebrations of Argentine independence by Italians show that "Italian-Argentine brotherhood is not limited to the exchange of international politeness or to the pretense of official state sentiments; this fraternity is a fact; it is in the heart that loves as it is in the brain that thinks." The Argentine newspaper *La Razón* considered the relationship between Italy, "the ideal friend," and Argentina, a "community of sentiments, of impulses, of memories of a brotherhood of the two people," while noting that "there are no bonds more robust that those of affection."[42] Such emotional declarations of fraternity and love reflected both Argentina's real appreciation for the contributions made by Italian labor, agricultural, and professional migrants, and the country's significant dependence on them as the largest foreign-born group.

Depictions of Italian migration to the United States—another important receiver of overseas Italian migration—served to further fortify the intimate ties of Latin brotherhood produced by Italian migration in the southern Atlantic. Unlike Argentina, the United States was neither Latin nor brotherly, the migrant press pointed out. In the United States, an Italian government publication noted in 1910, the Italian migrant "finds himself among people who seem to be of another race, that has diverse customs."[43] The Italian-language press in Argentina asserted that it was the absence of brotherhood that explained instances of Anglo-American hostility toward Italians and increasingly restrictive immigration laws designed to keep "Latin" migrants like themselves out of the United States. As Emily Pope-Obeda found in her exploration of US deportation policy during in the early twentieth century, the language of emotions could just as easily be used to articulate exclusion and difference as it could inclusion and belonging.[44] In the early 1920s, *La Patria* reported on the Argentine travels of an Italian emigration administrator who noted that "Italians are embraced like siblings by the Argentines." It made sense, he discovered, that Italians opted to work and settle in Argentina rather than in the United States, because unlike their Anglo neighbors to the North, Argentina "speaks to his [the Italian emigrant's] heart."[45] In the early twentieth century, as US businesses like Ford Motor Company, Armour and Company, and Goodyear Tire increasingly looked to Argentina as an outlet for consumer goods and a site of capital investment, *La Patria* called on the Italian-Argentine brotherhood established through decades of Italian migration to stop "Yankee imperialism." *La Patria*, which represented the interests of Italian merchants who felt increasingly threatened by US capital, encouraged the formation of a "Latin alliance." This alliance was intended to publicize and condemn US encroachment on Argentine economic and political independence as well as on Argentina's economic connections to European countries like Italy.[46]

The large majority of scholarship on the history of emotions, especially as it relates to the construction of nationalism and patriotism, has been done within the context of a single nation-state or region. In his work on the cultural roots of nationalism, Benedict Anderson shows how the press enabled emotional connections that cultivated a shared love of country among a heterogeneous and distant people.[47] Historians of the great revolutions that swept the Americas and Europe in the late eighteenth and early nineteenth centuries, for example, have utilized the family as a metaphor for examining revolutionary opposition to authority and new, emerging understandings of citizenship practices, national identity, and gender roles.[48] Transnational migration, because it links multiple nation-states, offers an opportunity to enlarge scholars' geographical framework.[49] While Argentina's Italian-language *La Patria* highlighted exchanges of brotherly love to promote a sense of common Italian identity and patriotism among a diverse group of migrants from Italy, it also facilitated transatlantic solidarities between Italians and Argentines. This was especially evident during World War I, during which the migrant press used the language of fraternal love to reinforce a transnational sense of belonging between Italians and Argentines.

Beginning in 1915, when Italy entered the Great War to win back its "unredeemed" territories from Austria-Hungary, the migrant press mobilized Italians as well as Argentines in support of Italy.[50] The paper hinted that Argentines who expressed encouragement and love for Italy during the war did not have to worry about betraying their own country, or their country's official commitment to neutrality, since ties between Argentines and Italians were familial. *La Patria*, for example, reported proclamations of Argentine support, such as an article in *El Diario*, an Argentine newspaper, which argued that the history of Italian migration made Argentine neutrality impossible. "It is not possible to be neutral and even indifferent to this conflict that affects our brothers." Such brotherly love, built on "ties of affection, of common lifestyles, of customs, and culture" obligated Argentines as well as Italians to support Italy. The *El Diario* article concluded, "We follow Italy, like a favorite sister, in her most serious trials," asserting that Argentines were obliged to "adopt an attitude of solidarity with her [Italy's] cause and her fate."[51]

That Argentines were joined together in support of Italy, their "sister," demonstrates how family metaphors sometimes included feminine depictions of Italy and Argentina and the relationship between them. The press forged transnational wartime intimacies around women in ways that departed from the consistently masculinized expressions before the war. In 1915, *La Patria* lauded the work of the Private Italian-Argentine Sewing Club, formed by a group of Argentine and Italian women in Rosario "where Italians and Argentines live in fraternal agreement." These women gathered together to raise money, collect wool, and to knit warm clothing like socks, face masks, and sweaters for soldiers on the cold Alpine front. The paper described these Argentine and Italian women as "sisters" who "bequeath to their work all the noble spirit of the people of the Latin race, understanding the grand cause of Italy and following with hope the fate of our army."[52] Such displays of Italian-Argentine solidarity, the paper asserted, demonstrated that "our saintly war does not only move and excite us Italians, but it makes everyone's heart beat who knows Italy and knows the spirit of justice that guides the conquest of the irredentist land."[53]

Before the war, Italian-language newspapers utilized women mainly to represent the Italian nation in its unique singularity. Portraits of "Italia," the female embodiment of the Italian nation, proliferated in *La Patria*, especially on Italian holidays such as Venti Settembre commemorating the culminating battle of the Risorgimento, the Italian unification movement. The cover of *La Patria*'s September 20 issue in 1911 features an image of a crowned and armored Italia draped in the red, white, and green colors of the Italian flag and a garland of pink roses. Her powerful yet celestial physique is set against an image of Rome, with Castel Sant'Angelo (the Mausoleum of Hadrian) and the Vatican in the background (see figure 5.3). Other illustrations paired Italia with depictions of the she-wolf suckling the infant twins Romulus and Remus in reference to the mythological founding of the city of Rome.[54] Feminized depictions of nation-states could be found in many national contexts, especially from the eighteenth through the twentieth centuries, when romanticized image of the homeland were often used to promote nationalism and unity.[55] The Italian-language press, therefore, cast gendered versions of familial relationships for its migrant readers; one envisioned intimate transnational partnerships between Italy and Argentina—on both a state and individual level—as a predominately manly bond between brothers; the other associated the elemental and primeval love migrants have for their homeland, their "ancient mother," as feminine and maternal.

During the war, however, changing migration patterns, shifting demographics, and women's work on behalf of the war effort opened up some room for the creation of feminized depictions of Italian-Argentine relations as one of sisterly love. The war produced a temporary balance in the gender ratios of Italian migration to Argentina as overseas migration decreased, and as Italian men in Argentina were called back to fight in Italy. These changing demographics meant that Italian women left behind, new female arrivals during the war, and, importantly, the substantial number of second-generation Italian women born in Argentina became critically important to mobilizing support for Italy.[56] Women spearheaded a number of transnational wartime campaigns to collect and send home money and supplies to Italian relief organizations and to help the "families of the recalled," women and children in Argentina left behind by their male relatives who returned to fight for Italy. During the war, *La Patria* began paying much more attention to female readers, as evidenced not only by the regular coverage of women's wartime activities, but also by the increased number of columns, articles, and advertisements directed toward women, including a women's page established during the war that focused on fashion, hygiene, and homemaking.[57] The press employed migrant women's transnational work to celebrate migrants' love to Italy, and to forge sisterly love between Argentine and Italians. As "brotherly people" in "sister nations," the press by World War I depicted Italy and Argentina as members of a Latin family that extended across the Atlantic and that sometimes included migrant and Argentine men *and* women.

Prominenti newspapers like *La Patria* reveal what Marcelo J. Borges, Sonia Cancian, and Linda Reeder call the "emotional landscapes" of migration, one

FIGURE 5.3. *La Patria degli Italiani* (Buenos Aires, Argentina), September 20, 1911, cover. Courtesy of the Hemeroteca, Biblioteca Nacional de la República Argentina.

that fostered emotional communities of Latin "brothers" (and sometimes "sisters") among everyday Italian and Argentine readers, but one that was simultaneously circumscribed by Italian and Argentine elites, and appropriated by nationalists, especially during World War I.[58] Investigating foreign relations through the prism of family relations opens up an exploration of how emotions and affective ties were used to make sense of Italian transoceanic migration and to fashion gendered and racialized connections between sending and receiving countries. The Italian press shaped a specific "emotive," a brotherly love used by Italian *prominenti* to legitimize predominantly male migration, to forge positive foreign relations between Italy and Argentina, and to promote harmonious bonds between Italians and Argentines.[59] The transnational ties crafted through brotherly love, however, did not diminish the centrality of the nation-state in these relationships. Ironically, in the hands of middle-class *prominenti* concerned with unifying the culturally diverse peoples of Italy and with Argentine citizenship laws that counted the children of Italians born in Argentina as Argentine rather than Italian, the transnational brotherhood served to promote distinctly Italian national identities. Despite the shared racial Latinness, it was a relationship built on an appreciation of and respect for inherent national differences between Argentines and Italians.

NOTES

I would like to thank the History Department at Old Dominion University for providing me the funds to attend the Social Science History Association's 2016 conference, where I first presented this work.

1. "Il centenario dell'independenza Argentina a Roma," *La Patria degli Italiani* (Buenos Aires, Argentina), May 23, 1910, 3 [hereafter *La Patria*].

2. "Situazione generale," *Il Bollettino Mensile* (Buenos Aires, Argentina), April 1910, 5. See Elizabeth Zanoni, *Migrant Marketplaces: Food and Italians in North and South America* (Urbana: University of Illinois Press, 2018) for a broader analysis of race, gender, and nationhood in Italian migrations to Argentina and the United States in the late nineteenth and early twentieth centuries.

3. On transnationalism from "above" and "below," see Michael Peter Smith and Luis Eduardo Guarnizo, eds., *Transnationalism from Below* (New Brunswick, NJ: Transaction Publishers, 1998); Donna R. Gabaccia, *Foreign Relations: American Immigration in Global Perspective* (Princeton, NJ: Princeton University Press, 2012), 1.

4. See the introduction by Marcelo J. Borges, Sonia Cancian, and Linda Reeder to this volume.

5. Rudolph J. Vecoli, "The Immigrant Press and the Construction of Social Reality, 1850–1920," in *Print Culture in a Diverse America*, ed. James P. Danky and Wayne A. Wiegand (Urbana: University of Illinois Press, 1998), 17–33. On the

Italian press in Argentina see Ronald C. Newton, "Ducini, Prominenti, Antifascisti: Italian Fascism and the Italo-Argentine Collectivity, 1922–1945," *Americas* 51, no. 1 (1994): 41–66; Mirta Zaida Lobato, "*La Patria degli Italiani* and Social Conflict in Early-Twentieth-Century Argentina," in *Italian Workers of the World: Labor Migration and the Formation of Multiethnic States*, ed. Donna R. Gabaccia and Fraser M. Ottanelli (Urbana: University of Illinois Press, 2001), 63–78.

6. Anna D. Jaroszyńska-Kirchmann, "As If at a Public Meeting: Polish American Readers, Writers, and Editors of *Ameryka-Echo*, 1922–1969," in *Letters across Borders: The Epistolary Practices of International Migrants*, ed. Bruce S. Elliott, David A. Gerber, and Suzanne M. Sinke (New York: Palgrave Macmillan, 2006), 200–220; Suzanne M. Sinke, "Marriage through the Mail," in *Letters across Borders*, 75–94; Elizabeth Zanoni, "'A Wife in Waiting': Women and the 1952 McCarran-Walter Act in *Il Progresso Italo-Americano* Advice Columns," in *New Italian Migrations to the United States*, Vol. 1: *Politics and History since 1945*, ed. Laura E. Ruberto and Joseph Sciorra (Urbana: University of Illinois Press, 2017), 80–104.

7. Many of the chapters in this collection examine how migrants employed, as Marcelo Borges writes in his contribution, "a language of transnational affect" in letters to stay linked to families left behind. Chapters by Marcelo J. Borges, Mirjam Milharčič Hladnik, and Suzanne M. Sinke discuss letters as a medium not only for exchanging practical information and remittances, but also for reestablishing personal and familial bonds and for renegotiating gender roles after migration. For the Italian migration case, see especially Sonia Cancian, *Families, Lovers, and Their Letters: Italian Postwar Migration to Canada* (Winnipeg: University of Manitoba Press, 2010).

8. Samuel L. Baily, *Immigrants in the Lands of Promise: Italians in Buenos Aires and New York City, 1870–1914* (Ithaca, NY: Cornell University Press, 1999), 73–75; Eugenia Scarzanella, "L'industria argentina e gli immigrati italiani: Nascita della borghesia industriale bonaerense," in *Gli italiani fuori d'Italia: Gli emigrati italiani nei movimenti operai dei paesi d'adozione, 1880–1940*, ed. Bruno Bezza (Milan: F. Angeli, 1983), 204–30, 283–91.

9. While circulation data is not available for *La Patria*, subscription information shows that by 1915, the Buenos Aires–based paper was sold and distributed throughout the country, as well as in Uruguay, Paraguay, Chile, Peru, Bolivia, and Colombia. *La Patria*, January 1, 1915, 1. There is disagreement over the ideological bent of the paper, with some scholars calling *La Patria* republican, even radical, with others insisting that it was monarchist. See for example, Lobato, "*La Patria degli Italiani* and Social Conflict in Early-Twentieth-Century Argentina," 66.

10. See Jose C. Moya, "Italians in Buenos Aires's Anarchist Movement: Gender Ideology and Women's Participation, 1890–1910," in *Women, Gender, and Transnational Lives: Italian Workers of the World*, ed. Donna R. Gabaccia and Franca Iacovetta (Toronto: University of Toronto Press, 2002), 190–216; Donna R. Gabaccia, "Worker Internationalism and Italian Labor Migration, 1870–1914," *International*

Labor and Working-Class History 45 (1994): 63–79. For radical Italian print culture in the United States see Marcella Bencivenni, *Italian Immigrant Radical Culture: The Idealism of the Sovversivi in the United States, 1890–1940* (New York: New York University Press, 2011).

11. Barbara H. Rosenwein, *Emotional Communities in the Early Middle Ages* (Ithaca, NY: Cornell University Press, 2006), 2.

12. Baily, *Immigrants in the Lands of Promise*, 64. Portugal and Spain also sent many male migrants to Argentina and other parts of Latin America. See Marcelo J. Borges's chapter on Portuguese migrants, many of whom made their way to Latin America, especially Brazil, in the late nineteenth and early twentieth centuries.

13. On Italian migration to Argentina see especially Baily, *Immigrants in the Lands of Promise*; Fernando J. Devoto, *Historia de los italianos en la Argentina* (Buenos Aires: Biblos, 2006); Gianfausto Rosoli, ed., *Identità degli italiani in Argentina: Reti sociali, famiglia, lavoro* (Rome: Edizioni Studium, 1993); Fernando J. Devoto and Gianfausto Rosoli, eds., *L'Italia nella società argentina: Contributi sull'emigrazione italiana in Argentina* (Rome: Centro Studi Emigrazione, 1988); Eugenia Scarzanella, *Italiani d'Argentina: Storie di contadini, industriali e missionari italiani in Argentina, 1850–1912* (Venice: Marsilio, 1983).

14. Donna R. Gabaccia, "In the Shadows of the Periphery: Italian Women in the Nineteenth Century," in *Connecting Spheres: Women in the Western World, 1500 to Present*, ed. Marilyn J. Boxer and Jean H. Quataert (New York: Oxford University Press, 1987), 166–76.

15. On Italian transnational family economies, see Linda Reeder, *Widows in White: Migration and the Transformation of Rural Italian Women, Sicily, 1880–1920* (Toronto: University of Toronto Press, 2003).

16. See María Bjerg's chapter in this collection.

17. "Il Centenario Argentino," *La Patria*, June 22, 1910, 7.

18. M. Gravina, ed., *Almanacco dell'italiano nell'Argentina* (Buenos Aires, 1918), 86.

19. "Babele economica," *La Patria*, January 4, 1910, 3.

20. On Italy see, for example, Olindo De Napoli, "Race and Empire: The Legitimation of Italian Colonialism in Juridical Thought," *Journal of Modern History* 85, no. 4 (2013): 801–32; Giulia Barrera, "Patrilinearity, Race, and Identity: The Upbringing of Italo-Eritreans during Italian Colonialism," in *Italian Colonialism*, ed. Ruth Ben-Ghiat and Mia Fuller (New York: Palgrave Macmillian, 2005), 98–108. See also Charlotte Laarman, "Family Metaphor in Political and Public Debates in the Netherlands on Migrants from the (Former) Dutch East Indies 1949–66," *Ethnic and Racial Studies* 36, no. 7 (2013): 1232–50; Elizabeth Buettner, ed., *Empire Families: Britons and Late Imperial India* (Oxford: Oxford University Press, 2004); Anne McClintock, *Imperial Leather: Race, Gender, and Sexuality in the Colonial Conquest* (New York: Routledge, 1995); Ann Laura Stoler, ed., *Haunted by*

Empire: Geographies of Intimacy in North American History (Durham, NC: Duke University Press, 2006).

21. Ruth Ben-Ghiat and Mia Fuller, "Introduction," in *Italian Colonialism*, ed. Ben-Ghiat and Fuller, 2. See also Nicola Labanca, *Oltremare: Storia dell'espansione coloniale italiana* (Bologna: Il Mulino, 2002); Patrizia Palumbo, ed., *A Place in the Sun: Africa in Italian Colonial Culture from Post-Unification to the Present* (Berkeley: University of California Press, 2003).

22. Since the 1990s, Italy has become a significant immigrant-receiving rather than immigrant-sending country. See Roberta Ricucci's chapter on how new information and communication technologies are influencing intrafamily expressions of love and intimacy among Moroccan and Latin American immigrants in Italy today.

23. Mark I. Choate, *Emigrant Nation: The Making of Italy Abroad* (Cambridge, MA: Harvard University Press, 2008).

24. Richard J. Bosworth, *Italy, the Least of the Great Powers: Italian Foreign Policy before the First World War* (New York: Cambridge University Press, 1979); "L'emigrazione italiana nel lo. semestre 1908," *Il Bollettino Mensile*, October 15, 1908, 6.

25. "Solidarietà italo-argentina," *La Patria*, September 16, 1915, 6; "La formazione della razza argentina," *La Patria*, September 3, 1915, 4.

26. Peter D'Agostino, "Craniums, Criminals, and the 'Cursed Race': Italian Anthropology in American Racial Thought, 1861–1924," *Comparative Studies in Society and History* 44, no. 2 (2002): 319–43.

27. D'Agostino, "Craniums, Criminals, and the 'Cursed Race'"; Paulina L. Alberto and Eduardo Elena, "Introduction: The Shades of the Nation," in *Rethinking Race in Modern Argentina*, ed. Alberto and Elena (New York: Cambridge University Press, 2016), 1–22.

28. "Il centenario dell'independenza Argentina a Roma," *La Patria*, May 23, 1910, 3.

29. "Il centenario dell'independenza Argentina a Roma."

30. Donna R. Gabaccia, "Making Foods Italian in the Hispanic Atlantic," unpublished paper, University of Minnesota, November 1, 2006.

31. See, for example, "Nel nome di Colombo," *La Patria*, April 17, 1910, 7; "Monumento a Cristoforo Colombo," *La Patria*, April 24, 1910, 11; "L'arrivo dell'Onorevole Martini," *La Patria*, May 20, 1910, 5; "1810–25–Maggio 1910," *La Patria*, May 25, 1910, 5.

32. "Babele economica," *La Patria*, January 4, 1910, 3.

33. "Sull'America Latina," *La Patria*, April 14, 1910, 5.

34. Comitato della Camera Italiana di Commercio ed Arti, *Gli italiani nella Repubblica Argentina* (Buenos Aires: Compañia Sud-Americana de Billetes de Banco, 1898), 213; see also "Establecimiento vitivínicola Domingo Tomba," *La Nación*, Número del centenario, 1810–1910, 1910, 241–43.

35. Eugenia Scarzanella, *Italiani malagente: Immigrazione, criminalità, razzismo in Argentina, 1890–1940* (Milan: F. Angeli, 1999); Julia Rodríguez, *Civilizing Argentina: Science, Medicine, and the Modern State* (Chapel Hill: University of North Carolina Press, 2006); Nancy Leys Stepan, *The Hour of Eugenics: Race, Gender, and Nation in Latin America* (Ithaca, NY: Cornell University Press, 1991).

36. D. Bórea, "La vastitá del problema agrario nella Repubblica Argentina," *La Patria*, April 4, 1910, 3.

37. The Spanish were the second largest group of foreign-born in Argentina in the late nineteenth and early twentieth centuries. Some prominent Italians, especially merchants whose livelihoods depended on Italian-Argentine trade, felt particularly threatened by the large presence of Spanish migrants and trade goods. For comparative statistics on Argentina's various migrant groups see Dirección General de Inmigración, *Resumen estadístico del movimiento migratorio en la República Argentina, años 1857–1924* (Buenos Aires: Talleres Gráficos del Ministerio de Agricultura de la Nación, 1925).

38. Jose C. Moya, *Cousins and Strangers: Spanish Immigrants in Buenos Aires, 1850–1930* (Berkeley: University of California Press, 1998), 346–84.

39. The red tip most likely refers to the red Phrygian cap, an ancient symbol of freedom and liberty. While the Phrygian cap was not on the official Argentine flag when it was adopted in 1812, the cap had appeared on early iterations of the Argentine flag and is currently on the coat of arms of the Argentine Republic.

40. Elizabeth Bartman, "Eros's Flame: Image of Sexy Boys in Roman Ideal Sculpture," *Memoirs of the American Academy of Rome, Supplementary Volumes*, vol. 1: *The Ancient Art of Emulation: Studies in Artistic Originality and Tradition from the Present to Classical Antiquity* (Rome: American Academy of Rome, 2002): 249–71; David M. Halperin, John J. Winkler, and Froma I. Zeitlin, eds., *Before Sexuality: The Construction of Erotic Experience in the Ancient Greek World* (Princeton, NJ: Princeton University Press, 1990).

41. "Fra l'Italia e l'Argentina," *La Patria*, January 18, 1910, 5.

42. Quoted in "Voci affettuose," *La Patria*, February 20, 1910, 5.

43. "Emigrazione," *Il Bollettino Mensile*, December 1910, 2.

44. See Emily Pope-Obeda's chapter in this collection.

45. S. Magnani Tedeschi, "Argentini e Italini per il trionfo della *latinità*," *La Patria*, August 18, 1925, 4.

46. "L'America Latina per Enrico Piccione," *La Patria*, August 3, 1906, 3.

47. Benedict R. Anderson, *Imagined Communities: Reflections on the Origins and Spread of Nationalism*, revised and extended edition (New York: Verso, 1991).

48. Lynn Hunt, *The Family Romance of the French Revolution* (Berkeley: University of California Press, 1992); Suzanne Desan, *The Family on Trial in Revolutionary France* (Berkeley: University of California Press, 2006); Mary Lowenthal Felstiner, "Family Metaphors: The Language of an Independence Revolution," *Comparative Studies in Society and History* 25, no. 1 (1983): 154–80.

49. Susan J. Matt and Peter N. Stearns, "Introduction," in *Doing Emotions History*, ed. Matt and Stearns (Urbana: University of Illinois Press, 2014), 7.

50. John Starosta Galante, "The 'Great War' in Il Plata: Italian Immigrants in Buenos Aires and Montevideo during the First World War," *Journal of Migration History* 2, no. 1 (2016): 57–92.

51. Quoted in "L'Italia e Argentina," *La Patria*, May 28, 1915, 4.

52. "L'offerta del 'Costurero Italo-Argentino'," *La Patria*, September 18, 1915, 5. See also "Solidarietà italo-argentina," *La Patria*, September 16, 1915.

53. "Costurero privado Italo-Argentino," *La Patria*, September 12, 1915, 6.

54. See, for example, cover pages, *La Patria*, September 20, 1905, and *La Patria*, September 20, 1910.

55. Stephen Gundle, *Bellissima: Feminine Beauty and the Idea of Italy* (New Haven, CT: Yale University Press, 2007), 48–54.

56. For chapters in this collection that focus on emotions and mobility as they relate to women migrants or female migration for work and marriage see those by Margarita Dounia, Mirjam Milharčič Hladnik, and Alexander Freund.

57. Examples include "Cronache femminile," *La Patria*, April 14, 1915, 4; "Cronache femminile," *La Patria*, May 23, 1915, 4. By the end of World War I, the column had expanded slightly and changed its name to "Vita femminile" (Feminine life). See "Vita femminile," *La Patria*, June 1, 1917, 4; "Vita femminile," *La Patria*, January 1, 1920, 8.

58. See the introduction by Marcelo J. Borges, Sonia Cancian, and Linda Reeder to this volume.

59. William M. Reddy, *The Navigation of Feeling: A Framework for the History of Emotions* (New York: Cambridge University Press, 2011).

CHAPTER 6

"Let Them Deport Me, I Will Come Back to Him Again"

Romance, Affective Relations, and the US Deportation Regime, 1919–1935

EMILY POPE-OBEDA

A large 1922 spread in the *San Francisco Chronicle* told of the "Puzzling Escapade" of one young Canadian, Beatrice Hebert, who was "thrice . . . deported" in the course of pursuing her love, William Zinser of Philadelphia.[1] The two had met on a tour in China, and though he claimed to have immediately spurned her advances, she pursued him with a single-minded persistence. Each time, despite apprehension and removal, she swore her determination to persevere. The fact that her beloved "doesn't want her, that he is moving heaven and earth to keep out of her sight, that he has yelled for the police to protect him and has besought the aid of two governments," had not deterred her advances, the paper reported. In spite of her repeated deportations, "the whole force of the United States government cannot keep her from forcing her attentions upon Zinser." Her case allegedly attracted the attention of "alienists" who labeled her the "strangest case in modern history." Her story was undoubtedly heavily sensationalized by the press, which crafted her as a delusional, but compelling young woman, suffering from "an acute case of 'loveitis.'" And yet, the role that deportation plays demands attention.[2] Deportation served on one hand as the most logical governmental recourse to the situation, and on the other hand, a federal power rendered woefully inefficient against the depth of passion and love-fueled mania.

Like so many of the romanticized deported heroines of news accounts of the era, Hebert was described as a strikingly attractive figure, "tall, slender... dark-haired, lithe, and powerful," while her beloved was portrayed as physically unworthy of her attractions, being "rather small, mild and inoffensive of manner."[3] Hebert, who was being held at Moyamensing Prison while awaiting action by the immigration officials, was said to have declared, "Let them deport me, I will come back to him again. He cannot resist my love forever. I will get him."[4] Indeed, reports circulated the following spring that after a two-month stay at the Detention House at Gloucester, New Jersey, Hebert was being deported to Canada for the fourth time. But by that point, Hebert seems to have had her fill of encounters with the US immigration bureaucracy, and allegedly claimed that she had been "cured" of her affections and would not attempt another surreptitious entry.[5]

To describe her misguided persistence, reporters referred to her in a variety of gendered terms that emphasized her predatory nature: a "determined vamp," a "huntress," etc.[6] But the coverage was remarkably sympathetic, generally depicting her as woefully afflicted with an overabundance of passion. Given the treatment of so many other deportees of her era, it seems likely that had Hebert not been a white, well-off Canadian, her quadruple deportation would have hardly seemed so charming or quirky to the public. She might have at best been assumed seriously mentally ill, and at worst been characterized as a dangerous criminal. In fact, one journalist reported, in spite of her conduct, she was examined by a police surgeon to be "perfectly sane—'that is, if anyone deeply in love can be called sane.'" Instead, the surgeon declared, Hebert was "simply... determined to capture and win this man."[7]

When reporters debated what drove her to these actions and concluded that she was struck by an extreme case of "love-itis," they were doing more than simply dismissing her actions as frivolous. They were also eliding the fact that while they fretted over her fabricated disease, thousands of individuals were being barred and removed from the country for real medical and mental afflictions, with remarkably little coverage or interest among the public. In 1922, for instance, the year of Hebert's third deportation, 464 immigrants were deported post-entry for a variety of mental illnesses, including diagnoses of "feeble-minded," "insanity," "constitutional psychopathic inferiority," and "other mental conditions" and many more were prevented from entering the country.[8] In an era when so many foreign-born women were caught in the deportation machinery for transgressions no greater than extramarital relations, a child out of wedlock, or even poverty, Hebert's role as the passionate and rather glamorous protagonist of a deportation love story is revealing.

Deportation policy gives the state the power to literally tear loved ones apart and as such, its practice has always been fraught with emotion, longing, and heartbreak. Unlike the choice to migrate, in which families weigh considerations of separation, alienation, and opportunity, deportation wrenches the choice away, and empowers the government not only to determine immigration status, but also to pass judgment on family and romantic relations. Throughout the post–World War I decades the argument that deportation was a cruel and unusual punishment because of family separation gained traction. So, too, however, did government assertions that immoral, improper, and un-American versions of love among immigrant populations created the need for more deportations. By bringing romance, sexuality, and familial love into the conversation about deportees, the press also decentered the stereotypical immigrant or deportee as male and generated a new image of the female deportee.

The immediate post–World War I moment represented a new prominence for the American deportation apparatus, which was growing not only in terms of legal criteria for removal but also in practical infrastructure for enforcement. Post-entry deportations grew steadily throughout the 1920s and reached a new high of 16,631 by 1930.[9] At the same time, deportation became newly prominent in the national imagination. Increasingly, commentators came to understand deportation not only through a lens of politics, but through a lens of affect. As Susan Matt and Peter Stearns explain, "rather than examining merely the external behaviors of individuals—the traditional subject of history," scholars must attend to "the anger, the envy, the love, and the greed that prompted such behaviors."[10] It was precisely these emotional valences to which contemporary observers frequently turned to explain the growing social reality of immigrant removal. Romance, jealousy, and heartbreak became common tropes in the coverage of high-profile deportation cases. Deportation, again and again, was narrated as a love story, and a frequently tragic one at that. As observers of the newly powerful deportation regime sought to make sense of this phenomenon, they increasingly created an emotional framework to discuss deportation. In cultural and journalistic representations of the early deportation state, love, sometimes sanctioned and protected, and sometimes disparaged and condemned, figured prominently.

The Press and the Tragic Romance of Removal

Beatrice Hebert's story was followed in unusual detail by the press, but it was not a total anomaly. Instead, it was one particularly colorful example of a broader media emphasis on deportee love stories in the era. The following year, journalists traced the similar story of Mrs. Gertrude Temperley of England, who was reported to have been deported for insanity three times from the United States to England, but who continued to return out of romantic obsession with a former employer. Temperley's case, which one journalist described as "an unusual story of unrequited love," echoed Hebert's in many ways, and she too was described in a flattering light, as a "tall, erect, and well-dressed woman" who "appeared unusually intelligent, dignified and refined."[11] But the obsessive repeat deportee was not the only type of deportation love story that emerged in the press during this era. While these tales followed a variety of different tropes throughout the period, headlines like "Lovers Parted by Immigration Law," "Wedding Is Delayed by Alien Laws," and "M'ms'lle, Love Blighted, Weeps When Deported" frequently appeared in major newspapers.[12]

How did love stories come to be such a prominent form of discourse around deportation? What compelled reporters to frame deportation through its impact on affective ties? Throughout the decade, there were hundreds of stories about jilted girls deported when their unscrupulous lovers deserted them, men who tried to seduce women of the wrong race or class and were removed for their transgressions, stalkers who were deported after repeatedly harassing unreciprocating lovers, and lovelorn youths who were caught when a jealous rival reported them to the immigration authorities. While the sensationalizing of deportation was not new (these stories came on the heels of a press frenzy around deportations of radicals during the so-called "first Red Scare" of 1919–20), the form of that sensationalism was evolving in new and telling directions.[13] Although it is clear that this media coverage was motivated by a desire to sell papers, it is also telling of a society trying to disentangle and control the narrative about what the rise of a modern deportation state meant. Often, newspapers made sense of it as a series of personal tales of heartbreak and separation, dissociating it from the broader labor control and racial policing agenda behind it.

Deportation was an ever-more important function of the state during the 1920s, even if it was rarely as dramatic as the depictions that dominated the media. Instead, the largest numbers of deportations were based on the criteria of "likely to become a public charge" (basically poverty, disability or other suspected vulnerability to becoming dependent on public welfare), and immigration violations.[14] While deportation did operate in fundamental ways as a mechanism to police morality, allowing an administrative agency of the state to decide and enforce the boundaries of normative sexuality and family structure, this practice also took on a distorted, but significant place in public discourse. Amanda Wise and Selvaraj Velayutham make the fruitful observation that "affects can and do produce inclusions and exclusions (forced or voluntary) from transnational social fields," and I would argue that they also provide a framework for the public to make sense of exclusions, and indeed, expulsions, from the national body.[15]

As immigrants circulated through the carceral spaces of the expanding bureaucratic state, stories circulated in newspapers around the nation. One case of a butler who dared to attempt a romance with a wealthy Pittsburgh heiress, and whose deportation was speculated to have been arranged by her family, spurred at least eighty articles discussing his sordid story alone.[16] Some deportation love stories were depicted as tragedies, while others were presented with a comic air. Many included an entertaining cast of characters, as in the 1924 case of Olga Yosipovitch, who was described as a "beautiful Serbian cloak model." Yosipovitch had been brought to the United States by the Serbian International Education Association to study, with the expectation that she would return to Serbia and use her education to serve the nation. When she instead fell in love and married Sidney Wolf, described as a popular young Yale professor, the head of the association requested her deportation. As she awaited expulsion, she explained to reporters that in spite of the intended purpose of her stay in the United States, she "hated relief work and wanted to marry and settle down in America."[17] Stories like Yosipovitch's, which pitted the immigration bureaucracy against starry-eyed young lovers, provided a captivating narrative.

In another unusual case from 1935, love was not enough to save the day. Instead, envy and romantic competition were attributed with ruining a young woman's chances at happiness. The woman, Ruby Eugene Ford, was deported to Barbados after being brought by an employer to the United States from Canada, unknowingly violating immigration law. The young woman had become engaged in New York City, but was apprehended shortly before her wedding, when she "learned to her surprise that a rival for the affections of her lover had written a letter exposing her illegal entry." The case gained the attention of the press aboard the ship on which she was being deported, where Ford was described as being "discovered heartbroken in the second-class division" of the boat. Her story, which was described by one newspaper as "an interesting case in which international chicanery was instituted to wreck the romance of a young girl," was only one of many in which deportation loomed as a potential threat to romance, able to be manipulated by any number of cruel characters: jealous roommates, overbearing parents, or scorned exes.[18]

Oftentimes, deportation stories gained the spotlight because the immigrants involved were deemed to defy social conventions of love in shocking ways. Frequently these featured subjects who attempted to cross either class (as in the case of the infamous butler) or racial lines in their amorous relations. In one memorable tale of racial miscegenation, the wealthy parents of young Mabel Van Den Akker attempted to keep her from marrying Farid Simaika, an Egyptian Olympic diver who had entered the United States on an athletic visa. Her parents, it was reported, disapproved of the union and attempted to get him expelled from the nation in order to prevent it. Mrs. Van Den Akker was quoted as saying, "Yes, I'll admit that I told the immigration authorities that Mr. Simaika should be deported . . . I think I'm a modern mother, but I object to Mr. Simaika's race. I don't want my daughter to marry an Egyptian—or any other foreigner." In fact, she dismissed her daughter's affections as nothing more than a passing and irrational fancy, responding to a reporter's query: "Mabel in love? No, she's not in love. She's just in love with the idea of a honeymoon to Egypt—to the Nile."[19] In short time, however, the couple wore down the parents' resistance, and they were married, at which point the bride's mother claimed to the press, "All's well that ends well . . . I did all that I could to stop it . . . but I'm sure now that everything will turn out all right. They do love each other."[20]

One of the most prominent stories of the period was the 1926 case of the Countess of Cathcart, which added the additional allure of torrid affairs among the British nobility. The countess was held at Ellis Island for deportation because of being designated as guilty of "moral turpitude" on account of her affair with the Earl of Craven. Widespread sympathy was mobilized on her behalf, and financial support and even marriage proposals were offered. The *Washington Post* described the incongruous figure she cut at Ellis Island, stating, "With sharp features, quick-moving, defiant brown eyes and dark hair, the countess is slim and smart. Today she wore black satin, lace and pearls." The countess herself was quoted as having found such moral strictures to be quite galling: "Adultery is not a crime in England. If it were, all the English nobility would be in jail. And if England had the same entrance laws as America, I don't think many American women would get in."[21] Around the country, observers expressed shock and dismay that such a high-class, Anglo-Saxon emblem of femininity could be subjected to the outrages designed for the more common deportable immigrant, reflecting the uneven application of romantic ideals.

Whether these fancifully narrated stories were precisely true as reported is hard to know, but regardless of their veracity, their very existence suggests the importance of attending to the affective angle of deportation practice. As Tyler Carrington explains regarding turn-of-the-century Berlin, newspapers "had immense power and influence" in setting the "emotional lexicon." In the early-twentieth-century United States, they provided a critical opportunity for Americans to process the removal of foreign-born residents. The prevalence and tone of reporting on love, marriage, affairs, and deportation suggests that something of deportation's growing social power had registered with the public in a disconcerting, if ultimately facile and romanticized, way. Observers of the deportation state engaged in a form of sentimentalism that integrated the disciplinary potential of the state into accounts of intimate relations. These stories, which focused on outliers to the normal business of deportation (the policing of racialized labor and immigrant poverty) dominated how much of the public received their information about the expansion of deportation machinery. As Daniel Wickberg has explained, "the life of emotions, desires, and inclinations is oddly absent from most concepts that historians have used to understand the deep structure of belief systems."[22] Deportation scholars must begin to explore how emotional language provided a mechanism for observers of the era to formulate and enunciate their readings of both immigrants and the modern state.

Removing Moral Threats: Policing Relationships through Deportation

However, deportation coverage demonstrated a striking disjuncture from what was actually happening on the ground. As Americans increasingly encountered deportation in the press, their exposure to it was, unsurprisingly, heavily racialized. Immigration restriction based explicitly on racial criteria was expanded and solidified through the Quota Acts, which added on to earlier Asian exclusion laws. Alongside these exclusionary parameters, post-entry, deportation increasingly operated to police the racial composition of immigrant populations that had already crossed the borders. Throughout the decade, rates of deportation of Mexican, Afro-Caribbean, and Asian immigrants were disproportionately high in relation to overall numbers of deportees.[23] As the racial project of post-entry removal accelerated (exponentially in the case of the mass repatriation of Mexicans and Mexican Americans during the 1930s), the public face of the deportation state's victim was often highly unrepresentative. As upper-class white women from Europe or Canada dominated the deportation love stories of the era, they reflected the distance between the realities of migration control and its perceptions. Sara

Ahmed notes that "love is conditional, and the conditions of love differentiate between those who inhabit the nation, from those who cause disturbances," an observation that is borne out in the unevenness of discourses on love and ideas about "desirable" or "undesirable" immigrants who might come to inhabit the nation throughout this period.[24]

The vast majority of deportations looked nothing like the sensationalized accounts in the press, whether they be centered around romance, anarchism, or crime. Instead, they were the routine and highly unglamorous removals of migrants who were impoverished, had violated immigration law, or both. While the press ate up dramatic tales of lovers torn apart, the Immigration Service quietly expanded its infrastructural capacity for removal. This involved the systematization of institutions, the expansion of detention capacity, the streamlining of transportation practices, and extensive coordination with foreign nations to ensure permission for reentry of migrants.[25] Deportation was not, primarily, the spectacular roundup of radicals, the raiding of brothels, or the conniving agendas of jealous lovers—it was a steady and more mundane process of determining national fitness along locally influenced ideas about poverty, useful labor, racial assimilability, moral transgressions, public health, and bodily hierarchies.

But deportees did often become entangled in the deportation state because of their romantic or sexual behaviors, which served as the rationales for their removals. Although exclusion at the border had long been used to reject those who were deemed unfit to reside in America, post-entry removals increasingly allowed officials to control the sexuality of immigrant populations even after long periods of residence. Bodies and behaviors were increasingly under surveillance and control, requiring expanded coordination between government and a wide array of institutions. Therefore, deportable immigrants were often referred to the immigration service by doctors, directors of mental asylums, or prison attendants. At these intersections of medicine and government, officials used the language of crime, public health, and medical knowledge to justify imposing moral codes through exclusion and deportation. The rising scientific study of perversity and abnormal sexuality gave an air of official knowledge to immigration agents' persecution of homosexuality, bigamy, and other forms of love that were deemed transgressive.[26]

As Deirdre Moloney explains, "the regulation of women's non-marital sexuality at the borders . . . was a means to ensure that admitted immigrant women would become both moral citizens themselves and the mothers of moral future citizens."[27] This process reached aggressively into the interior of the nation, not only preventing the admission of "immoral" women, but also creating the ever-present threat of castigation through removal. Eithne Luibhéid notes that when women whose "sexualities presented a threat to the nation" were admitted to the country, "immigration procedures ensured that they became incorporated into webs of surveillance that disciplined them and produced them as 'good' citizens, in gendered, sexualized, racial, and class terms."[28] Such work gestures to how critical the new era of surveillance and documentation was for tracking immigrants after their entry, and how deeply the institutions of the modern nation-state scrutinized the personal, private recesses of noncitizen lives. As the examples below reveal, women were often drawn into deportation proceedings because of a whole range of unsanctioned sexual or emotional activities including prostitution, extramarital affairs, having children out of wedlock, or "promiscuity." Men's sexual and moral behaviors were policed through deportation as well, with concerns emerging over immigrant men acting as procurers or pimps, failing to support wives and children, and engaging in bigamous relations. Indeed, immigrant bigamists such as those María Bjerg discusses in this collection were the subject of deportation investigations throughout the era, and the effort to build new affective ties in the United States could be cause for removal for "moral turpitude."

While immigration officials demonstrated a great deal of anxiety about immigrant sexuality, the constraints of the law often forced them to use other criteria for removal. The 1924 deportation of Lillian Mary Irene Johnson demonstrates how the designation of "likely to become a public charge" (LPC) could be used to mask a much broader agenda of moral policing.[29] The official deportation warrant for Johnson, a seventeen-year-old Canadian citizen of the "African black race," states only that she was to be deported as "LPC" and entry without inspection. However, her case file reveals a much more complicated case. Johnson had entered the country the year before at Detroit before traveling to the home of her uncle in Cleveland. Once she was in Cleveland, she took work as a domestic, but was reported to the Cleveland police "as an incorrigible" by her uncle. The investigation revealed that her sexual behavior had come into question, and Johnson had admitted to having prior sexual relations with two men, although she asserted she had been assaulted in both cases. In a deportation investigation ostensibly about the risk of the alien becoming a public charge, the fact that a great deal of attention was paid to her sexual history and impropriety (with no concern for her allegations of sexual assault), suggests the flexibility of LPC as a criterion for deportation. In fact, the only mention of the immigrant's economic standing was in the observation that she acquired work as a domestic once entering the country, with no indication that she had lost the position or had become unable to work.

As the inspecting officer searched for sexual improprieties, including whether she had ever had children, whether she was currently pregnant, and whether she had ever contracted a venereal disease, Johnson continued to maintain her innocence. After entry to the United States, the report stated, "the alien admits to having sexual relations with one man on three occasions since entering the United States, but denies having practiced prostitution." These encounters, she stated, were with a man with whom she had been "keeping steady company," denying that she had ever accepted money from him for sexual intercourse, but explaining that he had paid to take her to "dances and picture shows."[30] Scholars have noted that working-class women of the era, like Johnson, often engaged in romantic relationships with some element of material support, which were not understood by their participants or communities to be prostitution, a nuance that was scorned by immigration bureaucrats.[31] In the summary of her hearing, the immigrant inspector wrote nothing in the recommendation section regarding her LPC status or entry without authorization, instead reporting on her "immoral relations" both before and after her entry to the country. The unsubstantiated accusations levied against her were enough to color the immigration officials' view of her character, and they succeeded in finding an alternative basis for her deportation to Canada.[32] Johnson was particularly vulnerable due to her age, race, and the fact that her own family had reported her, but her case was far from unique.

The 1922 case of Mary Sarafin of Poland reflected the frustration authorities felt when they could not force legal categories to conform to their moral judgments of immigrant women. Sarafin successfully fought the charge of practicing prostitution after her entry to the country. She had, it was ascertained, given birth to "three illegitimate children by three different men, at least two of these men being married" since arriving in the United States. Although the commissioner of the Montreal district acknowledged that she had not technically "prostituted herself for hire," he concluded caustically that "she is guilty of the practice of offering her body for indiscriminate intercourse with men, which is defined in Webster's Common Sense Dictionary as prostitution." However, the Board of Review decided that because there were no charges other than prostitution that could be applied in her case, they must cancel her warrant, leading the commissioner at Montreal to lament that "it is greatly to be regretted that this alien, highly undesirable from a physical, moral and social standpoint, is to be allowed to remain in the United States."[33] His language is deeply tinged with language of emotion ("undesirable," "regret," etc.), reflecting the extent to which even bureaucrats processed deportation cases through a framework of emotional connection or repulsion to the subjects of the cases they handled.

In other cases, and in particular in cases of black Caribbean immigrants and other nonwhite immigrants, women failed to gain reprieve against deportation. After Hilda Christian of Antigua gave birth to an illegitimate child in the Harlem Hospital, she was accused by the baby's father of having been paid for their sexual relations. Although she denied it, the fact that she had given birth to another child out of wedlock before leaving Antigua was used against her, and the board determined that "since this alien has had two illegitimate children she has shown a propensity to disregard the moral law and consequently it is probable that she may have another illegitimate child and at such time would undoubtedly again become a public charge."[34] Such cases demonstrated the tight connection immigration authorities made between racist stereotypes about unrestrained reproduction, moral "criminality," sexual transgressions, and the policing of poverty.

Severed Affective Ties: Deportation Critiques and Familial Separation

While sexual behaviors attracted the attention of immigration officials, more often than not, deportees (especially nonwhite deportees) were treated by the immigration authorities as though they were without families or affective relations. In the press as well, Latin American and Asian immigrants, rather than being depicted as the protagonists of romantic escapades or torrid affairs of the heart, were generally presented as lacking ties to families or communities. Such articles assumed single, male deportees were identifiable primarily as laborers, criminals, or paupers, not lovers, husbands, or emotional beings. As many of the essays in this collection demonstrate so eloquently, however, even populations of disproportionately male laborers who migrated without their families were deeply embedded within networks of affective ties.

While the press frequently focused more on romantic love than familial love, deportees and their families structured their demands for relief around the cruelty of family separation through deportation. In case after case, family members, friends, and community and religious leaders wrote in to highlight the emotional as well as material suffering that would be brought about by the removal of a loved one. In the 1924 case of Eva Rojas, a Trinidadian immigrant who suffered from mental illness in the aftermath of childbirth and the death of her baby, her husband tried to fight the case, engaging a lawyer and offering to take out a bond to ensure that she would not become a public charge. Faced with the prospect of her removal, he stated, "I feel sure that it is not the intention of the American Government to deal harshly with such a case, thus breaking up a family." Sadly, his pleas were unsuccessful, and Rojas was returned to Trinidad.[35]

Such familial entreaties for relief from the hardship imposed by separation from loved ones were routinely acknowledged by immigration officials, but they were rarely seen as compelling enough to overturn deportation orders. In the 1926 case of Salvatore Capabianca, "various interested parties" attempted to intervene, citing the suffering that would befall his American-born wife and child. However, while the commissioner general responded to one such party that although "the Bureau deeply sympathizes with the wife in the hardship which the deportation of her husband will naturally cause," he concluded that "there is nothing that can be done here to alleviate her trouble."[36]

In the press, when Chinese or Mexican deportees were acknowledged as lovers or family members, it was most often for crossing the boundaries of "moral" behavior—generally for engaging in prostitution, bigamy, or cross-racial relations. In the rare instances that Chinese deportees were highlighted for their affective relations, it was often in alarmed tones, because of their relationships with white women. In 1925, the *Washington Post* featured the front-page headline: "White Wives Plead for Tong Suspects." It explained that after a roundup of suspected criminals in New York's Chinatown, many women were lobbying to keep their husbands in the United States. "Dozens of the suspects were found with white women, who said they were the men's wives," it reported, betraying the skepticism about the legitimacy of such unions, and explaining that some of the women produced marriage licenses to prove their otherwise dubious claims.[37] Another article, entitled: "Host of White Wives Found in New York Chinese Raids: Oriental Brides Plead for Their Husbands," cited the studies of Dr. Carleton Simon, an "honorary deputy police commissioner" studying the Chinese, who claimed that "while most of the woman certainly would not be classed as the best in American womanhood," their devotion to their Chinese husbands was certainly loyal.[38] And yet, even though it was the Chinese men being deported, the press could only imagine emotion, heartbreak, and loyalty among their white wives, while the men's own feelings went unmentioned.

Some family separation cases, however, garnered even more public attention. Scholarship on deportation has heavily emphasized the deportation of radical activists. Often, these prominent deportees are construed as being simply political beings, rather than emotional ones.[39] But they were part of a critical debate around deportation and affective relationships too. Even as radical activists fought back against deportations as violations of political freedom, justice, and free speech, they also decried deportations as violations of human decency because of the destruction of families. In a 1932 "Resolution of Protest against the Increased Terror, Persecution, Discrimination and Deportation of the Foreign Born," one group explained: "Families are broken up by the deportation of their members to different parts of the glo[b]e. Parents are torn from their children, wives from their husbands, thus causing inhuman cruel suffering."[40] As government agents failed to adequately account for radical deportees as members of family unit, activists like Elizabeth Gurley Flynn strove throughout the years following to raise awareness and support for family reunification. Flynn explained the plight of one of these families in a 1921 fundraising letter: "Luigi Parenti, has a family,—a wife and three small children . . . He must deposit with the Department of Labor the transportation expenses for his wife and children to accompany him, which will amount to about $400.00 . . . Now friends, it's no use to tell us the Government ought to pay this . . . If we refuse or fail, it means that Parenti stays in prison indefinitely, while his family literally starve outside."[41] After the famous "Red Ark" upon which Emma Goldman, Alexander Berkman, and roughly 250 other radicals were removed at the end of 1919, activists demanded attention for those loved ones left behind. Many of the deported had wives and children who remained in the United States, and because of the secrecy and speed of their removal, many found themselves suddenly torn from their families. A group of their wives massed at the harbor police station, demanding answers, and one, Clara Books, was reported to have cried out: "They have taken my husband and are taking the husbands, brothers, and fathers of all of us away!" Another woman explained, "They arrested my husband . . . I pleaded with them to let me talk to him, but they refused to let me see him. Now when I come back here I learn he is gone on the sea. I'll never see him again."[42] Although, as Kenyon Zimmer explains, some were ultimately able to secure transportation to join their husbands in Russia, this came only through protest, and others remained left behind.[43] Even as immigration officials policed affective relationships that fell outside of the traditional heterosexual, monogamous family structure, they demonstrated a consistent disregard to the damage done to those very relationships by deportation of spouses, parents, and children.

Conclusion

Throughout the period, immigration officials separated thousands of actual families through their deportation practices. Simultaneously, deportation came to occupy an important space in the national imagination, a space that allowed for both sentimental notions of longing and romantic obstacles, and harsh censure of relationships that didn't conform to normative morality. But these stories reflect how deportation enforcement has always impacted different immigrant communities unequally. As officials and commentators expressed outrage at nonnormative expressions of love among working-class immigrants, not all migrant love stories were met with public shaming, and in some cases, the press and public came to the defense of potential deportees. In the case of upper-class northern and western European or Canadian migrants, the discourse often centered sympathetically on their romantic ties to American residents. While immigrant organizations focused primarily on deportation as a practice that destroyed families, depictions in journalism and fiction tended to emphasize deportation as a possible obstacle to epic romances. In film, as well, love stories featured prominently, and overcoming the threat of expulsion to reunite with a lover allowed for a gratifying cinematic ending.[44]

One journalist, who was allowed to ride aboard a deportation train in 1930, described his trip as follows: "Under it all a romance that Maupassant might have made immortal flowered and withered, shot with beauty, ironic, not a little terrible. Here in these cars was a complete, if limited world, with its valiant ones, its lovers, its philosophers—and its confirmed, congenital villains."[45] Such sentimental language, alongside the recognition of deportees as, among other things, lovers, reflected a new emphasis on the emotional resonance of deportation. As authors and journalists sought ways to narrate deportation for the public, romances were often the chosen genre. While the "coming to America" trope is certainly more common, it is critical to begin to think about what the appearance of a "forcibly leaving America" trope reflected about the space deportation had come to hold in the national imagination.

Perhaps one of the most striking examples of the public visualization of the power, and the romance, of the nascent deportation state was the 1935 novel *Strange Passage* by Theodore Irwin. The novel traces a motley group of deportees on their journey of expulsion, first upon the train taking them to the coast for removal, and then culminating in their detention at Ellis Island before deportation. The novel is centered on a love story between Paul, an artistic Austrian, and Stephanie, a young Belgian woman being targeted by the government for her father's crimes. They fall in love aboard the train, where Paul protects Stephanie from the cruel conditions. In an immigration control twist on the classic mid-book crisis among lovers, there is an uprising and mass escape aboard the deportation train, and Paul and Stephanie are separated in the fray. But, of course, they are serendipitously reunited many years later across the country. Having just rekindled their love, they are reapprehended and brought to Ellis Island together to wait deportation.[46]

Perhaps no one encapsulated the rhetoric of the time more clearly than the reviewers of Irwin's odd novel, who fixated on the romantic storyline. One reviewer characterized the novel as a "romantic love story."[47] Another described its style as "blending romance with sociology," and in fact criticized that "in his preoccupation with the romantic theme of his novel Mr. Irwin has not delved as deeply as he might have into the sociological aspects of a problem which becomes increasingly important as a rising tide of nationalism threatens to inundate the world."[48] Yet another reviewer, John Chamberlain, summed up the bizarre plot succinctly: "we have the strange picture of the deportation squad playing cupid." Chamberlain, though remaining somewhat dismissive of the "liberal agenda" in the novel, explains that "the point that Theodore Irwin wants to make in his remarkable novel . . . is that deportation campaigns have a very human cost."[49] Though critiquing the structure of the novel, he concluded that "sticklers for form may forget their rules in their interest in a problem that is new to American fiction." Deportation, as a "new" problem for American fiction (and, I would argue, journalism), registered on a particular emotional plane. It was, in fact, through the romanticization of deportation that many were able to make sense of this rising "sociological" phenomenon. While so much of the press and media on the early deportation state reduced expulsions to stylized, tragic love stories, such stories do reveal that they were grappling with this social force and its "very human cost" in new and complex ways.

NOTES

1. "Chases 'Her William' Around the World and He Doesn't Want Her," *San Francisco Chronicle*, January 15, 1922, 11.

2. "Chases 'Her William' Around the World and He Doesn't Want Her."

3. "Girl, in U.S. to Woo Tourist Agent, Says He Can't Escape," *New York Tribune*, January 22, 1921, 18.

4. "Canadian Girl Whom Love Lured to America, Will Be Deported," *Baltimore Sun*, January 22, 1921, 1.

5. "Woman Again Deported: Canadian Says She Is Cured of Infatuation for Philadelphian," *New York Times*, March 27, 1922, 2.

6. "'Vamp' Pursues Victim on Ocean and by Airship: 'Will Get Him Yet,' She Tells Court," *Chicago Daily Tribune*, January 21, 1921, 3.

7. "British Columbia Letter: A Determined Huntress," *North-China Herald and Supreme Court and Consular Gazette*, March 5, 1921, 595.

8. *Annual Report of the Commissioner General of Immigration* (Washington, DC: Government Printing Office, 1922), 118–20.

9. *Annual Report of the Commissioner General of Immigration* (Washington, DC: Government Printing Office, 1930).

10. Susan J. Matt and Peter N. Stearns, eds., *Doing Emotions History* (Urbana: University of Illinois Press, 2013), 1.

11. "Deported 3 Times, She Is Back Again: Mrs. Temperley's Strange Story of Unrequited Love Revealed at Ellis Island," *New York Times*, May 19, 1922, 12.

12. "Lovers Parted by Immigration Law: Girl Says Jealous Suitor Caused Fiance's Arrest," *Daily Boston Globe*, February 13, 1929, 32; "Wedding Is Delayed by Alien Laws: Dutch Girl Is Ordered Deported But May Come Back in Next Quota," *Los Angeles Times*, June 2, 1924, 7; "'M'Ms'lle, Love Blighted, Weeps When Deported," *Chicago Daily Tribune*, September 26, 1922, 3.

13. For scholarship on deportation and the first Red Scare, see Torrie Hester, *Deportation: The Origins of U.S. Policy* (Philadelphia: University of Pennsylvania Press, 2017); Kenyon Zimmer, "The Voyage of the *Buford*: Political Deportations and the Making and Unmaking of America's First Red Scare," in *Deportation in the Americas: Histories of Exclusion and Resistance*, ed. Kenyon Zimmer and Cristina Salinas (College Station: Texas A&M University Press, 2018); Emily Pope-Obeda, "Expelling the Foreign-Born Menace: Immigrant Dissent, the Early Deportation State, and the First American Red Scare," *Journal of the Gilded Age and Progressive Era* 18, no. 1 (2019): 32–55; William Preston Jr., *Aliens and Dissenters: Federal Suppression of Radicals, 1903–1933* (Cambridge, MA: Harvard University Press, 1963); and Harlan Grant Cohen, "The (Un)Favorable Judgement of History: Deportation Hearings, the Palmer Raids, and the Meaning of History," *New York Law Review* 78, no. 4 (2003): 1431–74.

14. Scholars such as Rachel Ida Buff and Natalia Molina have increasingly paid important attention to the ways in which the expansion of deportation produced not only actual removals, but a condition of deportability that impacted far more immigrants than the removal numbers suggest. See Rachel Ida Buff, "The Deportation Terror," *American Quarterly* 60, no. 3 (2008): 523–51; and Natalia Molina, "Constructing Mexicans as Deportable Immigrants: Race, Disease, and the Meaning of 'Public Charge,'" *Identities: Global Studies in Culture and Power* 17, no.

6 (2010): 641–66. Contemporary studies of deportation have expanded the theoretic framework of deportability and provided critical insight into the social and political projects it serves. See Nicholas De Genova and Nathalie Peutz, eds., *The Deportation Regime: Sovereignty, Space, and the Freedom of Movement* (Durham, NC: Duke University Press, 2010); Hester, *Deportation*; Daniel Kanstroom, *Deportation Nation: Outsiders in American History* (Cambridge, MA: Harvard University Press, 2007); Hidetaka Hirota, *Expelling the Poor: Atlantic Seaboard States and the Nineteenth-Century Origins of American Immigration Policy* (New York: Oxford University Press, 2017); and Deirdre M. Moloney, *National Insecurities: Immigrants and U.S. Deportation Policy since 1882* (Chapel Hill: University of North Carolina Press, 2012).

15. Amanda Wise and Selvaraj Velayutham, "Transnational Affect and Emotion in Migration Research," *International Journal of Sociology* 47, no. 2 (2017): 125.

16. The 1922 case of August Probst, a former butler at the Rolling Rock Country Club, became particularly prominent, and newspapers across the country aggressively debated his case, including the question of whether the romance for which he was targeted had been real and reciprocated, or in his mind alone. See "Probst Deported Vowing Love for U.S. and Hoping to Return," *New York Tribune*, June 7, 1922, 22, which featured the subtitle "Romantic Butler Admits He May Have Been Slightly Mistaken about American Girls."

17. "Yale Professor Weds Serbian Cloak Model Almost Deported," *New York Tribune*, February 27, 1924, 4.

18. Ralph Matthews, "Deported Girl Says Rival Squealed to Win Lover: Former Roommate Gave Evidence of Illegal Entry, Girl Says," *Baltimore Afro-American*, May 11, 1935, 10.

19. "Egyptian Love Wins Daughter: Miss Van Den Akker Will Wed Olympic Swimmer," *Los Angeles Times*, February 9, 1929, A3.

20. "Course of True Love Smoothed: Film City Girl Weds Arab," *Los Angeles Times*, February 12, 1929, A20.

21. "Deporting of Earl in Countess' Case Is Being Discussed," *Washington Post*, February 14, 1926, 1.

22. Daniel Wickberg, "What Is the History of Sensibilities? On Cultural Histories, Old and New," *American Historical Review* 112, no. 3 (2007): 670.

23. See Mae M. Ngai, *Impossible Subjects: Illegal Aliens and the Making of Modern America* (Princeton, NJ: Princeton University Press, 2004); Natalia Molina, *How Race Is Made in America: Immigration, Citizenship, and the Historical Power of Racial Scripts* (Berkeley: University of California Press, 2014), Moloney, *National Insecurities*.

24. Sara Ahmed, *The Cultural Politics of Emotion*, 2nd. ed. (Edinburgh: Edinburgh University Press, 2014), 16.

25. See Hester, *Deportation*; Ethan Blue, "Building the American Deportation Regime: Governmental Labor and the Infrastructure of Forced Removal in the

Early Twentieth Century," *Journal of American Ethnic History* 38, no.2 (2019): 36–64.

26. See Eithne Luibheid, *Entry Denied: Controlling Sexuality at the Border* (Minneapolis: University of Minnesota Press, 2002); Moloney, *National Insecurities*; Margot Canaday, *The Straight State: Sexuality and Citizenship in Twentieth-Century America* (Princeton, NJ: Princeton University Press, 2009); Martha Gardner, *The Qualities of a Citizen: Women, Immigration, and Citizenship, 1870–1965* (Princeton, NJ: Princeton University Press, 2005).

27. Deirdre M. Moloney, "Women, Sexual Morality, and Economic Dependency in Early U.S. Deportation Policy," *Journal of Women's History* 18, no. 2 (2006): 96.

28. Luibheid, *Entry Denied*, xxvii.

29. File 55401/8, RG 85, National Archives and Records Administration, Washington, DC (hereafter NARA).

30. File 55401/8, RG 85, NARA.

31. See Kathy Peiss, *Cheap Amusements: Working Women and Leisure in Turn-of-the-Century New York* (Philadelphia: Temple University Press, 1986); and Joanne J. Meyerowitz, *Women Adrift: Independent Wage Earners in Chicago, 1880–1930* (Chicago: University of Chicago Press, 1991).

32. File 55401/8, RG 85, NARA.

33. File 55210/52, RG 85, NARA.

34. File 55227/788, RG 85, NARA.

35. File 55382/430, RG 85, NARA.

36. File 55475/79, RG 85, NARA.

37. "White Wives Plead for Tong Suspects: Federal Authorities Send 134 Men to Tombs; Are to Be Deported," *Washington Post*, September 16, 1925, 1.

38. "Host of White Wives Found in New York Chinese Raids: Oriental Brides Plead for Their Husbands," *Atlanta Constitution*, September 21, 1925, 2.

39. Indeed, as Zimmer notes, there was a common perception among antiradicals that single men were more predisposed toward radicalism, while familial ties provided a tempering impulse. See Zimmer, "The Voyage of the *Buford*," 145.

40. "Resolution of Protest against the Increased Terror, Persecution, Discrimination, and Deportation of the Foreign Born," March 27, 1932, US INS Files 71–42, Immigration History Research Center, University of Minnesota.

41. Letter from Elizabeth Gurley Flynn and the Workers Defense Union, October 13, 1921, Elizabeth Gurley Flynn Papers, Immigration History Research Center, University of Minnesota.

42. "U.S. to Ship Reds' Wives on Next 'Ark': 150 Women Riot at Ellis Island Ferry," *New York Tribune*, December 23, 1919, 1.

43. Zimmer, "The Voyage of the *Buford*," 146.

44. I have tracked down records of a small number of films from the period in which deportation played a role in the central love story, including *Anybody Here Seen Kelly?* (1928), in which a young woman immigrates to be with her lover, only

to have a jealous former flame, employed as a customs official, attempt to have her deported before the wedding can take place. In the 1925 *The Mystic*, a reformed criminal follows the woman he loves abroad after her deportation, while in the 1931 *Delicious*, lovers are separated but ultimately reunite aboard the young woman's deportation ship.

    45. Alan MacDonald, "A Trip on the Deportation Special: Unwanted Aliens Headed Home," *Baltimore Sun*, March 9, 1930, SM1.

    46. Theodore Irwin, *Strange Passage* (New York: H. Smith and R. Haas, 1935).

    47. Fred T. Marsh, "Strange Passage," *New York Times*, August 18, 1935, BR6.

    48. Joseph M. Smith, "Strange Passage," *New York Herald Tribune*, August 18, 1935, F8.

    49. John Chamberlain, "Books of the Times," *New York Times*, August 19, 1935, 13.

CHAPTER 7

The Emotions of War

Italian Emigrant Soldiers and Love of Country

LINDA REEDER

In 1916, Luisa Macina published a collection of essays for students entitled *Arms and Faith of Italy: Conversations with Youth.* Over the course of fourteen short chapters, Macina speaks of duty, justice, heroism, solidarity, and above all, love. Love is the central emotion underpinning Macina's pedagogical justification for war: love for the Italians still living under Austrian tyranny; love for the dead heroes of the Risorgimento; love for God, family, and country. The love of country, she insists, is felt among the young men leaving for the frontlines, the old who wish they could go, and the women who watch them leave. This love spreads across oceans, stirring the hearts of the "millions and millions of emigrants . . . in France, England, and faraway America, who rush to the flag, shouting: —Viva L'Italia!"[1] For Macina, Italians living abroad embodied the deep abiding love of country that defined Italians everywhere:

> Even beyond the ocean, my children, there beats the soul of Italy, and now more than ever we feel it vibrant, ardent, ready. Moreover, we must rejoice in this strengthened correspondence of affections and admire it, for how much heavier are the sacrifices of the earlier European war, and our war today, on our emigrants, who live almost exclusively on commerce. Wealth, accumulated with years of privation and fatigue, they now see diminished or destroyed: flourishing businesses now languish; the young, who hear the cry of their country, leave their profitable jobs,

cross an ocean more treacherous than ever, and rush to the aid of their homeland, wondering if they will ever return.²

Mixed with their selfless acts of sacrifice and patriotism is the "bitterness of exile, nostalgia for their country, and the incurable pain of separation. There was, perhaps, until yesterday, also rancor versus their stingy birthplace, that did not have bread for them: versus the fortunate rich to whom the country offers kindness and privileges. Today, all their emotions blend into one: Love for a common country."³ Macina's evocation of emigrants, men and women who chose to leave their homeland, as symbolic of Italian love of country seems an odd choice. In the decades before the war Italian men had left in ever-growing numbers; many from the South left, in part, to avoid, or at least postpone, the draft. Italian critics commonly dismissed emigrants as the least loyal of the newly minted Italian citizenry. Yet, fifty years after unification the country expected Italian men living abroad to return and serve, and thousands did. Why would these men return, what motivated them, and how did their experiences alter the emotional bonds linking emigrants to the Italian nation?

In reading through wartime memoirs, diaries, and letters of Italian soldiers love of country is fused with love of family. On the eve of the Great War, the conviction that Italian emigrants loved their homeland, and remained bound by love of family to the world they had left behind had become a truism. The intimate and political affective language that informed experiences of emigrants and war was anchored in nineteenth-century gendered notions of citizenship, and shaped understandings of late-nineteenth-century Italian emigration. Since the late 1890s, the state had consciously sought to strengthen diasporic affection by fusing the emotions of patriotism and emigration in ways that filtered an emigrant's personal feelings of anger, relief, adventure, sadness, and loss into what was generally considered a more noble sort of love—a theme explored by Elizabeth Zanoni in her study on brotherly love in Italian Argentine communities included in this volume. As illustrated by Macina, in 1916, the conviction that love motivated men to sacrifice their lives for their nation seemed immutable, yet, just a few years after the war ended, love faded from the nationalist rhetoric and from emigrant debates. The war appeared to fracture a fragile sentimental landscape that had placed love at the center of public political sentiment.

The history of emotions is a complicated field. In 1941, Lucien Febvre urged historians to seriously consider the importance of emotions in understanding the past, insisting that attending to the sentimental and affective expressions and modes of a particular moment could reveal a deeper understanding of society and politics. Writing in the midst of Nazi-occupied Europe, Febvre contended that the study of the history of emotions could help us understand why seemingly irrational passions suddenly upended social order. Febvre's plea seemed to fall on deaf ears. Only in the 1980s did historians, informed by the theoretical changes accompanying new trends in social and cultural history, begin to look at how emotions shaped individual and collective norms. Much of the early work focused on the social and institutional power to regulate emotion; more recently, historians have sought to understand emotion as both an analytic category and a subject of history.[4] The shift has not been easy. The historian of emotion faces an array of definitional and intellectual difficulties. What is an emotion? What does it do? How is it generated? What is the relationship between individual and collective emotions? Although still divided on the definition of emotions, and far from agreed on their physical or cultural origins, historians have increasingly recognized that emotional expressions, like political or economic languages, are critical to understanding social, cultural, and political change. Informed by works in gender history and the history of sexuality that made visible how changing meanings of desire, love, and attachment transformed social relations and political institutions, historians of emotion have looked at how historically contingent meanings of love, lust, anger, and fear give meaning to social and political change. Increasingly, historians are recognizing that emotional frameworks are central to the ways in which individuals and communities navigate through moments of change and upheaval, including wars, revolutions, industrialization, and urbanization.[5]

This chapter brings the insights of historians of emotion to bear on the experiences of Italian emigrant soldiers who "voluntarily" returned from the Americas. I argue that the rhetorical power of love to motivate emigrants to return and fight was grounded in gendered notions of male Italian citizenship and the construction of Italy as an "emigrant nation." The fusion of love of country and family underpinned both nationalist and radical politics until World War I. For emigrants, the sentimental language of nineteenth-century liberal politics transformed the myriad emotions underlying individual decisions to stay or go—fear, resignation, and homesickness—into love of country. For both sending and receiving societies familial and patriotic love marked individual men as worthy of full citizenship. The experiences of modern warfare, combined with transnational lives, fractured this emotional calculus. By the end of the war, emigrants and Italians had to reconstruct the emotional ties between individual and nation, citizen and state.

The Italian Diaspora and World War I

Between 1861 and 1915, over 14 million Italians left Italy, over 7 million traveling overseas and the rest seeking work in Europe. Although it is difficult to calculate the number of draft-age men living abroad in 1915, scholars estimate that nearly 9 percent of the class of 1886 (nineteen-year-olds) were out of the country when the state issued its first call to arms.[6] Considering that over 80 percent of the migrants were male, most between the ages of fifteen and forty-five, certainly a large proportion were eligible for the draft. Additionally, according to Italian law, the children of Italian emigrants born abroad were required to serve, regardless of their citizenship status. Factoring in the descendants, the Italian overseas army was numerically formidable. Over the course of the war, Italy called up all men between the ages of eighteen and forty, drafting them for war or territorial service. Based on the limited sources available, historians have estimated that roughly, of the 1,200,000 Italian emigrants called for active service, approximately 304,000 returned to fight, while nearly two-thirds remained abroad. The United States reported the highest proportion of "*renitenti*" or shirkers. In November of 1915, Italian American newspapers reported that only 15 percent of the 400,000 Italian reservists in the United States had responded to the call.[7]

Contrary to the numerical evidence, the Italian press insisted on depicting emigrants as loving and loyal citizens. In 1918, Alessandro Pomilo, a sharp critic of Italian foreign policy, described how the emigrants, abandoned by their country, "never forgot their faraway motherland, to whom they sent home their savings, and to whom in her hour of need, give their lives."[8] As one journalist from the nationalist weekly *L'Idea Nazionale* wrote, "No one forced them to return as soldiers. Many had evaded the draft, refusing to interrupt their work when Italy was at peace." Yet, as soon as they heard the news that Italy was at war, they "left their offices, abandoned their houses, bid adieu to their family and rushed to the Consulate to say: We want to fight."[9] Draped in the tricolor, sporting cockades and ribbons, the returning migrants disembarking from ships in the port of Naples, Palermo, and Genoa made visible their patriotic love to all.

In the United States, newspapers reported that the "war spirit" permeated Italian communities, and thousands of young men were rushing to enlist. Stories of thousands of eager recruits standing for hours outside consulate offices eager to return home to fight for their homeland appeared in newspapers across the country. In June of 1915, the *Brooklyn Daily Eagle* described how Antonio Cuti had been willing to abandon his wife and children in his eagerness to return to Italy. His wife reported him for desertion, and he was arrested when he tried to book passage back to Italy. Found guilty in court for failing to provide for his wife and children, he paid the bond and left. Cuti's story, according the *Daily Eagle*, proved that "with the Italians, patriotism is more than skin deep."[10] While the stories in the American press were tinged with anxiety over the effects of the sudden loss of immigrant labor, and the possible violation of US neutrality law, the underlying sentiment was satisfaction in the patriotism of Italian migrants, evident as communities mobilized in support of the Italian war effort. Throughout the Americas, Italian immigrants responded to the call to arms, established war committees, raised money, and sent clothes and supplies back to Italy.[11]

The memories and history of the role of the diasporic communities in the making of the nation of Italy remained deeply rooted among Italians abroad, shaping notions of patriotic love and enmity. Emigrants and exiles played central roles in shaping notions of Italian independence, and during the Wars of Unification (1848–1861), exiled patriots found support and safety among Italians abroad. Giuseppe Garibaldi, a founding father of modern Italy, known as the "hero of the two worlds," spent decades in exile first in South America and later on Staten Island in New York. Giuseppe Mazzini lived and died in exile in London. Emigrant Italians defined themselves within this history of transnational nation-formation as loyal Italians and enemies of the Bourbons and Austrians and friends to France and Great Britain. By 1914, only Austria still controlled lands that Risorgimento patriots considered part of the Italian nation. In the years leading up to the war it was clear that diplomatic efforts, including signing onto the Triple Alliance, had failed to advance Italy's territorial ambitions, and had fueled a growing nationalist *irredentista* movement stoking anti-Austrian sentiment at home and abroad.[12]

When World War I broke out in 1914, the past merged with the present among Italians living in the United States, reinforcing the historical narratives of the abiding love of emigrants and exiles for the nation. In 1914, Ricciotti Garibaldi, the grandson of Giuseppe Garibaldi, announced the formation of a volunteer legion to serve in France. US newspapers celebrated Ricciotti's efforts, reminding readers of the heroic escapades of his grandfather, the "hero of two worlds," and paying homage to sacrifice and bravery on the part of Italian emigrant soldiers, willing to die for liberty.[13] Leading papers in both the United States and Italy followed the exploits of Ricciotti and his brothers as they gathered 5,000 volunteers from America willing to don red shirts and fight with the French Army for the liberation of Italy. The deaths of Garibaldi's great-grandsons in the Argonne Forest testified to the patriotic love that flowed through the Italian diaspora. In the months after Italy entered the war, the affective references to Garibaldi grew more intense. In June, the *New York Times* published a poem by Katherine Drayton Mayrant Simons Jr., entitled "Garibaldi's Promise." Referencing Garibaldi's famous speech on the eve of fleeing the Italian Republic in 1848, the poet asked: "I promise cold and hunger / in the stead of drink and meat! / I promise death my brothers / shall be yours before defeat! / O sweetheart of the Nations / In the hour of your pain / Does Garibaldi's promises / to Italia hold again?"[14]

The love of country and family underpinning nationalist patriotic rhetoric also informed the radical opposition. *Cronaca Sovversiva*, an anarchist weekly in Massachusetts, published a series of letters appearing to be from soldiers at the front, family members in Italy, and emigrants challenging the equation of familial love and love of country. Nicola Palmiotti wrote to his father:

> [Y]ou beg me to return to Italy, because you do not want me to be labeled a shirker, and you urged my cousin to convince me to do my duty toward my country because "who abandons their country forgets their parents" and you fear I will end up in jail ... of the first I have no doubts; regarding the second I don't agree ... the more one loves their parents, the less one is taken with official patriotism ... where is my country I have no country, because the exploited slaves have no country. At the age of 16, I was forced to abandon my birthplaces, at the moment that I felt the most affection for the blue skies that smiled on me as a boy ... I had to abandon all those who I first felt the strongest and purest affection in my life? Why did I have to leave my godmother, why was I forced to emigrate? Because I meant nothing to my country ... and now it demands a sacrifice, a duty that I do not owe.[15]

In July of 1915 the paper published a long letter signed by "mothers of Italy," pleading "Sons, do not return [*figli, non tornate*] ... do not surrender to the lies ... for the sacred love of your mother who conceived you in torment, and gave birth to you in pain, and brought you up amidst tears, blood, kisses, and who does not live, does not think, does not suffer except by you and for you, for our love ... sons, do not return."[16] In challenging the equation of familial and national love, the anarchists acknowledged the central emotional bond underlying the liberal state.

Love and the Liberal State

Stories of Italian emigrant devotion to country and family were anchored in gendered ideals of nineteenth-century Italian nationalism and state formation. The Italian Risorgimento was an inherently gendered process, committed to the revitalization of a degenerate man. In the eyes of Italian nationalists and foreigners, centuries of living under tyrannical rule and its attendant corruption of marriage had turned Italian men into women, rendering them weak, servile, and unfaithful. According to patriots and political theorists, conjugal love and fidelity attested to a man's ability to love his country.[17] Italian nationalist insistence on fusing heterosexual, monogamous, loving marriage onto notions of good male citizenship was deeply embedded in liberal political theory, associating the health of the nation with a well-ordered family life. As early as 1834, Silvio Péllico linked a man's ability to love his country to domestic fidelity. A faithless husband, or an adulterer who dishonors another man's vows of marriage, is incapable of loyalty to his country. "If a man scorns the altar, the sanctity of holy matrimony, decency, probity, and cries 'Fatherland! Fatherland!' do not believe him! He is a patriotic hypocrite, the worst kind of citizen."[18] Marriage and fatherhood transformed men's egotistical love into an altruistic, self-sacrificing love. Woman, "the angel of the house," in Giuseppe Mazzini's words, exerted a mystical moral force on her husband and sons, transforming them into willing, obedient citizens. As the protagonist of Giuseppe Levi's fictional memoir (intended for use in the classroom) concluded after recounting his transformation from a hedonistic bachelor to a loving husband: "I now fully understand why, when a nation begins to rot and decay, the bachelor triumphantly replaces the family. The family needs order, justice, and virtue to live and breathe; when these are lacking, it languishes and dies."[19]

In particular, publicists and politicians identified the south of Italy and the southern man as a formidable challenge to building a strong nation. A wealth of pedagogical, medical, and political treatises insisting on the intimate affective ties that bound a man to the nation circulated throughout Italy in the decades after unification, informing discussions about the "problem" South and deficiencies of the southern man. The difficulty for southern Italian men lay, in part, in a disordered domestic life. The despotic rule of the father, which nineteenth-century ethnographers associated with southern Italian family forms, inhibited wives and mothers from exerting the moral force necessary to transform their husbands and sons into good men. Southern domestic arrangements transformed men into petty tyrants who, when slighted or attacked, took the law into their own hands. Whether a consequence of bad government or bad blood, experts generally agreed that the authoritarian, insular family posed a barrier to the transformation of southern men into self-sacrificing, loyal, and loving Italian citizens.[20]

By the 1880s, growing mass migration from the southern provinces heightened concerns about the moral condition and patriotic love of southern Italians. Faced with difficulties in stitching together the new nation-state, Italian politicians first paid little attention to the question of emigration. However, as the number of emigrants began to grow, critics began to turn their attention to the potential benefits and dangers posed by emigration. While recognizing the role of emigration as a kind of safety valve, tempering the social unrest that accompanied endemic unemployment and poverty, pundits grew increasingly concerned about the moral and military impact of emigration. Fears of the effects of emigration on the social fabric, on family ties, on public health and the strength of new military recruits colored public discourse. Descriptions of abandoned and forsaken women forced into prostitution, or left to die, accompanied statistical evidence of rising rates of adultery, illegitimate births, and infanticides, as proof of the dangers posed by unrestricted migration. The loyalty and "love of country" of southern Italians who left for the Americas, already rendered suspicious by virtue of geography, became an impossibility. The effects of emigration would erase whatever little sense of duty, obligation, sacrifice that remained in the migrants, and the effects, often measured in terms of heightened alcoholism, illness, and greater rates of draft evasion, seemed to prove that migration left men unfit to carry the burdens of citizenship.[21]

The tenor of the discourse began to shift in the late 1890s, after the defeat of the Italian forces at Adua by the Ethiopian army, and the collapse of Italy's dreams of formal empire. Italian statesmen began to look to the Italian diaspora as a means of realizing its imperial ambition. The reconsideration of the emigrant communities accompanied new understandings of the transformative possibilities of emigration. Rather than assuming mobility as a corrupting force, experts focused on the ability of emigration to turn southern Italians into Italians. In government inquiries and sociological studies, officials and experts focused on the deep love these men evinced for their homeland, despite being forced to abandon their homes by corrupt and brutal landowners.[22] Far from abandoning their parents, wives, and children, these husbands and sons were emigrating in order to provide for their families. As Giovanni Lorenzoni, the author of a government inquiry into conditions in Sicily, wrote, emigrants "have demonstrated that Sicily is not a depressed land, or miserable, or decadent, or reduced to dull immobility; but a region full of new life and rapidly rising . . . they are the obscure peasants who by emigrating, are conquering for the country the means to remake themselves."[23]

Nationalists contended that emigrants should be considered Italian colonists, representatives of the nation abroad, and that the experience of emigration itself could prove instrumental in fusing local attachments to family and birthplace into a love of Italy. Rather than leaving emigrants to flounder, the state had to take a more active role in constructing its "emigrant empire." If the Commissariat of Emigration could prove to the emigrants that the state had their best interests at heart, could strengthen their ties to those who remained behind, fuse the local and national through consulate networks, language courses, cultural programs, and even the Church, they could transform the emigrants into good husbands and citizens.[24] The Libyan war in 1911 seemed to offer evidence that their plan worked. Nationalists celebrated the apparent return of migrants filled with enthusiasm to fight the desert wars.[25] On the eve of World War I, the contours of the emotional landscape surrounding Italian immigration tied Italian men to the nation through their love of family. Even the most "Americanized of migrants" responded to their country's plight with such enthusiasm that no one could doubt Italy's "spiritual strength."[26] Italy's efforts to solidify affective ties with its emigrants generated some concern among receiving societies. The ability of homelands to maintain claims to the hearts and minds of their emigrants unnerved American statesmen, undermining the effectiveness of assimilation and naturalization in the creation of loyal American citizens.[27]

Changing Emotional Landscapes

Reading through the letters and diaries of the emigrant soldiers it becomes apparent that acceptance or rejection of public expressions of patriotism and love of country were created from a wider range of sentiments; alongside love of country stood fear, familial affection, and obligation. Boarding the ships for Italy, many returning migrants spoke of patriotism, but within a short time after they landed in Italy, cracks widened the gap between the political and private emotional landscapes. Giovanni Arru returned after two years in New York City because he feared he would not otherwise be able to come home. In his memoir, he recalled how newspapers kept reporting that whoever did not return home to serve would not be allowed back in Italy for thirty years. "To tell the truth," he wrote, "I did not feel as though I could remain outside my country for thirty years, so I thought and thought." In the end, anxious for his family, he decided to return, but nearly as soon as he landed, he began to regret his decision. Italian consulate officials had promised Arru, and all emigrant soldiers, that they would have time to see their loved ones before they had to report to duty. Yet, as soon as they disembarked they were sent to the front.[28] Within months of enlisting, emigrant soldiers counseled their brothers, friends, and kinfolk to stay in the Americas.

The war fractured the emotional landscape of emigrant soldiers. Even those who left convinced by the rhetoric legitimizing Italy's war ambition by calling on Risorgimento ideals of territorial liberation soon found their faith fading. The love that buoyed them up as they crossed the ocean disappeared in the trenches. In August of 1916, in a letter home to a friend, an unnamed soldier who had answered the call to return to Italy described the horrors of war, the constant sound of artillery, the mud, the lice, and the brutality of the officers. "To those who write to say that one does not feel the burden of this suffering when it is done for one's country, I respond to them in this manner, I wish you were next to me, and then after two days I would ask you the question and see what your answer would be—I was one of those patriots or I would never have left Buenos Aires." He told his friend, "By now I am no longer in the fog, as I was when I was drawn to so many things that sparkled in my sentiment, now that I have seen and tried them they have all vanished, all failed."[29]

The erosion of patriotic sentiment among emigrants is visible in diplomatic correspondence, as emigrant soldiers and their families turned to the US law for assistance in extricating themselves from the Italian army. By 1916, soldiers' kin sought assistance from United States congressional representatives in their efforts to bring their sons and husbands home. In many of these letters, sentimental attachment to the family trumped expressions of patriotic affection. Love of country gave way to the material and emotional needs of the family. In the spring of 1917, Alfio Carta, just shy of eighteen years of age, left his home in Washington, DC, to return to Italy and fight. His distraught mother immediately wrote to the State Department urging the government to detain her son at the border. Alfio's father had taken out naturalization papers, but had been too ill to complete the papers, though, she pointed out, "he purchased his home here," evidence of his commitment to his new land.[30] The willingness of Italians in America to draw on the resources of the US government suggests a more tenuous emotional attachment to Italy than was trumpeted in the media. Parents and wives were quick to highlight their material contributions to America and downplay their sentimental ties to Italy in their efforts to reclaim their men from the Italian army.

In the US State Department records, family members drew on familial affection and economic distress in their efforts to mobilize US government resources.[31] In the summer of 1918, Provvidenza Cutrufelli wrote to the US secretary of state, pleading for the department to effect the release of her husband, a US citizen, from the Italian army. "At the time Italy entered the present war, my husband, in order not to be considered as a deserter by his native country, and with true patriotic spirit, sailed for Italy to join the army and fight the invaders of the Italian soil." He left behind his wife and four children. Provvidenza went on to recount the sufferings the family endured in the absence of her husband. Apart from securing Red Cross assistance, however, the US government could do little.[32] Alvey Adee, the assistant secretary, expressed his sympathy for Provvidenza's plight but reiterated that since her husband voluntarily returned there was little to be done. According to Italian law, all Italian men were required to fulfill military service regardless of citizenship and the United States had no power to demand a soldier's discharge. The willingness of Italian emigrants to turn to the diplomatic networks of the United States speaks to their shifting loyalties and the erasure of love from notions of citizenship. Legal status, residency, economic investment, and work justified civic rights and obligations. The emotional attachment to homeland did not disappear, but was detached from the nationalist visions of an emigrant empire. Love of home conjured up family, kin, and community, but no longer defined national belonging or required wartime sacrifices.

The insistence of love as the prime motivator for patriotic sacrifice was further undermined by the willingness of the Italian government to forgive those who did not return to fight. The consequences for those who chose to remain abroad were minimal. Although failure to respond was classified as desertion, most men never appeared in court, their sentences suspended for the duration of the war and generally repealed afterward. While they still were required to serve, they no longer faced imprisonment if they did not. Those who chose to join allied forces, fighting for France or the United States, were generally exonerated.[33] By the mid-1920s, the Italian government awarded military honors to those Italians who had fought in allied armies. The fulfillment of civic obligations no longer corresponded to patriotic sentiment.

The emotional shift in Italian emigrant patriotism, marked by the separation of love of country from civic obligation, becomes clearer a few years after the war. When Italy first entered the war, the editors of the nationalist magazine *Il Carroccio* urged emigrants in the United States to respond to the call to arms out of their deep love of nation and family. In the June 1915 issue, the editors announced on the front page, in bold black letters, that Guglielmo

Marconi had left America to return to Italy and join the war effort as soon as he heard that Italy had joined the war. After extolling Marconi's love of country and personal sacrifice, the editors reminded their readers that Marconi left "with the certainty of knowing that Italians in America stood united, strong and generous in the face of the enemy. In Rome, he brings to Mother the promise of the love of sons who feel they must love her and defend her *usque ad mortem*."[34] The fusing of familial and patriotic love continue in the following article entitled "The Voices of the Father Call Us," written by Agostino De Biasi, who answers those who may wonder why they should return to fight, how their presence could affect the war, by insisting that "you could be the one fated by the heavens to repel the man who, once [he] has penetrated your house, violates your woman and leaves you with children who are not yours. . . . Italy calls you . . . your grandparents call you with examples of suffering martyrs." De Biasi recognized the multiplicity of ways Italians abroad could show their love—some could return and fight, others could defend their homeland from accusations of disloyalty, still others could raise money to care for the wounded.[35] Throughout the efforts of the Italian community to assist the motherland, they drew on the language of affective kinship.

By the 1920s, the patriotic rhetoric changed. In an article addressing the question of nationalism and Americanization, De Biasi argued that American citizens of Italian origin remained spiritually part of the Italian nation. Anchored in history, the nation now emerged is a sacred entity, timeless and eternal, not defined by kin. Italy's newfound position as a great power, a consequence of the war, means that all Italians, but especially emigrants, "have today, the mission of reflecting on the actions and valorizing in the world the Victory of Italy."[36] While not completely abandoning the foundational power of love that linked each individual to family and country, De Biasi distinguished between that primary love and the emotions that defined the nation. Lurking in De Biasi's rhetoric exists a distinctly different emotional pull on the migrant, invoking a kind of religious devotion to the sacred altar of the nation. The sacralization of the nation, as Emilio Gentile has long argued, was central to the nationalism of the postwar Italian right. Italian Fascism embraced the new patriotism that conflated military valor, patriotic sacrifice, and the mystical sacred love of man for God.[37] In the aftermath of the war a new form of diasporic nationalism replaced sentimental patriotism.

The Great War pushed love to the margins of patriotic rhetoric, requiring the Italian state to once again reconfigure its relationship with the emigrant communities. In the postwar social and economic chaos and political polarization, liberal Italy's vision of the emigrant nation anchored in love came under attack by the nationalists. Fascist supporters insisted that mass migration was a sign of a weak state, a failed democracy. The Fascist state would rehabilitate Italy, and as a sign of its newfound health, emigrants would become colonists. Embarking on spectacularly unsuccessful colonial schemes, and the *fascitizing* of existing emigrant communities, Benito Mussolini sought to bind the emigrants to Italy through Fascism. Italians abroad largely refused to play along, rejecting any association with the totalitarian regime, particularly after 1940. For the emigrant soldiers of World War II, familial devotion and Italian identity was best expressed by taking up arms against the state.

NOTES

1. Luisa Macina, *Armi e fedi d'Italia: Conversazioni coi giovani* (Turin: S. Lattes, 1916), 13.
2. Macina, *Armi e fedi*, 43–44.
3. Macina, *Armi e fedi,*, 44.
4. Lucien Febvre, "La sensibilité et l'histoire: Comment reconstituer la vie affective d'autrefois?" *Annales d'histoire sociale (1939–1941)* 3, no. 1/2 (1941): 5–20. For some examples see Carol Zisowitz Stearns and Peter N. Stearns, *Anger: The Struggle for Emotional Control in America's History* (Chicago: University of Chicago Press, 1989); Anne Vincent-Buffault, *The History of Tears: Sensibility and Sentimentality in France* (Basingstoke, UK: Macmillan, 1991); Steven Seidman, *Romantic Longings: Love in America, 1830–1980* (New York: Routledge, 1991); Sophia Rosenfeld, "Thinking about Feeling, 1789–1799," *French Historical Studies* 32, no. 4 (2009): 697–706.
5. Barbara H. Rosenwein, "Worrying about Emotions in History," *American Historical Review* 107, no. 3 (2002): 821–45. For a general history of emotions see Jan Plamper, *The History of Emotions: An Introduction* (New York: Oxford University Press, 2015).
6. ISTAT, *Serie Storiche*, Table 2.9—Espatriati e rimpatriati per destinazione e provenienza europea o extraeuropea—Anni 1869–2014." Emilio Franzina, "Emigranti ed emigrati in America davanti al primo conflitto mondiale (1914–1918)," in *Stati Uniti e Italia nel nuovo scenario internazionale 1898–1918*, ed. Danile Fiorentino and Matteo Sanfilippo (Rome: Gangemi Editore, 2012), 141, 143. Fiorello B. Ventresco, "Loyalty and Dissent: Italian Reservists in America during World War I," *Italian Americana* 4, no. 1 (1978): 93–122.
7. Franzina, "Emigranti ed emigrati in America," 141, 143; Vanda Wilcox, *Morale and the Italian Army during the First World War* (New York: Cambridge University Press, 2016), 173. For more on the history of Italian citizenship see Sabina Donati, *A Political History of National Citizenship and Identity in Italy, 1861–1950* (Stanford, CA: Stanford University Press, 2013).

8. Quoted in Franzina, "Emigranti ed emigrati in America," 144; Alessandro Pomilio, *Delitti d'oblio: Storia dell'azione italiana negli Stati Uniti* (Rome: Tip. L'Italiana, 1918), 99.

9. Quoted in Macina, *Armi e fedi*, 44–45.

10. *Brooklyn Daily Eagle*, June 6, 1915, 16.

11. See the work of John Starosta Galante, "The 'Great War' in Il Plata: Italian Immigrants in Buenos Aires and Montevideo during the First World War," *Journal of Migration History* 2, no. 1 (2016): 57–92.

12. For a discussion of the *irredentista* movement and migration see Mark I. Choate, *Emigrant Nation: The Making of Italy Abroad* (Cambridge, MA: Harvard University Press, 2008). On the history of Italian unification see Lucy Riall, *Risorgimento: The History of Italy from Napoleon to Nation-State* (Basingstoke, UK: Palgrave Macmillan, 2009). On exiles and emigrants in the Risorgimento see the discussion in Donna R. Gabaccia's *Italy's Many Diasporas* (London: Routledge, 2005); and Maurizio Isabella's *Risorgimento in Exile: Italian Émigrés and the Liberal International in the Post-Napoleonic Era* (New York: Oxford University Press, 2009).

13. Richard Conover, "True Battling Scions are these Garibaldi Fighting Qualities of the Italian," *Tampa Tribune*, October 25, 1914, 33.

14. Katherine Drayton Mayrant Simons Jr., "Garibaldi's Promise," *New York Times*, June 15, 1915, 10.

15. Quoted in Luigi Botta, *Figli, non tornate! (1915–1918): Lettere agli emigrati nel Nord America* (Turin: Aragno, 2016), 112–13.

16. Quoted in Botta, *Figli, non tornate!*, 142–44.

17. Linda Reeder, "The Making of the Italian Husband in Nineteenth-Century Italy," in *Italian Sexualities Uncovered*, ed. Valeria P. Babini, Chiara Beccalossi, and Lucy Riall (New York: Palgrave, 2015), 272–90.

18. Silvio Péllico, "Discorso dei doveri degli uomini," in *Opere complete di Silvio Pellico da Saluzzo*, vol. 1 (Lipsia: Ernesto Fleischer, 1834), vi.

19. Giuseppe Levi, *Autobiografia di un padre di famiglia* (Florence: Le Monnier, 1868), 99.

20. Alfredo Niceforo, *L'Italia barbara contemporanea: Studi ed appunti* (Milan: Remo Sandron, 1898), 247–48. On the psychological differences between the northerners and southerners see Alfredo Niceforo, *Italiani del nord e italiani del sud* (Turin: Bocca, 1901), 116–24; M. Levi-Bianchini, "Amore e morte nelle psicologia calabrese," *Rivista d'Italia* 7, no. 2 (October 1904): 605. For a general discussion of race and modern Italy see Aliza S. Wong, *Race and the Nation in Liberal Italy, 1861–1911: Meridionalism, Empire, and Diaspora* (New York: Palgrave Macmillan, 2006).

21. For debates on the social effects of mass migration see Giovanbattista Raja, *Il fenomeno emigratorio siciliano con speciale rigurado al quinquennio 1902–1906* (Palermo: Tip. Imp. Affari Pubblicità, 1908), 54–72; Giuseppe Bruccoleri, *L'emigrazione siciliana: Caratteri ed effetti secondo le più recenti inchieste* (Rome: Coop. Tip. Manuzio, 1911), 19–20; Francesco Coletti, *Dell'emigrazione italiana* (Milan:

Ulrico Hoelpi, 1912), 253–54; Lorenzoni, *Inchiesta parlamentare sulle condizione dei contadini nelle province meridionali e nelle Sicilia*, vol. 6, *Sicilia*, vol. 1, pt. 5 (Rome: Tip. Naz. G. Bertero, 1910), 852. On the gender implications of the debates see Linda Reeder, *Widows in White: Migration and the Transformation of Rural Italian Women, Sicily, 1880–1920* (Toronto: University of Toronto Press, 2003).

22. Choate, *Emigrant Nation*.

23. Giovanni Lorenzoni, *Inchiesta parlamentare sulle condizioni dei contadini nelle province meridionali e nella Sicilia, Sicilia*, vol. 1, *Relazione del delegato tecnico*, vol. 6 (Rome, 1910), 861.

24. Choate, *Emigrant Nation*.

25. *Rivista coloniale organo dell'Istituto coloniale italiano* (Rome: Unione coop. editrice, 1912), 200–201.

26. Gino Charles Speranza and Florence Colgate Speranza, *The Diary of Gino Speranza, Italy, 1915–1919*, vol. 1 (New York: Columbia University Press, 1941). Also see "La prova del fuoco," *Il Carroccio* 3 (March 1916): 1.

27. Choate, *Emigrant Nation*, 226–27.

28. The digital image of Arru's diary is available on *L'Espresso*'s Great War exhibit (http://espresso.repubblica.it/grandeguerra/index.php?page=estratto&id=44). For the complete text see Giovanni Arru, *Diari*, Fondazione Archivio Diaristico Nazionale, Pieve Santo Stefano.

29. Giovanna Procacci, *Soldati e prigionieri italiani nella Grande guerra: Con una raccolta di lettere inedite* (Rome: Editori Riuniti, 1993), 439. For a comparison with the reaction of the Italian community in Argentina, see María Inés Tato, "Italianitá d'oltremare: La comunità italiana di Buenos Aires e la Guerra," in *Fronti interni: Esperienze di guerra lontano dalla guerra*, ed. Andrea Scartabellati, Matteo Ermacora, and Felicita Ratti (Naples: Edizione Scientifiche Italiane, 2014), 213–26.

30. United States, Department of State, "Luis Costaggini to Hon. Robert Lansing, State Department, Letter, March 27, 1917, file 865.2225/5," *Records of the Department of State Relating to Internal Affairs of Italy, 1910–1929*, RG 59, Film 6:10.

31. The ways in which family members, in particular women, responded to the fractured landscapes by issuing emotional appeals to the state to help them find or care for their families appears in María Bjerg's chapter in this volume on bigamy in Argentina during an era of mass migration. Migrant women in Argentina appealed to state officials in the search for their migrant husbands. It is also evident in Sonia Cancian's chapter on the emotional impact of World War II in Italy.

32. United States, Department of State, "Provvidenza Cutrufelli to the Secretary of State," Letter, June 14, 1918, file 865.2222/13, *Records of the Department of State Relating to Internal Affairs of Italy, 1910–1929*, RG 59, Film 6:10. Consulate records Italy–US, 1914–1922, Letter to the Secretary of State, New York, NY, June 14, 1918.

33. Wilcox, *Morale and the Italian Army*, 173.

34. "Il più grande emigrato che accorre sotto la bandiera," *Il Carroccio* 1, no. 5 (June 1915): 2.

35. Agostino De Biasi, "La voce dei padri ci chiama," *Il Carroccio* 1, no. 5 (June 1915): 5–7

36. Agostino De Biasi, "Il nazionalismo e americanizzazione," *Il Carroccio* 6, no. 5 (May 1920): 435–42.

37. Emilio Gentile, *Il culto del littorio: La sacralizzazione della politica nell'Italia fascista* (Rome: Laterza, 1993); Emilio Gentile, *La grande Italia: Il mito della nazione nel XX secolo* (Rome: Laterza, 2006).

CHAPTER 8

Maintaining Relationships and Creating Epistolary Personae

(Not) Articulating Emotions in the Letters of a Viennese Family of the Mid-Twentieth Century

SUZANNE M. SINKE

When the Nazis took over Austria in March 1938, the ensuing dictatorship rapidly upended many lives. This chapter studies the mid-twentieth-century letters of one Viennese family who found themselves classified as Jewish and increasingly in danger as anti-Semitic regulations multiplied. As it was for many other Jewish families, escape meant a protracted search for visas to countries around the world, and the dispersal of individual family members to distant locations, not knowing when and if they could reunite. Organizing escape required correspondence, but correspondence also became the primary form of communication and the bedrock of emotional community.[1] In this tumultuous era, the exiled family members wrote letters in order to maintain relationships.[2] If uncertainty, fear, and anger lurked behind the words, letter writers sought to reassure one another, to express care and love, to offer a modicum of normality, and this meant foregrounding specific roles through epistolary personae. Articulating the language of love often meant withholding, expressing only certain kinds of emotions and sharing only certain kinds of information. The choices of which things to share reflected the writers' individual personalities, but also accepted ideas regarding particular kinds of relationships, and broader social understandings of generational roles, gendered behavior, and mental health, understandings built on the cosmopolitan world and psychoanalytic models of mid-twentieth-century Vienna.

To explore epistolary personae of this era I dig deep into the Hine Collection from Florida State University's Institute of World War II and the Human Experience. It contains thousands of letters from multiple family members and several friends, and provides a particularly useful example of how people demonstrated love through silences.[3] The letter collection originates with Giulia Hine, who was just entering adolescence as the Nazi edicts totally upended her bourgeois and slightly bohemian (but still Catholic) life. Giulia and her family members sought refuge in many different locations, from Kenya to Switzerland to England to the United States. A few of the writers remained in Austria. One prominent correspondent perished in a concentration camp. Dictatorial and later wartime censorship (seen in ominous swastika stamps on the envelopes) contributed to the mix of silences; fear of causing emotional trauma fostered many more; and the desire to maintain generational and gendered roles undergirded others. By cross-referencing information between correspondents in multiple types of relationships as well as contextualizing them with further sources on this family, we can uncover the epistolary personae the writers chose for particular settings.

In addition, the Hine Collection documents the difference age and the changing circumstances of wartime made. Though some writers conducted business, arranged for money transfers, provided affidavits of support and the like,[4] one of the most striking characteristics of the correspondence is the emotional support community it fostered, while nonetheless acknowledging the literal and figurative distance separating correspondents.[5] This chapter examines the epistolary personae that several writers created, maintained, and manipulated, and it demonstrates some of the strategies correspondents adopted to cope with their situations, in particular the emotions they expressed and some that they repressed, at least in certain exchanges.

Chronologically, the letters fall after the fin de siècle era Berlin described by Tyler Carrington elsewhere in this book, though they share a cultural connection to psychological models, developed even more over time in the Viennese context. Further, at times they pick up on the "emotional revolution" of romantic relationships James Hammerton describes for a slightly later time period in Britain, though he also noted foreshadows of the revolution for some individuals in the 1920s. The two primary adult women in the Hine Collection, Giulia's mother and aunt, demonstrated a particularly independent female model from the early twentieth century, even more so than that in Mirjam Milharčič Hladnik's Slovenian case.

These Hine Collection writers embraced the gendered and generational roles that tied them to one another in particular constellations. Letters followed the expectations of familial and friendship patterns as well as broader cultural standards.[6] Persecution and migration forced reformations of class, religious, and gender identities. Letters provide important insights into those personal transformations and tragedies and how the writers adjusted epistolary personae in light of them for particular audiences. The adjustment included holding back information and emotions for a variety of reasons, some explained in other materials in the collection. Some of the silences echo the personal avoidance described by David Gerber in a book chapter devoted to epistolary masquerades.[7] Moreover, the silences in the letters demonstrate what Joanna Bourke described as "emotion-work" of sorting people into categories of social hierarchy.[8] In this vein, writers chose whether to mention the dangers they faced, the disappointments they endured, and the pain they suffered. They articulated—or silenced—love and loss, the everyday and the extraordinary, at least in part according to their status in relation to the recipient.

Historians differ in evaluating wartime correspondence. Martha Hanna described the veracity of letters from French soldiers on the front to spouses at home during World War I. In her estimation "intimate correspondence offered in their daily letters the consolation and commiseration that made endurance possible."[9] In contrast, Judy Barrett Litoff noted how US couples during World War II often obscured the unpleasant in their correspondence.[10] This appears more often the case in the Hine Collection. In this, it offers similarities to the self-censorship described by Ann Goldberg in her study of one family under Nazi and Stalinist rule. Goldberg noted extensive use of silences and coded language to convey information between family members, in significant part due to the fear of censorship.[11] Censorship stamps did not need to be present on the envelopes for people to worry about the content. We can speculate that when the general news of dictatorship and war entered a negative spiral, one that hints of the Holocaust exacerbated, the perceived need to underscore positive information increased. For those remaining under Nazi control, calling out the dangers could serve as motivation for family members elsewhere to intensify rescue efforts. Yet if the correspondents could not assist, then the sharing of pain might cause emotional pain to a loved one reading the letter. For those already outside dictatorial control, avoiding too much attention to the loss of a way of life, family roles, and a homeland could serve important psychological purposes—love demonstrated through silence.

Unlike the letters that appeared in newspapers, or the writings that less-affluent migrants of the nineteenth century sent, the epistolary exchange embodied in the Hine Collection generally did not assume a public audience. At times, the writers anticipated censorship, but they were as likely to self-censor due to nonpolitical motives. The standard epistolary ethics of a mid-twentieth-century letter appear, with greetings and thanks for the previous correspondence and sometimes a specific theme such as a birthday greeting.[12] Writers in the Hine family possessed solid literacy skills and a conception of emotional life based on psychological models, meaning they could and did write detailed descriptions of their feelings at times. Beyond the expected epistolary forms, writers made it clear what they would or would not share with certain individuals or categories of people. Unlike letters of earlier times, these writers also depended on telegrams and phone conversations in some situations. Within the letters the authors did create and sustain personae, as David Gerber has suggested elsewhere, but the recipients also expected as well as feared omissions.[13] The circumstances of dictatorship and wartime exacerbated this tendency: focusing on information that would connect, rather than separate the correspondents, in a time when circumstances imposed barriers to continuing ties.[14] These family members shifted their self-perceptions over time. Age, experience, and the exigencies of living apart shaped new identities, ones the authors then embraced into the epistolary personae they shared with their correspondents.[15]

The correspondents in the Hine Collection embraced the gendered and generational roles that tied them to one another in particular constellations, sustaining an emotional community. We might speculate that writing about emotion was less likely to catch the eye of a state censor, but the Hine Collection exemplifies how writers themselves could and did impose limits on which emotions to share. To demonstrate in a bit more depth how the writers created epistolary personae I divide my coverage into three categories of relationships: lovers or former lovers, siblings, and cross-generational family members.

Lovers

Maria Hasterlik won the love of many men in her life. She sought a divorce from her first husband after they had one child. Her second husband died under circumstances that hinted at suicide. By the late 1920s she engaged in a romantic relationship with a man who at times anticipated marrying her and with whom she would carry out an emotionally intimate correspondence for most of the rest of her life. During the late 1930s she grew closer to another man and eventually married him, though her connection to her former lover remained.

Nearly four hundred letters in this collection are part of an exchange between Maria Hasterlik, or Mia, and her sometimes lover Heinrich Kopetz, or Boni, the nickname that appears most often in the letters. Once the war started, Boni stayed in Vienna and wrote to Mia using coded language about people and places, but open expressions of love. So in his letter of November 2, 1939, he mentions family members in Switzerland and the United States, two families who immigrated to different parts of South America, another person headed for London, and several friends in Vienna looking for a way out. Boni never included the full names, relying instead on first names, nicknames, or initials. He omitted place names as well, getting around it by using other information the two shared. In fact he admonished Mia for putting a woman's return address on the letter, making it clear he did not "need it." Perhaps this reflected fear, perhaps anger, perhaps frustration. His ongoing efforts to guide Mia faced the barriers of time, distance, and censorship. Other letters reveal that in the past Boni often entertained Mia and others, and the letters indicate he tried to maintain that role, through storytelling or jokes, which sometimes appeared in his letters. He employed a pet phrase known to the family to negate one part of his letter. "I heard from Oser that the food supply is plentiful and strictly distributed and no black market could exist, especially lately." When Giulia translated the phrase she knew "Oser" was an expression her family used indicating "ha, ha, this is not true."[16] Boni utilized the code in other letters as well, typically to make the Nazi regime sound good (and thus bad to those who understood the inside joke) and perhaps to assuage censors who might read it.

Boni expected to give Mia advice and assistance and for her to follow his instructions, as she had to some degree in the past. He had begun that practice at least a decade before, in 1929, when Mia went into drug rehabilitation and he had to communicate with her via correspondence for a time.[17] He expressed emotions openly in those earlier letters: "You must know with what fervor I wish you every success, and how elated I am when you manage to do that. Then it enables me to be successful as well. The large distance has not and will never be able to divide us." Or later: "My dearest Maunzerl, again my best wishes for you. Do everything I asked you and be kissed a thousand times by your old Minz. In the night from the 3rd to the 4th I dreamt of you so lifelike."[18] Not just these two, but Mia's family more generally used cat-related nicknames for one another in letters across the years. They also regularly reported on the antics of the family pets in Vienna. Finding links to the past and any semblance of normality in an otherwise abnormal time became a key part of Boni's letters leading up to the war.

Once Mia left Austria for good in the summer of 1939, Boni recognized the possible implications of the distance and the likelihood that it would shift the relationship. "Goodbye my dear, if we might not be able to write to each other for some time, please always think of your Boni, who never, even for a minute, will forget these eventful last 12 years which we lived through together. And who never stopped loving you and always finds you delightful again and again, during every minute of all these times in happy and sad situations, even when we squabbled. Stay always as you are, be good—you promised me. Am already very curious of all that you will recount to me when we see each other again."[19] The promise, as Giulia recounted in her translator's notes, was to remain drug-free. The letters continued regularly for a time. Boni helped organize a boisterous group that celebrated Mia's fortieth birthday in Vienna the following spring despite her absence.[20] Joy at a birthday celebration, care for a lover, humor in the everyday, disapproval of actions he could not control: many emotions Boni expressed followed the patterns already in place in their relationship. Yet other elements of the letters made the dictatorial context more evident—including the need for self-censorship.

That Mia accepted Boni's guidance and love appeared in her letter to him in late 1940, once she had made it to the United States: "Of one thing you can be assured: you are always with me. With all my actions, decisions, attitudes etc. etc. I always think: Would Boni approve if he saw me now? And this is exactly what makes me sad. Never before had I followed your spirit as diligently as in this last year. But I did it without being allowed to hear your beloved voice which is so good, encouraging, praising and a little proud of its own product when it says: 'My Maunz'! My life—good or bad, is lived for you. You are the one who is my invisible leader, who gives me strength."[21]

Boni continually had to negotiate this leadership from afar without irritating Mia—not an easy task. In a letter from November 1939 he expressed his concern: "I have to again implore you not to write uncle K's [Robert Koritschoner, in Kansas City] address to me. How often do I have to tell you this. You know that I don't usually belong to the overly cautious, and you have to believe me if I tell you that this could have the most disagreeable consequences for me."[22] He later apologized for this reprimand, and then went on to mention how much he missed her social skills while attending a recent holiday gathering: "During the party I talked with Ellen about you and constantly thought with what graciousness your parties had proceeded and how such things can become a nightmare if not led by a charming hostess such as you, who can smooth rough spots."[23] He wrote at different times of his dreams of her and of how much he missed her. Boni, however, remained in Vienna.

Though wartime meant letters went astray or took unfathomable amounts of time to arrive via third parties, the two continued to write. In November of 1941, Boni expressed his love again: "More and more do I feel that you are the only person with whom I could live and who I miss so terribly as no other. I cannot find anything or anybody who would mean even a fraction as much to me as you do."[24] Once the United States entered the war the letters increasingly did not get through, despite their trying various methods of third-country transmission. By the end of the war Mia had no idea if Boni was alive. Then came the news—yes, and he still loved her. So she replied—in English, ostensibly so it would get through the censors: "My Darling, my beloved darling." Later she continued in this vein: "Darling, I can only say it time and again I much I love your [sic]. Nothing has changed in my feelings toward you, in the contrary. I feel like being born again, since I know you alive and still thinking on me."[25] This came with a touch of irony, for Mia had married another Viennese refugee in the meantime. Despite this, which she explained in another letter to Boni, the two continued to send intimate letters for years beyond the war.

The letters of Mia's soon-to-be third husband, Thomas Heller, share some of the characteristics of those from her former lover, but in general they tended to include fewer references to emotion and more attention to other topics. Thomas appeared to ground this in a conscious choice: "My depressing letters are giving you a false picture of my situation. One should never write such letters in the first place because by the time they arrive they are not valid any longer: so I am really very well. Business is up and running again and my savings book is already showing more totals than when you left. But I am also working like a fiend and enjoying my work tremendously." The attention to business and requests for her assistance in making his business function appeared as a regular part of his correspondence, and so too did requests to contact other people and share news. Yet Thomas also included some romantic language: "No matter how long it will take I will remain true to you and keep on believing in a happy reunion. For Heaven's sake stay healthy and I too will take care of myself. We belong together and will stay together no matter what the future might bring. With my most tender love and fervent kisses your Thomas."[26] Writing from London, Thomas still could face censorship, but fewer challenges to postal transmission than a letter crossing into National Socialist territory.

Both Thomas and Boni wrote in loving language. Both tended to request that Mia do things. Both sought to keep Mia from falling into depression by stressing how she must be good and stay healthy. The circumstances of when they wrote meant they had more or less to say about emotion. Boni, in Vienna, faced increasing difficulty reporting on the political or economic activities around him. His hinted warnings about censorship made this clear. Under the eyes of a censor, it appeared that love was an acceptable topic of conversation. The letters from Thomas came from his period as a refugee in London when Mia was in the United States, hence he may have assumed less censorship. He also had the assurance of having shared Mia's bed while she was still living at her father's home in Vienna and in London prior to her departure. They corresponded until he made it to the United States as well. Both men provided Mia with directions for how to live, acting as a dominant partner in the heterosexual relationship. Each used an epistolary persona to promote a potential role as future husband.[27]

Sisters

Two sets of sisters corresponded in this collection as well. Mia wrote to her sister Auguste, or Gusti. Mia's daughters Suzanne and Giulia wrote to each other. Both sets of sisters tended to share news of their romantic interests with one another, information that typically did not appear in as much depth if at all in letters to others. Mia, shortly after getting her one daughter off to Switzerland, and while preparing to send the other daughter to Kenya in 1939, wrote her older sister Gusti: "I heard that during my absence they had arrested Thomas. Of course he was completely innocent. I need not tell you how sad I am because you know how much I am attached to him, in spite of some proofs to the contrary. In addition, I feel so sorry for him, he has stomach ulcers and: how many people never get out of jail!"[28]

While in London, Mia wrote to her sister of an admirer who was taking her out to dinner and buying her presents. Mia went along with this relationship to some extent, reporting she traded the expensive perfume he gave her for something more useful. "It is rather questionable whether this matter could furnish some income. Mostly because I don't cotton to him and also because he is pretty crazy—as usual. Have I ever been admired by a normal man?"[29] The same letter reported on what she cooked for dinner for Thomas, with whom she was living. With her sister, Mia shared candid comparisons of the men in her life: "I was immensely spoiled by Boni in this sense, he always entertained me and was the sweetest being and now I miss him so. Thomas is a good man, I can't really complain, but he is boring and always grumpy. I am already used to it, still it is out of place here where one is constantly in danger of sliding into sadness. Sometimes I get furious at him and could practically kill him—but then I realize how glad I am to have him, not being all alone, which would be even worse."[30] Mia's report came in part as a response to romantic news that Gusti shared. This we learn from Mia's letter: "Who is Lawatsch—you lucky one! I haven't fallen in love for the longest time and believe such emotions not to be possible anymore."[31] That Mia could report going out with one man, living with another, and pining for another, with the sense that she could no longer fall in love, hinted at her own volatility, but also to the wartime circumstances that upended her life. At the same time, the fact that Mia reported on her romantic life to her sister allowed for one element of apparent continuity in their relationship, a way to reinforce sibling bonding. She did not share this level of information about the men in her life with most others.

After Mia arrived in the United States, she entered into a sexual relationship with Peter Heller, Thomas's younger brother. Reporting on her "expectations," Mia explained: "I haven't told Peter anything about Thomas, but it's possible that [Thomas] would want to marry me. I think I would rather not—it would be too horrible for the three of us.—Only, it is very hard for me to give up Peter. Nobody else is as entertaining and maybe as hurtful, or rather was, in the past—not any longer. He is an abundant source of real fun, a bit à la Boni who is, of course, unrivalled but 'often copied'—one has to add."[32] Mia went on to note how she was trying to rid the apartment of evidence of her intimate relationship with Peter.

Though the sisters sometimes requested the other give specific people information, they nonetheless gave the impression that they meant the letters for the recipient alone. Two exceptions stood out: first, when the authors anticipated state censorship; second, when family members shared a home (as Mia did with her father for a time before fleeing Austria). In the latter case, family writers assumed others would read the letter itself. In various epistles the sisters requested their information remain confidential. The plea not to share information at least with certain people appeared several times in regards to their father, who did his own share of withholding information. Mia writes: "This is a private letter to you without Papi's knowledge. Please answer me to c/o Ellen Christiansen here because I don't want Papi to read the answer."[33] Ellen also shared the house, but as Mia's former housemate, not a family member, Mia could assume that a letter would not automatically also go to her father. Likewise Mia, writing in September 1939, asked her sister *not* to share news of her situation with her daughter Suzanne because "Suserl is still too young to hear certain things."[34] The authors engaged in a significant amount of self-censorship and convincing others to withhold information.[35] The combination of distrust and fear regarding a family member the two clearly cherished, expressed both in text and in action, demonstrated a form of communication that might easily have been conversational in other circumstances. Distance required a different means. Through selective silence to certain individuals, the sisters could demonstrate their love for those individuals. They could sustain their emotional community and retain epistolary personae that fit their sibling roles.

Mia's two daughters, Suzanne and Giulia, wrote to one another as well, specifically after Giulia made the trek to Switzerland. Their banter about romantic relationships and experiences developed as Suzanne married, then divorced, and then remarried in Kenya. Prior to leaving Europe, Suzanne wrote her sister sharing news of her husband-to-be and her interest in having a little more fun prior to marriage. On the boat on the way to Africa, she shared how she had fallen for one of the officers: "Pupperl [little doll], aren't you missing my talks about love, or do you have to listen to the same stuff from your new sister? To return to the officer, I resolved to not let him kiss me, I have to always remember that I have a fiancé. Robert is writing glowing love letters, isn't this a riot? He writes, he is crazily in love with me. What will happen when he actually gets to know me?"[36] Letters between the two sisters dwindled as Suzanne faced domestic abuse and chose not to report about it at first, in part because around the same time Giulia developed polio and was fighting for her life and then recovery. As conditions improved, Suzanne shared news of her escape from domestic "tyranny" in depth once she had a stable new setting. It took longer for Giulia to regain her health and resume correspondence. Both sisters, in other words, withheld important but extremely troubling information from one other for a time.

By the latter years of the war, Giulia entered her late teens, and had things to report to her sister as well. Suzanne continued to promote sharing news of one's love life: "I am so glad, Pupperl, that health-wise you are doing fine and are still improving. I am not surprised over your escapades, after all, none of us have been nuns. Especially not your older sister. Enjoy as much as you can, one is only young once. I am the one who understands you the best and am so glad that we are in contact again, our break in correspondence was long enough."[37] How much Giulia shared remains uncertain, for none of the surviving letters even mention the romantic friendship Giulia shared with Sister Luise, a staff member at the convalescent home where Giulia made much of her recovery from polio. Giulia's diary notes how she unburdened her heart about her family and struggles as well as her dreams to this slightly older confidante, and how she presented Sister Luise with the ring she had received from Suzanne.[38]

In addition to the regular news and the more detailed reports on some romances, the sisters Suzanne and Giulia also tried to bond over their generational status. Suzanne noted her reluctance to consider going to the United States: "In Mutti's view—everything should be less important as long as we are together. But on the other hand, we have to think of our future."[39] That attitude, which Giulia shared to some degree, led to a rather uncomfortable reunion for Giulia in the postwar period.

At least in the surviving letters, both sets of sisters, Mia and Gusti, Suzanne and Giulia, tried to maintain a degree of intimacy, a level of sharing about their romantic lives and generational fears that did not appear in the same form in other letters. The unusual circumstances that prompted them all to write created an even greater than normal need for emotional stability, but one that letters alone could not sustain. Strains in the relationship grew over time. Mia and Gusti, once on the same continent and for a time the same city, retained a greater lore of shared childhood compared to Suzanne and Giulia. The war, thus, created a rather stark break as Suzanne and Giulia faced some of their greatest life transitions and challenges geographically apart from family and with limited emotional support from family at least for the most crucial crises of this era. Gusti helped sponsor Mia into the United States and served as a financial and emotional support for her sister, listening to her horror stories from the Blitz in London, her fears for her daughter, and her distress at the war more generally. This also guided her role as aunt to the younger generation.

Older and Younger Generations

The letters across generations took on slightly different contours, with obvious recourse to hierarchy at times. Gusti's letter to niece Giulia made this abundantly clear when the aunt prohibited Giulia from writing to her mother about having polio: "It is very very difficult for me to write you this letter. . . . Unfortunately I must ask you for this sacrifice to not receive any letters from Mutti [Mama] regarding your illness until we here can tell her about it at the same time as we can tell her about your complete recovery. Otherwise your poor mother will go completely crazy from pain and longing and from desperation that she won't be able to see you." She ended, "Mutti is desperately yearning for news from you and I can't think of any more excuses every day why there is no mail from you. But there can't be a word about your being sick in this letter, just some schmoosen and dear and sweet so that she knows that you too are thinking of her a lot."[40] Gusti wrote about the ban to other family members as well, but getting Giulia to go along with it required a strong will. In her diary, Giulia expressed her pain at this enforced silence, but stay silent she did. The expectation of care across generations also went in the other direction. For example, Suzanne wrote to her Aunt Gusti "Please console my Maunz whenever she gets depressed as she so often had been in Vienna."[41]

Mia and Gusti's father, Paul, made a point of not sharing certain news with his daughters. He did, however write very regularly to those who emigrated, at least until the war interrupted options.[42] Before Mia left Austria, she wrote to Gusti about Paul's new love, as well as about his streetcar accident, both of which he downplayed or omitted from his epistles.[43] When daughter Gusti wrote of trying to get an affidavit of support that would allow him to emigrate, he was a bit dismissive: "They will surely leave the old folks alone. If not, then not and I will leave."[44] Shortly afterward he underscored his disagreement with his daughter about timing: "Things are very complicated, and you know that we have our hands full with Susi's trip so how can we think of our own problems, especially when there is no rush—except in your imagination."[45] For months he put off the decision. His letters barely hint at the increasing anti-Semitic measures going into place in Vienna. He also feared that his daughter was not forthcoming about her life and news she received from others: "Sometimes I think you know much more but want to protect me which would not be very wise."[46]

According to Boni, who also got to read the letters, Paul had good reason to assume the letters left out some things: "Haven't had a personal letter from you in ages. From a letter to Papi I learned that you liked the beach on the Atlantic. Your letters to Papi are always tinted in rosy hues, therefore I put more value on the ones to me. It is a little like Karl Tsch . . . The agreeable things to the right, the disagreeable things to the left."[47] So father protected daughters by not sharing the evils of life around him, and daughters focused on the positive so as to support him emotionally as well as entice him to emigrate.

One element of the epistolary personae people created was gender identity.[48] For Paul, Giulia's grandfather and a retired physician, increasing Nazi persecution robbed him of his home, his income, and various other markers of status. In this, the regime sought to destroy not just his economic, but his gendered social status. The elite version of masculinity he had lived crumbled in practice. The letters to his daughters and granddaughter, however, rarely hint at this. Instead, they continued to exude confidence and strength. Though his correspondents wrote in increasingly panicked terms of his need to leave, and offered assistance in this process, he demurred. He continued to present a competent and positive version of himself, though his letters over time hinted it might be impossible to continue life as he knew it. In the end, he waited too long to leave. The Nazis shipped him to a concentration camp.

Conclusion

Gusti and Mia had to take on leadership roles for the family, organizing migration and earning money. Mia clearly felt uncomfortable in this role and sought out men to assist her. Her marriage to Thomas appeared as much a means to gain a more stable income, and then be able to petition for Giulia to join them, as a romantic choice. Likewise, Suzanne and Giulia appeared to rely to a significant degree on others to take charge at this point in their lives. In Kenya, Suzanne replaced one man with another in quick succession after her arranged marriage fell apart, even before the divorce was final. Giulia struggled to find herself in a foster family with others sending her hither and yon.

In their letters, the Hine family members sought to sustain emotional bonds through difficult circumstances. The community of letters they fostered continued to some degree, but it also suffered and crumbled in some cases. Paul died in Theresienstadt. Giulia joined her mother in the United States after the war only to soon move out, in part a reflection of the personality she developed in the years when they were apart. Suzanne eventually returned to Austria, sometimes hinting that the family had somehow abandoned her in Africa. The letters chronicle a part of that process of shifting identity, the shaping of new personae on paper, and the emotional expression and repression that those entailed. They exemplify how individuals enforced norms of emotional expression within their small segment of an emotional community.

NOTES

1. Barbara H. Rosenwein explores the concept of emotional community, particularly for much earlier eras, in "Worrying about Emotions in History," *American Historical Review* 107, no. 3 (2002): 821–45. She explores the variability of emotions across time and group in her *Generations of Feelings: A History of Emotions, 600–1700* (Cambridge: Cambridge University Press, 2016).

2. David A. Gerber emphasizes how British migrants used correspondence to maintain a sense of self and personal connections in *Authors of Their Lives: The Personal Correspondence of British Immigrants to North America in the Nineteenth Century* (New York: New York University Press, 2006). See also the chapters by

Borges and Milharčič Hladnik in this anthology for letters maintaining and negotiating family ties among Portuguese and Slovenian migrants.

3. Institute on World War II and the Human Experience, Hine Collection, Florida State University. A note on translations: Giulia Koritschoner Hine translated most of the letters and added commentary from her family knowledge. She also looked over the translations of a family friend who assisted on a few other translations. As a native speaker of German and an acquired native speaker of English (with decades of residence in the United States), Hine represented an ideal translator. I consulted the originals and translations and changed a word or two very rarely, only when it would assist readability in current American English. Hine's translations fall closer to the literary than literal end of a translation spectrum, reflecting the level of vocabulary and ability to articulate thoughts of the writers in the originals, but still remaining close to the information conveyed.

4. The literature on refugees from the Nazis is voluminous. For some examples of policy positions see Louise London, *Whitehall and the Jews, 1933–1948: British Immigration Policy, Jewish Refugees, and the Holocaust* (Cambridge: Cambridge University Press, 2000); Guido Koller, "Entscheidungen über Leben und Tod: Die behördliche Praxis in der schweizerischen Flüchtlingspolitik während des Zweiten Weltkrieges" [Decisions about Life and Death: Official Praxis of Swiss Refugee Policy during World War II], *Studien und Quellen, Veröffentlichungen des Schweizerischen Bundesarchivs* 22 (1996): 17–104.

5. A further exploration of how letters functioned to provide emotional support appears in Suzanne M. Sinke, *Dutch Immigrant Women in the United States, 1880–1920* (Urbana: University of Illinois Press, 2002), particularly chap. 4, "In Sickness and in Death."

6. On this see Jan Assmann and John Czaplicka, "Collective Memory and Cultural Identity," *New German Critique* 65 (1995): 125–33; see also Babs Boter and Suzanne M. Sinke, "Adjusting and Fulfilling Masculine Roles: The Epistolary Persona in Dutch Transatlantic Letters, 1870s–1920s," *History of the Family* 21, no. 3 (2016): 337–49.

7. David A. Gerber, "Epistolary Masquerades: Acts of Deceiving and Withholding in Immigrant Letters," in *Letters across Borders: The Epistolary Practices of International Migrants*, ed. Bruce S. Elliott, David A. Gerber, and Suzanne M. Sinke (New York: Palgrave Macmillan, 2006), 141–57.

8. Joanna Bourke, "Fear and Anxiety: Writing about Emotion in Modern History," *History Workshop Journal*, no. 55 (2003): 124.

9. Martha Hanna, "A Republic of Letters: The Epistolary Tradition in France during World War I," *American Historical Review* 108, no. 5 (2003): 1361.

10. For example Judy Barrett Litoff and David C. Smith, "Since You Went Away: The World War II Letters of Barbara Wooddall Taylor," *Women's Studies* 17, no. 3/4 (1990): 263.

11. Ann Goldberg, "Reading and Writing across the Borders of Dictatorship:

Self-Censorship and Emigrant Experience in Nazi and Stalinist Europe," in *Letters across Borders*, ed. Elliot, Gerber, and Sinke, 158–72.

12. David A. Gerber, "Epistolary Ethics: Personal Correspondence and the Culture of Emigration in the Nineteenth Century," *Journal of American Ethnic History* 19, no. 4 (2000): 3–23.

13. Gerber, *Authors of Their Lives*.

14. This mirrors some of the insights of Barbara Henkes in "Letter-Writing and the Construction of a Transnational Family: A Private Correspondence between the Netherlands and Germany, 1920–1949," in *Life Writing Matters in Europe*, ed. Marijke Huisman, Anneke Ribberink, Monica Soeting, and Alfred Hornung (Heidelberg, Ger.: Universitätsverlag, 2012), 177–92.

15. This goes along with the discussions of shifting personae in Vera Sheridan, "Letters of Love and Loss in a Time of Revolution," *History of the Family* 19, no. 2 (2014): 260–71; and in Kathleen DeHaan, "Negotiating the Transnational Moment: Immigrant Letters as Performance of a Diasporic Identity," *National Identities* 12, no. 2 (2010): 107–31.

16. Letter 1503, Heinrich Kopetz to Maria Koritschoner, Vienna to London, November 2, 1939, Hine Collection. Kopetz letters translated by Richard Bloedon.

17. See for example letter 1311, Heinrich Kopetz to Maria Koritschoner, Vienna to Attersee, Austria, September 1929, Hine Collection.

18. Letter 1501, September 23, 1939, Heinrich Kopetz to Maria Kortischoner, Vienna to London, Hine Collection.

19. Letter 1398, August 26, 1939, Heinrich Kopetz to Maria Kortischoner, Vienna to Schaffhausen, Switzerland, Hine Collection.

20. Letter 0569, Heinrich Kopetz to Maria Kortischoner, Vienna to London, May 16, 1940, Hine Collection.

21. Letter 3792, Maria Koritschoner to Heinrich Kopetz, Dayton, OH, to Vienna, November 1940, Hine Collection.

22. Letter 1508, Heinrich Kopetz to Maria Koritschoner, Vienna to London, November 13, 1939, Hine Collection.

23. Letter 1510, Heinrich Kopetz to Maria Koritschoner, Vienna to London, December 25, 1939, Hine Collection.

24. Letter 0295, Heinrich Kopetz to Maria Koritschoner, Vienna to New York, November 1941, Hine Collection.

25. Letter 0253, Maria Koritschoner to Heinrich Kopetz, New York to Vienna, December 8, 1945, Hine Collection.

26. Letter 0166, Thomas Heller to Maria Koritschoner, London to Dayton, OH, December 14, 1940, Hine Collection.

27. Compare Boter and Sinke, "Adjusting and Fulfilling Masculine Roles," 337–49.

28. Letter 3113, Maria Koritschoner to Auguste von Doderer, Vienna to New York, NY, January 24, 1939, Hine Collection.

29. Letter 3095, Maria Koritschoner to Auguste von Doderer, London to New York, NY, September 13, 1939, Hine Collection.

30. Letter 3607, Maria Koritschoner to Auguste von Doderer, London to St. Paul, MN, February 5, 1940, Hine Collection.

31. Letter 3607, Maria Koritschoner to Auguste von Doderer, London to St. Paul, MN, February 5, 1940, Hine Collection.

32. Letter 5045, Maria Koritschoner to Auguste von Doderer, New York to Cascade, MD, July 4?, 1943, Hine Collection.

33. Letter 3071, Maria Koritschoner to Auguste von Doderer, Vienna to New York, NY, April 23, 1939, Hine Collection.

34. Letter 3095, Maria Koritschoner to Auguste von Doderer, London to New York, NY, September 13, 1939, Hine Collection.

35. On this element of the letter collection see Suzanne M. Sinke, "A Family Dispersed: Maintaining Unexpected Transnational Ties—American Ethnicity and Austrian Exile," *Studia Migracyjne-Przeglad Polonijny* 41, no. 4 (2015): 143–57.

36. Letter 0004, Suzanne Weiss to Giulia Koritschoner, Massaua, SS *Sabbia*, to Schaffhausen, Switzerland, March 22, 1939, Hine Collection.

37. Letter 0356, Suzanne (Weiss) Wolff to Giulia Koritschoner, Nairobi, Kenya, to Schaffhausen, Switzerland, July 18, 1944, Hine Collection.

38. Interview, Edith (Koritschoner) Cory-King with Giulia Hine, June 1998, Dorset, England, Cassette 6, Hine Collection; Giulia Koritschoner Diary, December 14, 1942, Hine Collection.

39. Letter 1240, Suzanne (Weiss) Wolff to Giulia Koritschoner, Nairobi, Kenya, to Schaffhausen, Switzerland, July 4, 1945, Hine Collection.

40. Letter 0550, Auguste von Doderer to Giulia Koritschoner, New York, NY, to Schaffhausen, Switzerland, September 10, 1941, Hine Collection.

41. Letter 0119, Suzanne (Weiss) Seemann to Auguste von Doderer, Kenya to New York, NY, November 23, 1940, Hine Collection.

42. In a letter from May 1939 he notes that he has written to his daughter twenty-eight times in the previous six months. Letter 3085, Paul Hasterlik to Auguste von Doderer, Vienna to New York, NY, May 15, 1939, Hine Collection.

43. Sinke, "A Family Dispersed."

44. Letter 3110, Paul Hasterlik to Auguste von Doderer, Vienna to New York, NY, February 2, 1939, Hine Collection.

45. Letter, Paul Hasterlik to Auguste von Doderer, Vienna to New York, NY, February 11, 1939, Hine Collection.

46. Letter 3625, Paul Hasterlik to Auguste von Doderer, Vienna to Dayton, OH, September 24, 1940, Hine Collection.

47. Letter 1513, Heinrich Kopetz to Maria Koritschoner, Vienna to New York, NY, August 13, 1941, Hine Collection.

48. Compare Sonia Cancian, "The Language of Gender in Lovers' Correspondence, 1946–1949," *Gender and History* 24, no. 3 (2012): 755–65.

CHAPTER 9

Love at the Threshold of War and Migration

A War Orphan's Story

SONIA CANCIAN

"*Io qui non voglio stare!*" ("I don't want to stay here!") Maria recalls tearfully screaming behind the dark looming door that stood between her and her mother, Rosina.[1] With the lock firmly latched, the school director ushered Maria away from the hall's entrance. As Maria was led to the main room, her mother and aunt walked back to the station of Nocera Umbra (province of Perugia), where they boarded the next train on their journey home to San Giovanni in Galdo and Matrice, two neighboring towns on the outskirts of Campobasso. It was 1946, barely a year since the end of the Second World War, and food and shelter were still hard to find. Local officials and the village priest urged women like Rosina to benefit from a state provision for children whose fathers or mothers had perished in the war.[2] Yes, mother and daughter would be apart, but Rosina would not need to worry about her daughter starving or being led astray. In boarding schools or colleges, she would be cared for, educated, and taught fundamental life skills.[3] Maria would be offered a life that her mother never had, one she could not afford. Still, there would need to be that separation. What did this and subsequent separations signify—materially and emotionally—for both mother and daughter?

This is a story about multiple migrations in the life of a young girl born in the throes of the Second World War. Maria's narrative of migration is distinguished by filial separation exacerbated by three critical events of disruption over the course of her life. These events were the death of her father in the Second World War, her exile within her homeland to educational institutions away from home, and her transatlantic migration with the objective of joining her mother and her new family. In 1946, as the dust settled from the ravages and destruction of the war in her mother's agro-village, San Giovanni in Galdo, six-year-old Maria embarked on a trajectory that was the beginning of multiple migration journeys. Migration, in this case, was experienced both internally and transnationally, beginning with Maria's journey from her home to two boarding schools for orphans in central Italy, and several years later, in southern Italy, followed by her mother's migration to Montreal, Canada, to her own migration to Canada, and finally to her mother's subsequent return to Italy two years later.[4]

Love and separation form the nexus of analysis, and as part of love's emotional constellation, silence, guilt, nostalgia, regret for what might have been, loss, and resilience run through the narrative of this story.[5] By attending to love and its unravelling between a mother and her orphaned daughter, I untangle the tensions that distant love engendered among intimate family relations. Memory and emotions are interwoven in the analysis, undergirding one another in my mother's telling of her story.[6] With the passage of time, the memories and emotions reevoked during our conversations in recent years have become more vivid, and, at times, more raw. Similar to the "boundary crossings," collected and analyzed by Michelle Mouton and Helena Pohlandt-McCormick, in the historical narratives recounted in this essay, it is not only "the exceptionally vivid story that emerges, but also one that shows all the signs of the wounded individual who, in the remembering and the telling, surrenders the injury and anguish of the self that are part of the individual experience of the historical."[7] Memory is critical here. As Luisa Passerini notes, memory has not only recorded the repercussions, that is, the suffering due to inequalities, frustrations endured or witnessed, but memory also speaks from today. It looks through the lens of a constructed identity, a political identity in the old sense of the term: a citizenship conferred and not easily canceled; a shared identity, participation in the creation of one's life and in the invention of a culture.[8] Within this constructed and political identity, there is resilience and agency in my mother's narrative; resilience and agency in her struggle, resilience and agency in her determination to recollect the past and acknowledge it, and finally, to get the story right, to reflect on it, voice it, and engage in a meaning-making process. By bringing these vivid memories to the surface, she acknowledges her individuality and her subjectivity.[9] In retelling her narrative, my mother situates her memories in dialog with an emotional community that shares similar memories of narratives of loss and separation in wider social and historical contexts.[10]

In this essay, I employ an auto/biographical, personal narratives approach to explore questions about love and distance emerging in the contexts of war and migration in the mid-twentieth century, a period which James Hammerton refers to as "postwar migration of austerity."[11] I show how the notion of love served as a driver of migration and as a legitimizer of separation between mother and daughter in dialog with several chapters in this volume whose focus is also on transnational love in other intimate relationships.[12] At the root of my interest in this family story is both the story itself and the powerful lifelong effects of multiple separations of mother and daughter at a critical moment in a young woman's life. Moreover, the ways in which my mother tells the story—and the emotional impulses that have underpinned our meetings when she speaks about her past—have urged me to untangle her story and examine it more closely. In their concise discussion of personal narratives resulting in forms of knowledge that are accessible through intersubjective or dialogic processes, Mary Jo Maynes, Jennifer Pierce, and Barbara Laslett suggest, "Sometimes this knowledge emerges only because of the emotional responses triggered by the interview situation itself."[13] Interviewers' emotional responses can reveal themselves more intensely when the researcher and participant share strong, filial bonds, as in this case. Emotions and memory are interwoven, as memory frequently narrates through emotions and tones of actual experience.[14] It is in the vivid tones of Maria's retelling that we encounter the emotional depth of loss that she experienced as both a war orphan and as a young woman.[15] A single story examined through a personal narrative lens offers important "insights from the point of view of narrators whose stories emerge from their lived experiences over time and in particular social, cultural, and historical settings."[16] In this case, the story of my mother and my grandmother affords a gaze into the interior, affective worlds "from the inside out" through the emotional memories that each has constructed and passed on to me.[17]

* * *

In 1946, over 13 million children in Europe had lost one or both parents in the Second World War.[18] Italy was the country with the third highest number of orphaned and displaced children.[19] The astounding figure of 390,000 known orphans or homeless children reported in 1945 was only a fraction of the total numbers. By 1945, the state had reportedly placed 115,000 orphans in 693 institutions, 250,000 were supported by private charitable organizations, and 25,000 were divided among 114 institutions, with over 40,000 in Milan, 65,000 in Rome, and 75,000 in Naples.[20] In late 1945, most of Italy's cities and much of its countryside were in a state of chaos. The country appeared to be on its knees. Those who survived the war endeavored to come to terms with ration cards, evacuations, bombed-out and gutted houses, forced cohabitation arrangements, rationed electricity, reduced mobility and transportation, and a dearth of wage work.[21] Added to the devastation was the loss of over 444,500 Italians killed in the war, one-third civilians. In the mid-twentieth century, UNESCO and other humanitarian organizations and psychologists like Anna Freud and Dorothy Burlingham documented their concern over the effects of war and violence on children. Freud and Burlingham noted in 1945, "All of the improvements in the child's life may dwindle down to nothing when weighed against the fact that it has to leave the family to get them."[22] Family separation was understood as a catastrophe, and as one historian writes, "Children were widely identified as the main victims of the conflict and the creation of new welfare states by democratic regimes seemed to imply an urgent necessity to create solid networks of support for the young victims of atrocities committed by the older generation."[23] In response, an estimated 200,000 children were provided assistance in roughly three thousand institutions.[24] Among these children were orphans, which each *comune* (municipality) and each of its villages listed "in order of need." This list was then submitted to the National Association for War Orphans (Opera Nazionale per gli Orfani di Guerra) in order for the very neediest to receive distributions of clothing and other necessities.[25] In Arezzo, and throughout the peninsula, temporary care for war orphans was sought in boarding schools and orphanages, a centuries-old practice.[26]

Rosina's Story

My grandmother, Maria Domenica, also known as Rosina Moscato, was born in October 1922 in San Giovanni in Galdo, Campobasso. She was the third of six children born into a family of *contadini* (farm laborers). On September 2, 1939, Rosina married my grandfather, Domenico Lemmo (born in August 1920) originally from the neighboring town of Matrice, roughly five kilometers from her hometown. In the first year, the couple lived in Matrice where their daughter Maria was born. The following year, they moved to Rosina's hometown where they rented a small two-room dwelling in the oldest quarter of San Giovanni in Galdo, known as "il morrutto." In January 1942, Domenico was drafted in the Italian military. He returned home on leave in November

1942 for sixty days, rejoined his company on January 27, 1943, and entered the battlefield on February 10, 1943. In September 1943, he was captured by the German army. Following Italy's signing of the armistice with the Allies on September 8, 1943, he became one of the approximately 600,000 Italian soldiers, known as Italian Military Internees (IMIs), transported by train to Germany where they were catapulted into a harsh life of forced labor.[27] Italians employed in the Third Reich were "regarded as traitors to the cause by the German authorities and civilians who supervised them."[28] This attitude led to the proliferation of poor working conditions and rough treatment of Italian prisoners of war, which contributed to higher levels of mortality among Italians than other captured nationals.[29]

When asked if she remembers anything about receiving the news of her father's death, my mother looks back: "Do you think they would have advised her with me there? I was just a child. I do remember the time when my mother learned of the news. I don't know how it is that I remember it, but I do. I recall relatives of my father from Matrice visiting my mother, bringing some food and comfort in the light of the family's loss. After that, nothing."[30] With the war over, Rosina found herself widowed at twenty-five years of age, with no property, no savings, no education, no allowance, and no assistance. In the words of my mother, "she had no support, not even from her mother who had her other children still at home needing attention and care. Her mother was very poor, and she could not think of helping her now-married daughter who had left home."[31] Rosina and Maria seemed fated to live a life mired in poverty, much like the millions of other Italians who had survived the war and now faced an unending struggle.[32]

There was no time to grieve. Unprepared to provide for herself and her child, Rosina turned to the tireless agricultural work she had known as a child. In addition to working the land for other families, she, like the other women in the village, "did various forms of manufacturing, making items like soap for direct consumption by the household."[33] In exchange for the irregular, precarious, and physical labor of endless hours in the fields, she received "the little that there was to survive for the evening. There was no money; they bartered instead; they would give her some cheese with supper, and a small part of the crops."[34] In the meantime, Maria was sent to *l'asilo* (preschool) where lunch consisted of nothing more than a small slice of bread dabbed with olive oil and a piece of fruit. There was little to live on, and while Rosina made every effort to provide for her daughter, the future appeared steeped in misery. Rosina rejected this future for Maria, and upon the advice of the local elite, she agreed to send Maria to Nocera Umbra.

In 1951, Rosina remarried, and made plans to leave the village. The groom was a widowed fellow villager, a tailor who had immigrated to Montreal in 1949. My mother recalls, "she told me when she came to visit me at the orphanage, and she asked me, 'Maria, are you happy that I am getting remarried?' adding, 'I am going to *America*, and after that, you will come too.' Here was the dream, it all felt so positive, and so she left."[35] Rosina married her second husband by proxy in 1951 and made plans to join him in Montreal.[36] A few days prior to her mother's departure, Maria returned home for a brief visit. The day Rosina left was dramatic, my mother recalls, "I remember that morning as though it were today. In this tiny home of hers, all the chairs were placed against the walls for the visitors my mother was expecting to pay her a visit and wish her farewell. Because at the time, when someone left for America, it was like saying goodbye forever, at the time there was no possibility of knowing whether she would ever return. One was leaving and that was that. The people started to fill the home to bid her farewell."[37] Shortly after her arrival in Montreal, Rosina found work in the garment industry, working five days per week, in addition to cooking, cleaning, and tending to her husband. In March 1954, Maria joined her mother in Montreal.

Maria's Story

The only child of Rosina Moscato and Domenico Lemmo, Maria was born in September 1940 in Matrice, Campobasso. Most of her memories date back to a life lived apart from her parents, in the *collegi* [boarding schools] in Nocera Umbra and Chianciano and the orphanage closer to home in Montagano, Campobasso. Maria vividly recalls her first separation: "When you are there, you cry today, you cry tomorrow, but after a few days you stop crying. The teachers were nice to me. And then, you begin to forget while you are playing with the other girls. Do you know what I mean? That was the way life was at that age, and it felt fine. I missed nothing, absolutely nothing. I was fine, I had everything and more. I remember it as though it were today."[38] Maria remembers being very excited about a parcel arriving at the school for her. It was from her mother. She could hardly contain her happiness: homemade cookies and a ball to play with. In Nocera Umbra, Maria attended first grade with girls of her age group. Once in Chianciano in 1948–49, she was placed in a *collegio* with over 200 girls attending. Maria remembers comparing her visits home to her mother and grandmother over the summer months with the family visits of her classmates. As Maria watched her classmates and their families rejoicing in their reunion on the school grounds, she became aware

FIGURE 9.1. Maria in Chianciano, 1948–49. Author's family archive.

of what a "real" family constituted. An ideal of family and maternal love was emerging for Maria, one that was defined by affective openness, care and presence, one that was not so worn down by the plights of poverty and hardship.[39]

The first separation from her mother in 1946 informed Maria's understanding of family and love. Recalling the day her mother left for Canada: "And, there I was. As friends and family said goodbye, they cried. And I observed the scene, I don't remember if I was terribly sad, or not, or if I was trying to make myself feel sad, there was this too, inside of me I was feeling a little sad and a little indifferent. Then, she left on that same day. My uncle, her brother, took the responsibility of accompanying me back to the orphanage," in Montagano.[40] Maria did not openly mourn or rebel against staying: "In the end I convinced myself to stay there. I didn't miss my mother so much, whether I lived in *America* or in the town, it was the same for me, I didn't live with her."[41] Having lived, by then, over six years separated from her mother in residential institutions, Maria had learned to make do without the material and affective support of her mother.

Despite her loneliness, my mother recalls that in Chianciano, "I missed no one, it seems to me, I was doing well. I had everything and more, even in Chianciano. Christmas and the day of *La Befana* were important holidays for us, even New Year's Day. What joyful memories I have of my time in Chianciano. We were all friends. They would put on small plays and many other activities in which I participated. Classes were held there."[42] Immersed in a life in two Catholic boarding schools run by lay teachers and administrators, Maria aspired to become a teacher herself. The dream changed once she was transferred to a local Catholic orphanage in Montagano, run by the nuns of San Giovanni Battista, and a mere 10 kilometers from her grandmother's home in Matrice. There, Maria was required to comply with the rigorous rules of a Catholic orphanage administered and taught by nuns. Once she had completed the five years of mandatory schooling, she had to focus on mastering needle trade skills: "They taught you to sew, embroider, all things that could be useful to me in the future. In some ways, it was a way out for the future. In training to become a seamstress, well, you became a seamstress."[43] Maria showed talent and speed in needlework, and the nuns soon relieved her of domestic chores to focus on needlework projects for the benefit of the orphanage. While the nuns encouraged Maria to think about joining the order, Maria yearned to join her mother in Canada.

Three years later, on March 18, 1954, Maria boarded the S.S. *Vulcania* in Naples and set sail for Montreal. When asked about the day of her departure, Maria describes the enthusiastic good wishes tinged with envy of her teachers, nuns, and fellow classmates, the fuss made over her new clothes (white gloves, jacket and skirt of elegant style, and a fashionable hat) made for the journey, the emotional farewell to her paternal grandmother and aunt. She also felt excitement and renewed optimism around reuniting with her mother: "the desire to come to *America*, to join my mother, you see, inside of me I had this mother whom I wanted to live with, that's it, even knowing that I was a stranger to my mother, she was still my mother."[44] Following ten harrowing days of nausea at sea, Maria finally arrived in Montreal where her mother and stepfather awaited to greet her at Windsor Station. From the first night, however, it was clear that reality was a far cry from her dreams. With acute awareness, thirteen-year-old Maria perceived tensions at home among her stepfather's children, her stepfather, her mother, and herself.

Her mother and stepfather lived in tight, dark quarters shared with her stepfather's children who neglected to show any sign of affection or familial tie as a welcoming gesture toward her. Long working hours in the factories, indifference and neglect, coupled with the challenges of recent migration and the "forced" living arrangements of two families brought together under one roof strained relations between family members. Disagreements inevitably flared. It became clear to Maria that "it was not a family who was together. There were many tensions, since we were two families living under the same roof, that is, he [stepfather] and his daughters lived with us, but they did everything on their own, including cooking and eating in turns. They prepared their meals first, then, my mother cooked for us. It wasn't healthy. The family was not together."[45] While reflecting on the family's habit of eating separately—evidenced from her first night in Montreal—she recalls: "They had a nice bedroom of their own. Mine was comprised of a small cot sectioned off by a curtain in my mother's and stepfather's bedroom.... There, I felt like Cinderella."[46] Daily life underscored the feelings of loneliness, injustice, and neglect that she experienced at her new family's home. Maria watched her older stepsisters jealously guard for themselves the special foods and groceries that her stepfather denied to her and her mother on the premise that they were too costly. Her stepsisters rarely included her in family visits or Saturday shopping trips along St. Hubert Street, a popular shopping avenue at the time. Her stepfather insisted on keeping a tight hold on the household purse-strings and rarely gave Maria or her mother spending money. Anything that was deemed an extra expense was denied. Her stepfather's stinginess was one reason why Maria decided to quit school after successfully passing the year: "During the summer I started working with my aunt . . . When September arrives, I don't go to school, what can you expect, I had a stepfather who would not give me not even 5 cents to buy a notebook. His point was that since his daughters had not continued school beyond grade five, why should I . . . And I said to myself, 'It's better if I go to work.' Who knows why I did [not] insist, my mother did not insist, maybe because she did not want to argue with him, no one insisted, and I went to work."[47]

We cannot tell from Rosina's silence if she wanted Maria to stay in school or not, but we can glean insight into the family dynamics. Maria's suggestion that her mother did not advocate for her schooling because she did not want to fight with her husband is reasonable. First, given the tensions at home, to raise this issue on Maria's behalf would have added a point of conflict between husband and wife and their respective children. Second, despite being well aware of her husband's grip on the household purse-strings, she (along with her daughter) was his dependent and probably did not feel comfortable making the request, and by extension, in asserting herself and her priorities toward her daughter. While mother and daughter sustained a silence on these memories over the course of their lives, their emotional ties remained strong. Yet, the impact on Maria has been significant. Even after sixty years, whenever Maria speaks about her first years in Montreal, a look of hurt and sadness is gleaned from her eyes.

In 1956, two years after Maria's arrival in Montreal, her mother and stepfather decided to return to Italy. After Rosina's miscarriage, other health concerns erupted, and Rosina's husband, Biasile, grew increasingly frustrated with the financial burden of healthcare costs. As my mother recalls, in an effort to curb such costs, Rosina and her husband decided to return to Italy. By then, the dream of family unification had deteriorated for sixteen-year-old Maria who ultimately decided to remain in Montreal rather than follow her mother and stepfather to their village in Italy. Maria was offered a choice: "Stay in Canada with your uncle or return to Italy with your mother and stepfather."[48] Maria decided to stay. On whether she worried about missing her mother, Maria looks back, "It seems I didn't more than usual, otherwise, I too would have left. To me it felt more like a continued adventure, an adventure to come to Canada, an adventure in going to live with my uncle, that is, her brother— it was all part of an adventure." But when her parents returned home to San Giovanni in Galdo, Maria felt the loss: "Of the tiny home that they had [in Montreal], nothing remained. Even that was gone."[49]

Life in Montreal was not easy. Her uncle demanded she pay eleven dollars per week for her room and board, leaving very little for herself from the weekly stipend of twenty dollars. And then, there was the sadness and melancholy

FIGURE 9.2. Maria and her family in Montreal, 1974. Author's family archive.

that accompanied her mother's departure, which was reinforced by the kin networks of her friends and acquaintances. My mother recalls, for instance, that one of her friends "had left her mother and her father in Italy, but she had a brother and sister in Montreal, and as a result lived with her married brother. She had support from her family even though she would confide in me that she wasn't happy, but I had no one. Staying with my uncle was like being on my own. I was lonely, very lonely."[50] At seventeen, she moved out and went to live with another Italian family on a room-and-board arrangement.

In 1958, my mother met my father, "and in one year, we married and I was very happy, he was handsome, we loved each other, and I wanted to have my own home ... I wanted some security, something I had never had before." No sooner had she married my father in July 1959, that family and motherhood became a priority for Maria: "My dream was to have a family," she echoes in our conversations, "I very much wanted children so that I could give them the affection they needed, because I needed it from them too. So, I give to you, you give to me ... I had always dreamed of having a brother and sister ..., since my father died very young. So, my family had to be a family. I can say that at least I have had the gratification of having children, I brought them up, and I do not feel alone like I once did when I had no one. I now have a real family. My greatest achievement is my family."[51] Four years following their wedding on July 25, 1959, Maria was expecting the first of their four children. Her dream was to have a large family, "I brought you up. Your father worked, always, always, and I stayed at home as a wife and mother."[52]

My mother's story is fraught with complex issues around family, affection, ties, separation, maternal love, war, loss, and orphanhood. The story's complexity is further amplified by my own emotional tensions and ties as a transnational mother and daughter reflecting on questions of love, separation, and migration. In the remainder of this essay, I focus on the narratives of love in separation and distance in my mother's story.

"I Did It for Her"

For as long as I can remember, my grandmother abstained from discussing in detail her initial separation from my mother when she first brought her to the boarding school in Nocera Umbra in 1946. In my memory, it was especially in her final years that she declared that she did it in the best interest of my mother. She did it, she would iterate, to ensure a better future for my mother. "L'ho fatto per lei" ("I did it for her"), she declared whenever the discussion came up. What lies behind my grandmother's five-word justification? What other emotions emerged then and later from her decision to accompany her six-year-old daughter to a boarding school, a full day's travel away, at a time when destitution, poverty, and woe accompanied her loneliness and devastation? My own vivid recollections of my grandmother's response urge me to associate the meaning of her words to notions of selflessness, altruism, sacrifice, all part of a maternal love that she had learned coming of age during Italy's Fascist years combined with the long-held view of Italian collegi and orphanages. In return, Rosina hoped and expected that her child would reciprocate with respect and affection. The state and the emotional community around Rosina had encouraged her to let her child go for the sake of her child without the burden of guilt. My grandmother came of age in the twenty years of Fascist rule. It would not be unreasonable for us to assume that she—like myriad other women—would have been influenced by the policies and ideologies espoused by the country's Fascist dictatorship.[53] As a member of the lower class, Rosina was among the countless women who, as Victoria De Grazia notes, were "the targets of specific fascist programs, the most reliant in their services and the most vulnerable to their overall impact."[54] In Rosina's and Maria's memories the act of sending her six-year-old daughter away was an act of love.[55] This choice is rationalized by my mother over a decade following my grandmother's passing: "My poor mother, maybe she gave me what she could, as much as I could give to her, and she gave me what she could give to me."[56] While the sorrow over the mother-daughter separation was significant, the relationship endured.

My mother's description of her story, as "it's a long story, a story that is like so, I have been a war orphan all my life, an orphan in everything, a real orphan," is significant. The phrase epitomizes the loss and sorrow she has felt for much of her life. It encompasses the absence of her father, a childhood away from her mother, and the overall lack of material and social support that accompanied living for years in a boarding school and an orphanage. The incremental separations and disruptions between mother and daughter engendered by intra-national and transnational migrations have had a lasting impact, even though the ties were negotiated over time and were restored. Still, regrets infuse my mother's narrative: "Perhaps the only regret, remorse that I have toward her is that even though she did not demonstrate affection toward me, I didn't either toward her, it was reciprocal. This is the way I was, I did everything for her, I loved her, but to embrace her and tell her how much I loved her, I don't think I ever told her."[57]

Deep-rooted loss and separations pointed to an intense desire to have a family she could call her own. In retrospect, my mother concludes: "I can say this, everything happened because I was a war orphan, because I didn't have a family to call my own, I never knew my father, I barely knew my mother, I had lived away from home, and worse of all, I have never felt affection, never, I have been an orphan all my life. If it weren't for all of you who give me immense gratification, I don't know . . . but even today when I think of it, my sorrow returns." Toward the end of one of our conversations, my mother summed up her experience with the words, "Today, now, I feel complete and happy, as a woman, a mother, and a grandmother of six grandchildren whom I adore."[58]

Concluding Remarks

Familial love and distant love are central to this narrative. As Ulrich Beck and Elizabeth Beck-Gernsheim suggest, "distant love is defined by geographical distance."[59] Although this definition of distant love is applied in the current global context in which virtual, instantaneous communications are normalized, the term provides a window on explicating the impact of love at a distance precipitated over seventy years earlier. The distant love experienced by a mother and her child today is described by Beck and Beck-Gernsheim as "the dilemma of a mother who abandons her own child out of love for it [he/she] in order to earn money abroad so as to pay for its [his/hers] food, healthcare, and education."[60] It refers also "to the situation of the children who have been left behind and who yearn for closeness, human warmth and security, and who miss their mother."[61] These dynamics of distant love—coupled with familial love, and emotions of loss, guilt, and abandonment—resonate within the narrative of love and separation examined in this chapter.

From the viewpoint of the history of emotions, Barbara Rosenwein's notion of emotional community provides a useful lens for examining the sociocultural context surrounding my grandmother.[62] This is especially the case when I consider my mother's recollection of her mother's silence with regard to her father's death in the Second World War. Rosina's silent response betrays a need to conform to an emotional community who required her to be stoic, work hard, support herself and her daughter while mourning the loss of her husband. Her separation from her daughter at a young age alludes, moreover, to Arlie Hochschild's notion of "managed heart" when the endemic poverty of the immediate postwar and her own grief and worries weighed her down as she undoubtedly struggled with her decision to send her daughter away to a boarding school in the interest of the child. Embedded in the notions of familial and distant love are emotions associated with loss, abandonment, guilt, regret, sadness, and disappointment. They are emotions that contributed to strains in family relations, and were likely exacerbated in contexts of long-distance migration.[63]

Despite the emotional strains induced by migration and distance, the bonds of love shared by Maria and her mother proved strong enough to endure, resisting any form of rupture. Underneath this love is Maria's lifelong struggle with abandonment and loss coupled with her resilience and agency in ensuring profound bonds of love with her children and her husband as well as her mother and half-brother. In this family's story, war and death juxtaposed by internal and transnational migration characterized the separation of a child from her parents. In this chapter, we learn how narratives of love are closely interwoven with war, mobility, and separation, themes examined in Linda Reeder's and Suzanne M. Sinke's chapters as well. Moreover, in conversation with many essays in this volume that analyze love, families, and migration, this essay affords insight into the affective long-term impact of war and migration on the children and adults who endured disruption and forms of trauma during and immediately after the Second World War.

NOTES

1. This chapter tells the story of my mother. It is a story I remember us both discussing since I was a little girl, around the kitchen table, usually just the two of us. There we are: I curiously asking about our family, my grandfather, my grandmother, and my step-grandfather, as I came to grips with a family story that was different from my friends'. Every time I explained that I had a step-grandfather, my friends would look at me awkwardly, awaiting some kind of explanation. While to them it was not a common story, to me it was my family's story, a story that I had learned to normalize, a story that exemplified some of the ways in which war and migration had unleashed their havoc onto my family. This essay exists because of my mother's agreement to share her story, and I am deeply grateful to her. I dedicate this chapter to my mother and to my late grandmother Rosina.

As someone who has lived in a transnational family, the emotions associated with distance and separation have weighed heavily on me. As my earlier work shows, to work through as a scholar what these emotions mean is to provide a critical, yet intimate understanding of the affective tensions that contract and expand in separation and migration. See, for instance, Sonia Cancian, *Families, Lovers, and Their Letters: Italian Postwar Migration to Canada* (Winnipeg: University of Manitoba Press, 2010). Access to the memories of emotions opens a window into examining more deeply an understanding of the emotions-narrative nexus in the telling and interpretation of our life stories in relationship to distance and separation. The emotions and their memories help us to create a narrative we can live with to make that distance bridgeable and to survive the separation. Throughout the writing and research, I have held conversations with my mother at her home in Montreal and Fort Lauderdale, sometimes in person, most times over the telephone and digital technologies, like Skype and WhatsApp while I was in Dubai and Berlin. In addition, a formal interview was held in Montreal in August 2016. The conversations and interview were held in Italian. All translations into English are mine.

2. While exact details on the criteria that determined the selection of my mother among the neediest of children in San Giovanni in Galdo in 1945–46 to be accepted in a *collegio* in Nocera Umbra and Chianciano remain to be uncovered, what we do know is that "Italy's children constituted one infinitely large, directly suffering category of postwar needy victims. . . . Each commune and each village within the

communes listed its orphans 'in order of need' to submit to the National Association for War Orphans [Opera Nazionale per gli Orfani di Guerra], as only the very neediest might receive distributions of clothing and other items." Victoria C. Belco, *War, Massacre, and Recovery in Central Italy, 1943–1948* (Toronto: University of Toronto Press, 2010), 143. As Giovanna Da Molin notes, in the eighteenth and nineteenth centuries, children who were starving or whose parents were unable to provide the means to support their children in their first years were placed in state-funded orphanages and boarding schools. Giovanna Da Molin, *Storia sociale dell'Italia moderna* (Brescia: Editrice Morcelliana, 2016), 192. For more on the historical practice of seeking temporary shelter and care for children in orphanages, foundling homes, and *collegi*, see also: Andrea Falcomer, "Gli 'orfani dei vivi': Madri e figli della guerra e della violenza nell'attività dell'Istituto San Filippo Neri (1918–1947)," *Deportate, esuli, profughe* 10 (2009): 76–93; David I. Kertzer, *Sacrificed for Honor: Italian Infant Abandonment and the Politics of Reproductive Control* (Boston: Beacon Press, 1993); David I. Kertzer, "The Lives of Foundlings in Nineteenth-Century Italy," in *Abandoned Children*, ed. Catherine Panter-Brick and Malcolm T. Smith (Cambridge: Cambridge University Press, 2000), 41–56; Nicoletta Roman, ed., *Orphans and Abandoned Children in European History: Sixteenth to Twentieth Centuries* (New York: Routledge, 2018); and Tara Zahra, *The Lost Children: Reconstructing Europe's Families after World War II* (Cambridge, MA: Harvard University Press, 2011).

3. This point echoes a traditional view on the opportunities that orphanages and boarding schools offered in nineteenth-century Italy. Da Molin writes, "Whoever was admitted in an orphanage, an institute that assumed the role of both mother and father, was [viewed] as fortunate in his/her misfortune, because often, the legitimate yet poor children of the same age who remained at home, did not benefit from the same level of nutrition, education, training, and vocational outlet." Da Molin, *Storia sociale dell'Italia moderna*, 210.

4. This migration includes Maria's mobilization from her hometown, San Giovanni in Galdo, to the *collegi* in the *comune* of Nocera Umbra (Perugia) and Chianciano (Siena), and an orphanage in Montagano, Campobasso.

5. I am inspired by the work of scholars Luisa Passerini, Luisa Del Giudice, Vishanthie Sewpaul, and others who have been forthcoming in acknowledging the ways in which our personal lives and experiences shape our scholarly work. See, for example, Luisa Passerini, *Autobiography of a Generation: Italy, 1968*, trans. L. Erdberg (Middletown, CT: Wesleyan University Press, 1996); Luisa Del Giudice, ed., *On Second Thought: Learned Women Reflect on Profession, Community, and Purpose* (Salt Lake City: University of Utah Press, 2017); Vishanthie Sewpaul, "The Power of Biography: Shifting the Boundaries of Knowledge through Emancipatory Pedagogy and Critical Consciousness," *Social Work/Maatskaplike Werk* 42, no. 2 (2006): 101–16; and Christa Santina Wirth, *Memories of Belonging: Descendants of Italian Migrants to the United States, 1884–Present* (Leiden: Brill, 2015).

6. As noted by Maynes, Pierce, and Laslett, "Personal narrative analysis can never be disconnected from the analyst." Mary Jo Maynes, Jennifer L. Pierce, and Barbara Laslett, *Telling Stories: The Use of Personal Narratives in the Social Sciences and History* (Ithaca, NY: Cornell University Press, 2008), 100. The documenting of a historian's or ethnographer's positionality with regards to the individuals or groups they study or whose stories they collect illuminate and enrich their findings.

7. Michelle Mouton and Helena Pohlandt-McCormick, "Boundary Crossings: Oral History of Nazi Germany and Apartheid South Africa–A Comparative Perspective," *History Workshop Journal* 48, no. 1 (1999): 58.

8. Passerini, *Autobiography of a Generation*, 23.

9. Ute Frevert, "Defining Emotions: Concepts and Debates over Three Centuries," in *Emotional Lexicons: Continuity and Change in the Vocabulary of Feeling 1700–2000*, ed. Ute Frevert et al. (Oxford: Oxford University Press, 2014), 5.

10. Aleida Assmann and Sebastian Conrad, "Introduction," in *Memory in a Global Age: Discourses, Practices, and Trajectories*, ed. Assmann and Conrad (Basingstoke, UK: Palgrave Macmillan, 2010), 2.

11. A. James Hammerton, *Migrants of the British Diaspora since the 1960s: Stories from Modern Nomads* (Manchester: Manchester University Press, 2017), 7 and 27. See also Hammerton's chapter in this volume.

12. In this volume, see particularly the chapters by María Bjerg, Marcelo J. Borges, Mirjam Milharčič Hladnik, Suzanne M. Sinke, Margarita Dounia, and A. James Hammerton.

13. Maynes, Pierce, and Laslett, *Telling Stories*, 9.

14. Passerini, *Autobiography of a Generation*, 23.

15. While trauma is related to the experience of displacement and migration affecting both mother and daughter, in this essay my focus is on love, which is central to the narrative that Maria has constructed about her life story.

16. Maynes, Pierce, and Laslett, *Telling Stories*, 16.

17. Maynes, Pierce, and Laslett, *Telling Stories*, 16.

18. Zahra, *The Lost Children*, 6. The term orphan here refers to a child whose mother or father, or both parents have died. The definition of orphan is informed by the *UNESCO Report on the War-Handicapped Children*, which defines an orphan as a "not only a child who has lost his father and mother or one of them; it also covers a child who, for practical purposes, has no home, and for material or moral reasons, cannot receive from his parents the care to which he is entitled and who therefore must be looked after by society." Thérèse Brosse, *War-Handicapped Children: Report on the European Situation* ([Paris]: UNESCO, 1950), 58. This definition is in synchrony with the definition provided by the Italian state since 1917 as "the person, whose father, mother, or legal guardian has died serving the state at war" (*"colui, di cui il padre, o la madre esercitante la patria potestà o la tutela legale, sia morto in dipendenza dello stato di Guerra"*). *Gazzetta Ufficiale del Regno d'Italia*, no. 177, chap. 1, art. 2 (July 27, 1917).

19. Brosse, *War-Handicapped Children Report*, 24.

20. Brosse, *War-Handicapped Children Report*, 29.

21. Paul Ginsborg, *A History of Contemporary Italy: 1943–80* (London: Penguin, 1990); Luca Gorgolini, *L'Italia in movimento: Storia sociale degli anni Cinquanta* (Milan: Bruno Mondadori/Pearson Italia, 2013); Linda Reeder, *Italy in the Modern World: Society, Culture, and Identity* (London: Bloomsbury, 2019).

22. Freud and Burlingham, *War and Children*, cited in Zahra, *The Lost Children*, 18.

23. Stefania Bernini, *Family Life and Individual Welfare in Postwar Europe: Britain and Italy Compared* (New York: Palgrave Macmillan, 2007), 78.

24. Bernini, *Family Life and Individual Welfare*, 82. Originally cited in I. Pini, "Duecentomila bambini negli Istituti Italiani per l'Infanzia," Ministero dell'Interno, 2, March–April 1951, 6.

25. Belco, *War, Massacre, and Recovery in Central Italy*, 143. The precise names of the schools and orphanage that Maria attended from 1946 to 1954 have not yet been recovered. The description of the school and social activities bears a remarkable resemblance to the academic program in place in the Convitti scuola della Rinascita, a series of nine schools established in 1946 across northern Italy for young partisans and other children of the war to continue their studies that had been interrupted during the war. See specifically, Luciano Raimondi, *I convitti scuola della rinascita* (Milan: Aurora, 2016); and Fabio Pruneri, "The Convitti Scuola della Rinascita (The Boarding Schools of Rebirth): An Innovative Pedagogy for Democracy in Post-war Italy (1945–1955)," *Paedagogica Historica: International Journal of the History of Education* 52, no. 1–2 (2016): 188–200. Over the years, many of these orphanages and boarding schools were presumably converted into public schools or fell into disuse.

26. Belco, *War, Massacre, and Recovery*, 143.

27. S. P. MacKenzie, "The Treatment of Prisoners of War in World War II," *Journal of Modern History* 66, no. 3 (1994): 487–520; and Bob Moore, "Enforced Diaspora: The Fate of Italian Prisoners of War during the Second World War," *War in History* 22, no. 2 (2015): 174–90. An official report issued from the military district of Campobasso indicates that my grandfather died on September 5, 1945. The records also note that his death was officially recognized on April 3, 1947. It seems my grandmother was advised of his death before this date. My mother vividly remembers my grandmother telling her that he had died of illness in a prison camp with the priest by his side. Few other details were provided to my grandmother about his life and death in a German prison camp. More research is required on this score as I endeavor to make sense of this information.

28. Moore, "Enforced Diaspora," 186–87.

29. Moore notes that Italians employed in the Reich were "regarded as traitors to the cause by the German authorities and civilians who supervised them, and were

branded as 'Badoglio-Schweine,' an image that was reinforced by the idea that Italy had betrayed Germany twice—in 1915 as well as in 1943.... There was a tension between the need to feed the workers sufficiently to maximize their productivity and a desire to punish them for their betrayal." Moore, "Enforced Diaspora," 186–87.

30. Interview with Maria Lemmo, August 3, 2016.

31. Interview with Maria Lemmo, August 3, 2016.

32. The abject poverty and sense of neglect that Maria and Rosina felt in postwar Italy following the death of Maria's father in the Second World War remarkably resonates in other historical contexts in the twentieth century. For instance, Joy Damousi notes that in Australia in the aftermath of the Second World War, "The legacy of the war for the children, as well as for their mother, was in the grinding poverty many of them endured in a family without a male breadwinner." Joy Damousi, *The Labour of Loss: Mourning, Memory, and Wartime Bereavement in Australia* (Cambridge: Cambridge University Press, 1999), 145. See also Perry Wilson, *Women in Twentieth-Century Italy* (London: Palgrave Macmillan, 2010), 19.

33. Wilson, *Women in Twentieth-Century Italy*, 19.

34. Interview with Maria Lemmo, August 3, 2016.

35. Interview with Maria Lemmo, August 3, 2016.

36. Shortly after the Second World War ended, Italians began to emigrate abroad again in large numbers. They emigrated to countries like Canada, Australia, Argentina, Brazil, the United States, and other nations in Europe. Among the countries that welcomed Italian immigrants and their families, Canada introduced the Sponsorship Program in 1947. The program facilitated the immigration of roughly 440,000 Italians to Canada between 1949 and 1971. As Bruno Ramirez notes, of all the immigrant groups arriving in Canada during the period of the Sponsorship Program, Italians were the ones who benefitted the most. Bruno Ramirez, *The Italians in Canada* (Ottawa: Canadian Historical Society, 1989), 9. For a global history of Italian migration, see Donna R. Gabaccia, *Italy's Many Diasporas* (Seattle: University of Washington Press, 2000).

37. Interview with Maria Lemmo, August 3, 2016, and ongoing conversations.

38. Interview with Maria Lemmo, August 3, 2016, and ongoing conversations.

39. Notions similar to those expressed by Maria, including "what might have been," and the idealization of the family are also discussed in Heide Fehrenbach, "War Orphans and Postfascist Families: Kinship and Belonging after 1945," in *Histories of the Aftermath: The Legacies of the Second World War in Europe*, ed. Frank Biess and Robert G. Moeller (New York: Berghahn Books, 2010), 175–95.

40. Interview with Maria Lemmo, August 3, 2016, and ongoing conversations.

41. Interview with Maria Lemmo, August 3, 2016, and ongoing conversations.

42. Maria also completed the sacraments of Holy Communion and Confirmation in the boarding schools. Interview with Maria Lemmo, August 3, 2016, and ongoing conversations.

43. Interview with Maria Lemmo, August 3, 2016, and ongoing conversations.
44. Interview with Maria Lemmo, August 3, 2016.
45. Interview with Maria Lemmo, August 3, 2016.
46. Skype conversation with Maria Lemmo, February 8, 2018.
47. Interview with Maria Lemmo, August 3, 2016.
48. In October 1956, my grandmother and her second husband had a child of their own. Today, my mother shares close ties with her half-brother who immigrated to Montreal in the mid-1970s. Interview with Maria Lemmo, August 3, 2016.
49. Interview with Maria Lemmo, August 3, 2016, and ongoing conversations.
50. Interview with Maria Lemmo, August 3, 2016, and ongoing conversations.
51. Interview with Maria Lemmo, August 3, 2016, and ongoing conversations.
52. Interview with Maria Lemmo, August 3, 2016, and ongoing conversations.
53. Victoria De Grazia reports, "In the interest of promoting the race, the welfare of the mother was subordinated to that of the infant. Thus, while propaganda insisted that, by nature women were fulfilled only in motherhood, government social services cast doubt on whether women were naturally the best nurturers, especially when the women were unwed, delinquent, or simply impoverished." Victoria De Grazia, *How Fascism Ruled Women: Italy, 1922–1945* (Berkeley: University of California Press, 1992), 60. Part of the programs that contributed to making women feel inadequate and urged them to give up their children for a limited time was a full-scale mobilization of children to colonies in seaside, hill, or mountain resorts. De Grazia, *How Fascism Ruled Women*, 110–111. Whatever resistance families felt in complying with these initiatives, as De Grazia argues, "In the end, the unanimous voices of employers, social workers, medical experts, and political cadres must have overwhelmed familial reluctance." De Grazia, *How Fascism Ruled Women*, 111.
54. De Grazia, *How Fascism Ruled Women*, 55.
55. For more on choices immigrant women make within the structures they face, see Mary Patrice Erdmans, *The Grasinski Girls: The Choices They Had and the Choices They Made* (Athens: Ohio University Press, 2004).
56. Interview with Maria Lemmo, August 3, 2016.
57. Interview with Maria Lemmo, August 3, 2016.
58. Telephone conversation with Maria Lemmo, October 11, 2017.
59. Ulrich Beck and Elisabeth Beck-Gernsheim, *Distant Love: Personal Life in the Global Age*, trans. Rodney Livingstone (Cambridge: Polity Press, 2014), 45.
60. Beck and Beck-Gernsheim, *Distant Love* 51.
61. Beck and Beck-Gernsheim, *Distant Love*, 51.
62. Barbara H. Rosenwein, "Worrying about Emotions in History," *American Historical Review* 107, no. 3 (2002): 842.
63. See, for instance, A. James Hammerton and Alistair Thomson, *Ten Pound Poms: Australia's Invisible Migrants* (Manchester: Manchester University Press, 2005); Hammerton, *Migrants of the British Diaspora*; Loretta Baldassar and Donna R. Gabaccia, eds., *Intimacy and Italian Migration: Gender and Domestic Lives*

in a Mobile World (New York: Fordham University Press, 2011); Loretta Baldassar, "Transnational Families and Aged Care: The Mobility of Care and the Migrancy of Ageing," *Journal of Ethnic and Migration Studies* 33, no. 2 (2007): 275–97; and Loretta Baldassar, "Missing Kin and Longing to Be Together: Emotions and the Construction of Co-presence in Transnational Relationships," *Journal of Intercultural Studies* 29, no. 3 (2008): 247–66.

CHAPTER 10

Love, Sex, Feelings

Marriage and Transatlantic Migration in Postwar Germany

ALEXANDER FREUND

On October 15, 1948, the West German regional newspaper Westfälischer Kurier published the following advertisement in its classified section: "Correspondence for girls and women up to 60 years with Americans to initiate marriages in the USA. More information: International Marriage Initiation [Eheanbahnung] Agency Jutta Welke, Hamburg 20, Heilwigstrasse 14 (include stamped envelope)." Women from throughout postwar Germany wrote to the "marriage office" (Heiratsbüro) and bought American men's addresses for five German marks apiece. "I so much would like to have one from New York, because a girl from our village is already there," wrote Ferdinande K.[1]

Jutta Welke, a widow and orchard farmer who had fled from the Soviet occupation zone to the West in 1947 and opened her agency in November of that year, was more concerned about the expectations of the "heiratslustigen Amerikaner" (American men eager to get married). Men from Los Angeles and San Francisco wrote to Welke's friend and business partner, Baroness Edith Sieboldt, describing how they envisioned their future German wives. American men, Welke told her clients in a form letter, were looking for women who enjoyed keeping a house neat and clean. Sieboldt explained that the German candidates had to be "human beings of excellent character" and needed to conform to American men's image of German women: "The German woman is particularly esteemed here in America, because she is considered to be practical and modest as well as warm and natural." Next to character, physical features were important. One of Welke's German clients wrote of her pen pal, Mr. B.: "His greatest wish is to marry a woman with long, thick hair."[2] She did not say whether she fit this image, or what she thought of this male fantasy that reduced women to their bodily features.

For men and women on either side of the Atlantic, their correspondence about marriage and migration was their first international contact since the war in Europe had ended. It allows us a glimpse into the hopes, dreams, fantasies, desires, fears, anxieties, and intentions that German and American women and men associated with marriage and migration in the postwar world. Acting on a reemerging transatlantic marketplace of marriage and migration, the correspondents found their desires and needs obstructed by physical distance. In navigating the stormy seas of postwar migration politics and negotiating the fluid meanings of marriage and sexuality in postwar Germany, both sides mobilized and invested strong emotions in their struggles for a better life.

The German and American correspondents and mediating agents like Jutta Welke and Baroness Sieboldt, however, were not the only actors in the transatlantic emotion-migration-marriage triangle. The state, the church, and private organizations and individuals became heavily embroiled in negotiating the legal, moral, national, and emotional meanings of German women's postwar plans to migrate and marry. Male representatives of state and church agencies had concerns about single female migrants' "safety" that were deeply entrenched in sexualizing, racializing, and nationalistic discourses of previous decades and continued the social disciplining of women along traditional moralizing tracks. Such regulatory rhetoric created barriers and threatened livelihoods for women who wished to rebuild their lives after years of dictatorship, war, insecurity, and poverty.

This chapter argues that the sexualization of female migrants shaped how women in postwar Germany could envisage and use migration as a creative life strategy. Discourses about sexuality and migration were interlaced with an emotional rhetoric that state and church mobilized to control women, and that women employed to fight for autonomy. The chapter is based on documents of German government agencies and church organizations in the British and US zones of occupation that dealt with so-called scam agencies (Schwindelfirmen). These suspected Schwindelfirmen, alleged state and church officials, used advertising to con German women (and men) who wished to emigrate in the immediate postwar period—at a time when German migration was severely restricted.[3]

A Matter of Love?

Beyond sparse excerpts from letters, we do not know anything about Welke's female clients. We do know that they invested hope in the possibility of marrying an Amerikaner and immigrating to the United States. Many other things we do not know: their age or health; whether they were refugees from the East, had been evacuated from western German cities during the war, or had indeed never left their hometowns; whether they lived in a camp, a bomb-damaged apartment, or their intact family home; whether their background was urban or rural; whether they were widowed or divorced; whether they had ever been to the United States or even outside of Germany; we do not know their religious background, their class status, or their political convictions or affiliations. Did they have paid employment, perhaps even careers? We do not know anything about their life experiences or the emotions they had felt: had they experienced or committed violence? Had they loved? Had they hated? Had they feared for their lives or the lives of loved ones? Had they grieved for losses?

About a few other things we can make plausible assumptions. Quite likely, they lived in the same postwar conditions as millions of single women in occupied Germany. Hunger, poverty, displacement, and the breakdown of families may have shaped Welke's female clients' views of their future prospects in postwar Germany (which many saw as rather dim) as well as their high expectations of "Amerika." They may have also been influenced by Weimar images and postwar media reports about US culture and society. We can only speculate how much their courage to take this leap of faith that a transatlantic marriage to a foreigner entailed may have been influenced by the growing sense of independence German women found through "Girlkultur" and media images of the "New Woman" in Weimar Germany, through Nazi images of womanhood, or through the experience of having had to survive flight, bombing, rape, and starvation without the help of fathers, brothers, or husbands. The late 1940s saw "the hour of the woman," when German women took the initiative while their men—defeated soldiers—felt weak, tired, and emasculated. Encounters with GIs or enthusiastic reports from so-called war brides already in the United States may have further contributed ideas about Amerikaner. Most of the correspondents, however, wrote from locations in the British Zone of Occupation and likely had little or no contact with Americans. How the women thought and felt about their future lives may have also been shaped by the demographic shortage of men or, as it was portrayed by media and academics in the postwar period, the "surplus women." As historian Elizabeth Heinemann has shown, notions of marital status were in flux in the 1940s but nevertheless of great importance in postwar lives and politics. At the time Welke's clients were writing, West German society had not yet begun its efforts to restore traditional notions of family, but this does not tell us what Welke's clients thought and felt about the importance of getting married.[4]

Our knowledge of Welke's clients' thoughts and feelings is obscured by the problematic provenance of the letter collection, which is further complicated by "the question of audience."[5] The letters were shaped by two different audiences for two different occasions. First, the authors addressed Welke for specific purposes. Yet, we do not know how many clients Welke had and thus how representative the surviving letters were of this larger group. Second, later, Welke's lawyer selected letters to prove to authorities that she was not propagating emigration and impress upon them the idea that she was doing a good deed. Did Welke's lawyer select all correspondence or, perhaps more plausibly, only a particularly favorable sample? Did the lawyer embellish or even add to the letters? Further, the original letters were not in the archival file; we have only the transcribed excerpts, and we do not know whether they were transcribed by the lawyer or by agency officials.

Despite such limitations, we can say a few things about the women's writings. In their letters to Welke, the women thanked Welke, expressed joy, happiness, and anticipation, and indirectly confided their hopes and anxieties. They also used their letters to portray their relationships with the Amerikaner in explicitly nonsexual, nonmaterial, almost platonic and ethereal ways. Eleven of the twenty-seven women whose correspondence we have directly thanked Welke; nine spoke of happiness (Glück, glücklich, glückselig), and eight of their joy (Freude, froh). Eleven expressed their impatience, wishing to "get out" and "over there" as quickly as possible. While many of the women seemed to anticipate an eventual marriage to one of their pen pals, few spoke of love. Indirectly, however, several women implied a deep but nonphysical love had already formed on both sides of the Atlantic.

The women who thanked Welke and updated her on their transatlantic correspondence expressed their gratefulness, joy, and giddy anticipation in almost surprisingly similar ways. One may even speak of a fleeting "emotional community" that had crystalized around the promise of a better life via a marriage to an Amerikaner. An emotional community, writes Barbara H. Rosenwein, is a concept that helps researchers understand what members of such a community "define and assess as valuable or harmful to them (for it is about such things that people express emotions)."[6] What did the women consider valuable in their emotional relationships with their US pen pals? It seemed to be the immediacy and intensity with which their relationships had formed, as well as the pure, innocent, ethereal, nonsexual, nonbodily, nonmaterial quality of these relationships: the relationships were immediately "fulfilling" and directed by "fate." They were lifelong friendships with lifelong "acquaintances."

It seems that the women portrayed their relationships with the Americans as innocent and pure, more like platonic friendships and ethereal romances, certainly far removed from any carnal notions of sex that so disturbed German men about German women's liaisons with occupation soldiers.[7] Welke's clients portrayed their pen pals as courteous and gallant soulmates. A discussion of material benefits was almost completely absent. Through their use of language that implied an almost girlish, naïve giddiness, they portrayed themselves as similarly pure, innocent, nonsexual, and disembodied "girls" whose plans to go abroad and marry an American were completely guileless. This rhetoric seemed to be a direct response to Welke and Sieboldt's rhetoric that demanded "human beings of excellent character." Perhaps, the women's rhetoric was also shaped by what historian Frank Biess has described as an "emotional regime . . . of restraint and anti-intensity" that dominated postwar West German society and that constituted a response to the "emotional excesses of the wartime period."[8] There were other reasons for such a desexualized rhetoric: as we will see in the next section, women also responded to state and church agencies' attempts to derail their life strategies by linking their migration to social fears of immorality, sex, violence, and crime.

Yet, underneath the rhetorical positioning of their relationships as dignified and cultivated, the overwhelming emotion I sensed in this collection of letters was relief: relief that their lives were about to become better; relief that their hopes, wishes, and dreams were about to come true; relief that they might find happiness after almost having given up; relief that finally, their lives were back on track. Reading through the letters, I felt I could almost hear the women's collective sigh of relief that a heavy burden had been lifted from their shoulders. Yet, the relief I sensed in the women's letters was not one related to a possible feeling of Torschlusspanik or the sense that they were going to miss out on marriage because they were getting too old. The women did not seem to be afraid of not getting married. Rather, they seemed to be relieved that they were escaping a dead end, a bleak future, an unpromising society. In a few cases, as I will discuss in the final section, there was also Wanderlust.[9] The women's anticipation that migration (and perhaps marriage) promised some sort of relief was widely shared in postwar Germany.[10]

German women's immigration to the United States via marriage with US citizens in the postwar years was part of a longer history of international migration for the purpose of marriage and of international marriage for the purpose of migration. The US historian Suzanne M. Sinke argues that with its focus on labor migration, historians of transatlantic migrations in the long nineteenth century have neglected the role of reproduction and marriage within international migration. Marriage markets functioned like labor markets, providing opportunities for economically motivated people to negotiate both opportunities and obstacles in sending and receiving economies. Using examples of German women who immigrated to the United States in the nineteenth and early twentieth centuries, Sinke developed a matrix of diverse connections between marriage and migration, including migration as "a means to marry" and marriages as "a means to migrate": "A woman may want to marry and to migrate, but she may stress one more than the other. Further, these goals and means may change over time." Such strategies, wrote Sinke, were shaped by marriage opportunities and barriers in sending and receiving societies.[11]

Barriers to marriage in postwar Germany were particularly high for women. In 1946, there were seven million more women than men in Germany; despite the massive transformations of society, there continued to be great social pressures not to marry outside of one's class, religion, or region; a massive shortage of housing (as a result of wartime destruction) made it difficult for young people to start families; widespread poverty made it impossible for a great number of women to raise a dowry; poverty also discouraged men from proposing, because they felt they could not provide for a family. Furthermore, men and women had lost loved ones in the war and hesitated to commit to new emotional relationships. There were also concrete barriers: laws, a lack of transport, and insufficient funds restricted migration, closing off other regional or international marriage markets. Cultural and social norms and attitudes further restricted access to international marriage markets: some German women or their parents rejected foreign soldiers as potential spouses, either because they were seen as hated occupiers or they viewed Asian Red Army soldiers and African American GIs as racially unacceptable.[12] Marriage options and opportunities were greater for men than for women in postwar Germany, but for some German women, foreign occupation soldiers were more attractive than German men or at least an acceptable alternative; some parents even encouraged their daughters' relationships with occupation soldiers in order to access material goods, thus blurring the lines between voluntary and forced prostitution and rape.[13] In addition, German American and American men wished to marry German women for the reasons Welke and

Sieboldt cited, which opened further paths to migration. US immigration legislation privileged white women vis-à-vis Asian women as "war brides" while German men were largely shut out of this international marriage market.[14]

Considering the general desire to leave the war-torn continent and German women's particular difficulties in building livelihoods after the war, it is perhaps not surprising that the international marriage market played a prominent role in the transatlantic migration after 1945. About one million so-called war and occupation brides, who moved across the Atlantic and Pacific Oceans from 1946 to 1952, constituted a major migration stream.[15] For German women (and a few men), marriage to an American (or, in a few cases, a Canadian) was one among only a few paths to North America before those two countries once again began to admit German immigrants on a large scale in 1950. Until July 1, 1950, some 14,000 German women traveled to the United States under the War Brides Act (1945–52).[16]

Social norms and cultural values prescribed how men and women were to act on marriage markets. Women were to remain passive while men were active. This was particularly so in the context of reossifying traditional gender roles from the late 1940s onward. Single women seeking to emigrate had to contend with state and church agencies' attempts to control their mobility, by invoking social fears about female sexuality, morality, and security.

A Matter of Sex?

West German state and church agencies were deeply involved in the international postwar marriage market, whether skeptically observing, reluctantly facilitating, or actively obstructing German women's attempts to migrate. West German laws dating back to the 1890s, 1920s, and 1930s allowed state authorities to prosecute individuals and companies that actively promoted and facilitated emigration—even after the 1949 West German Basic Law's Article 2 gave everyone the right and freedom to move. Emigration scams (Auswandererschwindel) became a big business in postwar West Germany, at least in the eyes of state emigration authorities who saw their role as hindering rather than facilitating West Germans' emigration. Authorities viewed firms like those of Jutta Welke as emigration scams operating under the cover of promising to facilitate marriage. State agencies argued that such companies were not advertising marriage facilitation but emigration facilitation. Working within a postwar emotional regime of restraint, state and church officials mobilized emotions in their fight against Auswandererschwindel. Their tactics included stirring up historical fears, invoking male insecurities, and drawing on postwar Germans' desire for security.[17]

Historian Dagmar Herzog has argued that postwar West German reconstruction was based in part on social discourses that narrowly focused understandings of morality on sexuality while avoiding the moral implications of having been complicit in Nazi atrocities.[18] Biess has argued that such talk happened within an emotional regime of restraint in which "moral panics" served as safety valves for expressing otherwise taboo emotions. The alleged kidnapping of young German men into the French Foreign Legion during the 1950s generated one such moral panic. This abduction was constructed as "white slavery," leading to a sexualization of male bodies as well as feeding into Germans narratives of victimization.[19] Talking about sex and violence allowed West Germans to see themselves as present and future victims of Allied revenge and to avoid any talk of moral culpability for the Nazi period. Similar panicky talk about sex and violence occupied state and church officials who in the late 1940s positioned themselves as present and future gatekeepers of migration, female sexuality, and moral order.

Several Hamburg state authorities intervened in the case of Welke. Even though Welke had a business license and passed a security check by Hamburg police, the Hamburg Emigration Office (HEO) investigated her. The HEO cited the German Emigration Law of 1897 and argued that her business illegally promoted emigration. Welke's lawyer countered that the firm was simply providing addresses. The HEO conceded. The state prosecutor closed the case in December 1948. But the federal emigration office reopened the case in the summer of 1949 after Welke had advertised in several popular magazines. It asked the HEO to follow up. This time, Welke's lawyer provided thank-you notes from female customers. He also reassured officials that Welke's business partner in California would "only provide addresses of marriage-willing Americans in cases where one could rule out bad intentions or misuse of a marriage advertisement."[20]

Despite all attempts by the local and trans-zonal authorities and by a Westphalian "Association against Moral Corruption" (Vereinigung für Volksentsittlichung), Welke's firm continued to do business in the international marriage market. While authorities failed to stop several firms and individuals they suspected of trafficking, they were more successful in other cases, especially if victims of scam artists came forward and provided evidence. Furthermore, authorities successfully convinced part of the West German press not to publish such classifieds.[21]

The male, middle-class officials in state and church agencies, however, were not only motivated by a wish to protect the general population from scam artists. In the case of single women, they were driven by the desire to protect "innocent girls" from "moral corruption," in particular in the form of "white slave trafficking."[22] This fear of "girl trafficking" or "bad intentions" was pervasive in the correspondence among various state and church agencies, who often talked about "corrupt" and "dishonorable" intentions in the case of female emigrants. The specter of "girl trafficking" had scandalized society at the turn of the century.[23] Soaked in eugenic fantasies and racial ideology, Mädchenhandel, also described as "white slavery," touched ideas about masculinity and femininity, but also "reflected [West Germans'] intense feelings of powerlessness and inferiority," as Biess argues in his study of postwar moral panics.[24] Emigration authorities in the 1940s and 1950s were aware that the "German National Association of Female Friends of Young Girls" and countless other associations for helping young women find jobs had been founded in the nineteenth century in order to protect German girls and women from "moral corruption" and "decline into prostitution." Several such organizations continued this work after the Second World War.[25]

The recruitment of German maids to Great Britain in 1948 alarmed all of these private and public agencies that dealt with emigration and the protection of women. By that time, there were dozens of church and public information offices for emigrants in West Germany. The Permanent Secretariat for Emigration Matters was the pan-zonal agency in the three Western occupation zones that eventually became the first federal office to overlook emigration in West Germany. The secretariat advised all information offices to refer all single women wishing to emigrate abroad to the various societies for the protection of girls for more in-depth counseling.[26] "Action North Sea" was a British–West German initiative that recruited German women for domestic service in Great Britain. Several British and Irish private companies had jumped onto this bandwagon, advertising German maids in Great Britain as preferable to Irish maids, because they had been trained in domestic service during the Nazi period and the Catholic Germans, unlike the Irish, did not insist on Sunday mornings off. "Apart from this, the Germans are probably the most domesticated nation in Europe." A German law from 1935 forbidding the recruitment of German workers outside of Germany, still on the books in postwar West Germany, allowed German authorities to restrict the companies' recruitment activities from early 1949 onward.[27]

The attempts to protect children and women from human trafficking and forced prostitution were as justified in the nineteenth and twentieth centuries as they are in the twenty-first. At the same time, the raped woman continued to serve as "the allegorical image of the victimized nation," which meant that at stake was not the well-being of the individual person but the emotional economy of the nation."[28] In the 1940s and 1950s, several cases of "white slavery" made headlines. West German newspapers reported that some German women who had applied to work in Great Britain and Ireland "had fallen into the hands of international girl traffickers and been forced into brothels."[29] One company was charged because it had asked female applicants "about their dancing and musical skills rather than their cooking skills... Irish authorities confirmed the suspicion of 'white slave traffic,' that is, girls trafficking. None of the girls that had been procured by this agency was in a domestic service position. They could not be located. It is to be assumed that all girls were sent to brothels overseas. In the meantime, it was possible to prevent other German girls from emigration to Ireland via 'Continental Agencies' and thus save them from a ghastly fate."[30] Even agencies that actually sent women into domestic service made women financially dependent because of their high fees. This was inevitably "the first step into misery." Girls should think twice about emigration: "Once kidnapped to one of the world's port cities, there is no escape. Even if life at home is difficult, even if many people no longer have a home—no fate is harder than being young, naïve, and vulnerable in foreign lands."[31]

The postwar press as well as public and private agencies focused on women's sexual exploitation while ignoring their labor exploitation in a number of other labor migration schemes. Further, the potential for sexual exploitation and abuse in middle-class families that hired German maids was horrifying to the bourgeois "saviors" of "innocent girls." In their eyes, the only viable life strategy for single women was to stay put. The newspaper report insinuated that women would be protected in their *Heimat* (home or homeland), but it was silent on how this protection was guaranteed.

When church and state authorities heard about actual abuse, however, they were no longer willing to assume that the victims were "innocent." In September 1948, newspapers and Catholic clergy involved in emigration counseling learned that the owner of a recruitment agency had raped several of the women he had hired. In the discourse of the press and the priests, however, the owner had "seduced" them and one of the women was put into a psychiatric clinic. Although the company lost its license in Ireland, the owner's wife continued running it. Even when the police were already investigating the owner and had forbidden him to recruit any more women, the priest defended the owner by claiming that the recruited women may have been of "dubious character." Further, one of the women he interviewed, said the priest, was "surely at least partly at fault. It [the girl] seems to be somewhat hysterical. It is not proven that a subsequent suicide attempt with gas was really serious." Although judging the women, the priest refrained from judging the owner. One of the reasons the priest was reluctant to fault the owner was that he himself had helped him recruit the women, and therefore was implicated in the owner's crimes. The priest's condemnation of the women stemmed also from the image of girls and women among West German social workers in the postwar period that always saw them rather than men at fault for rape. Many, indeed, were convinced that even children could seduce men.[32]

This sexualization of female emigrants continually confronted women with male emigration counselors who associated single women's emigration with the international marriage market, the international labor market, and the trafficking of girls and women. All single women wishing to emigrate abroad for the purpose of marriage or work therefore required welfare state protection from male and female guardians. In early 1949, the department of refugees of the ecumenical council counseled the church conference: "The emigration of single women requires a particularly careful surveillance. Work in cleaning, social and church institutions is preferable for them. The emigration of individual girls and young women is only recommended in particularly safe cases and is to be considered a special task of care for the churches."[33] In the postwar period, the Evangelical and Catholic churches had significant social influence and played a crucial role in organizing international migration. The impact of such views can therefore hardly be overestimated. The same was true of similar statements by state agencies. The federal emigration agency reminded all associated information offices in the mid-1950s of the special care they had to take when advising single women: "In particular, no woman or girl should accept a position abroad before having gained further information about the employer through an information office."[34]

Thus, state and church officials inexorably linked the female body with the danger of moral corruption, abuse, and prostitution. Unlike the body of the male emigrant, the body of the female emigrant became sexualized. And even in a democracy, sexualized bodies required state regulation, in particular by muffling women's sexuality and directing it into paths laid out by the imaginations of bourgeois men and women. Society found it difficult to see women as innocent victims. As historians have shown, men often believed that women had not done enough to protect themselves from rape or that they even had seduced their rapists.[35] Male pastors and bureaucrats saw male rapists as victims of seduction by women of "dubious" character. Single women, confronted with such ideas and ideals, were restricted in pursuing emigration as a life strategy. They had to consider perceived and real dangers of sexual exploitation but also the risk of being seen as tramps or prostitutes. Simply thinking out loud about emigrating by herself might expose a woman to such stigmatization. Thus, state and society obstructed women's paths to a better life.[36]

The state agencies' actions, however, were contradictory in several ways. In the 1950s, German authorities fretted over single men emigrating overseas, because they were seen as vital to postwar Germany's reconstruction.[37] Single women's status, even in the late 1940s, was more ambivalent. The "surplus of women" was viewed not only as a demographic but also as a moral problem that complicated the construction of a new national identity. Emigration obviously would have been a solution to the demographic "surplus"—as it was pursued in the case of refugees who were encouraged to emigrate.[38] Yet, German men's memories of their failure to protect "their" women at the end of the war, their inability to compete with GIs in the postwar years, and the ongoing humiliating military occupation weighed heavily on them.[39] Protecting women by keeping them home became paramount. Further, bureaucrats and clergy sought to ensure and enhance their jobs beyond the transition from occupation to statehood in 1949 by positioning emigration as a major national concern about society and morality.

A Matter of Feelings?

The women who used Jutta Welke's services did not fit bureaucrats' and pastors' images of women as passive victims and sexualized bodies. They were not intimidated by press reports about "white slave traffic." Yet, they knew that the male bureaucrats' emotional reaction to their assertion of autonomy of their lives required, in turn, an emotional response from them.[40] Thus, they clad their alliances with the Amerikaner in rhetoric of asexual purity and innocence. Correspondence with American men offered the chance at social upward mobility. And in several cases, women viewed marriage as a means to migration rather than vice versa. Whatever the reason for migration, several of Welke's clients emigrated and married. Unfortunately, the archival documents do not tell us how many women eventually married or migrated to the United States.[41]

The diverse and competing languages of love employed by a range of actors restructured the emotional landscape of postwar Germany. In the post–World War II transatlantic migration system, marriage became deeply entwined with migration. But in the context of disparate economies and sexualized female identities, more was at stake than love and desire. Women and men as well as private and public agents and officials negotiated fears and anxieties about male and female sexualities that could be constructed as creative life strategies. Single women in postwar Germany faced poverty, stigmatization as "surplus women," sexualization as morally corrupted or prostitute bodies, and migration policies that limited their movements much more so than that of men. Yet, they negotiated paths to marriage and migration that allowed them to maintain some control over their bodies and thus over their livelihoods and lives. Emotional rhetoric was a key tactic, both for authorities invoking public fears of national violability and for women presenting themselves and their intimate relationships as no threat to the nation's moral order. Thus, discourses about love as a driving force of emigration intersected with broader regimes of emotion that sought to reorder gender relations and regulate remembrance in the reconstruction of postwar Germany. It was within this emerging emotional landscape that competing languages of love made and unmade possibilities for women's livelihoods.

NOTES

1. Staatsarchiv Hamburg [Hamburg State Archive] (hereafter StAH), H 33-8052, Behörde für Wirtschaft und Verkehr, Auswanderungsamt [Office for Economy and Traffic], File "Heiratsvermittlung in das Ausland" [Marriage Brokerage Abroad]. All translations from German to English by author. The file contains transcripts of twenty-seven letters, including one letter from the Soviet zone of occupation, one from the French zone, seven from the US zone, and eleven from the British zone; one letter was sent from England, three locales are unknown, and the rest of the transcripts do not mention locations. The documents are silent on the costs of these exchange services for US clients. The file does not contain correspondence from the male American customers, but there are some indirect quotes within the women's letters. The transcripts contain only anonymized names, including full or partial first names only; some authors' names are missing.

    The German mark was introduced in June 1948. The average hourly gross (pretax) wage for unskilled female workers was around DM 0.35, meaning that they would have had to work for two days to earn five marks. Heinz Schmidt-Bachem, *Tüten, Beutel, Tragetaschen: Zur Geschichte der Papier, Pappe, und Folien verarbeitenden Industrie in Deutschland* (Münster: Waxmann, 2001), 186.

2. StAH, H 33-8052, Heiratsvermittlung in das Ausland.

3. This chapter is based in part on my book *Aufbrüche nach dem Zusammenbruch: Die deutsche Nordamerikaauswanderung nach dem Zweiten Weltkrieg* (Göttingen: V and R Unipress, 2004) and on additional research. I thank the archivists in Bre-

men; Hamburg; Washington, DC; and Ottawa for their support. This research was made possible through funding from the Konrad Adenauer Foundation; the German Historical Institute, Washington, DC; the Department of History and Classics at the University of Edmonton; and the chair in German-Canadian Studies at the University of Winnipeg.

4. The relevant literature on postwar German society, "Americanization," and relations with Americans is discussed in Freund, *Aufbrüche nach dem Zusammenbruch*. More recent studies include Frank Biess, *Homecomings: Returning POWs and the Legacies of Defeat in Postwar Germany* (Princeton, NJ: Princeton University Press, 2009); Moritz Föllmer, "Auf der Suche nach dem eigenen Leben: Junge Frauen und Individualität in der Weimarer Republik," in *Die "Krise" der Weimarer Republik: Zur Kritik eines Deutungsmusters*, ed. Moritz Föllmer and Rüdiger Graf (Frankfurt am Main: Campus, 2005), 287–317; Francis Graham-Dixon, *The Allied Occupation of Germany: The Refugee Crisis, Denazification, and the Path to Reconstruction* (New York: I. B. Taurus, 2013); Elizabeth D. Heinemann, "The Hour of the Woman: Memories of Germany's 'Crisis Years' and West German National Identity," in *The Miracle Years: A Cultural History of West Germany, 1949–1968*, ed. Hanna Schissler (Princeton, NJ: Princeton University Press, 2001), 21–56; Elizabeth D. Heinemann, *What Difference Does a Husband Make? Women and Marital Status in Nazi and Postwar Germany* (Berkeley: University of California Press, 1999); Dagmar Herzog, *Sex after Fascism: Memory and Morality in Twentieth-Century Germany* (Princeton, NJ: Princeton University Press, 2005); Thomas A. Kohut, *A German Generation: An Experiential History of the Twentieth Century* (New Haven, CT: Yale University Press, 2012); Jessica Reinisch, *The Perils of Peace: The Public Health Crisis in Occupied Germany* (Oxford: Oxford University Press, 2013); Hester Vaizey, "Empowerment or Endurance? War Wives' Experiences of Independence During and After the Second World War in Germany, 1939–1948," *German History* 29, no. 1 (2011): 57–78; Hester Vaizey, *Surviving Hitler's War: Family Life in Germany, 1939–48* (Basingstoke, UK: Palgrave Macmillan, 2010).

5. Susan J. Matt, "Current Emotion Research in History: Or, Doing History from the Inside Out," *Emotion Review* 3, no. 1 (2011): 119.

6. Barbara H. Rosenwein, "Problems and Methods in the History of Emotions," *Passions in Context: International Journal for the History and Theory of Emotions* 1, no. 1 (2010): 11; Rosenwein, "Worrying about Emotions in History," *American Historical Review* 107, no. 3 (2002): 842.

7. Herzog, *Sex after Fascism*, chap. 2.

8. Frank Biess, "Feelings in the Aftermath: Toward a History of Postwar Emotions," in *Histories of the Aftermath: The Legacies of the Second World War in Europe*, ed. Frank Biess and Robert G. Moeller (New York: Berghahn Books, 2010), 34.

9. On *Torschlusspanik* and *Wanderlust*, see Tiffany Watt Smith, *The Book of Human Emotions: An Encyclopedia of Feeling from Anger to Wanderlust* (London: Profile Books, 2015).

10. See my *Aufbrüche nach dem Zusammenbruch* for a detailed study of this migration; see also Freund, "Contesting the Meanings of Migration: German Women's Immigration to Canada in the 1950s," *Canadian Ethnic Studies* 41–42, no. 3–1 (2009–2010 [2012]): 1–26; Freund, "Immigrants' Identities: The Narratives of a German-Canadian Migration," in *A Chorus of Different Voices: German-Canadian Identities*, ed. Angelika E. Sauer and Matthias Zimmer (New York: Lang, 1998), 187–208.

11. Suzanne M. Sinke, "The International Marriage Market: Theoretical and Historical Perspectives," in *People in Transit. German Migrations in Comparative Perspective, 1820–1930*, ed. Dirk Hoerder and Jörg Nagler (Cambridge: Cambridge University Press, 1996), 227–247, quote on 231.

12. Heinemann, *What Difference Does a Husband Make?*, 4; Atina Grossmann, "The Question of Silence: The Rape of German Women by Occupation Soldiers," in *West Germany under Construction: Politics, Society, and Culture in the Adenauer Era*, ed. Robert G. Moeller (Ann Arbor: University of Michigan Press, 1997), 33–52; Maria Höhn, *GIs and Fräuleins: The German-American Encounter in 1950s West Germany* (Chapel Hill: University of North Carolina Press, 2002); Tamara Domentat, *Hallo Fräulein: Deutsche Frauen und amerikanische Soldaten* (Berlin: Aufbau-Verlag, 1998). Margot Buchwald, interview by author, Abbotsford, BC, Canada, September 27, 1993; Peter Hessel, interview by author, Waba, ON, Canada, March 22, 1998; Gustav Anders, interview by author, Stittsville, ON, Canada, March 12, 1998. All interviewee names, except Hessel's, are pseudonyms. Interviews are accessible through the University of Winnipeg's Oral History Centre archives.

13. Höhn, *GIs and Fräuleins*; Michaela Freund-Widder, *Frauen unter Kontrolle: Prostitution und ihre staatliche Bekämpfung in Hamburg vom Ende des Kaiserreichs bis zu den Anfängen der Bundesrepublik* (Münster: LIT, 2003); Ute Frevert, *Frauen-Geschichte: Zwischen bürgerlicher Verbesserung und neuer Weiblichkeit* (Frankfurt am Main: Suhrkamp Verlag, 1986), 258.

14. Sinke, "International Marriage Market," 245.

15. Rita J. Simon, "Sociology and Immigrant Women," in *Seeking Common Ground: Multidisciplinary Studies of Immigrant Women in the United States*, ed. Donna R. Gabaccia (Westport, CT: Praeger, 1992), 26; Elfrieda Berthiaume Shukert and Barbara Smith Scibetta, *War Brides of World War II* (New York: Penguin, 1989), 1–2.

16. U.S. Dept. of Justice, Immigration and Naturalization Service (INS), *Annual Report, 1946–1960* (author's calculations). See also Frank L. Auerbach, "Who Are Our New Immigrants?" *I&N Reporter* 1, no. 1 (July 1952): 6; Elliot Robert Barkan, *And Still They Come: Immigrants and American Society 1920 to the 1990s* (Wheeling, IL: Harlan Davidson, 1996), 78.

17. On the link between fear and security, see Bettina Hitzer, "Emotionsgeschichte—ein Anfang mit Folgen," in H-Soz-Kult, November 23, 2011, http://www.hsozkult.de/literaturereview/id/forschungsberichte-1221, 23–24; on the political mobilization of emotion see Hitzer, "Emotionsgeschichte," 31–35.

18. Herzog, *Sex after Fascism*, esp. chap. 2.

19. Frank Biess, "Moral Panic in Postwar Germany: The Abduction of Young Germans into the Foreign Legion and French Colonialism in the 1950s," *Journal of Modern History* 84, no. 4 (2012): 811–12.

20. StAH, H 33-8052, Heiratsvermittlung in das Ausland, Amt für Hafen und Schiffahrt, Auswanderungsamt Hamburg, Lohmann, Aktennotiz, November 13, 1948; Lohmann, Vermerk, July 1, 1949; Wolff, Ständiges Sekretariat für das Auswanderungswesen [Permanent Secretariat for Emigration Matters] (hereafter StSekAusw) Bremen to Lohmann, June 15, 1949; Lohmann to Welke, June 29, 1949; Lohmann to StSekAusw, Bremen, July 5, 1949. A survey in January 1950 found that 40 percent of the population in the US zone (and up to 60 percent in cities) read journals. Axel Schildt, *Moderne Zeiten: Freizeit, Massenmedien, und Zeitgeist in der Bundesrepublik der 50er Jahre* (Hamburg: Hans Christian Verlag, 1995), 129.

21. StAH, H 33-8052, Heiratsvermittlung in das Ausland, Amt für Hafen und Schiffahrt, Ausswanderungsamt Hamburg.

22. StAH, H 33-8052.

23. Barbara Kluwen, "Die Bekämpfung des Mädchenhandels im Deutschen Kaiserreich (1897–1914)" (Master's thesis, University of Hamburg, 1996).

24. Biess, "Moral Panic in Postwar Germany," 805.

25. StSekAusw, Bremen, Rundschreiben August 12, 1949.

26. StSekAusw, Bremen, Rundschreiben, February 19, 1949.

27. StSekAusw, Bremen, Rundschreiben, February 19, 1949; Schwindelfirmen A–L, StSekAusw. Bremen, Rundschreiben March 29, 1949. See also Diana Kay and Robert Miles, *Refugees or Migrant Workers? European Volunteer Workers in Britain 1946–1951* (London: Routledge, 1992), 38; StAH, Raphaels-Werk, Schwindelfirmen M–Z, Caritas-Verband für Berlin e.V. to Raphaels-Verein Hamburg, November 30, 1948; StAH, Raphaels-Werk, Schwindelfirmen A–L, StSekAusw, Bremen, Rundschreiben March 29, 1949.

28. Biess, "Moral Panic in Postwar Germany," 806. Biess's claim that this image "shifted from the female rape victim in the interwar period to the abducted young male in the 1950s" (806, also 808) thus needs to be corrected.

29. StAH, Raphaels-Werk, Schwindelfirmen A–L [no date], "Opfer Internationaler Mädchenhändler," *Die Frau*, January 29, 1949, in StSekAusw. Bremen, Rundschreiben, March 29, 1949; StAH, Raphaels-Werk, Schwindelfirmen M–Z [no date], "Opfer Internationaler Mädchenhändler," in *Kölnische Rundschau*, January 29, 1949; according to a staff member of the Bishopric Youth Welfare Office of Berlin, further articles were published in *Hannoversche Presse, Allgäuer, and Neue Zeitung*; StAH, Raphaels-Werk, Schwindelfirmen M–Z, Rev. P. Josef Michalke, S.J., Abt. Frauenjugend, Beschöfliches Jugendseelsorgeamt Berlin to St. Raphaelsverein Hamburg, March 8, 1949.

30. StAH, Raphaels-Werk, Schwindelfirmen A–L [no date], "Opfer Internationaler Mädchenhändler."

31. StAH, Raphaels-Werk, Schwindelfirmen A–L [no date], "Opfer Internationaler Mädchenhändler."

32. StAH, Raphaels-Werk, Schwindelfirmen M–Z, Michalke to Raphaelsverein Hamburg, March 8, 1949; "Der Himmel auf Erden," in *Neue Zeitung* [no date; early February 1949]; StAH, Raphaels-Werk, Schwindelfirmen M–Z, Michalke to Raphaelsverein Hamburg, March 8, 1949; E. Hennig, "Flüchtlingsschicksal und -milieu als gefährdende Momente für die psychische Entwicklung Jugendlicher" (PhD diss., University of Kiel, 1951), cited in Albrecht Lehmann, *Im Fremden ungewollt zuhaus: Flüchtlinge und Vertriebene in Westdeutschland 1945–1990* (Munich: Beck, 1991), 153–58; Freund-Widder, *Frauen unter Kontrolle*, 181–258.

33. StAB, 3-A.4. Nr. 671, Neuregelung des Auswanderungswesens, 1947–1958, Flüchtlingsabteilung des Ökumenischen Rates der Kirchenkonferenz über deutsche Flüchtlingsfragen: Bericht und Empfehlungen der Arbeitsgruppe. Auswanderung und Binnenwanderung, Hamburg, February 22–25, 1949.

34. Bundesamt für Auswanderung [Federal Emigration Office], ed., *Merkblatt Nr. 12: Verzeichnis der Gemeinnützigen Auswanderer-Beratungsstellen*, 4th ed. (Koblenz, July 1954). The West German government continued this policy when dealing with the arrival of the first female "guest workers" from Italy and Turkey in the 1950s and 1960s. See Monika Mattes, "Zum Verhältnis von Migration und Geschlecht–Anwerbung und Beschäftigung von 'Gastarbeiterinnen' in der Bundesrepublik 1960 bis 1973," in *50 Jahre Bundesrepublik—50 Jahre Einwanderung. Nachkriegsgeschichte als Migrationsgeschichte*, ed. Jan Motte, Rainer Ohliger, and Anne von Oswald (Frankfurt am Main: Campus, 1999), 285–309.

35. Freund-Widder, *Frauen unter Kontrolle*; Grossmann, "Question of Silence."

36. On the ambiguity of welfare policies geared toward women in postwar West Germany, see Robert G. Moeller, *Protecting Motherhood: Women and the Family in the Politics of Postwar West Germany* (Berkeley: University of California Press, 1993).

37. Although "alleged enslavement in the Foreign Legion" (Biess, "Moral Panic in Postwar Germany," 808) may have symbolized greater fears, the actual recruitment by the United States, Canada, and Australia of hundreds of thousands of young men as immigrants in the 1950s was of much greater and real concern to postwar reconstruction. See Freund, *Aufbrüche nach dem Zusammenbruch*, 185–91, 201–44, 411–35.

38. Freund, *Aufbrüche nach dem Zusammenbruch*, 204–12.

39. Biess, "Moral Panic in Postwar Germany," 796, 806.

40. Anna M. Parkinson, *An Emotional State: The Politics of Emotion in Postwar West German Culture* (Ann Arbor: University of Michigan Press, 2015), 4.

41. StAH, H 33-8052, Heiratsvermittlung in das Ausland.

CHAPTER 11

"When I Came to Canada, All I Did Was Cry"

Emotions and Migration of Greek Women in Postwar Montreal

MARGARITA DOUNIA

Alexandra returned from school one day to receive the news of her imminent engagement and marriage. The decision was reached between Alexandra's parents and the groom's mother, who had returned to Greece from Canada to find a wife for her son. Though Alexandra was upset because "her opinion was not considered," she conceded to her parents' wishes.[1] The groom, an established migrant in Montreal, sent an approving telegram, stating that he agreed to "marry Alexandra." The engagement took place in the village, with the groom "represented" by his kin. In 1956, Alexandra met her husband at the airport, recalling "but he was handsome, a very attractive and tall man. I instantly liked him!" Her story reveals the intersections between emotions felt ("I instantly liked him"), suppressed (upset), expressed (according to parents' wishes) and confirmed (agreement in marrying her) in the context of migration.

By focusing on personal recollections of migrant women, this chapter discusses a dimension of the Greek migration experience articulated by Greek migrant women themselves. It focuses on emotions as evaluative judgments, "inner feelings," and practices in the context of Greek female migration to Montreal.

Over the past two decades, scholarly interest in emotions has seeped into a plethora of fields, accompanying a growing insistence on inter- or multidisciplinarity. Building on this work, this study explores emotions associated with migration through the multiple lenses of history, anthropology, and gender and migration studies. It applies the methodological tool of oral history, a trusted fieldwork friend.[2] Over the summer and early fall of 2016, I interviewed eighteen female Greek migrants located through a snowballing technique, who provided accounts of their migratory experience in postwar Montreal.[3] Resting on the strong correlation between migration studies and oral history,[4] I have no illusions about the limitations of treating interviews as the ultimate or "privileged access" to a culture's past.[5] Further, I admit giving up on the quest for objectivity, echoing Susan J. Matt's point that "even in firsthand accounts of sentiments, attitudes, and emotions, nothing is raw or unfiltered."[6] Finally, my position as a researcher constitutes another important point for reflection: a Greek woman myself,[7] and sometimes a fellow villager, I felt every word of Catherine Lutz and Geoffrey M. White's observation that "emotion is ineffable and understanding requires 'walking in the other person's shoes.'"[8] Yet, there were clear limitations to such rapport, created by my position as a researcher. In particular, my status as a "Greek woman from Greece" asking questions introduced power dynamics of representation that often left me ambivalent.

Arriving in Canada: Hope and *Misemos*

Women migrants, especially southern Europeans, have often been depicted as appendages to male migrating pioneers. In the case of Greek migrants, women, if identified at all, have little agency. Women's actions are inscribed in the gender expectations shaped by Greek culture or prevalent decision-making patterns in patriarchal households.[9] Interviews of unmarried Greek women who migrated between the ages of fifteen and twenty-five (the majority in this study), however, reveal more complex, actor-centered narratives.[10]

In Canada, all interviewees were received by family members, compatriots, fictive kin, or friends. Despite their common familiar welcome, the women's first impressions of the new country varied significantly. While Phaedra emphasizes the "terrifying winter," Christina remembers feeling mesmerized by the shop windows lit up for Christmas on the way to her brother's apartment. Differing initial reactions to Canada reflect the variety of ways women invested their own emotions into migration. Even when family members were heavily involved in a woman's emigration, rarely was the decision finalized without considering her wishes or enthusiasm.[11] Anastasia, for example, not only emphasizes her own desire to migrate, but also challenges the widely held notion of migration as a painful separation, captured by the Greek concept of misemos.[12] She states: "It was not hard for me to leave Greece. I always had the dream of leaving Greece and going to live somewhere else."

Even when conforming to the Greek gender norms of the time, female migrants' narratives are not void of agency. As Ioanna Laliotou points out, "the subjects insist on descriptions of their own desire and their will to migrate."[13] This position is illustrated by Xenia, whose story of departure unravels both her desire to migrate and her family's involvement in that decision. She states: "I arrived in Canada on the 27th of July 1957, the unforgettable day of Santa Paraskevi, together with two 'chaperons,' Peter and Nick. I went to Montreal with an invitation from my female cousin. I wanted to go and work, to live a better life, of course. A better life."[14] Xenia's story shows that economic motives were not exclusive to men. References to poverty as a prime reason for their desire to leave their homeland abound in participants' stories.[15] This is the case, for example, for Christina: "My brother Vangelis invited me and I went. I wanted to leave from here. I wanted it," she says—stressing her own desire with the use of an emphatic first-person pronoun—"because I did not like life here, the outdoor labor, I wanted to leave. I mean, poverty, such poverty."

Extending economic motives to a broader household strategy also involved single women acting as the initial link in the migratory chain that would eventually facilitate the migration of other kin. Stefania and Ioli, among others, followed their sisters, established as live-in domestics in Montreal. Ioli narrates: "I wanted to go somewhere else, away from Greece and my sister was sending me letters, telling me how beautiful life is here [in Montreal], so I wanted to leave."

In the 1950s and 1960s, single women inhabiting the Greek periphery witnessed an ever-growing desertion of villages due to massive urbanization, turning village life harsher in terms of opportunities. Anna admits, "I left in 1968, and to tell you the truth, it was out of jealousy. Because all the girls had left the village and I did not want to stay here alone. That was it. Jealousy [laughter]." Among married women, if many appear to have yielded to their husbands' migration plans, interviews reveal that, in most cases, wives shared their husband's desire for a better future. They acknowledged the limited opportunities available to them in Greece and sometimes even put forward a family plan for migrating, as Argyro vividly recalls: "Those were very difficult years, my Margarita. My husband was working, making little money. We lived in my mother-in-law's apartment, together with her, my brother-in-law and sister-in-law. One of them left for Canada and then I told my husband: 'Vangeli, why don't we go too? We don't even have a house here to stay.'"

Living in Montreal: Nostalgia and *Stenahoria*

Characterized by Stearns as "an emotional characteristic of modernity," nostalgia refers to homesickness, longing, and yearning in relation to time, space, or people.[16] As an emotional state, it has often been linked to migrants and people on the move. In Greek, the word comes from nostos (from coming home or reaching the homeland) and algos (pain or grief). In Greek cosmology, nostalgia, expressed as "love for the country," is an expected reaction when one is away from the homeland.[17] Various forms of artistic expression, in particular Greek folk songs, refer to this lingering ache and its resulting somatization and emotionalization, termed marasmos or marazi.[18] For Greeks, a related concept is xenitia, which refers to living in a foreign country. Xenitia is seen as a point and process of rupture, not only due to spatial dislocation, but most importantly because of a migrant's distancing from socially and culturally familiar settings, and from networks of support.[19]

Greek migrants in Montreal often have felt the devastating effects of nostalgia; the physical symptoms of "inexplicable" distress landed some in the hospital.[20] Traditionally considered as more emotion-driven by nature, women were seen as particularly susceptible to nostalgic feelings when faced with the new challenges that their migration laid bare.[21] Longing appears to hold a central position in most informants' narratives in relation to place, to people, to time, but also to a self-perception that gradually or abruptly faded away.

Most migrant women in this group refer to "place" as the object of their nostalgia. Locations vary among participants: a specific village community, an island or broader region, their home country, or a combination of places. Manifestations of strong nostalgic sentiments idealizing the homeland center on Greece's climate and landscape, which they contrast with those of Canada. This contrast serves them to present the place left behind as the antithesis of what women seem to dislike in Canada. Stefania recalls her first holidays in Greece after migrating to Montreal: "When I first visited the island after such a long time I went to see the sea, and there I started crying… The beach was right next to my house. Now compare this with having to walk to work in Montreal's snow."

Place is highly associated with people in these narratives. In stories, women attribute kin qualities to the whole village community, and idealizing the place contributed to a stronger "feeling of loss."[22] Zoe's comments are an example of the shifting boundary between people and place in migrants' minds and hearts: "I feel nostalgia. For the people, for the village we grew up. Yes, primarily for the village we grew up. We cannot forget it. Our mind is forever there." Speaking of her home village as a living entity, Zoe's words further reveal her anguish over the loss of the social function of place and her role in it. Zoe's socializing in her village is contrasted sharply with the initial social marginalization she faced in urban Montreal. The homeland is thus perceived as a community of emotional belonging, where people shared bonds of solidarity, support, recognition, and safety usually attached to kin. Feeling rules, moral codes, gender roles, and social behaviors were established, predicted, and overt.[23] The transition to urban living thus signified not only new spatial arrangements in women's efforts to settle down, but most importantly a new perception of the social contours of place whose significance is equally recognized by informants of both rural and urban backgrounds.

Overcoming the potential social and emotional trauma of this transition to an unfamiliar urban environment, many Greek migrants in Montreal opted for living in ethnic enclaves close to family, friends, and coethnics.[24] Most interviewees, like Fotini, cherish their experience of "Greek neighborhoods," especially in Park Extension and Laval where they first settled: "In every balcony there was a radio playing Kazantzidis and other Greek songs."[25] "The melodies of xenitia made you feel at home," she recalls. Shopping in Greek-owned stores, speaking their native language, attending the Greek Orthodox Church, and frequenting Greek-owned restaurants provided a sense of social and emotional continuity, while also allowing an intercommunity mobility that would otherwise be questioned or even rebuked outside the context of migration.

Replicating social behavior inscribed in the use of space back in the homeland proved to be another effective strategy in dealing with feelings of loss, rupture, and discontinuity. Argyro and Alexandra, two highly sociable interviewees, exuberantly refer to their homes as "very central" and "close to the Greek Church" allowing them to re-create socialization practices from Greece. Argyro explains: "I leave my door open, I like it, whoever walks by, any woman walking by, I will call her inside to have coffee together. I will make the coffee and start chatting. Even if I don't know her, especially an old lady, I will call out 'hey compatriot, where are you going? Come over here, my dear.' And so I have met so many women." The type of housing and living arrangement among Greek immigrants in Montreal also had an impact on emotional management, reflected in the Greek word *stenahoria*. Used to describe sadness, *stenahoria* translates literally as "limited space," and as such it can also refer to a place that makes you feel uncomfortable.²⁶ In this way, the Greek language hints at a strong correlation between spatial confinement and negative feelings. Though houses are not always explicitly mentioned in women's nostalgic narrative, as Margaret Lock and Pamela Wakewich-Dunk explain, "the combination of a small apartment and the Montreal climate added to a sense of loss and confinement when compared with the warmth of an airy Greek house."²⁷ This is corroborated by most informants, for whom migration signified their first experience of apartment housing. Ioli could find no consolation for "living in a house without a garden!"; while Christina vividly recalls her negative reaction when her brother drove her to his apartment: "I said, 'is that it?' I did not like it at all."²⁸

A practical and affordable solution embraced by many migrants, cohabitation further contributed to a feeling of stenahoria. Cohabitation frequently included both family members and boarders. Fotini explains: "We rented a room and took in my future husband as boarder. And then it was my sister, my brother Kostas, my brother George and his wife, myself, we all lived in one apartment to share the rent. We were poor back then; we could not afford any luxuries." Cohabitation among kin was not new to women from rural Greece, where extended families living together were common. Yet, the same housing setup in a small tenement introduced negative changes from traditional practices, namely a deviation from the standard spatial gender segregation. Having to share a single room with three men, Christina laments: "In one room, my brother-in-law, my two brothers, and myself! Our privacy was separated by a curtain!" In addition, power dynamics and emotional distancing are described by the women interviewed as highly challenging.²⁹

For young women in particular, cohabitation had its oppressive side, as Greek families devised alternative ways to supervise them and protect their reputation. As Evangelia Tastsoglou explains, in the case of migrant women, "living with brothers meant the transfer of the Greek patriarchal family structure into Canada."³⁰ Fotini and Christina attest to the expectation of asking for permission to go out, or to be accompanied to work by their elderly brothers. Stefania justifies why her sister would act as the "paterfamilias" by confining her to the house: "She was responsible for me. Father entrusted me to her, so she wanted me out of trouble."³¹ Similar restrictions were also encountered among the cohort of married women.³²

Cohabitation, however, should also be viewed as a way of effectuating social continuity as well as fulfilling emotional needs. Most interviewees speak fondly of cohabitation and use with relief the phrase "I found the table set" when describing how they walked into an extended family household upon their arrival in Montreal. Cohabitation provided women with feelings of love, protection, respect, and joy. Alexandra recalls: "Thirteen people in one house, to share the rent. Every night was a party. One night we would play cards, the other night we would sing." Cohabitation also contributed to increased solidarity among women, rather than competition, as household chores for the extended family were usually shared among them. Even for those managing housework alone, there was purportedly a sense of pride in their household skills.[33] As Argyro proudly recalls: "I had my husband in the house and my four brothers. I would cook for them, clean their clothes, have everything ready for them! And I had to work. But I would have been depressed otherwise."

Among migrants, there is often a feeling that is stronger than nostalgia and that is described by Loretta Baldassar as "a type of heartache, of longing and missing that is commonly expressed as a desire to be with kin."[34] Missing family members, and in particular parents, often casts a heavy shadow on migrant women's emotions. "I might be living here, but my heart is there. Everything I love is there," cries Ioli. In many cases the interviewees' eyes turned tearful or their voice cracked, somaticizing the discursive narrative of longing: "Your own people stay behind. Your very own, the ones you are closest to," laments Panagiota; while Aliki explains how migration deprived them of their loved ones: "We left and were not given the time to enjoy our parents or our brothers." Attachment to kin is accentuated along gendered lines, with women expressing special bonds of affection for their mothers. This sentiment was expressed by the several women:

> When I came to Canada, every day I was crying. "I want to go to my mother. I want to go to my mother," I used to say: "How will you do that?" My brother would tease me. "I will walk if I have to!" (Christina)

> The beginning was very difficult. I had a very difficult time (emphatically).... I used to say, "I am going back. I want to go back to my mother." (Xenia)

All interviewees agreed that an exacerbated feeling of nostalgia and homesickness affected women who traveled alone or migrated single. Migrating with kin helped mitigate their sense of longing for home. Sophia points out: "I adjusted easily because all of my husband's family was here. So they were affectionate and helpful. If you come alone, when the first difficulty presents itself, you want to go back." Attaching oneself to emerging loyalties in Montreal also contributed in appeasing the feeling of longing, as Anna describes: "First we missed out parents, yes. But then we lived our best years here, we created ourselves and our families here." For other participants, the remedy for nostalgia and longing for kin was the eventual "invitation" extended to kin in Greece in the context of family reunification, confirming the Greek saying that "the place is the people."

However, for most participants, separation from kin was meant to last. And it was mostly women who felt an aggravating pain toward those left behind. In the context of Greek feeling rules, it is women who are expected to care for kin and reciprocate obligations, especially toward aging parents. The resilience of such feeling rules in the changing contexts of migration is seen in many participants' efforts to extend care across borders and attempt to build "a sense of shared 'presence.'"[35] Communication with Greece was mostly left to women. Solidifying what Sonia Cancian calls an "emotional transnationalism," women sent letters or called home in order to "to bridge distances," physical as well as emotional.[36] Aliki explains:

> We always communicated with each other. Through the post office, because phone calls were not easy. I would have to set an appointment and ask the village mayor to call my parents to his office to receive the call. So I used to write two–three letters a month, without waiting for a response. I wrote both to my father and my father-in-law, and then years later I would send them cassettes and videotapes with my children singing Greek songs to them.

In addition to correspondence, contact with home was nurtured through remittances, the dispatch of objects; visits to the homeland during important Greek holidays; and "hands-on care" or "duty visits," especially in moments of family crisis, such as sickness or death.[37]

Creating a Home: *Eros, Agapi*, and Motherhood

If courtly love was characterized by what Luisa Passerini describes as "the insurmountable distances between the lovers," in the context of migration, romantic love also often mandated the overcoming of distance.[38] Falling in love was not only a reason for the arrival of many women in Canada, but also for their decision to stay. Marriage as the legitimizing context of romantic love or the desired outcome of shrewd matchmaking constituted one of the primary hopes of Greek migrant women in Montreal. For many, after marriage, motherhood gave way to new expressions of love. These different manifestations of love created tensions—among couples, between generations, and across sociocultural divides. Interviewees refer to these different manifestations of love by using the Greek words eros (which refers mostly to the state of "being in love" or to "romantic love") and agapi (which means to love in a more general sense that can include loving one's parents, loving one's job, etc.).

In the context of migration, romantic love could be seen both as an emotional practice and as a mobilizing feeling.[39] In the first case, romantic love was invoked in managing emotions through practices, rituals, and moods. In the second case, romantic love became the basis for a "relation that moves you," the reason for crossing borders, or the hindrance in recrossing them.[40] In a lyrical tone, a number of interviewees admit "listening to their heart" by following a spouse or a lover abroad, or falling in love while in Montreal and deciding to remain in Canada, despite their initial intention of eventual return to the homeland. Explicitly or not, all women agree that their ideal in finding love or a successful arranged match primarily meant "marrying a fellow Greek."

In the early years of Greek migration to Canada, marital unions were mostly the result of successful matchmaking by friends and family.[41] Arranged marriages sought to maintain the marital practices of the homeland, but also to ensure sociocultural reproduction and women's "good reputation." Upholding prevailing Greek moral codes meant embodying cultural continuity in the midst of change. There was an association of sexuality with the very maintenance of a sense of "Greekness" that rested on the patriarchal code of "honor and shame."[42] This is reflected in Christina's words: "Here you had opportunities to flirt, to date, but we were not used to that, we preferred to stay indoors."

Arranged matches have to be treated with some skepticism. Allegedly emotion-deprived, such marriages are often perceived as unions of convenience. The stories of Fotini, Xenia, and Marina, however, attest that in many cases emotions were present, if not from the outset, by the eventual consolidation of the conjugal agapi. Another misconception challenged by the condition of migration is the supposed passivity with which Greek women adhered to the matchmaking decisions made for them by kin. In some cases, migration allowed for a degree of agency that some did not hesitate to exert. As the cases of Fotini, Alexandra, and Phaedra show, the determination that brought migrant women to Canada could not be easily quenched when deciding with whom to spend their lives there.

Fotini recounts how her future husband, Petros, who rented a room in Fotini's family lodgings, "only had eyes for her." He invited her brother out for dinner, asking permission to marry her, and after dinner they returned home to deliver the good news to Fotini. Yet, to everyone's astonishment, Fotini would not come out of her room. She listened with hesitation to her future husband promising a life of happiness, only to reply "I need time to think about it." It was only some months later that the future couple started dating, and Fotini eventually consented to the marriage proposal. Fotini's story underscores her challenging tradition and her brother's authority over her life. She stated that, having lived and worked in Montreal as a nurse for some time helped her to fight for her "final say" in such a crucial decision.

Like other migrant women, some Greek women experienced a new independence in the context of migration that "opened opportunities to choose their own spouses on their own terms."[43] A number of young Greek migrant girls took the initiative to "invite," or sponsor, fellow Greeks to Montreal with the intention of marrying them. In this way, not only did they fulfill their desire to marry "a shoe from the homeland," as the Greek saying goes,[44] but most importantly, by extending a migration invitation they were relieved from the burdensome Greek custom of providing a dowry.[45] Such was the case of Christina, who narrates:

> Though from the same village, I did not know him, and he had only seen a photo. . . . Then my mother wrote me a letter . . . [saying] that he is a good man and orphaned. So I decided to write to him. I explained things clearly. "If you come here, you will have to work day and night, and to start a family we will have a hard time." He wrote back, asking if I was interested in another man there [laughter]. In the end, he came.

Migration provided a transformative context for migrant women who married out of love. This cohort includes women who migrated mostly in the 1960s and 1970s, a time when marital customs and gender roles in the homeland were undergoing decisive changes. Some informants experienced migration as "lovers who stay behind." In order to bear the pain of separation, they resorted to emotional practices such as the exchange of letters and photographs until they received the required invitation with the purpose of marriage. This was Lena's experience, who recalls:

> He promised me [he would marry me] and he kept his promise. He could have married any girl here in Canada and secured a permanent visa for himself. But no, he would not treat me indecently. He was not fooling around with me, just to give me a bad reputation. He brought me here and we were married . . . That's why I was happy to come here

... to George. I refused whoever they introduced me to on the island. My poor mother would tell me "For a man you will leave me here and migrate?" but I could not do otherwise.

Aliki smiles remembering her first meeting with her husband when he returned to Greece for a visit. She characterizes the rapid evolution of events, from meeting to marriage, as a "coup de foudre!" In just one month they were engaged, married, and on their way to Montreal. "I was going to a foreign country and I was not even thinking about it! Everything seemed en rose [rosy]." "All I cared about was our future together," she adds.

For some participants, the transformative context of migration included a renegotiation of gender roles and new opportunities to find love in Montreal. Maria, Rosie, Danae, Panagiota, Antonia, and Ioli had plans to return to Greece when they fell in love.[46] So did Stefania, who met her future husband when applying for a job in his small craft manufacture. She gave him her phone number and agreed to go out on a date, after asking permission from her older sister. Months later, Stefania was happily married. For all interviewees, finding love in the context of migration signaled sacrificing their dream of returning to their homeland. Such experience resonates with Anthony Giddens's observation that "passionate love ... uproots the individual from the mundane and generates a preparedness to consider radical options as well as sacrifices."[47]

Soon after marriage, motherhood shaped the roles and identities of many informants, bringing to the fore a combination of emotions. In the context of migration, Greek migrant mothers faced the demanding task of mothering without the help provided by kin, as was customary in the homeland.[48] Lack of help was compounded by social isolation, as young mothers were confined to their household. In order to escape this double burden, some women opted for co-mothering among friends and coethnics. Phaedra rejoices when she recounts her experience of collective motherhood in the company of other Greek migrant mothers. "Our children were very young so we would all go out together, let the children play while we chatted, played bingo, or enjoyed our coffee."

Concerns over raising a family also included the challenge of lost income, as some interviewees had to give up their jobs. "I had to stop working. I had nobody to attend my children. No relative, no kin," Zoe comments. Others resorted to sharing parenting duties with their husbands, despite viewing such an alternative as a reversal of Greek traditional gender roles. "I worked during the day and my husband worked at night so that we could switch shifts in taking care of our children," comments Maro.

For some women, hiring nannies for their children was their only option for returning to work. Yet the deviation from practices and ideas of full motherhood from the homeland created conflicting feelings. "I paid five dollars an hour for a trustworthy babysitter, but most were never really trustworthy. Some did not even bother to show up. And there I was heading to work with two young babies. Stress! Paralyzing stress!" bemoans Panagiota. Other women opted for home-employment, especially for garment labor, or abandoned their premotherhood position to join a family business such as a restaurant. Aliki, Argyro, and Alexandra continued sewing fur coats for twenty hours a day while caring for their small children.

Lack of alternatives also led several interviewees to what they saw as the "ultimate solution"—the heartbreaking decision of sending their children to Greece. Ioli's emotional management of this poignant decision is manifested in her words: "I sent my son to Greece and he stayed there with my mother for two years. I regret sending him, but at least I knew he was in good hands." As Rhacel Parreñas states, "without a doubt, mothering from a distance has emotional ramifications both for mothers who leave and children who are sent back or left behind."[49] Panagiota could not agree more: "I had to send my children to Greece; there were no helping hands here. And this is difficult! It is very difficult to be away from your children! I would worry all the time. . . . John was 17–18 months old!"

Working in a New Land: Stress and *Proodos*

As Paola Corti has reminded us, "women were labor migrants too."[50] In the case of Greek migration to Canada, the post–World War II years witnessed a growing number of female migrants arriving in Montreal and entering the labor market. In particular, in the 1950s and 1960s, there were "movements of exclusively female immigrant workers," such as domestics, and to a lesser degree nurses' aides and seamstresses.[51] For most Greek women, paid labor was not a new experience, nor did it lead to drastic changes in gendered practices of labor at home.[52]

Rosie, Kiki, Despoina, and Fotini arrived in Montreal in the late 1950s to work as domestics in affluent homes.[53] Domestic service is deemed by participants as the most exigent sector of Greek female paid labor primarily because of the lack of familiarity with work practices in a Canadian home and lack of English, but especially for the stress caused by the isolation from the outside world. Panagiota characterized her workload as "nerve-wracking," cooking and serving for fifteen hours a day, along with mothering her two toddlers. All women soon broke off their contracts. Some opened their own stores, while others worked in family-owned businesses.

Most Greek women in Montreal opted for factory labor, mainly in the garment industry. Rigorous factory labor contributed to Greek women's suffering of nevra (Greek for nerves). Interviewees who worked in industries unanimously mention the anxiety caused by expected performance quotas or by the challenges of operating heavy factory equipment.[54] Stefania remembers entering the factory floor with her sister "who was so stressed that she would get dizzy." Lena recalls: "the machine was difficult and too heavy. I was only 17 years old!" Piecework from home was not less stressful, with some informants getting admitted to hospitals after long days of exhausting home labor.

Despite these challenges, all informants also shared fond memories of camaraderie, laughter, and good company at work. Colleagues proved to be dear friends and helpful assistants in times of need. Established kin or friend networks were ranked first in job searches. Alexandra explains: "As women we did not care if we liked the job or not. We asked our friends: 'where are you working?' 'Are they hiring there?' And we would go." The vast majority of the interviewees treat paid labor as their own contribution to family progress and what they conceptualize in Greek as proodos, that is, "social success." Hard work contributed to their self-appreciation and the fulfillment of their initial hopes. As Alexandra puts it: "Canada offered me a job and helped me acquire all that I have ever aspired to."

Conclusion

The language of emotion contributes to understand migration as a gendered experience among Greek female migrants in Montreal. Considering emotions—felt, negotiated, expressed, or suppressed—allows for a different and more "personal" reading of the actors, one that also allows their own voices to be heard. Emotional management, as the effort to deal with feelings, or as actions and practices, are also prevalent in these stories. Cohabitation as a response to social isolation, new emotional loyalties to ease the pain of separation or to justify the decision to leave parents and siblings behind, were among the many adaptive emotional practices that migrant women employed. All such attempts manifest a strong emotional agency that enabled Greek women to deal with hardships and embrace their new lives. By integrating emotions into migration history, it may be possible to transform not only the relation between historians and sources, and the interplay between interviewer and interviewee, but also the very practice of history.

NOTES

1. I would like to express my gratitude to the women who participated in this study and gave me access to their worlds and narratives. I am particularly grateful to Christina and Aliki, who generously introduced me to their lovely friends and relatives. Also, I would like to thank Lena Korma, Nicholas Michelacakis, Konstantinos Christodoulou, and Panos Panopoulos for reading my work and sharing their very constructive comments. Translations from Greek are mine.

2. I also used oral history in my master's thesis: Margarita Dounia, "Your Roots Will Be Here Away from Your Home: Migration of Greek Women to Montreal 1950–1980" (Master's thesis, McGill University, 2004).

3. At the time of this study, all interviewees resided in Montreal, with the exception of one returned migrant who now lives in Laconia, Greece. I have used pseudonyms for purposes of anonymity.

4. Alistair Thomson and Paul Thompson problematize narratives produced primarily by external voices of authority rather than by migrants themselves, whose access to linguistic tools or academic discourses is often limited. Such assertion holds particularly true for the case of migrant women whose intersectionality creates further mutations to their own voices. Alistair Thomson, "Moving Stories: Oral History and Migration Studies," *Oral History* 27, no. 1 (1999): 24–37. Other classic works for the use of oral history include Paul Thompson, *The Voice of the Past: Oral History* (1978; rpt. New York: Oxford University, 2000); and Luisa Passerini, *Storia e soggettivita: Le fonti orali, la memoria* (Florence: La Nuova Italia, 1988).

5. Michael Eugene Harkin, "Feeling and Thinking in Memory and Forgetting: Toward an Ethnohistory of the Emotions," *Ethnohistory* 50, no. 2 (2003): 262–63.

6. Susan J. Matt, "Recovering the Invisible: Methods for the Historical Study of the Emotions, in *Doing Emotions History*, ed. Susan J. Matt and Peter N. Stearns (Urbana: University of Illinois Press, 2013), 44.

7. Espín's words—"When the researcher's experiences share characteristics with those of the researched trust may increase"—further consoled me. Oliva M. Espín, *Women Crossing Boundaries: A Psychology of Immigration and Transformations of Sexuality* (New York: Routledge, 1999), 41.

8. Catherine Lutz and Geoffrey M. White, "The Anthropology of Emotions," *Annual Review of Anthropology* 15 (1986): 415.

9. Evangelia Tastsoglou, "The Margin at the Centre: Greek Immigrant Women in Ontario," *Canadian Ethnic Studies* 29, no. 1 (1997): 128.

10. For a discussion of an actor-centered approach, see Vasiliki Galani-Moutafi, "From Agriculture to Tourism: Property, Labor, Gender, and Kinship in a Greek Island Village (Part 1)," *Journal of Modern Greek Studies* 11, no. 2 (1993): 244–45.

11. The concept of "economy of family" is also encountered in Milharčič Hladnik's chapter in this volume. Some sources on Greek female migration emphasize more the forced character of Greek female migration. For example, Stefanos Kon-

stantinidis, *Η παρουσία των Ελλήνων στον Καναδά* [*The Presence of Greeks in Canada*] (Rethymno, Greece: E.DIA.M.ME, 2004); Deirdre Meintel, Micheline Labelle, Geneviève Turcotte, and Marianne Kempineers, "Migration, Wage Labor, and Domestic Relationships: Immigrant Women Workers in Montreal," *Anthropologica* 26, no. 2 (1984): 135–69.

12. *Misemos* is a Greek word that comes from the verb μισεύω (misevo = to depart from my country). It is a synonym for departure, immigration, and separation from one's country. Some female participants, however, do not describe their departure in dramatic tones, as would often be expected. This may be due to a variety of reasons: their perception of migration as the result of their own personal decision-making; their close ties with the homeland (frequent visits, communication with loved ones, etc.); a positive evaluation of their overall experience of migration; a negative evaluation of their prospects, had they stayed in their homeland; and the time that has passed since their departure and its possible effect on lessening or softening earlier feelings of pain, loss, rupture, and separation.

13. Ioanna Laliotou, "'I want to see the world': Mobility and Subjectivity in the European Context," in *Women Migrants from East to West: Gender, Mobility and Belonging in Contemporary Europe*, ed. Luisa Passerini, Dawn Lyon, Enrica Capussotti, and Ioanna Laliotou (New York: Berghahn Books, 2010), 53.

14. Xenia refers to two male kin members accompanying her to Montreal in order to "protect" her from any danger or misfortune that could be encountered during her transatlantic trip.

15. An interesting discussion on migration of austerity can be found in the chapter by A. James Hammerton in this volume.

16. Peter N. Stearns, "Modern Patterns in Emotions History," in *Doing Emotions History*, ed. Matt and Stearns, 30.

17. In her study of homesickness in the American context, Susan Matt explains that the term originally had a negative connotation, seen as an atavistic emotion that hinders adaptation, independence, and progress. During the twentieth century, what was celebrated were "those who can separate and move on" while those who could not were seen as "pathological and maladjusted." Susan J. Matt, *Homesickness: An American History* (New York: Oxford University Press, 2011), 8. For most Greeks, however, nostalgia and homesickness are seen as "proof" of love for one's country, despite its potentially harmful effects. Beatriz Macías Gómez-Estern and Manuel L. de la Mata Benítez make a distinction between two kinds of nostalgia: "nostalgia as desire (often called homesickness) regarded as a 'negative form,' considered to be typical of migrants, and whose function would be to maintain the basic scopes and values in the new setting. The second form, related to memory, is regarded as more positive and not so intense; its function would be to reconstruct identity and to promote self-cohesion." Macías Gómez-Estern and de la Mata Benítez, "Narratives of Migration: Emotions and the Interweaving of Personal and Cultural Identity through Narrative," *Culture and Psychology*

19, no. 3 (2013): 348–36. However, I am skeptical about the applicability of this distinction to the women interviewed for this study, and I also question whether either notion of nostalgia could be "felt" by such broad categories as "migrants" or "women," ignoring individuality.

18. The Greek word *marasmos* describes the feeling of depression and grief. Its sense is metaphorical, with its literal meaning describing the withering of flowers. *Marazi* in particular could be best explained as a lingering pain that eventually wears off the sufferer. In Greek, it is usually used metaphorically with the verb "to eat," to show that someone is slowly, gradually (and sometimes secretly) "consumed" by this pain.

19. The Greek word *xenitia* has its root in *xenos* (foreign, alien). It means living and being in a foreign land. The term is broad in content and implies uprootedness, dislocation, and suffering.

20. Citing evidence from studies about Greek immigrants in Canada, Margaret Lock and Pamela Wakewich-Dunk conclude that "there is a propensity for somatization among Greek patients, to the extent that it could be considered as an 'ethnic characteristic.'" Lock and Wakewich-Dunk, "Nerves and Nostalgia: Expression of Loss among Greek Immigrants in Montreal," *Canadian Family Physician* 36 (1990): 254.

21. Beyond popular culture and popular literature, also of Greek origin, various academic studies hold women as emotion-driven or "instinctive." For example, Matt discusses how, in early-twentieth-century United States, "observers maintained that a variety of different ethnic groups as well as African Americans, Native Americans, and women of all races were unsuited to movement and independence because of their alleged vulnerability to homesickness." Matt, *Homesickness*, 6.

22. Espín, *Women Crossing Boundaries*, 30–31.

23. I borrow the concept of "feeling rules" from the work of Arlie Russel Hochschild, *The Managed Heart: Commercialization of Human Feeling* (Berkeley: University of California Press, 2012), 56.

24. The pattern can be seen as a continuation of traditional residential patterns, particularly in Greek villages. But familiarity and socializing among neighbors or schemes of household proximity with kin were also common in Greek urban centers of the first post–World War II years. See, for example, Renée Hirschon, "Open Body/Closed Space: The Transformation of Female Sexuality," in *Defining Females: The Nature of Women in Societies*, ed. Shirley Ardener (London: Croom Helm, 1978), 51–72; Renée Hirschon, *Heirs of the Greek Catastrophe: The Social Life of Asia Minor Refugees in Piraeus* (New York: Berghahn Books, 1998).

25. Stylianos ("Stelios") Kazantzidis was a popular Greek folk singer, whose repertoire included many songs about the pain of migration.

26. Hirschon explores the binary of open/closed space, people, and emotions. Closed is associated with confinement and negative feelings. She mentions that "a person in this mental state is typically in low spirits, subdued and turned in upon

himself." Hirschon, "Open Body/Closed Space," 61. Extending this discussion, I deem stenahoria as a type of emotional as well as spatial cramping.

27. Lock and Wakewich-Dunk, "Nerves and Nostalgia," 254.

28. While visiting the homes of some interviewees in Montreal, I noticed that many maintained a small Greek-style garden in their backyard, with flowers, fruits, and vegetables that could be grown in Montreal's climate, including some that are used for cooking traditional Greek dishes.

29. What is meant by this is mostly distant cousins or siblings with a significant age difference who had been already abroad for some time, and who were not so close to the newly arrived migrant. For example, two interviewees stressed emphatically the difficulties they had developing a relationship with their much older and "estranged" sisters.

30. Tastsoglou, "The Margin at the Centre," 138.

31. Trouble in this case is associated with spending time outside the house, either unchaperoned or without apparent purpose. Greek mentality of the time associated women's morality and good reputation with staying at home, while the opposite could be seen as promiscuous, immoral, and harmful for family reputation. See Hirschon, "Open Body/Closed Space," 57; and Lock and Wakewich-Dunk, "Nerves and Nostalgia," 256.

32. For young unmarried women, such restrictions depended on women's age, on familial, educational, and economic status, on social entourage, and on time of arrival in Montreal. Women who migrated prior to World War II faced greater restrictions, as migrant families carried with them more traditional social and gender ideas. Those who arrived in the postwar decades enjoyed a great degree of independence for young unmarried women, as Greek society was also undergoing drastic transformations in social and gender norms—at least in urban centers. Therefore, postwar migrants had witnessed, and even embraced, these new ideas before their departure for Montreal.

33. Researchers have emphasized the importance of household skills (*noikokyrosyni* in Greek), especially for Greek communities in the first half of the twentieth century. Women's hard work and their role in maintaining cleanliness and order were considered as marks of their moral character. See Hirschon, "Open Body/Closed Space," 66; and Lock and Wakewich-Dunk, "Nerves and Nostalgia," 256.

34. Loretta Baldassar, "Missing Kin and Longing to Be Together: Emotions and the Construction of Co-presence in Transnational Relationships," *Journal of Intercultural Studies* 29, no. 3 (2008): 252.

35. Baldassar, "Missing Kin," 252.

36. Sonia Cancian, *Families, Lovers and Their Letters: Italian Postwar Migration to Canada* (Winnipeg: University of Manitoba Press, 2010), 6. Further exploration of the multiple connections between correspondence and emotions in family settings in context of migrations, and the tensions created by separation, can also be seen in the chapters by Bjerg, Borges, Milharčič Hladnik, and Sinke in this volume.

37. For a discussion of these terms, see Baldassar, "Missing Kin," 261–62.

38. Luisa Passerini, "Introduction," in *New Dangerous Liaisons: Discourses on Europe and Love in the Twentieth Century*, ed. Luisa Passerini, Liliana Ellena, and Alexander C. T. Geppert (New York: Berghahn Books, 2010), 1.

39. For the concept of emotional practice, see Monique Scheer, "Are Emotions a Kind of Practice (and Is That What Makes Them Have a History?)," *History and Theory* 51, no. 2 (2012): 193–220.

40. I borrow the term from Laliotou, "'I want to see the world.'"

41. Efie Gavaki, "The Greek Family in Canada: Continuity and Change in the Process of Adjustment," *International Journal of Sociology of the Family* 9, no. 1 (1979): 9.

42. Espín, *Women Crossing Boundaries*, 7. For a discussion of honor and shame, see Vasilikie Demos, "Maintenance and Loss of Traditional Gender Boundaries in Two Greek Orthodox Communities," *Journal of the Hellenic Diaspora* 16, nos. 1–4 (1989): 77–93; and Alice Scourby, "Three Generations of Greek Americans: A Study in Ethnicity," *International Migration Review* 14, no. 1 (1980): 43–52. For a discussion of the moral code of honor, see Ute Frevert, *Emotions in History—Lost and Found* (Budapest: Central European University Press, 2010).

43. Suzanne M. Sinke, "Migration for Labor, Migration for Love: Marriage and Family Formation across Borders," *OAH Magazine of History* 14, no. 1 (1999): 19.

44. Greek proverb that encapsulates the favored Greek marital pattern of endogamy. In Greek it is "παπούτσι από τον τόπο σου και ας είν' και μπαλωμένο." It could be translated: "It is better to have a shoe from your homeland, even if it has been resoled."

45. For a comparative discussion of dowry, see also Milharčič Hladnik's chapter in this volume.

46. Maria and Rosie were not interviewed, yet extensive references to them were made by their interviewed kin.

47. Anthony Giddens, *The Transformation of Intimacy: Sexuality, Love, and Eroticism in Modern Societies* (Stanford, CA: Stanford University Press, 1992), 38.

48. De Tona observes the same situation among Italian mothers and migration. Carla De Tona, "Mothering Contradictory Diasporas: Negotiation of Traditional Motherhood Roles among Italian Migrant Women in Ireland," in *Intimacy and Italian Migration: Gender and Domestic Lives in a Mobile World*, ed. Loretta Baldassar and Donna R. Gabaccia (New York: Fordham University Press, 2011), 109.

49. Rhacel Salazar Parreñas, "Mothering from a Distance: Emotions, Gender, and Intergenerational Relations in Filipino Transnational Families," *Feminist Studies* 27, no. 2 (2001): 362.

50. Paola Corti, "Women Were Labour Migrants Too: Tracing Late-Nineteenth-Century Female Migration from Northern Italy to France," in *Women, Gender, and Transnational Lives: Italian Workers of the World*, ed. Donna R. Gabaccia and Franca Iacovetta (Toronto: University of Toronto Press, 2002), 133–59.

51. Evangelia Tastoglou, "'The Temptations of New Surroundings': Family, State, and Transnational Gender Politics in the Movement of Greek Domestic Workers to Canada in the 1950s and 1960s," in *Women, Gender, and Diasporic Lives: Labor, Community, and Identity in Greek Migrations* (Lanham, MD: Lexington Books, 2009), 85. See also Peter Chimbos, *The Canadian Odyssey: The Greek Experience in Canada* (Toronto: McClelland and Stewart, 1980); Mina Noula, "Taming and Training Greek 'Peasant Girls' and the Gendered Politic s of Whiteness in Postwar Canada: Canadian Bureaucrats and Immigrant Domestics 1950s–1960s," *Canadian Historical Review* 94, no. 4 (2013): 514–39.

52. Most participants were skilled upon arrival and many had exercised their profession while in Greece.

53. I did not interview Kiki or Despoina, yet their stories were also discussed by their sisters in their respective interviews.

54. These observations are corroborated by studies of work in the garment industry. See Lock and Wakewich-Dunk, "Nerves and Nostalgia," 257; and Evangelia Tastsoglou and Valerie Preston, "Gender, Immigration, and Labour Market Integration: Where We Are and What We Still Need to Know," in *Emigration: Economic Implications*, ed. T. R. Shastri (Hyderabad, India: Icfai University Press, 2007), 48.

CHAPTER 12

Stories of Love and Marriage in the Modern British Diaspora

Themes of Change and Continuity

A. JAMES HAMMERTON

Matthew Lee's celebration of his new life—and his love—in Australia is perhaps as bald a statement of migration driven by love as we are likely to find:

> I left [England] in August 1999, after nine months apart, with my family's somewhat emotional blessing, not really at any time thinking about the enormity of what I was going to do, but more that it had always felt right and I should always go with what my heart told me.... I now have a passion for this wonderful country, and am always thankful for what it has given me, mainly my beautiful wife, daughter, and a fair go in life. It was for these reasons I completed my Australian citizenship papers in 2004, and I am proud to call myself an Australian.
>
> If I hadn't met Mirella, and done what I've done, I don't think I would have had the impetus to move.[1]

Matthew's statement is also a product of the modern contexts of migration between developed countries, in this case between Britain and Australia. Matthew fell in love with Mirella in 1997 during a twelve-month "working holiday" in Melbourne, under a late-twentieth-century policy that facilitated youth mobility, albeit with strict controls on overstaying and few opportunities for permanent settlement. After his reluctant return to England, the couple struggled to find strategies for being together, first through Mirella's brief Christmas visit to Britain, and later their marriage in Australia during Matthew's second visit on a tourist visa. While that brought no guarantee of his permanent settlement, they were ultimately able to satisfy immigration officials that their marriage was "genuine," finally yielding the treasured residence visa, and eventually citizenship.

Here, then, was a happy sequel to a quintessentially late-twentieth-century transnational love story. It bore all the hallmarks of modernity, such as courtship-friendly working holidays, the ease—and relative cheapness—of multiple return visits, the struggle to obtain the precious visa, and, crucially, the elevation of love and longing to a prime motivator in migration decisions. Only a generation earlier, in the decades following World War II, such considerations would have been almost unthinkable. Postwar conditions in "austerity Britain" left limited scope for impulsive, emotion-driven migration decisions like Matthew's, let alone multiple returns and short visits. Receiving countries like Australia sought—and often subsidized—skilled migrants and young families. The most obvious link between love and migration was, for a few, to embark on the migrant journey to Australia or New Zealand immediately following a wedding, then enjoy a six-week honeymoon on the ocean for only ten pounds each, although they risked having to endure sex-segregation in dormitory cabins during the voyage. More commonly, families, overwhelmingly from the skilled working class, first strove to obtain a passage, then struggled further to establish themselves after arrival, constrained by the requirement to stay for two years or repay the subsidy. The stresses often tested love and put relationships at risk during rough hostel living, homesickness, and housing shortages, although interviewees frequently insisted that the challenges "brought us together" rather than "drove us apart."[2]

Love, Migration, and an Emotional Revolution

By the 1980s the mobility of modernity had transformed this migration landscape, particularly for a generation for whom extended travel could merge seamlessly with permanent resettlement. Rising affluence from the 1960s had created an expanding educated middle-class with disposable incomes and enhanced capacity to pursue overseas opportunities. Revolutions in transport facilitated mass travel, enabling prospective migrants to "sample" prospective destinations, alongside the rise of expatriate employment and new mobile industries like information technology. The pursuit of migration as consumerism, dominated by the upwardly mobile middle class, was an unsurprising product of these conditions, best reflected in the rise of "lifestyle migration" among a young generation who were intent on individual self-realization.³ This represented a shift from a postwar migration of austerity to a migration of prosperity, a discretionary phenomenon in which financially ambitious migrants might decide to move from a mixture of motivations, some rational, some deeply emotional, some simply on a whim.

I use the term "mobility of modernity" here with reference to these material changes in the later twentieth century, and the expansion, in the developed world at least, of forms of discretionary migration less driven by economic imperatives. The shifting contexts of prosperity, social mobility, education, mass travel, and mobile employment helped to facilitate more casual attitudes to global mobility now taken for granted. These attitudes were one product of what Charles Taylor calls a more pronounced "culture of modernity, . . . a culture which is individualist . . . : it prizes autonomy; it gives an important place to self-exploration; and its visions of the good life involve personal commitment."⁴ Its visions of the good life also provided space for intense pursuits and expressions of emotional life, notably love, romance, and unchaperoned courtship. Travel and migration offered fertile fields for these pursuits, and the resulting migrant stories have been among the more dramatic products of a mobility of modernity, increasingly visible toward the end of the twentieth century.

Modernity and discretionary migration thus made love more public, but this was a work in progress throughout the postwar decades. It is no accident that historians of love in Britain have targeted the 1940s and 1950s as a key moment of transformation in emotional life, the culmination of an "emotional revolution" starting in the 1920s. For Claire Langhamer this was when ideas of marriage as a romantic ideal, based on individual commitment, love, mutual sexual satisfaction, and companionate marriage, overwhelmed traditional prescriptive conceptions of marriage as an institution: "These were decades when the emotional landscape changed dramatically for large numbers of ordinary people; a period that witnessed a revolution in the value attached to emotional intimacy within heterosexual encounters," and a commitment to ideals of monogamous marriage. She then traces the fate of postwar ideals from the 1970s, when social relations framing mid-century love "were reconstituted" under the pressure of contradictions: "a mid-twentieth century of quiet emotional instability and gentle subversion of established norms: a story of discontinuity and relative speeds of change." "Love and marriage," she argues, "were about to change once again, heralding the rapid decomposition of short-lived mid-century ideals" amid rising divorce levels and alternatives to heterosexual marriage.⁵

The concept of an emotional revolution and its disruptive power in postwar Britain is useful for exploring intimate relations among late-twentieth-century migrants, with particular reference to courtship, romantic love, and marriage. It fits well with patterns of change implicit in the transformation from a postwar migration of austerity to one of prosperity. But personal migrant testimony takes us a step further by complicating the relationship between the big-picture framing ideals and actual behavior under the pressures of transnational mobility. Matthew's romantic story, for example, could belong to the 1950s in the couple's ardent yearning for marriage, yet its transnational elements, its evolution from a casual to committed relationship and their unremarkable premarital overseas travel together situate it more firmly in the later decades.

Langhamer's emotional revolution typology rests on evidence of ideals expressed in media and prescriptive literature, together with behavior, drawn from volunteers' extended diary entries written for the Mass Observation Society established in 1937. She makes a fair claim that actual behavior and language mirrored changing ideology. But elsewhere the relationship between ideals and practice is not invariably so obvious. Other essays in this volume illustrate the routine resort to forms of intense romantic language from the late nineteenth century to the 1980s, the same forms that were so popular at the height of the emotional revolution; arguably such language was even common well before the nineteenth century. Yet in the earlier periods the highly charged language rarely reflected prevailing ideals and forms of marriage, as an economic institution, at the time. María Bjerg's essay, on bigamy cases of Italian and Spanish husbands sued by their wives in the nineteenth-century Argentinian courts, surveys spousal letters that employed frequent romantic language, but the dominant themes dwell on the economic basis of marriage, on husbands' hard work and obligations to transmit adequate remittances back to their wives. Similarly, Marcelo J. Borges's essay, spanning the 1870s to 1920s, on Portuguese migrants' letters to their wives, mostly focused on remittances, explores a "gendered language" blending concepts like "love, interest, sacrifice, and reciprocity," classic components of traditional constructions of marriage before the emotional revolution.[6] Such inconsistencies should not be surprising.

Like the emotional revolution, the transformation from a migration of austerity to one of prosperity was never smooth and linear. In Britain, it encountered new obstacles, like the recession of the 1980s, which motivated a generation eager to flee Britain. Mostly unemployed, and echoing the urgencies of postwar austerity, many described themselves as "Thatcher's refugees," referring to mass unemployment and political alienation under Margaret Thatcher's Conservative regime from 1979 to 1990.[7] A further obstacle was the loss of relatively unhindered free access of the British, since colonial times, to the old white Commonwealth countries of Australia, Canada, and New Zealand. In contrast to a postwar era of generous subsidy and easy access designed to develop Commonwealth economies, from the 1970s prospective immigrants, like Matthew, faced increasingly rigorous visa restrictions to meet tighter entry standards for skills and education.[8] Still, by 2000, British emigration surged to levels recalling those of the 1960s. While the British Empire was a distant memory, the British—like other Anglophones—still enjoyed the benefits of the colonial dividend: a global lingua franca in a wide choice of congenial settlement locations, including the United States.

In less than half a century, the changes had been deep and enduring, but not all of them were wholly new. One of the largest examples of love-driven migration occurred in the immediate aftermath of World War II with the migration of "war brides" between various countries after demobilized male troops married local women and took them "home."[9] Moreover, postwar assisted migration schemes, designed to attract skilled working-class families, enabled young singles to access cheap fares and pursue subsidized working holidays. These youthful sojourners, precursors of modern backpackers, many from tightly knit working-class families, could enjoy the freedoms of uncontrolled courtship on extended ship voyages. Daphne Knights, who emigrated alone to Australia in 1956, recalled that, on the six-week voyage, "I came out of my shell, and anyone wanted me to join in I joined in. . . . And it was a ratio of six men to every woman! So, from having no boyfriends, no experience, it was wonderful. . . . And I took to it; I loved it. . . . And so, by the time I got off the ship, you know, I was a totally different person. I was outgoing, ready for anything."[10] Most of these sojourners settled permanently, some returned or moved on to other destinations, but their part in a mass migration movement signaled the democratization of youthful global mobility, with highly charged prospects of romance and marriage abroad, although, as Daphne hinted, contemporary moral standards exercised a powerful influence: "I'd had all this high time on the ship and, luckily, kept my head, shall we say! [laughter] Arrived intact, as they say! [laughter]."[11] Langhamer's emotional revolution is on full display here, still subject to traditional moral restraints, but with the freedoms of mobility pointing to a different future.

As Langhamer observes, the meaning of love is mediated by contexts of time and space and shaped by the interplay of change and continuity.[12] I have explored aspects of this process in two books based mainly on oral testimony, one on the postwar British migration to Australia, the other on the modern British exodus to several countries.[13] In the second book the interrelationship of migration and issues around love, marriage, family, and divorce were prominent in the emergence of a mobility of modernity and its impact on migrant experience. So it is timely to review some of the main themes and to reflect on degrees to which the link between intimate relationships and migration are inflected differently over a relatively short time when social contexts change.

The Lens of Retrospective Testimony: Love and National Identity

A methodological observation is appropriate here, given the reliance of this research on oral and written testimony. For the recent past we can speak to migrants themselves and tap their memories in extended interviews, sometimes supplemented with revealing written autobiographical accounts. Invaluable as they are, for insights into intimate relationships the drawbacks are undeniable, particularly compared to the emotional language we encounter in love letters. Moreover, those interviewed in the early twenty-first century, whether recalling events of the 1950s or 1990s, tend to employ similar language. While accounts of intimate relationships can be extended and deeply felt in interviews, and sometimes even more in measured written accounts, only rarely do they capture the emotional depth and immediacy expressed in private correspondence or diaries. Retrospective emotional expression necessarily yields different kinds of emotional evidence compared to contemporaneous discourse, which demands careful historical awareness.[14] A more pragmatic difference can stem from reticence, especially in front of a microphone, and there is invariably interviewee caution about the uncertain audience beyond, who may become privy to the intimate aspects of their lives. An account spanning four decades, from 1961, illustrates the point. Elizabeth Taylor, in England, met Michael, a visiting Australian, when she was sixteen and he was twenty-two; both acknowledged love at first sight and vowed, eventually, to marry. This was realized only forty years later in Melbourne, after Michael had married three times, Elizabeth once, and both had had children, punctuated by recurrent visits back and forth. Here was a fluctuating, tempestuous, profound affair, a story of love defying distance, told by Elizabeth with candor and sincerity. Yet the most emotionally charged language she used occurred in this description of their meeting in England during one of Michael's visits: "With Paul's knowledge [her husband] I got myself into an affair with Michael and we re-kindled all the feelings, which culminated in my coming to Australia [in 1975] for two months."[15] This is, indeed, revealing, but a history of their transnational relationship might look very different if it was based instead on the turbulence of their forty-year correspondence; it might yield different insights about the possibilities faced by lovers contending with the tyranny of distance as well as their divorces.[16]

Despite these limitations there are compensating benefits to be gained from retrospective testimony compared to sources like correspondence. For migration historians with an eye to issues of intimate relationships one overriding advantage is the opportunity to locate matters of love, marriage, and divorce within the shifting settings of individual life stories and the larger social context. In an extended life narrative a migrant's intimate adult experience can be seen, for example, against events of childhood like family breakdown, the shifting impact of transnational marriages, and the evolution of mentalities and identities under the long-term tensions of migration. There remain the well-rehearsed cautions around the vagaries of memory, of retrospective reconstruction, especially of exaggerating or downgrading the passions of the past under pressure of later events. Some of these issues can never be fully resolved, like those which affect other sources, but are more likely to come under scrutiny, with gently probing questions, during long, sometimes revisited, interviews, an aid to detecting inconsistencies. Moreover, personal memories are invariably recalled with more vivid and articulate certainty than those of more general and accessible public background matters.[17]

Matthew Lee's fuller story provides an instructive example, and takes us further into the modern nature of his transnational marriage. In the opening quotation he associated his passion for his wife and daughter with his appreciation for "a fair go in life" in "this wonderful country." The causative link between his love and his life transformation dominated much of the interview, although marriage, let alone romance, was never part of his travel plans. Born in 1977 in the north of England into a close middle-class family, he owed an early sense of independence to his parents, traveling twice to Canada at the age of twelve and thirteen with an older friend and an older sister, "and I loved it, I've always had an independent spirit." Looking back, he reflected, "I actually thought, at some stage in my life, I would end up living somewhere out of England." He left school and home at eighteen, partly at the prompting of his parents: "My parents have an approach, which was, seventeenth birthday you got the suitcase, eighteenth it was packed.... My dad was told at eighteen: "Right, go off and see the world, learn who you are, go and see the world." I was told the same thing, but instead of seeing the world I just immersed myself in work." Keen to save money—he decided not to attend university—for about two years his life revolved around work and a close relationship that began when he was sixteen. The fraught ending of that relationship inspired his Australian working holiday; an example of lost love driving mobility, it was intended strictly as a temporary escape from his sadness, and from growing disillusion with the English class system and right-wing government in the shadow of Thatcherite politics, which had impelled him to join the Labour party. "I'd lived all my life under Maggie, and I had an absolute hatred of everything she stood for."

Matthew's time in Australia in 1997–98 was colored dramatically by his relationship with Mirella, begun within two weeks of arrival, moving promptly from casual to serious, but with the looming shadow of his eventual forced return to England.

> Truthfully we were just having a bit of fun, we could see we got on straight away, and we had a really good time together, but I'd just come out of a revolting relationship, that I was very hurt from, and I wasn't in the mood for anything serious. . . . But as we got closer and closer it became a bit more obvious to me and her that it wouldn't work, we couldn't continue as we were, but we just kept ignoring the fact that I was leaving at some stage, and just trying to enjoy it.

Matthew's return to England was softened by Mirella's short visit over Christmas, but he recalled his nine-month wait as the most painful in his life, albeit eased by an enjoyable job with British Airways. But it was a formative time too: "We had nine months apart, and that nine months apart has shaped our marriage, because, never should we have to go through that again, whatever we go through, nothing will be as bad as the time that we spent apart. . . . So we've gone through some tough times, but we've always gone back to the basis: "Well, we still want to be together, because, we don't want to go back to the situation that we had before, we've fought too bloody hard to be together."

The bond was cemented, on Valentine's Day, by an international telephone proposal Matthew left on her answering machine at work, promptly accepted. The wedding that followed in Australia was a multicultural affair. He had warmed immediately to Melbourne, its atmosphere and nightlife, with little culture shock to hold him back, but faced a challenge stemming from Mirella's family background. Her parents were Sicilian migrants, initially suspicious of him from fear that he might take her back to England. They resisted her plan to spend three weeks with him in England, but came around when the plan was expanded to include a visit to relatives in Sicily. His parents traveled to Melbourne for the wedding and both families warmed to each other, but Matthew had not anticipated the depth of cultural adaptation that lay ahead. Close contact, not just with Mirella's parents, but with uncles, aunts, and cousins, tight-knit and within easy proximity, initially caused doubts as he discovered the "huge amount of cultural differences between my very English family, and her very traditional Sicilian clan." For the first two years he resisted being drawn into Mirella's family orbit. "I clung to my identity here," he insisted, "kind of fighting against the system, I didn't want to go to all these bloody functions and things with [her] family. . . . I wanted to be on my own." But family immersion, and especially the birth of their first child, wrought a change, as he realized that:

> I can't fight this; I've got to try and develop it a little bit . . . and I got much closer to my mother-in-law, and realized that we've actually got an awful lot in common, and really got *on* with my mother-in-law, but culturally there's some pretty impressive differences. Well, my mother-in-law says now that I've become one of them. She says: "You've become more of a wog than us," because I've kind of adapted, I've had to. . . . I've got used to it, the fact that my mother-in-law is virtually at my house every day.

Matthew's multicultural adaptation went deeper, extending to a shifting national identity that began to minimize his British origins; again the catalyst was the value he placed on his marriage. "Oh, I still know where I came from, I still know what shaped me, my Britishness is what shaped who I am. . . . What's made me a better person is Australia, it's my wife, my life here, . . . and therefore I do cling to my Australianness more. If you asked me in the street: "What nationality are you?" "I'm Australian," and that to me is very important. . . . I wanted to become an Australian citizen as soon as I was eligible to become one."[18]

The conjuncture here of physical and marital mobility, encompassing a transnational marriage, is dramatic but hardly uncommon, although Matthew's rapid shift in national identity amid the glow of a happy marriage is an unusual, more modern, development. National identity and loyalty among British migrants in Anglophone countries is traditionally malleable, but change usually followed many years of adjustment in the new country. Matthew's shift was avowedly inseparable from his attachment to Mirella. It underlines the way in which his narrative is a migration story told through an emotional lens. If narrated through a traditional demographic framework, his story would serve to illustrate the global trend of working holidays as prelude to permanent migration. But here the love story is the prime migration story, and, like his newfound Australian identity, barely comprehensible without it. Migration narratives informed by love are more palpable in stories like Matthew's, when the power of new love remains in the relatively recent past. Fuller life stories, seen from a greater age, might give a more subtle impression of evolving relationships, but the larger point remains that a history of migration written through a framework of the emotions contributes quite different perspectives compared to others, like those structured around personal improvement narratives. Matthew's account is infused with emotion and emotional language, moving from the loss of one love to the discovery of another. It suggests that both migration and love demand a psychic shift, each with the capacity to enhance the experience of the other. It is also significant that this very modern migrant love story was told by a young man, when no such stories structured around love interests emerged from male interviewees for the earlier postwar project from the 1940s to 1960s.[19] By contrast, postwar women interviewees were more likely to elaborate on courtship and marriage; their husbands, though often expansive on family matters, gave more attention to issues of work and career. Might it be that by the end of the century men were joining women in ascribing a driving priority to love in their migration stories? A diminished gender distinction in this respect would be consistent with Langhamer's emotional revolution, where both men and women were exposed to the new ideals of romantic love. But the later timing in Matthew's case, when those ideals had long been under challenge, points to a less linear set of changes.

Matthew's newfound Australian loyalty, driven expressly by his emotional life, was consistent with shifting attitudes to national identity among British migrants in the late twentieth century. Tanya Piejus, for example, who had lived in Italy and Australia as well as Britain in the 1990s, finally settled in Wellington, New Zealand, in 2001 and reflected on the insignificance of her dual British–New Zealand citizenship compared to her sense of local belonging: "I'm a citizen of both countries and a native of neither, but it doesn't matter to me at all. I finally feel like I belong somewhere."[20] Similarly, Andrew Mackie and his wife settled in Melbourne in 1992 after "sampling" both Australia and Canada; Andrew wore his sense of global citizenship like a badge: "but really, I consider myself a citizen of the world above a British person. Why wouldn't you?"[21]

This casual cosmopolitanism was just one element of a more discretionary migration in the late twentieth century, distinguished sharply from the experience of the previous postwar generation. It was consistent with the emergence of more continuous mobility, or serial migration, when decisions to move on to further destinations might be taken lightly, especially for the young without children. Its most extreme expression is found in migrants' pragmatic evaluations of different destinations for courtship and marriage prospects. Catherine Seddon emigrated with a partner to Wellington, New Zealand, in 2001, an adventure followed by a painful breakup. By 2007, still single, she contemplated a second move to Melbourne. "Finding a future partner in Wellington just seems impossible [laugh] . . . and as I'm single, I want to live in a bigger city and all that the critical mass can offer."[22]

Courtship-Friendly Mobility from the 1950s

These examples contrast sharply with earlier stories beneath the shadow of World War II, and particularly from those young married couples who struggled to establish themselves and obtain a cheap passage abroad, then pursued opportunities for their families in the new country. Their stories rarely include reference to romantic courtship, which disappears inside narratives of struggle and achievement. Some women could pursue a migration project as a means to save a marriage, most poignantly those who took their husbands to Australia to solve the man's drinking problems, invariably a forlorn hope.[23] In such cases the wife's initiative, a form of emotional work, signaled shifting power balances within the marriage, but a materially successful migration could be undermined by a husband's susceptibility to a strong drinking culture. More generally these postwar patterns of family migration, characterized by traditional gender distinctions and pride in multiple third-generation grandchildren, have much in common with nineteenth-century migration narratives, so often dominated by foundational family stories of striving and material transformation in colonial settings.

It is among the postwar single sojourners of the 1950s and 1960s, rather than married couples, where we are most likely to find early signs of changing experiences and attitudes, particularly among women. The cheap fares aimed at young families were available equally to young singles, assuming that most would settle permanently, marry, and contribute to the economy. But easy admission created unprecedented prospects of the two-year working holiday. In the longer term it began to democratize opportunities for extended global travel and serial migration. Young women with mobile qualifications, for example in nursing, physiotherapy, hairdressing, and secretarial work, seized the opportunities for adventure and short-term expatriate experience, perhaps yielding some of the best-known images of the Australian "ten pound Pom" scheme. Maggie Campbell fit this pattern explicitly when she followed a childhood dream and left alone, aged twenty-four, for Sydney in 1969. She was an experienced nurse from Oxford, accustomed to work at a teaching hospital, with an international mix of "medical staff, doctors from Sydney, New Zealand, lots of places." She was barely touched by the 1960s rebellious youth culture but recalls the sixties in Oxford as "a very easy cultural decade, . . . my social life was all around the colleges in Oxford," for Maggie a safe place to be a single woman. She was resolute that her trip was to be an adventure, strictly limited to two years. "I was certainly going to travel extensively around Australia, do my two years, but then I could go back." In Sydney, where she moved straight into a prearranged job, the work culture was similar to Oxford, and offered an instant network of friends and social life. "I latched into a group very quickly after arriving here, I had my friends I came out with and I instantly was adopted by all these others who liked the way I spoke, or whatever, and so for me it was very lucky." The "others," within a few weeks, included her future Australian husband.

With large numbers of single sojourners arriving in Australia at the time, marriage to a locally born spouse was a strong possibility, and for most it brought an abrupt change of plan from working holiday to permanent settlement—like Matthew Lee's experience three decades later. For women the experience could be similar to that of war brides, with risks of culture shock and rejection by the husband's family. Maggie's experience was different, as she warmed to the country and her welcoming in-laws. Her only distress flowed from her parents' inability to face the prospect of a trip to attend her wedding. Moreover, when her husband's work later took them to various English hospitals for nearly three years it raised the possibility of permanent return to England. But it was Maggie who pressed for return to Australia, despite attachment to her close-knit family. Back in Australia she withdrew from the workforce for ten years to raise three children, and enjoy an apparently harmonious family life, with shared domestic tasks, especially child-rearing. But as the children grew older intense conflict emerged in the marriage, leading to a painful separation. Maggie insisted this had nothing to do with her migrant past, rather with temperamental differences stemming from her husband's critical and controlling personality, although he had observed that migration was unhealthy for mixed marriages: "he spoke once about how you shouldn't marry somebody from another country."

Maggie's migration, her abrupt change of mind to stay and marry a local, had much in common with patterns like Matthew's a generation later, although she never employed his emotional language, possibly a product of the long passage of time rather than gender difference. She embarked during the "youth revolutions" of the 1960s, but more importantly when new birth-control options and rising female employment were facilitating greater independence and mobility for women, although deeper changes in gender relations were in their early stages. A wider, more international, choice of marital partners was a predictable consequence. At the same time, Maggie's experience was a product of the postwar generation, still to witness the full explosion of mass travel and the global aspirations of backpacking youth. She was emphatic that her migration would go no further than Australia, with no plans for onward movement. There was still an air of the exotic for her about Australia: "I was still a bit of a pioneer, it was still a bit adventurous, and I think these were the things that attracted me about it." Even telephone calls home remained an expensive luxury, and the back and forth movements of Matthew and the multiple country "sampling" enjoyed by others were inconceivable. Marriage to a local involved settling down and committing to the new country, just as the policy-makers of the postwar migration schemes intended. Love and marriage must have reinforced her resolve to stay in Australia, but more likely it simply reinforced a decision she was close to reaching anyway. Indeed, despite later holding dual citizenship, Maggie became a proud Australian citizen, with diminishing attachment to Britain; only much later did she become attracted to the modern trend of an international identity.[24]

Maggie's story marks the turbulent years of the late 1960s as a point of transition in the experience of young women migrants. But similar processes had been under way a decade earlier. We can trace single women itinerants and migrants back to prewar years and even earlier; many modern migrants spoke of female family forebears who pursued overseas adventures, settled and married abroad at times when it was challenging for women to travel alone.[25] But the accessible mass migration programs after 1945 democratized those opportunities beyond the affluent, and freedom of movement and social mixing on shipboard and afterward were a measure of how much had changed for single women at the end of the war.

A book published in 1957 by a return migrant to Australia offers some insights into the changing possibilities. Eunice Gardner, a hairdresser, used the ten-pound scheme to launch her childhood dream to travel the world, starting with a two-year working holiday in Australia in the early 1950s. Soon after arrival she joined a like-minded British nurse, Diana Williams; they worked for five months in Sydney, traveling the country together, later returning across Asia and Europe, partly hitchhiking. Eunice's book, *The World at Our Feet: The Story of Two Women Who Adventured Halfway across the Globe*, provided a rich account of people and places and engaging character sketches of traveling companions.[26] Many of these were British single women sojourners; she was intrigued, too, by Englishwomen she met who had married Australians and settled, even in the Outback, singing its praises as "a grand place, and there's so much space."[27]

There was no hint that Eunice was remotely interested in allowing love to divert her travel adventure. But she was alert to romantic possibilities, as their hitchhiking threw them together with male drivers and other travelers, often for extended periods, and at various stops they joined mixed groups of itinerants in an intense social life. In a chapter titled "Ruined Romance," she recalled her time in the hot, tropical climate of Darwin, when she and Diana had teamed up with two young Australian truck drivers. At a romantic coastal restaurant "above the whispering moonlit sea on either side," the foursome "sat lazily sipping glasses of Pimms. . . . 'This is the life for me,' I whispered contentedly, the glorious tropical night beginning to cast its spell." Later, on the dance floor,

> the spell continued as I swayed in Joe's powerful arms, . . . two powerful figures beneath the star filled sky, and from wherever we looked, a golden pathway shimmered across the dark water from below the full moon. "I think I should like to live in Darwin," I said to Joe. "It could be a real paradise with someone you loved." He laughed rather cynically, but clasped me tighter and, his body close to mine, he said: "Why don't you stay? I need a wife in Darwin." I wanted to believe him, but something in the way he paused before saying "Darwin," or maybe the strange secretive part of him, that appeared frequently, made me know instinctively he didn't fully mean what he said.

Later her disillusion melted as the two couples strolled along a moonlit beach "'Now I know what moon magic is!' I laughed softly. . . . Joe drew me into the shadow of the cliffs. . . . Then his mouth was hard and hot and his hands a part of the wonder of the night and although I tried to reason with him, I began to realize the reason for the lack of morals we had been amazed at even in this little while in a hot tropical climate." The heated moment came to an abrupt halt when Eunice spotted an approaching army of giant crabs, "their pincers waving for an attack." For Joe it was a laughing matter, but for Eunice "the beauty of the still night was shattered." The other couple, too, had been preoccupied with crabs, and later the two women laughed, "but Merv and Joe were quiet. They hadn't realized how crabs could react on those who weren't used to them!"[28]

This romantic vignette is the only one of its kind in the book, otherwise preoccupied with engaging traveler's tales and descriptions. The language of love here seems to borrow from the popular Harlequin romantic fiction, embroidered with alluring tropical settings.[29] Such language provided one of few easily available means of describing romantic encounters, thoroughly consistent with ideals of the emotional revolution. Eunice's comments were firmly located in the contexts of her time, like the easy association of a "lack of morals" with a tropical climate, which echoes classical environmental determinism. The book speaks to a 1950s sensibility, and would have been attractive to prospective readers open to similar dreams of migration and adventure, with possibilities of exotic romance thrown in. It recalls Alistair Thomson's observation that, at the time, "the ten pound passage offered perhaps the only way apart from marriage that an unmarried working-class woman in her mid-twenties could leave the family home and create an independent life."[30] An equivalent book written by a woman in the 1990s might focus more on family relationships, career intentions, further travel and prospective partners, extending even to politics. Love and its travails might play more of a part, more explicitly, with new, often serial, mobile partners. Prospective interviewees routinely dwelt on such subjects when writing for the modern diaspora project.

Eunice might have embroidered her romantic episode with literary license, but it remains pertinent to modern readers, particularly in her knowing evaluation of Joe's cynical proposal, and the implicit suggestion that love might bring her to contemplate, albeit briefly, shifting her identity from single sojourner and explorer to married migrant. This is a strong message about the power of the exotic awaiting unsuspecting young sojourners. Even without the exotic, thousands of young assisted migrants, like Maggie Campbell intent only on a two-year working holiday, ended up marrying and becoming permanent migrants. More generally, Eunice's celebration of youthful female sojourning anticipates the greater global reach of modern backpackers, often with open-ended travel and migration ambitions. Just as Daphne Knights felt newly liberated, "outgoing, ready for anything" after her romantic 1956 ship voyage, Matthew Lee could convert his 1997 Australian working holiday into a love story and permanent settlement. Either story, with variations, could be common to both periods. Here continuity in the migrant experience, during and after the emotional revolution, dominates.

Yet profound changes did occur in British migrant experience over half a century, not least in the transition from motivating contexts of austerity to prosperity, modern preoccupations with lifestyle change, enhanced freedoms for women and greater opportunities for routine mobility. Viewed from a distance, the mid-century emotional revolution and its disruptive aftermath suggest two sharply distinguished emotional landscapes, most starkly illustrated in the late-century visibility of love as a driver of migration, exemplified in the popularity of working holidays facilitated by regimes hungry for a young workforce. But the stories canvassed here suggest that the course of the emotional revolution in migrants' lives was never straightforward, and that there was no single moment when love became a prime motivating driver, or indeed lost its purchase. Rather, as material conditions fostering an individualist "culture of modernity" intensified from the 1960s, the space for overt emotion to complicate the transformative potential of migration was enhanced gradually, as contexts shifted. Migrant testimony illustrates how life experience might resist the dominant ideals at the heart of an emotional revolution and its demise. Maggie's independent migration leading to marriage was quite unremarkable by the late 1960s, and Matthew's rapid change of direction under the influence of love for Mirella in Australia half a century later was both a modern and traditional story. Yet Eunice's Australian story suggests that, even in the 1950s, changes were already well under way, not least in women's abilities to use independent migration to manage opportunities for romance. The migrant experience, always a creature of its time, is a subtle mixture of the complexities of change and continuity; the push and pull of love and private life, of shifts from one emotional landscape to another, is subject to even greater variations in its social meaning over time, with the potential to unsettle definitions of migration. Unscrambling the mutual influences of each on the other is a challenge for migration historians, but one with potential to enhance our understanding of migrant lives.

NOTES

1. Matthew Lee, written account and interview by James Hammerton, October 27, 2007, Melbourne, Australia, British Diaspora Oral History Project, La Trobe University, Melbourne (hereafter BDP), file DL40.

2. A. James Hammerton and Alistair Thomson, *Ten Pound Poms: Australia's Invisible Migrants* (Manchester: Manchester University Press, 2005), 230–37.

3. Karen O'Reilly and Michaela Benson, "Lifestyle Migration: Escaping to the Good Life?" in *Lifestyle Migration: Expectations, Aspirations, and Experiences*, ed. Michaela Benson and Karen O'Reilly (Farnham, UK: Ashgate, 2009), 1–13; Michaela Benson and Karen O'Reilly, "Migration and the Search for a Better Way of Life: A Critical Exploration of Lifestyle Migration," *Sociological Review* 57, no. 4 (2009): 608–25.

4. This private culture of individualism is one element only among a large diversity of interpretations of the development of modernity, but central in Charles Taylor, *Sources of the Self* (Cambridge, MA: Harvard University Press, 1989), 305.

5. Claire Langhamer, *The English in Love: The Intimate Story of an Emotional Revolution* (Oxford: Oxford University Press, 2013), 7–9. See also Simon Szreter and Kate Fisher, *Sex before the Sexual Revolution: Intimate Life in England, 1918–1963* (Cambridge: Cambridge University Press, 2010).

6. Similar dissonances are evident in Mirjam Milharčič Handlik's essay on Slovenian women's migration to Egypt in the 1920s and 1930s. Most of these essays raise questions about ethnic-specific differences given the uneven pace of modernity in different countries compared to the Anglosphere, but note Tyler Carrington's essay on "chance encounters" in the new urban mobility in Berlin at the beginning of the twentieth century, where romantic language mirrors transforming modernity, but without any suggestion that expectations of marriage itself have been transformed.

7. A. James Hammerton, *Migrants of the British Diaspora since the 1960s: Stories from Modern Nomads* (Manchester: Manchester University Press, 2017), 82–104.

8. Hammerton, *Migrants of the British Diaspora*, 54–65.

9. Marjory Harper and Stephen Constantine, *Migration and Empire* (Oxford: Oxford University Press, 2010), 243–44. There is a substantial memoir and oral history literature of individual war bride experience. See, for example, "The American War Bride Experience: GI Brides of World War II," http://uswarbrides.com/WW2warbrides/wbbooks.html; last updated August 2012.

10. Daphne Knights, interview, quoted in Hammerton and Thomson, *Ten Pound Poms*, 255–56.

11. Knights, interview.

12. Langhamer, *The English in Love*, 11.

13. Hammerton and Thomson, *Ten Pound Poms*; Hammerton, *Migrants of the British Diaspora*.

14. Thanks to Claire Langhamer for sharing discussion on these issues.

15. Hammerton, *Migrants of the British Diaspora*, 170.

16. Oral history projects designed expressly to probe memories of sexual behavior and attitudes, selecting mostly willing volunteers, can be more successful; Szreter and Fisher's *Sex before the Sexual Revolution* is a recent example.

17. Alessandro Portelli, "What Makes Oral History Different?" in *The Oral History Reader*, ed. Robert Perks and Alistair Thomson, 3rd ed. (London: Routledge, 2016), 48–58; Hammerton and Thomson, *Ten Pound Poms*, 18–19.

18. Matthew Lee, interview by James Hammerton, October 27, 2007, Melbourne, Australia, and written account, BDP, DL40.

19. The postwar "Ten Pound Poms" project included 66 male and 115 women interviewees. "Ten Pound Poms" Oral History Collection, National Library of Australia, Canberra.

20. Tanya Piejus, interview by James Hammerton, November 30, 2006, Wellington, New Zealand, and written account, BDP, DP15.

21. Andrew Mackie interview by James Hammerton, November 23, 2007, Melbourne, Australia, and written account, BDP, DM15.

22. Catherine Seddon, interview by James Hammerton, Wellington, New Zealand, November 28, 2006, and written account, BDP, DS20.

23. Hammerton and Thomson, *Ten Pound Poms*, 200–201, 291.

24. Maggie Campbell, interview by James Hammerton, Mosman, New South Wales, Australia, July 14, 1998, "Ten Pound Poms" Oral History Collection.

25. Hammerton, *Migrants of the British Diaspora*, 45, 99, 188.

26. Eunice Gardner, *The World at Our Feet: The Story of Two Women Who Adventured Halfway across the Globe* (London: W. H. Allen, 1957).

27. Gardner, *The World at Our Feet*, 47, 73, 78.

28. Gardner, *The World at Our Feet*, 89–91.

29. I am indebted to Professor Gail Savage for pointing out the similarity in language to romantic scenes in Nevil Shute's novel *A Town Like Alice*, published in 1950, seven years before Eunice's book and set partially in Australia.

30. Alistair Thomson, *Moving Stories: An Intimate History of Four Women across Two Countries* (Sydney: University of New South Wales Press, 2011), 320.

CHAPTER 13

"I Can Express My Feelings with Just a Tweet"

Language, Emotion, and the Digital Divide among Immigrant Families in Italy

ROBERTA RICUCCI

Until a few decades ago, migrant families in their places of settlement were studied mainly from two perspectives. In the first, the family, whether reunited or formed as a result of emigration, was the lens through which researchers examined the processes of integration and settlement in the arrival society.[1] The second area of inquiry explored the links between insertion dynamics and notions of identity among younger generations.[2] A major focus of these studies has been parent-child relationships, specifically regarding parental authority, the languages used and their impact on intergenerational communication, and the new lifestyles adopted by the children.

Today, these research paths converge and expand, taking into account two new, interconnected elements. On the one hand there is transnationalism,[3] one aspect of which is "less wished-for but more endured—the growing phenomenon of people and family units who make an effort to keep alive emotional and family ties in spite of the borders and distances that separate them."[4] On the other, there is the role of the new media, as the widespread use of information and communication technologies (ICTs) among migrants has become fundamental in maintaining bonds with friends and family in the distant homeland and members of the diaspora in other countries.[5]

While ICTs offer extraordinary opportunities for staying in touch, they have also generated challenges. The younger generation is especially adept at seamlessly navigating the internet moving from one social network to another. Their parents, by contrast, are less versed in using the internet and other digital technologies. As a result, a widening gap has emerged between the younger generation (sometimes the second generation of immigrants) and their parents (first generation of immigrants, usually).

Like many of the chapters included in this volume, this chapter examines emotions among immigrant families and the challenges that ensue as a result of mobility. Specifically, I look at the ways in which language, ICTs, and cultural backgrounds intersect with affective ties among migrant families in the city of Turin (Italy). Drawing from more than eighty interviews with parents and young adult children of Moroccan and Peruvian immigrant families living in Italy, this study offers a sociological perspective on how technology disrupts continuity in the affective language between parents and children.[6] In relationship to the language divide that has emerged between parents and children in immigrant families, I show how four emotional factors influence affective distance in familial relationships: alienation, loneliness, frustration, and in a few cases, obligation.[7] The lack of cultural capital and low investment in understanding the function of ICTs in children's lives are two key issues that contribute to explaining why, in today's knowledge society in immigrant families, as well as in native Italian families, interactions between parents and children are increasingly marked by emotional distance. In the next section, I offer a brief theoretical overview followed by an introduction to Moroccan and Peruvian immigrant families as ideal case studies for comparing two current immigrant communities in Italy.

Theoretical Framework

The family is a key locus for analyzing the migration process and relations between parents and children. For the children of immigrants, the family represents the environment in which they grow up and settle. In the new arrival setting, they learn local behaviors and rules. Conflict emerges more easily when family members live separate lives, where "both parents and children are involved in a parallel and interrelated process of change in self-definition, with ambivalent tensions between 'over here' and 'over there,' toward the country of origin and that of residence."[8] Three main issues intervene in hampering youth's skills in interacting—by means of language, values, norms, and habits—with the host society where they attend school and socialize with peers, and, eventually, distance themselves from the family environment where they grew up.

First, the distance between parents and children may occur as a result of school attendance, language acquisition, and friends from outside the migrant community; children tend to acquire cultural and linguistic expertise faster than their parents. Many parents are "forced into silence"; their native language is looked down upon and banned because it is considered an obstacle to improving the children's learning of the language of the new country, a language wherein the parents remain quiet because they may be less versed in it.[9] In relationships where dialog and discussion of personal matters are rendered difficult by the lack of a common language, parental support tends to become more limited because, on the one hand, the language of care and affection, and, on the other, the opportunities for bonding through symbols, rites, and words of the parents' original culture have been diminished by the migratory experience.[10] Different levels of integration occur in a host society—from language proficiency to interiorized habits and values, from interaction with ethnic communities to detachment from all signals of ethnic identity.

The common use of ICTs, especially among younger generations, is linked to identity. As several scholars point out, identity is a complex concept, in which the concept of self interplays with group closeness and homogeneity, especially in the case of immigrants.[11] In this case, the term "belonging" appears more appropriate, in accordance with Constanza Vera Larrucea's argument that, "[t]he emotionally laden sense of belonging is intimately connected with collective identities. The experiences of descendants of migrants illustrate the blurred boundaries of group belonging with attachment to two or more groups."[12]

A second issue discussed in this chapter is intergenerational differences and the extent to which new technologies may interfere in managing emotions (for example, using Facebook and/or Instagram for expressing personal feelings). The emotional rhetoric created by ICTs creates a sense of overall closeness and proximity, a feeling of shared emotional experiences from posts on Facebook, photos on Instagram, and chats through Messenger. Children learn to construct a language of emotion in relation to their peers who have different backgrounds and a cultural knowledge of socialization that is more pertinent to their generation. However, ICT tools can produce emotional distance in parent-child relationships. In immigrant families, the risks of incomprehension and verbal distance are compounded. Words are missing from their shared emotional vocabulary, limiting the expression of feelings across generations—for instance, voicing anger about discrimination or elation in being considered no longer a foreigner.

Related to this discussion is the role of communication in transnational caregiving and obligations in immigrant families. One positive function of ICTs is the frequency of audio and visual contact via the internet at low cost among caregivers—doctors, family assistants, relatives, and neighbors, or other members of the community who take care of parents who remain in the homeland. ICTs also make possible the rapid delivery of money. Daily connections with family members in the homeland can have the effect of expanding the distance between the "ethnic" world in which one lives and the outside environment. Among the risks associated with ICTs that parents feel are the sense of "being elsewhere," of sharing joys, emotions, and pain in real time while on another continent. They tend to live in their present homes with a certain detachment, participating and sharing in everyday life in superficial ways. The vocabulary of immigrant parents points to their limits and their "confinement" in a timeless space. This divergence underscores a divide in integration which differs from the parents' heterogeneous social capital.

All of the above-mentioned issues are part of current debates in Italy on intergenerational relations among immigrant families, specifically among Peruvian and Moroccan families, two of the oldest communities whose presence dates back to the 1980s. In these communities, two dynamics coexist: cohabitation of members of two generations and transnational caregiving through ICTs. As a result, they provide excellent case studies on how language and the digital world influence affection and communication in parent-child relations.

Italy, a Country of Immigration

Italy is a country that generated over 26 million emigrants in the nineteenth and twentieth centuries.[13] By contrast, by the second decade of the new millennium, Italy has become a country of immigration. This transformation has taken on a structural—not temporary—nature. With approximately five million immigrants in Italy at the beginning of 2017, foreigners are an important part of the country's socioeconomic fabric. The intertwining of migrants of diverse origins, heterogeneous migratory itineraries, and diverse dynamics of social adaptation pose challenges. Immigrant experiences fluctuate from the lack of any conflict to episodes of religious discrimination and racism.[14]

Children and adolescents born in Italy or who arrive at a later age are part of a complex social landscape. Immigrant children vary in terms of ethnic background, age of arrival, family household composition, and future aspirations. From an educational perspective, more are attending senior high school and university. From the point of view of socialization, some are engaged in ethnic associations; others, in interethnic activities within their generational cohort in an effort to distinguish themselves from their parents' associations, which tend to be linked to nostalgia for the home country.[15]

Moroccan and Peruvian Families and Language

Identity is often tied to one's mother tongue and, as such, is central to the definition of the self.[16] Learning a language is never merely a question of grasping a set of grammatical rules and acquiring vocabulary. It is a long, arduous journey of discovering the world that the language relates to, describes, and animates. Similarly, losing a language means losing the world associated with it. In the case of one's mother tongue, it implies losing elements of one's original world.[17] Language is one of the principal ways to express a sense of belonging in a family circle and a broader community. Language transmits information and feelings, both positive and negative. In migrant families, negative feelings often arise in children who are reunited with their families after several years of separation: anger, resentment, and a sense of abandonment.[18] The children's reactions to their new living situation can swing from alienation (for example, perceiving themselves out of the loop due to the lack of language fluency and lack of familiarity with the slang used by peers) to frustration for not being in tune with their parents' habits, ways of acting, and approach to interpersonal relations. With the diffusion of digital technologies, immigrant children's feelings are expressed partly on the internet, where children tend to use different languages in expressing themselves. They do this by diversifying their communications—in words and images, with different social media accounts, and through different messages delivered to various audiences. Parents are generally excluded from this realm since most are familiar with neither the technology nor the languages their children use. This may lead to feelings of frustration and intergenerational tension. Migration compounds the challenges faced by parents and children.

As migrant children grow, they improve their mother tongue from attending ad hoc classes in mosques, in ethnic churches, and in cultural associations. Their mother tongue is an important means of communication for them and a marker of identity. Parents' weak proficiency in Italian is one of the main reasons for maintaining ethnic language among children of Moroccan origin, together with the annual periods spent in their country of origin and living in an area inhabited by coethnics.[19] As Krishna Pendakur and Ravi Pendakur argue, "in human capital theory, language knowledge is valuable because of its direct effect on productivity. However, language knowledge is an important dimension of ethnic membership."[20] Speaking the mother tongue can affect the level of interaction among young immigrants within the ethnic community not only in terms of their involvement in cultural activities, but also with respect to improving job opportunities. Ethnic enclaves may open job opportunities, contributing to overcoming discrimination that young people with a foreign background may encounter in mainstream society. Minority language knowledge may also mark the distance between "us" and "other"—between Italians and Moroccans, Peruvians, and all the other foreign collectivities living in Italy.[21]

Immigrants from North Africa were among the first to arrive in Italy in the 1980s, and for some time they have continued to be the most numerous among immigrant groups. Within this group, Moroccans have predominated both numerically and symbolically as an early immigrant group in the region of Piedmont and its capital, Turin. Today, the Moroccan population represents roughly 13 percent of the total number of foreigners residing in and around the city of Turin. This is an important figure in terms of settlement and community rootedness, and for the robust presence of the younger second generation. In these communities, marriage, family reunification, and children's schooling are part of the everyday life of families as parents worry about their children's well-being, their academic life, and opportunities for the future.

The Peruvian presence, on the other hand, has been shaped by over two decades of near-invisibility in public spaces where they have been closely identified with a Catholic culture similar to that of Italians. While a numerically smaller group (5.6 percent of total immigrants),[22] Peruvians in Turin, as in the rest of Italy, are characterized by the migration of middle- and upper-class women and men who used cultural capital to develop networks and migration projects in tune with their university education and specializations. Over time, this national group created its own ethnic associations before the migration of less skilled workers and workers with a lower cultural capital. Reunification of these less privileged parents with their children after years of separation has led to emotional strain. Many young adolescents feel abandoned because their mothers work long hours in residential elderly care. Older children feel they were called to a country that they did not choose, a country in which they are forced to share a home with new brothers and sisters born in Italy.

Speaking Arabic in an Unwelcoming Context: Not Only a Matter of Identity

Among the Moroccan families interviewed, the language used at home depends on the children's status. As a general rule, children born in Italy, or who arrived when they were very young, tend to use Italian with their siblings and parents. In contrast, those born in Morocco use Arabic in combination with a few Italian words. As one nineteen-year-old Moroccan woman who arrived in Italy at the age of ten noted: "My brother was born here and he is in the second year of middle school, so for him it is natural to speak Italian. He doesn't know much Arabic, he knows a little more of our local dialect, but don't ask him to speak it. My mother speaks only our dialect so she talks mainly to me, and I translate. We often use one of our languages when we don't want to be understood or when we are angry. It's an arm, a way of separating our world from that of our parents." Similarly, an eighteen-year-old Moroccan girl, who joined her father when she was nine and is currently attending a vocational school, reflected:

> We sisters prefer to use Italian among ourselves—that way it's better, we don't get confused. With our parents it depends on the situation. For example, if we are angry we speak Italian so that our mother doesn't know what we are fighting about because she speaks only dialect. Even when we are speaking on the phone with Moroccan friends, we often use Italian so that our parents do not understand. . . . Our father wants us to watch Arabic programs but we prefer Italian programs and music on TV, and when we can go online, which is not always, because our parents don't want us to waste time "chatting," even though they have no idea what it means. Internet, to them, is useful only for talking to our relatives in Belgium from time to time.

Language is thus a strategy for expressing disagreement; a way in which children unknowingly confess their frustration about living between two worlds, often running in parallel and rarely converging. The situation is intensified when neither parent is sufficiently familiar with the Italian language. Language in this case serves several functions: it performs as a barrier, as a marker of difference, and as an element of pride among children whose bilingualism helps them in their relationships within and outside the family. Paradoxically, parents are proud of their children's fluency while at the same time they often feel alienated from a world that speaks Italian and where their children seem to thrive better than in the family environment. The children feel frustrated as they feel more comfortable speaking Italian than the language of their parents, the language they associate with parental love. The feeling of not being "good enough children," of "mistrusting" their ancestral background, comes to the fore in this situation. As noted by a young Moroccan (aged twenty-one) who arrived in Italy at twelve years old and now works in a drugstore:

> We are trapped. We have to demonstrate that we are 100 percent Italian and we speak Italian all the time. When we are with our parents, our elderly aunts, our grandmother we feel like a fish out of water, we feel uncomfortable because we cannot really understand, not only several words and slang expressions, but also nonverbal expressions, cultural references. I feel 85 percent Italian and 15 percent Moroccan, and those who are younger than me, who are born here in Italy and growing up in a multicultural neighborhood, feel 100 percent Italian, I'm sure.

It is inevitable that the school experience underscores the prevalence of the Italian language in the family too, even more so if siblings share the same language. The lack of a common vocabulary increases the sense of loneliness, especially when children face episodes of bullying due to their ethnic or religious background or their family history. For instance, Fatima, an eighteen-year-old Moroccan girl born in Italy and enrolled in a technical school, highlights this point when recalling an episode that happened to her and her friends: "My mother knows very little Italian and I don't know our language. Sometimes I am not able to tell her what has happened to me on the street or at school, when someone says to me: 'Take off your veil' or 'Fucking Moroccan!' I haven't got the vocabulary to be angry in Arabic and if I speak Italian, she hears only incomprehensible sounds. Fortunately, I have friends, some who are Italian, that I talk to."

In situations where dialog and discussion are obstructed by the lack of a common language, parental support is limited as children grow. As Caterina Gozzoli and Camillo Regalia state, "the language of affection and the possibility of creating bonds through the original culture's symbols, rites, and language" have been diminished by the migration experience.[23] The following excerpt is drawn from an interview with a twenty-year-old Moroccan girl, who arrived in Italy when she was five years old. A student of biology at university, she discusses how she feels about not having the possibility to be fully open with her mother:

> Sometimes I would like to tell my mother what is happening to me but I'm at a loss for words. I don't know the words in Arabic and my mother doesn't know them in Italian. So, it's easier to say nothing. Occasionally I speak to my aunt, she's younger than my mother and she speaks Italian, but she's very busy because she just had a baby. When I was younger it was easier, but now the things I need to explain are more complicated.... They live here now and they should feel more integrated in this society. We need their support here. Do you know what I mean? I'm not speaking about money. We need parents who are able to play their role: How can they care for us if they do not really understand our Italian world? I cannot attend my sister's school meetings on behalf of them because my sister is ashamed of our parents and they are shy because of their poor Italian.

Many parents feel trapped. Their bodies are free to move to a new country but their heads are anchored in their homeland. It is the cohort of parents who arrived in Italy with little or no formal education who suffer most from the communication gap between them and their children. This is especially the case when immigrant children invest heavily in their schoolwork and the local language in order to find their own insertion and integration paths. A Moroccan father, forty-five years of age and in Italy since he was twenty-six, working as a waiter in a restaurant, discusses the frustration of parents not being able to help their children with their education:

> Having a common language is indispensable, especially in migration. But it does not always happen. In some families the parents are no longer able to control their sons and daughters because the children do not understand what they are saying. This happens frequently because many of our families are illiterate. Men who have been here for years have learned only enough Italian to get by. For their children who attend school, a new world is opened, a world in which their parents are excluded. They use the internet, they chat, they tweet, whereas their parents are limited to [the basic functions of] smartphones.

Language is not only a means of communication; it also unifies and protects people against social discrimination. Language is part of the ethnic capital which, as Alejandro Portes and Hao Lingxin show, can at the same time reinforce the individual's identity and facilitate integration into a host society.[24] Language can also help to develop life paths within one's ethnic community of belonging, for employment purposes, in the interaction with others in one's original language, and in the weaving of relationships, which in some cases might replicate the social structures of one's country of origin.

Spanish Is Not Italian: The Language Illusion

The case of Peruvian families is relevant in our discussion on the effects of language socialization and the effectiveness of the parental role according to a parent's language skills. In a majority of families, mothers were the first members of the family to leave their home in Peru and begin the process of migration. In many families, women controlled their integration and settlement. They sought the necessary income, accommodation, and fulfilment of legal requirements (for instance, residence permits) that were necessary for family reunification with their spouses and/or children.[25] When their children joined them, it became clear how different Italian society is from Peruvian society. As Elisabeth, an eighteen-year-old woman who joined her mother in Italy at the age of eleven, now enrolled in the last year of secondary school, reflects:

> My mother came here thirteen years ago. One of her cousins had told her that she could work for a lady. Since my father was unemployed, she left. She rang me every week, telling me that there were lots of Peruvians here, many girls like me who went to school, and that I would join her soon. She said not to worry: the language was practically the same and there were various associations helping young people to settle into Italian society.... Not at all. It is false. The language is not the same and speaking Itaniolo, a mix of Spanish and Italian, means to be different from your peers, it means being an immigrant, and as such, being bullied. And you know, migrants are not well accepted in these times in Italy.

While in the case of Moroccan families (especially mothers) the main theme is Italian-language acquisition, in the case of Peruvian families, the focus has been on how to avoid the common belief that Spanish and Italian are almost identical languages, a perception that has led many Peruvian children to neglect their studies and fall back on their community. This risk is usually compounded by the effects of living away from their mothers for several years, as Susana, an eighteen-year-old Peruvian woman who arrived in Italy at the age of six and is now enrolled in a vocational school, remarks:

> We siblings use Italian, partly to improve our use of the language, especially since we've only been here for five years and we are not yet perfectly fluent. We often speak Spanish with our parents: my father doesn't know Italian well, so we speak Spanish with him. Whereas my mother has been here for fifteen years and has never attended a language course, claiming

that she knows Italian—she says it's enough to change some Spanish vowels and consonants here and there.... It feels like a nightmare. During the week I'm half Peruvian and half Italian, speaking Spanish at home, trying to speak Italian at school. On Sunday, we go to the parish where there is a priest who says mass in Spanish, then we spend the afternoon together in a [parish] hall. The older ones organize [activities], and there are games for the children. For our parents it's important—it isn't for me.... This Italian world is our world now, Peru becomes farther away day-by-day.

This viewpoint is not an isolated case in the way it underscores shifting feelings from one world to another as an "alien." Among the young people interviewed, a common characteristic was asking themselves whether it was not anachronistic to try to replicate in a new country the same way of living as elsewhere, including the language used. Here we see a generational difference: Alongside the adults who are firmly anchored in the past while trying to understand and confront difficulties in the present, young people feel they are part of an Italian, European, and global context. For the latter, identity is part of a puzzle in which only a few pieces are related to their family background.

Peruvian mothers find support in their communities (religious or national associations) to navigate the difficult task of parenting after several years of distance from their children. Remaining in contact by telephone or Skype and purchasing expensive gifts for their children are expressions of love that are often insufficient in re-creating a strong relationship between parent and child after years of separation. Parents' efforts to bridge the distance by using the language of global brands like Nike, Apple, and Abercrombie & Fitch (the most popular brands according to the interviewees of the study), however, do not replace the lack of daily emotional and physical contact. Indeed, feelings of loneliness are commonly expressed after reunions between adolescents and mothers.[26]

Parents, especially mothers, try to win their children's affection back by making them want for nothing. It's almost as if they were trying to compensate with brand-name consumer goods for their lack of communication and availability in taking care of their children. This raises children's expectations, and is especially disappointing when family reunification leads to the discovery that the mother's economic situation is not flourishing.

Mothers plan for their children's arrival (school registration, free-time language courses) believing that the transition will be seamless and uncomplicated. "Everything will work out," many believe, especially because their children speak a language similar to Italian. As one Peruvian mother (aged forty-six, caregiver, with two daughters who joined her at the age of twelve and seventeen respectively, and who is in Italy since 2001) said, "All you need is a little discipline. We need to keep an eye on our children so they don't go off the straight and narrow."

But the departure of a mother or father leaves scars that are hard to heal. Indeed, having been "children left behind" influences subsequent intrafamily relationships, in areas such as parental authority, and the value attributed to the family in the present and later in life. Roberto, aged nineteen, who joined his parents six years after they left, and who is currently enrolled in a training course for bartenders, explains: "I don't have much to say to my parents. We don't get on. They want to tell me what to do, where to go and how to behave. They are thinking of an ideal son, Italian at school and Peruvian at home. That's not the way it is. At school I feel good, well-integrated in the classroom and with my schoolmates, except that I'm a foreigner. It's not like being in Peru, in my aunt's house, where I felt fine. That is my home, where I am a Peruvian."

The same unwritten rules of migration apply to family reunification. Immigrants usually present themselves to family members and others in the home country as cases of success. They rarely mention the obstacles they have encountered, and the legal challenges, lodging difficulties, and precarious employment they face.[27] The success of their migratory project is revealed as an illusion when family reunification demonstrates the family's true socio-economic condition.[28] The young protagonists' journey—not usually freely chosen, often imposed—becomes a source of disappointment.[29] The narrative of parents' success comes undone in the harsh light of reality, where both economic and social opportunities often are drastically reduced, as Juan, nineteen years of age, reflects:

> I arrived in Turin when I was fourteen. My mother left me behind in Peru, entrusting me to the care of my father and grandparents for three years, during which time I grew up immersed in the Peruvian environment and culture. And now here I am in Turin, in a completely different setting. ... It is not true that we Peruvians have a language advantage [in Italy]. Rather, we run the risk of not understanding and not being understood. This happens to my parents, who think they understand everything because they consider Italian and Spanish to be "similar": but then they ask me to translate or confirm what they just heard. Most of the time, it turns out to mean something different from what they had understood. It isn't easy. They live in Turin as if they lived in a Lima neighborhood, meet-

ing only Peruvians, going to a mass for Peruvians delivered by a priest who speaks only Spanish. They say that by now they are integrated; but that isn't integration, it's segregation. Is it possible that they don't realize this? On the contrary, they want me too to mix only with Peruvians and to marry a Peruvian girl, so that there will be no problems. My mother says to me: "Listen, if you marry an Italian or a Romanian or an Albanian girl, what will I do? I will lose our traditions and our bonds." . . . For our parents, we are not Italian, but extensions of themselves. We are expected to follow them. Only our bodies are in Italy while our hearts and minds should be in Peru. We are expected to speak Spanish, eat empanadas at least once a day, and hang around other Peruvians.

Geographical frontiers and distance have created intergenerational barriers that are not easy to knock down. Reunification between parents and children is a complex experience calling into question relations of authority, recognition processes, and roles within the family. This complexity is compounded by contact with the outside world, specifically the host society. The new arrivals feel alone when they cannot explain to their parents their feelings in Spanish without risk of being misunderstood. Children and parents refer to different worlds. After several years of absence, parents and their children have difficulty relating to each other. They use the same vocabulary, but they lack a common framework. As I noted in a previous publication, sometimes parents use Italian words without knowing exactly the meaning,[30] often resulting in misunderstandings and misinterpretations. For the parents, family reunions represent a success, an important step in the migratory experience, and they interact with their children in step with their knowledge and experience of their home country as well as new cultural habits learned in Italy.[31] For the children, and adolescents especially, the experience often feels like a failure due to the lack of sustained support in understanding the new rules, habits, norms, and languages (including their peers' slang) of Italy.[32]

An Increasing Gap: When Parents Cannot Check Their Children's Facebook

On the web, children create a world from which parents are generally excluded. This generational divide occurs both in Italian families and in immigrant families in Italy. However, as an Italian social worker points out, the effect is more devastating for immigrant adolescents: "The internet is part of young people's lives. They grow up in the web culture and if you haven't got a smartphone or a Facebook page, you're nobody. They come here to the association, they chat online, they surf on the internet to do their homework, and, above all, they use social networks. There is no difference among Italians, Peruvians, Moroccans, and Romanians. And their parents, especially those of a lower cultural level, are worried because they are not able to control what their children say or write on the World Wide Web." The media and the web serve as a means of learning and participating in the new culture, which immigrant children joined upon arriving in Italy. Social media offer access to a peer group and common spaces for relationships to thrive across differences. However, the role of media is far from neutral. The media serve as a means of inclusion, but also of exclusion—by stigmatizing or marginalizing particular cultures. A Moroccan father (aged forty-eight) whose two children were born in Italy, and who works as a cultural mediator in refugee welcoming centers, remarks:

> For some time, my children have been more interested in the subject of identity. They have been asking, "Who am I?" as a Muslim. They tell me that a lot is said about it on the internet. My daughter has shown me a video about the veil, in which some girls discuss the importance of wearing it in Italy and others ask why they have to put it on now [after a long period without it]. I'm a little outside of this. Other mediators and I have talked about the importance for women to identify as Moroccan and Muslim, and as foreigners in Italy. Ours, however, were face-to-face meetings, not on the web. We had met to write posters for demonstrations, not to "write a post." These are two different things. It is a good thing for our children to be aware of their identity, but I always think of the internet as a game, in which I don't think their points of view are taken seriously.

However, ICTs offer immigrants significant opportunities to stay in touch with their families and friends in the homeland and strengthen their relationships in the diaspora.[33] Beyond this, however, ICTs also generate challenges for the integration of younger generations. Parents can easily reinforce links with relatives in their places of origin or in other countries of immigration, feel emotionally supported and able to support and care for elderly family members transnationally. Many are not interested in learning the language of the receiving country, and as such, do not generally keep up with their children's linguistic progress. In these cases, parents unconsciously build day-to-day barriers between themselves and their children. To quote a Moroccan woman, aged forty-eight, who is a housewife with three children, and who has been in Italy since 1998:

> I feel more comfortable when I speak with my sister in Amsterdam than when I argue with my youngest daughter. It seems to be a dialog for the deaf. Words seem to have different meanings for us, and my interpretation of behavior seems extraordinary in the Italian context. There is a paradox: I feel much closer to my sisters, parents, and aunts living abroad than I do to my children in our little flat in Italy. I frequently discuss this feeling of loneliness with my friends at the *musalla* [space for praying]. This is one of the unexpected costs of raising children abroad, where they are exposed to cultural habits and influences that they would not have if they were living in Morocco, and breathing the millennial culture through internet and TV.

At the same time, immigrant parents who are not proficient in Italian have boosted the voice of children from the second generation, many of whom express their identity on the web—an identity that is at the same time global and local, ethnic and cosmopolitan. Virtual forums seem to have replaced real forums, enabling the children of immigration to discuss in public their points of view, asking not to be judged only on the basis of their past or their own or their parents' immigration status.[34] Young foreigners find spaces in these new arenas (social networks, specialized websites) to express themselves by adopting positions on matters that concern them, not only in Italy, but also in their home countries. Yet this movement excludes their parents who rarely use the internet and even more rarely follow their children in their virtual worlds. In this way, ICTs tend to bring faraway countries closer while driving an emotional wedge between people living under the same roof. As a result, digital divisions affect immigrant families twice as often as native Italian families. Parents and children are driven apart not only because of divergent communication codes but also because of the ways in which these codes reflect on their identity and how they present themselves to society.[35]

Immigrant children's familiarity with ICTs inadvertently results in the exclusion of their parents from the digital world in which they engage. Although similar situations occur among Italian native-born families, the effects on immigrant families, who in addition to their limited technological knowledge possess limited oral and written knowledge of Italian, are more devastating. The use of social networks highlights many interviewed parents' low language proficiency in Italian. Concerned about the ramifications of this communication divide, for instance, one Moroccan mother (aged thirty-nine), a housewife with three children and with infrequent contact with non-Moroccan women while living in Italy for five years, notes:

> At school we talk about Facebook, about how our children use the internet. We mothers speak among ourselves, but the problem is not to check, to have access to their pages. It is to read what they have written. It isn't just the Italian. Young people have their own language. It's always been this way. We did the same with our parents. But our incomprehension is greater now. We don't know Italian, we know very little about using social networks, we are too old to understand their slang. What's more, our children have learned Romanian, Arabic, and Albanian words from their friends. How can we keep an eye on them?

Several interviewed parents have expressed increased awareness about the need to learn Italian if they want to be successful as parents. The potential risks of parents' lack of familiarity with the Italian language and with digital languages are being recognized as important. Several initiatives have been organized in the city of Turin for helping migrant women (and especially women with few years of formal education) learn Italian and gain computer skills. For the interviewees, understanding the internet is linked to learning how to monitor their children's online activities.

In addition to acting as a vehicle for accessing peer groups and to building relationships that transcend cultural and other differences, the internet and social networks are becoming the stage on which "new ethnic identities" are being played out. There seems to be general agreement that media are playing a positive role in young people's development of "hybrid, "cosmopolitan," or even "floating" identities.[36] Young immigrants use media to "look back," to sustain ties with their country of origin, and to "look around" at their new culture. This is especially true in the case of girls who, by taking on a virtual identity, have become protagonists of a cultural debate on questions of gender in unprecedented ways. For instance, a group of girls has stirred up the argument about the hijab, explaining why they believe it should be worn for purposes of identity, history, and sense of personal belonging. Through web messages, they also have engaged in discussions about what it means to become a woman in a country where cultural differences may have frightening consequences, especially when connected to religion (in this case, Islam). Between posts and tweets, there seems to be a demand for voicing immigrant children's struggles in Italian society, as well as challenges faced in relation to their parents, whose members seem to drift—even if involuntarily—away from the more cosmopolitan identity that their children are embracing in the age of web 2.0.

Concluding Remarks

As I have endeavored to show with my focus on Peruvian and Moroccan immigrant families in Italy, four factors demonstrate how language and the digital divide shape emotional distance in familial relationships. The first is alienation, which derives from an unresolved generational conflict, accompanied by a multifaceted cultural conflict. The way this conflict plays out depends on the migration timing of parents and children, the relationship kept up with one's country of origin, and the investment made in the receiving country in terms of relationships formed with locals and co-nationals. The second factor is the sense of obligation among immigrant children due to their parents' limited grasp of the Italian language. While overcoming the language barrier does not always help with the cultural and/or generational divide, it nonetheless reinforces the feeling of care and responsibility. The third factor is a feeling of solitude and loneliness. Whether reunited or born in Italy, young individuals often find themselves coping with the absence of parental figures, who are heavily engaged in full-time work outside the home. The last one is a feeling of frustration derived, above all, from expectations of success that children were led to believe their parents had achieved and that have not been met.

As the chapters in this volume by Sonia Cancian, Linda Reeder, Suzanne M. Sinke, and Margarita Dounia also show, migration challenges intergenerational affective ties among families. Integration in host societies can have numerous effects on parent-child relations. Children can internalize social and cultural values in contrast to what their parents believe or how they behave. Among these cultural challenges, language plays an important role. Even in earlier migration experiences, the focus was devoted to investigating to what extent both first and second generations shared the host country language, while underscoring the role played by children in coping with the parents' limited language proficiency. The recent use of ICTs and social media has added a new challenge for interactions across generations and across countries. Among immigrant families, new technologies are reshaping emotional ties between parents and children both transculturally and transnationally. The focus on immigrant families provides an opportunity to study how proximity and speed of interaction can shape cultural distances and define intercultural misunderstandings, especially as far as feelings and expressions of intimacy are concerned.

NOTES

1. Michael Fix, Wendy Zimmerman, and Jeffrey S. Passel, *The Integration of the Immigrant Families into the United States* (Washington, DC: Urban Institute, 2001); Anna Triandafyllidou and Ruby Gropas, eds., *European Immigration: A Source Book* (Farnham, UK: Ashgate, 2007).

2. Maurice Crul, Jens Schneider, and Frans Lelie, eds., *The European Second Generation Compared: Does the Integration Context Matter?* (Amsterdam: Amsterdam University Press, 2012); Olga G. Bailey, Myria Georgiou, and Ramaswami Harindranath, eds., *Transnational Lives and the Media: Re-imagining Diasporas* (London: Palgrave Macmillan, 2007).

3. Peggy Levitt and Nina Glick Schiller, "Conceptualizing Simultaneity: A Transnational Social Field Perspective on Society," *International Migration Review* 38, no. 3 (2004): 1002–39; Lee Komito, "Social Media and Migration: Virtual Community 2.0," *American Society for Information Science and Technology* 62, no. 6 (2011): 1075–86.

4. Maurizio Ambrosini, *Un'altra globalizzazione: La sfida delle migrazioni transnazionali* (Bologna: Il Mulino, 2008), 99.

5. Loretta Baldassar, Mihaela Nedelcu, Laura Merla, and Raelene Wilding, "ICT-based Co-presence in Transnational Families," *Global Networks* 16, no. 2 (2016): 133–44.

6. The analysis is enriched by considering experiences and new practices developed by second generations in Turin, Italy, a city with well-established Moroccan and Peruvian communities. Turin represents an interesting case because the city was one of the first municipalities to make an effort to manage the increasing flows of immigrants. Turin has emerged as a national leader in designing integration policies from an intercultural perspective. Conversations with a number of interviewees took place during associational activities, social events (dinners, parties, and religious and ethnic cultural celebrations, such as processions in honour of various home-country manifestations of the Virgin Mary, national holidays, and the end of Ramadan). Respondents were reassured about the confidentiality of information and the ethical uses of the collected interviews. In the interview quotations, they are indicated in the following way: sex, age, age of arrival in Italy, occupation status, and citizenship. The occupational status serves as an indicator of whether the interviewees interact in a mono-ethnic job environment or in a job situation where Italian is the main language used. The sample was accumulated using a snowball method, starting from contacts at intercultural, religious, and ethnic associations. In order to avoid the risk of contacting only young people involved in organized activities, I also contacted young people across social contexts. I also interviewed ten parents and five stakeholders among psychologists, social workers, cultural mediators, and teachers. All the qualitative material was collected between 2014 and 2016.

7. Marjorie Orellana, Lisa Dorner, and Lucila Pulido, "Accessing Assets: Immigrant Youth's Work as Family Translators or 'Para-Phrasers,'" *Social Problems* 50, no. 4 (2003): 505–24.

8. Roberta Ricucci, "Famiglie italiane con bambini d'altrove: Scoprirsi interculturali," *Minorigiustizia* 2 (2012): 33.

9. Roberta Ricucci, "Senza una lingua in comune: Il ruolo genitoriale in emigrazione," *Minorigiustizia* 3 (2014): 94–101.

10. Marjorie Faulstich Orellana, *Translating Childhoods: Immigrant Youth, Language, and Culture* (New Brunswick, NJ: Rutgers University Press, 2009).

11. Charlotte Burck, *Multilingual Living: Explorations of Language and Subjectivity* (New York: Palgrave Macmillan, 2005).

12. Constanza Vera Larrucea, "Identity: Belonging, Language, and Transnationalism," in *The Integration of Descendants of Migrants from Turkey in Stockholm*, ed. Charles Westin (Amsterdam: Amsterdam University Press, 2015), 94.

13. The history of Italian emigration has generated a vast scholarship. For references and specific experiences, see the chapters by Bjerg, Zanoni, Reeder, and Cancian in this volume.

14. Istituto Nazionale di Statistica, *Bilancio demografico nazionale, anno 2017*, June 13, 2018.

15. Roberta Ricucci, *Second Generations on the Move in Italy: Children of Immigrants Coming of Age* (London: Lexington Books, 2014).

16. Andrew Fuligni, Melissa Witkow, and Carla Garcia, "Ethnic Identity and the Academic Adjustment of Adolescents from Mexican, Chinese, and European Backgrounds," *Developmental Psychology* 41, no. 5 (2005): 799–811.

17. Peggy Levitt, "Roots and Routes: Understanding the Lives of the Second Generation Transnationally," *Journal of Ethnic and Migration Studies* 35, no. 7 (2009): 1225–42.

18. Kara Somerville, "Transnational Belonging among Second Generation Youth: Identity in a Globalized World," *Journal of Social Sciences*, Special Volume no. 10 (2008): 23–33.

19. Maria Medvedeva, "Negotiating Languages in Immigrant Families," *International Migration Review* 46, no. 2 (2012): 517–45.

20. Krishna Pendakur and Ravi Pendakur, "Language as Both Human Capital and Ethnicity," *International Migration Review* 36, no. 1 (2002): 150–51.

21. Roberta Ricucci, *Cittadini senza cittadinanza: La questione dello ius soli* (Turin: Seb27, 2018).

22. Città di Torino, *Cittadini stranieri al 31.12.2015* (Turin: Città di Torino, 2016).

23. Caterina Gozzoli and Camillo Regalia, *Migrazioni e famiglie: Percorsi, legami e interventi psicosociali* (Bologna: Il Mulino, 2005).

24. Alejandro Portes and Hao Lingxin, "The Price of Uniformity: Language, Family, and Personality Adjustment in the Immigrant Second Generation," *Ethnic and Racial Studies* 25, no. 6 (2002): 889–912.

25. Paola Bonizzoni, *Famiglie Globali: Le frontiere della maternità* (Turin: Utet, 2009).

26. Arul Chib, Shelly Malik, Rajiv George Aricat, and Siti Zubeidah Kadir, "Migrant Mothering and Mobile Phones: Negotiations of Transnational Identity," *Mobile Media and Communication* 2, no. 1 (2014): 73–93; Mirca Madianou, "Migration and the Accentuated Ambivalence of Motherhood: The Role of ICTs in Filipino Transnational Families," *Global Networks* 12, no. 3 (2012): 277–95.

27. Mara Tognetti Bordogna, *Donne e percorsi migratori: Per una sociologia delle migrazioni* (Milan: Franco Angeli, 2012).

28. Carola Suárez-Orozco and Marcelo Suárez-Orozco, *Children of Immigration* (Cambridge, MA: Harvard University Press, 2001).

29. Among the interviewees who belong to the 1.5 generation, about half said they agreed with moving to Italy. The Peruvian girls interviewed had prepared by trying to learn a little Italian. For the rest, the reunion decision had been taken unilaterally by their parents. Interrupting studies, strong bonds with grandparents and other relatives, and breaking off friendships were among the principal reasons for loneliness given by the interviewees, followed by not knowing Italian.

30. Ricucci, "Senza una lingua in comune."

31. Roberta Ricucci, *Italiani a metà: Giovani stranieri crescono* (Bologna: Il Mulino, 2010).

32. Luca Queirolo Palmas, *Atlantico latino: Gang giovanili e culture transnazionali* (Rome: Carocci, 2010).

33. Steven Vertovec, "Migrant Transnationalism and Modes of Transformation," *International Migration Review* 38, no. 3 (2004): 970–1001.

34. Myria Georgiou, "Diasporic Communities Online: A Bottom-Up Experience of Transnationalism," in *The Ideology of the Internet: Concepts, Policies, Uses*, ed. Katharine Sarikakis and Daya K. Thussu (Cresskill, NJ: Hampton Press, 2006), 131–46.

35. Johan A. Bargh, Katelyn Y. A. McKenna, and Grainne M. Fitzsimons, "Can You See the Real Me? Activation and Expression of the 'True Self' on the Internet," *Journal of Social Issues* 58, no. 1 (2002): 33–48.

36. Hulf Hannerz, *Transnational Connections: Culture, People, Places* (London: Routledge, 1996).

Epilogue

DONNA R. GABACCIA

I do not consider myself to be a historian of emotions. Nevertheless, both my lifelong interests in international migration and my repeated experiences as an academic labor migrant have pushed me at times to consider the intellectual concerns addressed by contributors to this volume. I began my professional life as a letter-writing, blue-aerogram-purchasing temporary academic worker in Germany. At that time, I telephoned far-off loved ones only at extraordinary moments of death or birth. I am now retiring from my professorship in Canada as an email-writing user of social media, Google Hangouts, Skype, and WhatsApp. Personal experience has made me exquisitely aware of emotional differences in communication with diverse technologies and also made me an enthusiastic reader of this collection's essays (by Marcelo J. Borges, Mirjam Milharčič Hladnik, Suzanne M. Sinke, Sonia Cancian, and Roberta Ricucci) that touch on transnational communication and communication technologies.

In this epilogue, however, I will privilege a few elements of the entwining of love, hate, gender, and sexuality with mobility that began to engage me intellectually already twenty years ago. In particular, I have long remained interested in how migrants learned to "love" the countries where they lived and in whether or not concepts of honor or shame mattered in the rise of modern nationalism, especially in diasporic Mediterranean cultures.

* * *

In 2003, I wrote a paper titled "Honor and Shame in a Mobile World." It drew on the research of a scholarly network that had already published two edited collections (*Italian Workers of the World* and *Women, Gender, and Transnational Life*) and my own monograph, *Italy's Many Diasporas*.[1] I wrote "Honor and Shame" in hopes of moving beyond questions about the impact of work and labor mobilizations on the formation of modern nations and nation-states. I feared the focus on work and labor mobilization could not fully capture the dynamics of nation-building, especially for women, and that greater attention was required to develop a gendered analysis of diasporic nation-building. A subsequent collection of essays, coedited with anthropologist Loretta Baldassar, *Intimacy and Italian Migration*, ultimately did outline variations in how countries contributed to the construction of masculinities and femininities that were understood to be distinctive of the Italian nation, worldwide.[2] But even that volume left unanswered questions about how gendered emotions—symbolized in the paper through the Mediterranean complex of "honor and shame"—played a role. And even my 2003 paper failed to ask how nation-building might, in turn, have transformed gendered emotions.

The 2003 paper drew on a wide array of earlier scholarship, which I will not summarize here in any detail. Scholars had long observed that the earliest Mediterranean states, in order to survive and expand, had to wrest from kinship groups the power to monopolize interpersonal violence—for example, honor killings and vendettas—if they wished to control and legitimize reproduction and social solidarities in their own interests.[3] Other scholars have suggested instead that modern states modeled themselves on families, transforming national territories into fatherlands or motherlands that were much loved by their residents.[4] In my own work, I had portrayed Italy's migrants as characterized simultaneously by deep emotional attachments (*campanilismo*) to their home village (which Spanish speakers tellingly call *la patria chica*) and by ambivalence if not outright hostility toward the national Italian state. I hoped a diasporic study of Italians could reveal the many ways that migrants learned the "love of country" that is said to be characteristic of modern nationalism.[5] Understanding love of country was an urgent undertaking to me after a decade of teaching twentieth-century history, for what else could explain the willingness of soldiers and citizens to engage in its horrific levels of violence and warfare? It struck me as plausible that the mass migrations of the nineteenth century had encouraged states to assert in newly active ways their need for citizens who loved their country enough to sacrifice themselves as soldiers and mobilized civilians.

Ultimately, these plans were never fulfilled through scholarly collaboration. True, "love of country" did become the theme of a 2004 University of Pittsburgh workshop. The theme of honor killings also provided an opportunity for historians of Italian migration to meet in Bellagio in 2009 and to explore comparative perspectives of historical integration with settlement workers concerned with Muslim migrants and refugees in contemporary Europe. But for complex reasons, sadly, no further collaboration or publication emerged from either event.

I thus brought a sense of intellectual work unfinished to my reading of the essays collected in *Emotional Landscapes*. Although none of its essays focuses precisely on the questions of the 2003 paper, the collection nevertheless offers a provocative and overarching narrative of the evolution of nation-building through love and its "attendant constellation of emotions (loss, grief, guilt, nostalgia, hate, euphoria, and joy)" (page 3) from the nineteenth to the twentieth century. The narrative is a simple one, leaving much room for elaboration through future research. *Emotional Landscapes* makes the case that the entwining of material interests with love and the expectations of sacrifice within family and kin groups provided an emotionally firm foundation for nation-building. During the twentieth century, the full horror of the sacrifices extracted by nation-states at war then pushed interpersonal and familial love away from sacrifice toward a new emphasis on individual development, autonomy, and pleasure. Ironically, love motivated migration across two centuries even as its meaning shifted.

A first cluster of essays in *Emotional Landscapes* focuses on familial emotions during the nineteenth century. In his essay, editor Marcelo Borges uses "call letters" (which states required before authorizing women to follow their migrant husbands to the Americas) to show that familial love was defined largely through the emotions of obligation and duty; loving individuals expected to work and to sacrifice for the good of the family collective. Men felt obligated to support and to protect women; their migrations required their sacrifices and suffering in order to fulfill these duties. The money men sent home was literally "their blood," as they often wrote. Even then, according to Borges, "migrants' transnational affect" was reinforced by "national emotional regimes that equated love of family with love of country" (page 21). Although few of the letters analyzed were written by women, Borges suggests how sacrifice and suffering for the betterment of family may have been common concerns for them too. Migration also exacerbated fears that family members could neglect, escape, or even forget their obligations (a theme also taken up by María Bjerg in her essay, discussed below), reinforcing cultural messages about sacrifice.

Subsequent essays add depth and nuance to Borges's identification of the key familial emotions implicated in nation-building. Mirjam Milharčič Hladnik emphasizes how a courting and subsequently married couple reconciled themselves to temporary female labor migration (from Slovenia to Egypt) even as popular nationalism increasingly condemned female work and migration as morally threatening to women's role as "mothers of the nation" (page 60). The nationalist celebration of mothers who remained committed to domestic chores in private families silenced the matter-of-fact, pragmatic, and generally loving personal correspondence that spoke of women's desire to achieve dignity or independence through migration and work.

Elizabeth Zanoni reveals instead how emotions associated with fraternalism and the imagined blood brotherhood of racialized "Latin" men could be mobilized by both Italian migrants and Argentine natives as part of a nation-building strategy that linked love of Italy to love of Argentina. Men could creatively adapt their emotional attachments to nations as they moved—so long as the two countries remained at peace, that is. Not incidentally, perhaps, war shifted attention away from fraternalism among men as potential soldiers toward the construction of Italy and Argentina as "sister nations."

Finally, a chapter by Emily Pope-Obeda focuses on the flip side of emotional nation-building through metaphors of love. Nation-building always involved exclusion as well as inclusion. Noting that deportation was frequently reported through the circulation of tragic love stories, Pope-Obeda suggests the stories registered popular discontent with the spreading use of detention and deportation in the post–World War I imposition of American immigration restrictions. Simultaneously, the threat of deportation became an increasingly important mechanism for disciplining morality, sexuality, and proper family behavior among racialized or undesirable immigrants in the United States.

These essays' focus on love suggests not that nation-building broke the affective power of family and kin groups but rather drew on their strength in order to guarantee the sacrifice nation-states at war require. Those states, in turn, promised at least symbolically to protect women and children—as had patriarchal families before them. A US president's inaugural-address challenge to "ask not what your country can do for you—ask what you can do for your country" nicely sums up what love of family and love of country typically entailed for nineteenth-century migrants. As twentieth-century warfare revealed more fully the resultant levels of loss, guilt, and grief, the meaning of personal love began to change dramatically, and enthusiasm for romantic love based on individual autonomy and resistance to family control or sacrifice grew.

It is no accident that many chapters in this collection either focus on periods of warfare or mention war, which alongside state-building are two in a cluster of influences on the twentieth century's transformation and shifts in what volume editors call "emotional landscapes." In differing ways, chapters by editors Linda Reeder and Sonia Cancian provide support for an overarching narrative of wartime violence as an instigator of change in the key emotions associated with both national and familial solidarities. Love of country peaked during war years for both natives and migrants but for migrants this love was doubly marred by nostalgia and longing not just for the dead but for places and for people who had remained alive but who lived far away.

Reeder's article uses memoirs, letters, and diaries of Italian emigrant soldiers returned to fight for Italy in World War I to paint a powerful portrait of "love of country" during its peaking years of consolidation. In both sending and receiving countries, states celebrated the conflation of familial and patriotic love as markers of manhood "worthy of full citizenship" (page 133). Almost overnight, emigrant and immigrant populations that had long been disparaged as neglecting or ignoring their homelands, as racially indifferent to citizenship elsewhere, or as hostile to capitalism and states in general found acceptance as celebrated, patriotic soldiers. Reeder's chapter offers an excellent history of the kinds of state actions that made possible such a rapid transformation. She not only asserts that "the war fractured the emotional landscape of emigrant soldiers" (page 140) but also shows how emigrants began to separate "love of country from civic obligation" (page 141). That separation allowed for the possibility that a patriot Italian might take up arms against the state; emotionally, then, the foundation had been created for the next two decades of conflict between Fascist and anti-Fascist Italians, both claiming to be "true Italians." Sonia Cancian's focus on the life of a single war orphan (with a dead father and an indigent mother who could scarcely provide material care) then focuses readers' attention on the profound, immediate, and long-term emotional costs of love of country during and after World War II. In her chapter, one sees, in particular, how ordinary Italians reacted to the nation-state's failure to protect women and children. The Catholic Church offered better resources to an orphan than the state. By leaving impoverished families to cope as best they could (and in ways that could, as in the story told in this chapter, heighten the emotional stress of postwar poverty and emigration), even the once-firm and universal commitments to sacrifice for the family could begin to crumble.

As the editors argue in their introduction, the aftermath of twentieth-century warfare generated "a sharp shift in the relationship between love and migration" that "complicated ideas of obligation and love in connection with individual, family, and societal projects.... No longer did languages of love describe migration as an expression of love and sacrifice" (pages 8–9). Of course, the editors also acknowledge the longer history of this newer form of personal love—usually called romantic love—that replaced sacrificing familial love. Tyler Carrington's study of pre–World War I, urbanizing Berlin offers a compelling examination of how recently arrived rural migrants experienced the anxiety and excitement of seeking love in a cosmopolitan, modernizing industrial city already in the nineteenth century. Romance was also an important focus of the letters exchanged between sisters and cousins in Sinke's account of an Austrian Jewish family's war years. For the postwar era, Alexander Freund's analysis of Germany's emigrants reminds us how long anxiety and excitement about romantic love persisted—exacerbated by discussions of postwar "surplus women" and fears about the defeated and divided sovereign national body, they encouraged both church and state to begin vigorous efforts to protect the morality of postwar female migrants.

Still, it is A. James Hammerton's essay that provides the fullest exploration of the new transnational landscape of love. His chapter puts on full display the opportunities that travel and migration opened for those seeking escape from family obligations and exploration of self-development and autonomy. Migrating in search of love further unsettled love of country. Hammerton's migrants of the 1970s and 1980s exhibited a kind of casual cosmopolitanism, freed of responsibilities to any collectivity, whether family, nation, or radical, internationalist political movements. One female migrant (who had lived in Italy, Australia, and Britain before settling in New Zealand) even described herself as "a citizen of both countries and a native of neither, but it doesn't matter to me at all. I finally feel like I belong somewhere" (page 229). Another migrant declared: "But really, I consider myself a citizen of the world above a British person. Why wouldn't you?" (page 229). Hammerton does not consider the impact of such individualism and cosmopolitanism for late twentieth-century nationalism but it is hard to imagine these young migrants unquestioningly making sacrifices for their country as citizens or soldiers. The impact of this new landscape of love on love of country has long intrigued me as a teacher. For years, I have used classroom surveys to try to grasp the meaning of love of country for twenty-first-century students as they struggle to grasp fully the powerful rise of nineteenth- and twentieth-century nationalism. While most students declare themselves proud of their own nation and most also identify as patriotic, only a few have been willing to promise to fight or die "without question" for their country. Certainly, too, the casual cosmopolitanism Hammerton describes has helped to spark a recent backlash in a resurgence in populist nationalist movements.

In this volume's analysis of love of country, the emotions of honor and shame have exceedingly modest roles, even though a significant number of its chapters focus on migrants in or from Mediterranean countries. Borges's essay is important in refining older, anthropological understandings of honor as originating in male vigilance and control of female sexuality; the call letters instead reveal male honor as embedded in work and sacrifice to provide support for families. Bjerg's in-depth analysis of two bigamy cases involving migrants from Spain and Italy does suggest that *gente decente* risked dishonor if men failed to watch over female sexual conduct, demand female chastity, and value marriage. Nevertheless, she describes such a family overcoming even the dishonor threatened by a bigamous marriage. Honor was also not merely a concern of men. In the case she reports of a plebian bigamist, Bjerg reveals the two wives fighting over their own honor in ways violent enough to warrant the arrest of one of them. While the preservation of family honor among gente decente required the second wife to remain silent while legal counsel intervened, both plebian wives took action on their own behalf and found ways to reject the bigamist man they had both married. Reeder's essay, finally, shows that Italian nationalists explicitly linked familial and national expressions of honor, when they claimed "a faithless husband, or an adulterer who dishonors another man's vows of marriage is incapable of loyalty to his country" (page 137). Tellingly, of the essays that address the postwar world, by contrast, only Margarita Dounia's essay on Greek immigrants in Montreal mentions shame, and then only in passing. Thus, overall, *Emotional Landscapes* appears to confirm Ute Frevert's argument that the emotion of honor declined in importance during nation-building in most of the countries of Europe and that sympathy and empathy replaced it as the most desired emotions for building solidarity among co-nationals.[6]

Of course, the narrative of emotions, migration, and nation-building offered in *Emotional Landscapes* provides ample remaining challenges for future researchers. Since all the essays collected here focus on Atlantic migrations, Europe, or the English-speaking world, the collection leaves open the possibility that its history of nation-building and the transformation of love may be exclusive to the west or to the "neo-Europes" of the world. It is not at all clear that studies of migration, emotion, and nation-building around the Pacific or in Asian or African regions—marked by different civilizational origins, different kinship and family systems, and markedly different colonial histories of human mobility—would reveal similar transformations. On the contrary they might be expected to modify, reverse, or refute the narrative offered here. Read in conjunction with Luisa Passerini's provocative works (*Love and the Idea of Europe* and *Europe in Love, Love in Europe*),[7] *Emotional Landscapes* challenges area specialists to undertake case studies focused on other regions of the world. Studies of Asia and the Pacific and of postcolonial Africa would allow a future generation of scholars to write a truly global and comparative narrative of the rise and possible fall of nationalism as "love of country," while also resolving the complex issue of whether the heightened rates of mobility of the late twentieth and early twenty-first centuries are also effecting fundamental transformations in the meaning and experience of love itself.

NOTES

1. Donna R. Gabaccia and Fraser M. Ottanelli, eds., *Italian Workers of the World: Labor Migration and the Formation of Multiethnic States* (Urbana: University of Illinois Press, 2001); Donna R. Gabaccia and Franca Iacovetta, eds., *Women, Gender, and Transnational Lives: Italian Workers of the World* (Toronto: University of Toronto Press, 2002); Donna R. Gabaccia, *Italy's Many Diasporas* (London: UCL Press, 2000).

2. Donna R. Gabaccia and Loretta Baldassar, eds., *Intimacy and Italian Migration: Gender and Domestic Lives in a Mobile World* (New York: Fordham University Press, 2011).

3. From the extensive literature that influenced my early twenty-first century (unpublished) paper on honor and shame, see J. G. Peristiany, ed., *Honour and Shame: The Values of Mediterranean Society* (1965; rpt. Chicago: University of Chicago Press, 1966); John T. Campbell, *Honour, Family, and Patronage: A Study of Institutions and Moral Values in a Greek Mountain Community* (Oxford: Oxford University Press, 1964); and Peristiany's entry "Honor" in the *International Encyclopedia of the Social Sciences* 6 (New York: Macmillan/Free Press, 1968), 503–11. Critiques emerging in the 1980s and 1990s included Nancy Lindisfarne, "Variant Masculinities, Variant Virginities: Rethinking 'Honor and Shame,'" in *Dislocating Masculinity: Comparative Ethnographies*, ed. Andrea Cornwall and Nancy Lindisfarne (London: Routledge, 1994); David D. Gilmore, ed., *Honor and Shame and the Unity of the Mediterranean*, American Anthropological Association Special Publica-

tion 22 (Washington, DC: American Anthropological Association, 1987); Michael Herzfeld, "Honor and Shame: Problems in the Comparative Analysis of Moral Systems," *Man* 15, no. 2 (1980): 339–51; and Michael Herzfeld, "The Horns of the Mediterraneanist Dilemma," *American Ethnologist* 11, no. 3 (1984): 439–54. I was also influenced by the work of Latin Americanists Kristin Ruggiero, "Honor, Maternity, and the Disciplining of Women: Infanticide in Late Nineteenth-Century Buenos Aires," *Hispanic American Historical Review* 72, no. 3 (1992): 353–73; Lyman L. Johnson and Sonya Lipsett-Rivera, eds., *The Faces of Honor: Sex, Shame, and Violence in Colonial Latin America* (Albuquerque: University of New Mexico Press, 1998); Sueann Caulfield, *In Defense of Honor: Sexual Morality, Modernity, and Nation in Early-Twentieth-Century Brazil* (Durham, NC: Duke University Press, 2000); Ann Twinam, *Public Lives, Private Secrets: Gender, Honor, Sexuality and Illegitimacy in Colonial Spanish America* (Stanford, CA: Stanford University Press, 1999).

4. Thoughts on the relationship of honor, shame, and state- or nation-building included J. G. Peristiany, *Mediterranean Family Structures* (Cambridge: Cambridge University Press, 1976); Mariko Asano-Tamanoi, "Shame, Family, and State in Catalonia and Japan," in *Honor and Shame*, ed. Gilmore, 104–20; Franz X. Eder, Lesley A. Hall, and Gert Hekma, *Sexual Cultures in Europe: National Histories* (Manchester: Manchester University Press, 1999); J. Davis, "Honour and Politics in Pisticci," *Proceedings of the Royal Anthropological Institute of Great Britain and Ireland*, no. 1969 (1969): 69–81; John Davis, *People of the Mediterranean: An Essay in Comparative Social Anthropology* (London: Routledge and Kegan Paul, 1977), 89–90; Jane Schneider, "Of Vigilance and Virgins: Honor, Shame, and Access to Resources in Mediterranean Societies," *Ethnology* 10, no. 1 (1971): 1–24. And there was of course more theoretical work available also at that time: Andrew Parker, Mary Russo, Doris Sommer, and Patricia Yaeger, eds., *Nationalism and Sexualities* (New York: Routledge, 1992); Sita Ranchod-Nillson and Mary Ann Tétrault, eds., *Women, States, and Nationalism: At Home in the Nation?* (London: Routledge, 2000). From a large, and still growing bibliography, readers can usefully consult Nira Yuval-Davis, *Gender and Nation; Politics and Culture* (London: Sage Publications, 1997); Tamara Mayer, ed., *Gender Ironies of Nationalism: Sexing the Nation* (London: Routledge, 2000).

5. I originally borrowed the concept notion of "love of country" from Maurizio Virioli's analysis of patriotism and nationalism. See Virioli, *Per amore della patria: Patriottismo e nazionalismo nella storia* (Bari: Laterza, 1995).

6. Ute Frevert, *Emotions in History, Lost and Found* (Budapest: Central European University Press, 2011).

7. Luisa Passerini, *Love and the Idea of Europe*, trans. Juliet Hydock and Allan Cameron (New York: Berghahn Books, 2009); Luisa Passerini, *Europe in Love, Love in Europe: Imagination and Politics between the Wars* (New York: New York University Press, 1999).

CONTRIBUTORS

MARÍA BJERG is a professor of history at the Universidad Nacional de Quilmes, Argentina, and a researcher at the National Research Council (CONICET). A specialist in migration history, she is the author of *Entre Sofie y Tovellile: Una historia de la inmigración danesa en la Argentina* (2002); *El Mundo de Dorothea: La vida cotidiana en un pueblo de la frontera de Buenos Aires en el siglo XIX* (2004); *Historias de la inmigración en la Argentina* (2009); *El viaje de los niños: Inmigración, memoria e infancia en la Argentina de la segunda posguerra* (2012); and *Lazos rotos: La inmigración, el matrimonio y las emociones en la Argentina entre los siglos XIX y XX* (2019).

MARCELO J. BORGES is a professor of history and the Boyd Lee Spahr Chair in the History of the Americas at Dickinson College, where he teaches Latin American history and migration history. He has been a research fellow at the Netherlands Institute for Advanced Studies in the Humanities and Social Sciences and the Nantes Institute of Advanced Studies. He is the author of *Chains of Gold: Portuguese Migration to Argentina in Transatlantic Perspective* (2009) and coeditor of *Company Towns: Labor, Space, and Power Relations across Time and Continents* (with Susana Torres, 2012) and *Migrant Letters: Emotional Language, Mobile Identities, and Writing Practices in Historical Perspective* (with Sonia Cancian, 2018). He is the coeditor (with Madeline Hsu) of a forthcoming volume on modern migrations for the Cambridge History of Global Migrations.

SONIA CANCIAN is a historian affiliated with the Centre for Interdisciplinary Research on Montreal following a postdoctoral fellowship at the Max Planck Institute for Human Development in Berlin (2018–19). She is the author of *Families, Lovers, and Their Letters: Italian Postwar Migration to Canada* (2010), and coeditor of *Migrant Letters: Emotional Language, Mobile Identities, and Writing Practices in Historical Perspective* (with Marcelo J. Borges, 2018) and *Post-migration "Italo-Canada,"* special issue of *Studi Emigrazione* (with Bruno Ramirez, 2007). Her other articles and research interests include a focus on gender and family history, history of emotions, and transnational correspondence in twentieth-century migration history. With Donna R. Gabaccia, she has led the Digitizing Immigrant Letters Project at the University of Minnesota. She is the author of the forthcoming volume *With Your Words in My Hands: The Letters of Antonietta Petris and Loris Palma* (2021).

TYLER CARRINGTON is an assistant professor of German studies and history at Cornell College. His book, *Love at Last Sight: Dating, Intimacy, and Risk in Turn-of-the-Century Berlin* (2019), is a history of dating in 1900s Berlin told around the life and murder of an enterprising woman who used newspaper personal ads to find love, and the trial of the man accused of her murder. His other articles, reviews, and research interests revolve around the history of masculinity, urban life and culture, and legal history.

MARGARITA DOUNIA holds graduate degrees in history and social anthropology from McGill University and the National and Kapodistrian University of Athens. Her dissertation focused on the materialization of memory through correspondence, photography, and film among early twentieth-century Greek migrants to the United States. She teaches at the Hellenic American College where she held the Fylaktopoulos Chair (2013–14). She is a current fellow at the Royal Anthropological Institute, UK. Her interests focus on emotions, memory, transnational and diasporic communities as well as visual anthropology.

ALEXANDER FREUND is a professor of history at the University of Winnipeg, where he also holds the chair in German-Canadian Studies. He has published in migration history and oral history, including articles in *Canadian Ethnic Studies, Oral History Review, Oral History,* and *BIOS: Zeitschrift für*

Biographieforschung, Oral History, und Lebensverlaufsanalysen. Recent edited and coedited volumes include *Entangling Migration History: Borderlands and Transnationalism in the United States and Canada* (2015); *The Canadian Oral History Reader* (2015); *Oral History and Ethnic History* (2014); *Beyond the Nation? Immigrants' Local Lives in Transnational Cultures* (2012); and *Oral History and Photography* (2011). He is currently editing a collection of essays on *History, Memory, and Generations: German-Canadian Experiences in the Twentieth Century* and writing a history of refugees in Winnipeg.

DONNA R. GABACCIA is a professor emerita at the University of Toronto and past director of the Immigration History Research Center at the University of Minnesota. She is the author of fourteen books and dozens of articles on immigrant class, gender, and food studies in the United States; on Italian migration around the world; and on migration in world history. Her 2015 book *Gender and International Migration,* coauthored with sociologist and demographer Katharine Donato, was awarded an Honorable Mention from the American Sociological Association's Znaniecki Prize. In 2018, she received a Lifetime Achievement Award from the Immigration and Ethnic History Society. She is currently general editor for a forthcoming Cambridge History of Global Migrations.

A. JAMES HAMMERTON is an emeritus scholar at La Trobe University, Melbourne. His research ranges across nineteenth-century female emigration, the history of marriage and marital conflict in nineteenth-century England, the lower middle class in Victorian and Edwardian England, and emigration from Britain since 1830. His publications include *Migrants of the British Diaspora since the 1960s: Stories from Modern Nomads* (2017); *Ten Pound Poms: Australia's Invisible Migrants* (2005); *Cruelty and Companionship: Conflict in Nineteenth-Century Marriage* (1993); and *Emigrant Gentlewomen: Genteel Poverty and Female Emigration, 1830–1914* (1979). His current research focuses on the history of an English expatriate's extended family in Iran and Iraq in the early twentieth century.

MIRJAM MILHARČIČ HLADNIK is a research advisor at the Slovenian Migration Institute at the Research Center of the Slovenian Academy of Sciences and Arts in Ljubljana and an associate professor at the University of Nova Gorica. A passionate researcher of "the documents of life" and specialist in migration and gender studies in Slovenia, she is the editor of *From Slovenia to Egypt: Aleksandrinke's Trans-Mediterranean Domestic Workers' Migration and National Imagination* (2015), and the coeditor of *Going Places: Slovenian Women's Stories on Migration* (with Jernej Mlekuž, 2014). She is the author of the screenplay for the documentary film *100% Slovenian* (2005) and editor-in-chief of the academic journal *Dve domovini / Two Homelands.*

EMILY POPE-OBEDA is an assistant professor of history at Lehigh University. Her research and teaching center on late nineteenth- and twentieth-century US history, migration, race, and ethnicity, and labor and working-class history. She is currently working on her first book project, which focuses on American deportation practice in the 1920s.

LINDA REEDER is an associate professor of history at the University of Missouri. Her research focuses on gender, migration, and nation-formation in modern Italy. In addition to articles, her publications include *Italy in the Modern World: Society, Culture, and Identity* (2019) and *Widows in White: Migration and the Transformation of Rural Italian Women, Sicily, 1880–1920* (2003).

ROBERTA RICUCCI is an associate professor at the University of Turin, Department of Culture, Politics, and Society, where she teaches sociology of inter-ethnic relations and sociology of Islam. She is also a research affiliate at the Center for the Study of Religion and Society of the University of Notre Dame (United States), and a senior researcher and a member of the international network IMISCOE (International Migration, Integration, and Social Cohesion). As expert in several issues concerning migration in the Mediterranean areas, she is currently leading various international projects. She has a wide record of publications in English and Italian focused on migration, school integration, immigrant children, identity-building, and religion. Her publications include *Second Generations on the Move in Italy* (2014) and *The New Southern European Diaspora* (2017).

SUZANNE M. SINKE is the director of graduate studies and an associate professor in the Department of History at Florida State University. Since fall 2018, she has served as editor for the *Journal of American Ethnic History*. A specialist in migration and gender studies in the US context, she is the author of *Dutch Immigrant Women in the United States, 1880–1920* (2002), and coeditor of three additional books, including *Letters across Borders: The Epistolary Practices of International Migrants* (2006). Sinke's extensive list of journal articles includes venues such as *International Migration Review, OAH*

Magazine, *Gender Issues*, *Journal of American Ethnic History*, and *History of the Family*. Many of Sinke's publications link marriage and international migration across US history.

ELIZABETH ZANONI is an associate professor of history at Old Dominion University. She is the author of *Migrant Marketplaces: Food and Italians in North and South America* (2018) and has published articles on food, gender, migration, and consumption in edited collections and in academic journals including *Social Science History*, *Journal of American Ethnic History*, and *Global Food History*.

INDEX

affect, language of transnational, 22–23, 31–33
affect studies, 4
Ahmed, Sara, 118–19
Aldaz, Facunda, 40–44
Aldaz, Luis, 40–44, 46, 48–49
aleksandrinke. *See* Egypt, migration to
Amarante, Justina, 42–44
Amarante, Paulino, 43
Anderson, Benedict, 102
Arabic language. *See* digital divide in Italy
Argentina: Luis Aldaz and, 40–44, 46, 48–49; Andresa Barrachina and, 39, 40–44, 48–49; bigamy in, 39–52; Rafaela Fioretto and, 39, 44–46, 48–50; Italian-Argentine brotherhood in, 91–106; letter-writing and longing in, 46–50
Arms and Faith of Italy (ed. Macina), 131
Arru, Giovanni, 139
Australia, migration to, 220–35
Austria, migration from. *See* Hasterlik, Maria; Hine, Giulia

Baily, Samuel, 61
Baldassar, Loretta, 2, 22, 207, 260
Barrachina, Andresa, 39, 40–44, 48–49
Baudelaire, Charles, 79
Beck, Ulrich, 176
Beck-Gernsheim, Elizabeth, 176
Ben-Ghiat, Ruth, 95
Benjamin, Walter, 79
Berkman, Alexander, 124
Berlin, turn-of-the-century, 75–76; as dynamic modern city, 77–78; fate in, 85–87; finding love in, 78–82; romantic roadblocks of, 82–85
Berliner Lokal-Anzeiger, 84
Berliner Morgenpost, 80–81, 84
Berman, Marshall, 87
bigamy, 39–52
Bjerg, María, 9, 10, 93, 120, 223, 262, 265
Boccagni, Paolo, 22
Boddice, Rob, 4
Bolívar, Simón, 98
Books, Clara, 124
Borges, Marcelo J., 9, 104, 223, 259, 261–62, 265

Bottero, Angelo, 101
Brazil, migration of Portuguese to, 19–20, 25–26, 28, 29, 31
Bric, Neda R., 62
British diaspora, modern, 220–21; courtship-friendly mobility from the 1950s and, 230–35; love, migration, and emotional revolution in, 221–25; love and national identity in, 225–30
Brooklyn Daily Eagle, 134–35
brotherly love. *See* Italian-Argentine brotherhood
Burlingham, Dorothy, 166

Campbell, Maggie, 230–34, 235
Canada: deportation from the United States to, 113, 121; migration of Greeks to, 201–2, 213; migration of Italians to, 63, 164, 170, 172
Cancian, Sonia, 12, 13, 62, 63, 104, 208, 254, 259, 263
Capabianca, Salvatore, 123
Carrington, Tyler, 10, 118, 148, 264
Carroccio, Il, 141
Carta, Alfio, 140
Chamberlain, John, 126
Choate, Mark, 95
Christian, Hilda, 122
Christiansen, Ellen, 155–56
Columbus, Christopher, 96, 98
communities, emotional, 5–6, 32, 61, 93, 150, 176, 187
Corti, Paola, 212
Cronaca Sovversiva, 136
Cuti, Antonio, 135
Cutrufelli, Provvidenza, 141

DeBartolo, Domingo, 44–46, 48–50
De Biasi, Agostino, 142
del Valle, Aristóbulo, 44
deportation, 112–14, 125–26; familial separation and, 122–24; policing relationships through, 118–22; press coverage of tragic romance of, 114–18
Diario, El, 103
digital divide in Italy, 238–39; Arabic speaking and identity in, 244–46; Moroccan and Peruvian families and, 242–43; social media checking by parents and, 250–53; Spanish speakers and, 247–50; theoretical framework of, 239–41
Dinis, Júlio, 20
Dounia, Margarita, 13, 254, 265

economies, emotional, 5
Egypt, migration to, 9, 57–61, 66–67, 68. *See also* Koglot, Felicita, and Franc Peric
Elias, Norbert, 5
emotional communities, 5–6, 32, 61, 93, 150, 176, 187
emotional economies, 5
emotional landscapes, 6–8, 92, 104, 139–43, 260–66
emotional regimes, 5–6, 21, 32, 188, 190, 191
emotional revolution, 221–25
emotions: changing, 50–52; gendered mobility and, 59–62; language of affect in, 31–33; theoretical frameworks of, 3–8; understanding history of, 132–33, 259

Facebook, 250–53
familial love: between sisters, 154–57
Fascism, 70n1, 142–43, 174–75, 263
fate and love, 76, 79–80, 82, 85–87
Febvre, Lucien, 132–33
Ferri, Enrico, 96
Fioretto, Rafaela, 39, 44–46, 48–50
Flynn, Elizabeth Gurley, 124
Ford, Ruby Eugene, 116
Freud, Anna, 166
Freund, Alexander, 13, 264
Frevert, Ute, 5, 265
Fuller, Mia, 95
Fusinato, Guido, 91

Gabaccia, Donna R., 2
Gardner, Eunice, 232–33, 235

Garibaldi, Giuseppe, 96, 135
Garibaldi, Ricciotti, 135–36
gender, 7–8; deportation as policing of relationships and, 118–22; love, mobility, and, 8–15, 50–52, 59–62; and narratives of sacrifice, 30–31; and postwar migration from Germany, 184–96; societal roles, 60; and state authority, 190–95
gender paradox, 60
Gentile, Emilio, 142
Gerber, David A., 19, 61–62, 149, 150
Germany, female migration from postwar: advertisements for, 184–85; letters on, 186–90; love and, 195–96; state authority, sex, and, 190–95. *See also* Berlin, turn-of-the-century
Gianolio, Emanuele, 98
Goldberg, Ann, 149
Goldman, Emma, 124
Gozzoli, Caterina, 245
Greece, female migration from postwar, 201–2, 213; and *eros*, *agapi*, and motherhood, 208–11; and hope and *misemos*, 202–4; and nostalgia and *stenahoria*, 204–8; and stress and *proodos*, 212–13

Hammerton, A. James, 13, 14, 148, 165, 264–65
Hanna, Martha, 149
Hasterlik, Maria: daughters of, 156–57; letters across generations and, 157–59; lovers of, 150–54; sister of, 154–57
Hebert, Beatrice, 112–15; press coverage of, 114–18
Heinemann, Elizabeth, 187
Heller, Peter, 155
Heller, Thomas, 153–55
Herzog, Dagmar, 191
Hine, Giulia, 148–50
Hochschild, Arlie, 176
Hoerder, Dirk, 60
Holocaust, 149
"Honor and Shame in a Mobile World" (Gabaccia), 260

human trafficking, concerns over, 190–95

Idea Nazionale, L', 134
information and communication technologies (ICTs). *See* digital divide in Italy
intergenerational love, 157–59
Irwin, Theodore, 125–26
Italia del Popolo, L', 93
Italia e Argentina (Italian Colonial Institute), 98
Italian-Argentine brotherhood, 91–106; Argentine elites and, 97–98, 101; during the Great War, 103–6; Italian elites and, 95–97; Italian migration to the United States and, 101–2; language of, 94–95; liberalism and, 97–98; migration of Italians to Argentina and, 93–94; visual imagery of, 98–101
Italian emigrant soldiers, 131–33; changing emotional landscapes of, 139–43; love and liberal state and, 137–39; press depictions and narratives of, 134–36
Italy: as country of immigration, 241–42; emigrant soldiers of World War I, 131–43; migration from postwar, 163–77; migration to Argentina from, 44–46, 48–50, 91–106; migration to Canada from, 63, 164, 170, 172; migration to the United States from, 101–2; Moroccan and Peruvian families in, 242–54; speaking Arabic and identity in, 244–46; speaking Spanish in, 247–50; war orphans of, 163–77. *See also* digital divide in Italy

Johnson, Lillian Mary Irene, 120–21
judicial records, emotions in, 39–40, 47–50

King, Russell, 7
Knights, Daphne, 234
Koglot, Felicita, and Franc Peric, 57–59, 69–70; dreaming and longing in letters of, 62–66; gender roles and emotions

in letters of, 59–62; weeping and consoling in letters of, 66–69
Kopetz, Heinrich, 151–54
Kurdi, Aylan, 1

Lagoeiro, Joaquim, 20
Laliotou, Ioanna, 203
landscapes, emotional. *See* emotional landscapes
Langhamer, Claire, 221, 223, 224–25
language: of brotherly love, 94–95; digital divide and (*see* digital divide in Italy); of love, public, 10–11; of transnational affect, 22–23, 31–33
Larrucea, Constanza Vera, 240
Laslett, Barbara, 165
Lee, Matthew, 220, 226–29, 231–32, 234–35
Lemmo, Domenico, 166
Lemmo, Maria, 168–74
letter writing, 9–10; bigamy in Argentina and, 39–52; dreaming and longing expressed through, 62–66; by female German migrants, 186–90; gendered mobility and, 59–62; across generations, 157–59; by Maria Hasterlik, 150–54; between Felicita Koglot and Franc Peric, 57–70; in long-distance love, 58–59; love and national identity in, 225–30; narrative of responsibility in, 23–26; narrative of sacrifice in, 26–31; by Portuguese migrants, 19–33; weeping and consoling in, 66–69; during World War II, 147–59
lifestyle migration, 220–35
Lingxin, Hao, 246
Litoff, Judy Barrett, 149
Lock, Margaret, 206
Lomer, Georg, 80, 83
Lorenzoni, Giovanni, 138–39
love, 2–3, 7; changing feelings of, 50–52; deportation and, 112–26; fate and, 85–87; across generations, 157–59; German migrant women and, 186–96; in letter-writing by Maria Hasterlik, 150–57; in letter-writing by Portuguese migrants, 19–33; long-distance, 58–59, 176–77; longing and, 46–50; migration for, 57–70; mobility, gender, and, 8–15; in modern British diaspora, 220–35; narrative of responsibility and, 23–26; narrative of sacrifice and, 26–31; national identity and, 225–30; patriotism and, 137–42; public languages of, 10–11; between sisters, 154–57; in turn-of-the-century Berlin, 75–87; war orphans and, 163–77; written expressions of, 9–10. *See also* Italian-Argentine brotherhood
Love and Psychosis (Lomer), 80
Luibheid, Eithne, 120
Lutz, Catherine, 202

Macaya, Julia, 45–46
Machado, Benito, 43
Macina, Luisa, 131
Mai, Nicola, 7
Marconi, Guglielmo, 141–42
marriage: bigamous, 39–52; deportation in destruction of, 112–26; migration from postwar Germany to the United States for, 184–96; migration from postwar Greece for arranged, 201–13; in modern British diaspora, 220–35
Matt, Susan J., 61, 114, 202
Maynes, Mary Jo, 165
Mazzini, Giuseppe, 135, 137
migration and mobility: changing emotions and, 50–52; communication technologies and, 14; lifestyle, 220–35; modernity and, 13–14; public images of, 1–2; state controls on, 12, 190–95; urban, in Berlin, 75–87; of war orphans, 163–77. *See also* digital divide in Italy; war and migration
Milharčič Hladnik, Mirjam, 9, 149, 259, 262
Moloney, Deirdre, 119–20
Montreal. *See* Canada
morgadinha dos Canaviais, A (Dinis), 20
Moroccan migrants to Italy, 242–50, 254; social media use and, 250–53

Moscato, Rosina, 166–68; love for her daughter, 174–75; separation from her daughter, 168–74
Mouton, Michelle, 164
Moya, Jose, 98
Mussolini, Benito, 143

Nación, La, 101
Nathan, Ernesto, 96
national identity and love, 225–30
nationalism, 139, 140
New York Times, 136
New Zealand, migration to, 221, 229, 230
Novota, José, 40

orphans, war, 163–65; hopes and love for, 174–75; Maria Lemmo's story and, 168–74; long-distance love for, 176–77; Rosina Moscato's story and, 166–68; statistics of, 165–66

Palmiotti, Nicola, 136
Pan Americanism, 98
Parenti, Luigi, 124
Passerini, Luisa, 164, 266
Patria degli Italiani, La. See Italian-Argentine brotherhood
patriotism and love, 137–42
Paz y Haedo, José María, 98
Péllico, Silvio, 137
Pendakur, Krishna, 243
Pendakur, Ravi, 243
Peric, Franc. See Koglot, Felicita, and Franc Peric
Peruvian migrants to Italy, 242–50, 254; social media use and, 250–53
Pierce, Jennifer, 165
Pina, Mariano, 25
Pohlandt-McCormick, Helena, 164
Pomilo, Alessandro, 134
Pope-Obeda, Emily, 12, 102, 262
Portes, Alejandro, 246
Portuguese migrants, 19–21; emotions in mobility of, 31–33; narrative of responsibility in letters of, 23–26; narrative of sacrifice in letters of, 26–31; transnational affect of, 21–23
postwar migration: courtship-friendly mobility of the British diaspora and, 230–35; from Greece for arrange marriages, 201–13; from Italy, 163–77; of women from Germany, 184–96

Questione Sociale, La, 93

Ramella, Franco, 61
Razón, La, 101
Reddy, William, 5–6
Reeder, Linda, 12, 104, 177, 254, 263, 265
Regalia, Camillo, 245
responsibility, narrative of, 23–26
revolution, emotional, 221–25
Ricucci, Roberta, 14, 259
Rojas, Eva, 122–23
Rosas, Juan Manuel de, 96
Rosenwein, Barbara H., 5, 61, 176, 187–88

sacrifice, narrative of, 26–31
Sáenz Peña, Roque, 96
Salazar Parreñas, Rhacel, 60
San Francisco Chronicle, 112
San Martín, José de, 98
Sarafin, Mary, 121–22
Sarmiento, Domingo Faustino, 98
Seddon, Catherine, 230
Seymour, Mark, 20
Sieboldt, Edith, 184–85, 190
Simaika, Farid, 117
Simmel, Georg, 78
Simon, Carleton, 123
Simons, Katherine Drayton Mayrant, Jr., 136
Sinke, Suzanne M., 12, 177, 189, 254, 259, 264
Slovenia, migration from. See Koglot, Felicita, and Franc Peric
social media, 250–53
Spain, migration from. See Barrachina, Andresa

Spanish language. *See* digital divide in Italy
Spinetto, Davide, 97
state controls on migration, 12, 190–95
Stearns, Carol Z., 4–5
Stearns, Peter N., 4–5, 114, 204
Strange Passage (Irwin), 125–26
Strebel, Wilhelm, 80

Taylor, Charles, 221
Taylor, Elizabeth, 225–26
Temperley, Gertrude, 115
Thomson, Alistair, 234
Tomba, Antonio, 97
Tomba, Domingo, 97
transnational affect of Portuguese migrants, 21–23
transnationalism, 238

United States: deportation regime (1919–35), 112–26; Italian emigrant soldiers and, 131–43; migration of Germans to, 184–85; migration of Italians to, 101–2
urban migration, 10–11, 50, 58, 205. *See also* Berlin, turn-of-the-century

Van Den Akker, Mabel, 117
Velayutham, Selvaraj, 21, 116
Vienna, Austria: migration from. *See* Hasterlik, Maria; Heller, Thomas; Hine, Giulia
Viúvas de vivos (Lagoeiro), 20

Wakewich-Dunk, Pamela, 206
war and migration, 12–13. *See also* orphans, war; postwar migration; World War I; World War II
Washington Post, 117, 123
Welke, Jutta, 184–85; letters of female clients of, 186–90; love and women working with, 195–96; state authority and work of, 190–95
White, Geoffrey M., 202
Wickberg, Daniel, 118
Williams, Diana, 232
Wise, Amanda, 21, 116
Wolf, Sidney, 116
World at Our Feet, The (Gardner), 232–33
World War I, 103–6; Italian emigrant soldiers of, 131–43
World War II, 143; letter writing in maintaining relationships through, 147–59; migration from Germany after, 184–96; migration from Greece after, 201–13; war orphans of, 163–77

Yosipovitch, Olga, 116

Zanoni, Elizabeth, 11, 12, 132, 262
Zimmer, Kenyon, 124
Zinser, William, 112

STUDIES OF WORLD MIGRATIONS

The Immigrant Threat: The Integration of Old and New Migrants in Western Europe Since 1850   *Leo Lucassen*
Citizenship and Those Who Leave: The Politics of Emigration and Expatriation   *Edited by Nancy L. Green and François Weil*
Migration, Class, and Transnational Identities: Croatians in Australia and America   *Val Colic-Peisker*
The Yankee Yorkshireman: Migration Lived and Imagined   *Mary H. Blewett*
Africans in Europe: The Culture of Exile and Emigration from Equatorial Guinea to Spain   *Michael Ugarte*
Hong Kong Movers and Stayers: Narratives of Family Migration   *Janet W. Salaff, Siulun Wong, and Arent Greve*
Russia in Motion: Cultures of Human Mobility since 1850   *Edited by John Randolph and Eugene M. Avrutin*
A Century of Transnationalism: Immigrants and Their Homeland Connections   *Edited by Nancy L. Green and Roger Waldinger*
Syrian and Lebanese Patrícios in São Paulo: From the Levant to Brazil   *Oswaldo Truzzi, translated by Ramon J. Stern*
A Nation of Immigrants Reconsidered: US Society in an Age of Restriction, 1924–1965   *Edited by Maddalena Marinari, Madeline Y. Hsu, and Maria Cristina Garcia*
Ethnic Dissent and Empowerment: Economic Migration between Vietnam and Malaysia   *Angie Ngọc Trần*
Emotional Landscapes: Love, Gender, and Migration   *Edited by Marcelo J. Borges, Sonia Cancian, and Linda Reeder*

The University of Illinois Press
is a founding member of the
Association of University Presses.

———————————

Composed in 11/13 Arno Pro
with ITC Avant Garde display
by Jim Proefrock
at the University of Illinois Press

University of Illinois Press
1325 South Oak Street
Champaign, IL 61820-6903
www.press.uillinois.edu